Social Judgment
and Decision Making

FRONTIERS OF SOCIAL PSYCHOLOGY

Series Editors:
Arie W. Kruglanski, *University of Maryland at College Park*
Joseph P. Forgas, *University of New South Wales*

Frontiers of Social Psychology is a series of domain-specific handbooks. Each volume provides readers with an overview of the most recent theoretical, methodological, and practical developments in a substantive area of social psychology, in greater depth than is possible in general social psychology handbooks. The editors and contributors are all internationally renowned scholars whose work is at the cutting edge of research.

Scholarly, yet accessible, the volumes in the *Frontiers* series are an essential resource for senior undergraduates, postgraduates, researchers, and practitioners and are suitable as texts in advanced courses in specific subareas of social psychology.

Published Titles

Negotiation Theory and Research, Thompson
Close Relationships, Noller & Feeney
Evolution and Social Psychology, Schaller, Simpson & Kenrick
Social Psychology and the Unconscious, Bargh
Affect in Social Thinking and Behavior, Forgas
The Science of Social Influence, Pratkanis
Social Communication, Fiedler
The Self, Sedikides & Spencer
Personality and Social Behavior, Rhodewalt
Attitudes and Attitude Change, Crano & Prislin
Social Cognition, Strack & Förster
Social Psychology of Consumer Behavior, Wänke
Social Motivation, Dunning
Intergroup Conflicts and their Resolution, Bar-Tal
Goal-directed Behavior, Aarts & Elliot
Social Metacognition, Briñol & DeMarree
Social Judgment and Decision Making, Krueger

Forthcoming Titles

Group Processes, Levine

For continually updated information about published and forthcoming titles in the *Frontiers of Social Psychology* series, please visit: **www.psypress.com/frontiers**

Social Judgment
and Decision Making

Edited by
Joachim I. Krueger

Psychology Press
Taylor & Francis Group

New York   London

Psychology Press
Taylor & Francis Group
711 Third Avenue
New York, NY 10017

Psychology Press
Taylor & Francis Group
27 Church Road
Hove, East Sussex BN3 2FA

© 2012 by Taylor & Francis Group, LLC
Psychology Press is an imprint of Taylor & Francis Group, an Informa business

Printed in the United States of America on acid-free paper
Version Date: 2011916

International Standard Book Number: 978-1-84872-906-3 (Hardback)

Library of Congress Cataloging-in-Publication Data

Social judgment and decision making / editor, Joachim I. Krueger.
    p. cm. -- (Frontiers of social psychology)
   Includes bibliographical references and index.
   ISBN 978-1-84872-906-3 (hbk. : alk. paper)
    1. Judgment--Social aspects. 2. Decision making. 3. Social psychology. 4. Knowledge, Sociology of. I. Krueger, Joachim I.

BF447.S63 2012
153.4'6--dc23   2011036833

Visit the Taylor & Francis Web site at
http://www.taylorandfrancis.com

and the Psychology Press Web site at
http://www.psypress.com

Contents

SECTION I   THE PROCESSES OF JUDGMENT AND DECISION MAKING

SECTION II   MEASUREMENT ISSUES

SECTION III   ECOLOGICAL RATIONALITY

SECTION IV   APPLICATIONS

Prolegomena to a Social Psychological Approach to Judgment and Decision Making

"Never mind the formulas; we want you to *think* statistically."
Matthias Geyer (paraphrased, University of Bielefeld, ca. 1980)
"*Now* you tell me!" Student's response (after having taken the course)

Processes of judgment and decision making are essential activities for an organism to psychologically reconstruct the world, make sense of it, and respond to it adaptively. Some judgments are concerned with value (or utility), others with physical characteristics. Some judgments are absolute, others comparative. Decisions are concerned with preferences, that is, they are necessarily comparative. Typically, decisions entail actions. To say that "I decided that Joe was the better candidate for the job than Jane" makes little sense unless a job offer for Joe is forthcoming. Otherwise, the comparison lingers at the level of judgment. Typically, judgments precede and enable decisions.

It is not a trivial exercise to demarcate the domain of the psychology of judgment and decision making (JDM). At one extreme, a great range of behavior expressed by an organism can be described as judgment or decision. Where that range ends is less clear. Simple reflexes or internal, physiological reactions, for example, seem out of bounds. On the other hand, and contrary to folk wisdom, visual perception can be described as a clever act of creation that involves "inferences" (Helmholtz, 1867; Rock, 1983). Ordinary understanding does not incorporate the idea of unconscious inferences; it treats judgment and decision making as activities that humans pursue with purpose and deliberation. A jury's efforts to reach a verdict are prototypical in this regard. A jury, of course, is a group of people, whereas a judging and deciding individual can be alone.

Issues of individual versus group-level JDM as well as issues of deliberative versus nonconscious JDM, among others, are explored. Payne and Iannuzzi (Chapter 3) show how a process-dissociation model can yield separate estimates for the impact of controlled versus automatic reasoning on J and DM. The key to their method is that the two processes must be set in competition with each other, which can be done experimentally. Larrick, Mannes, and Soll (Chapter 13) survey issues or information aggregation within and across individuals. They show how, depending on the task and the information at hand, judgments and decisions can range from the egocentric to the wise.

As a scientific discipline, the psychology of JDM cannot be too constrained by folk psychology. Its objective is to model and explain how humans (and other animals) make all sorts of judgments and decisions, and do so with theoretical frameworks that are as parsimonious as possible. Ideally, there would be an overarching meta-theory, or at least a shared metaphor, guiding the research enterprise. The rational-actor model, computational models, evolutionary game theory, and various *homo* _____*us*-es (economicus, heuristicus) have been among the contenders. The continuing coexistence of these models and the controversies among them suggest, at minimum, that the study of JDM is difficult. Were it not so, a unified theory would have emerged by now. A somewhat dyspeptic conclusion is that some of the existing models must be false; a more optimistic inference is that many models probably do a good job accounting for some aspect of JDM. Whatever the case may be, it is no longer enough to simply ask people to describe their own thought processes and leave it at that.

In psychology, the temptation to simply ask always lurks near the surface. To most people their own J's and D's seem obvious, rational, and dictated by the stimulus or the task at hand. They tend not to see that many other individuals come up with different J's and D's that seem obvious to *them*. Social reasoning is fundamentally and inescapably egocentric, a theme that Gilovich, Cone, and Rosenzweig (Chapter 1) elaborate in new and interesting ways. Likewise, much of the cognitive work goes on underground, as it were, and remains inaccessible to introspection (see Payne & Ianuzzi, Chapter 3). Many of the stories people tell to account for their J's and D's are *post hoc* attempts to convince themselves and others of their own reasonableness (Kurzban, 2010). The advantage of the experimental method is that it confronts judges and decision makers with systematic variations in the problem that would otherwise go unnoticed, but that are critical in that they reveal the psychological processes supporting JDM.

To illustrate, consider the game of *balla*, which the Franciscan monk Fra Luca dal Borgo ("Paccioli," 1446–1517) used to study the "problem of points" (cf. David, 1962). The game involves a device that produces outcomes two players can bet on. In a classroom demonstration, I asked one student to flip a coin and two other students, A and B, to contribute $10 each to a stake. If the coin came up heads A won the round, otherwise B won the round. We agreed that whichever player was the first to win six rounds would take the entire stake. Paccioli's question was "How should you divide the stake if the game cannot be completed?" In the classroom demonstration, I stopped the game when player A was ahead five to two.

Polling the class on what to do, I found a large group that—like Paccioli—favored a proportional division: seven rounds had been played, and A had won five, therefore A was entitled to 5/7 of the stake. A minority asked that the $10 dollars each player had contributed should be returned. One student insisted that A should get the whole stake because he was closer to winning. In short, there was some variation in response, little empathy for the solutions proposed by others, and all of them were wrong.

Once the three numbers that constitute the game are varied, the flaws of these division rules become obvious. Suppose the criterion for winning all is 100 rounds and imagine yourself as player B in two games. In game 1, A has won one round and you have won none. In game 2, A has also won one round while you have won 99.* The proportional rule awards you nothing in game 1 and less than all ($19.80) in game 2. Across the two games, you are awarded less than A, although you have won 97 more rounds than he. That does not seem fair. How about the equality rule, then? This rule awards A as much as you, although you have done much better in the game overall. The player-ahead-takes-all rule entails the same unfairness. Over the two games, then, you only break even regardless of which of the three rules is applied.†

Seeing the inadequacy of the proposed rules does not guarantee that a better rule is found. It is necessary to take a counterintuitive step and ask *how close* the players are to winning. What would need to happen for each player to win the game in accordance with the original agreement if the game were to be continued? In other words, the players need to contemplate counterfactual realities; they need to create "mental representations of what *is not* in the immediate environment" (Hastie & Dawes, 2010, p. 3). In correspondence, this is what Pascal and Fermat did, thus solving the problem of points and laying the foundation of modern probability theory.

In the class game, there was only one way B could win all. It would have taken a series of four consecutive successes. The probability of that to happen is $.5^4$ or .0625, resulting in a claim of $1.25. Every other sequence of outcomes favors player A, thus entitling her to $18.75. Applied to your imaginary two games, the probability rule awards you a total of about $30 (a little more than half in game 1 and a little less than all in game 2, or about 3/4 of the pooled stakes).

The probability rule is rational, fair, and counterintuitive (Dawes, 1988). It is rational because it avoids contradictions, and it does so by incorporating the future into the JDM process. It is fair because only fools would complain once the rule is explained to them.‡ It is counterintuitive because experience (see above) and research (Krueger, 2000) show that people have little spontaneous insight into the past–future asymmetry.

None of the other three rules casts the problem of points as a judgment under uncertainty. Only the probability rule treats the problem of fair division as a betting problem. Betting focuses the attention on the future. It remains to be seen if people would intuitively grasp Pascal and Fermat's vision if they were asked to wager their own money on player A or B when the game is interrupted. Likewise, the problem of points could be reframed by telling the judges that "A and B have agreed to play *balla* until A has won one round or B has won four rounds, whichever comes first. A disruption prevents them from playing. How should the $20 stake be divided?"

The probability rule is easy to apply if one player is one round short of winning; it is difficult if many rounds are necessary. The progress of the scientific study of probability, uncertainty, and risk has been measured in generations (Bernstein,

---

* This example highlights the limits of thought experiments. Any sane person would question the assumption that the coin is fair.
† To help people appreciate rational solutions, it is sometimes necessary to appeal to their passions, be they moral or self-interested.
‡ I realize that this is an illogical, question-begging argument, but I like its pragmatic appeal.

1996). Insights into *what* should be calculated were hard-won and insights into *how* to make the calculations were not much easier to gain. Yet, the intuitions of ordinary people and their capacities to calculate have not changed much. In consequence, there has been a growing gulf between what formal models of JDM can handle and what human performance typically provides. This is a continuing challenge for JDM because much of its tension and excitement stems from the study of the discrepancies between the normative and the descriptive.

Shu, Tsay, and Bazerman (Chapter 14) argue that irrational judgments matter a great deal. Going beyond the conventional arena of personal JDM, Shu and colleagues explore the consequences of cognitive and emotional sources of bias on policy decisions. Baron (Chapter 15) is concerned with judgments of morality and their origins. His distinction between deontological and consequentialist reasoning maps nicely on Paccioli's problem of points. Its forward-looking nature gives consequentialist reasoning a better shot at being rational than inflexible categorical reasoning.

Every time ordinary humans are charged with having committed an error of judgment, the onus is on the claimant to show that the normative response was within psychological reach. In my chapter (Chapter 4), I argue that this criterion is seldom met. In theory, debiasing studies can serve this purpose. If study participants perform normatively after they have been warned of certain biases or promised monetary incentives for accuracy, it can be said that the expectation of normative responding itself was reasonable. In practice, however, the logic of inference is the reverse. Failed debiasing interventions are taken as evidence for the robustness of the error and the limitation of the mind.

Paccioli's problem, which marks the beginning of the modern conception of probability, also highlights what is social about JDM. An abstract or nonsocial version of the game would arouse little excitement. It is not even clear what such a game would look like. Paccioli's game confounds us not only because combination-based probabilities are more difficult to compute than simple ratios, but also because we feel the pull of the norm of fairness and the easy confusion of equality with fairness. Arguably, most of the psychology of JDM, as it stands, is social. Von Neumann and Morgenstern (1947) developed game theory from their analysis of strategic behavior among players trying to outwit each other. Tversky and Kahneman (1974) introduced the study of heuristics by asking how people categorize other *people* (Tom the engineer; Linda the bank teller). People vote in elections, invest their money, and find mates and abandon them. In the most recent *Handbook of Social Psychology* (5th edition), Gilovich and Griffin (2010) track the historical interplay of social psychology with "regular," *asocial* JDM psychology.

The social psychology of JDM is moving beyond the simple and equally untenable view that reasoning by heuristics is all bad or all good. Given today's state of the science, such characterizations must be rejected as caricatures. Hoffrage and Hertwig (Chapter 8) explore the interactions between JDM heuristics and different ecological contexts. Their perspective of ecological rationality emphasizes the *fit* between what is in the mind (e.g., capacities and modes of thinking, such as heuristics) and what is in the environment (e.g., the complexity or the structure of the task). When the fit is good, heuristics yield excellent results, often amazingly so, but they are not all-powerful. Recall that in the Paccioli situation, all the wrong division rules can be phrased as simple heuristics, whereas the Pascal–Fermat rule cannot.

Many social situations are high in complexity, in part because the person interacts with, and is interdependent with others who find themselves in the same situation. This complexity requires strategic thinking and behavior. Game theory, evolutionary and otherwise, has produced important insights here, but many questions remain unresolved. DeScioli and Kurzban (Chapter 12) focus on the issue of friendship. Taking an alliance of at least two against one as the basic structure of friendship, their theory assumes complexity, both in the structure of the task and the mental equipment needed to solve it.

The suite of social tasks is broad. If all JDM tasks containing at least one social aspect along the way were counted as social, the residual category would be small indeed. Yet, there is sometimes a sense that the "social" aspect is merely something that is tacked on to more foundational or essential types of "pure" process. The reductionist project is to strip away all that is social and describe the operations of the mind in an abstract fashion. Social JDM then is pure JDM plus garnish.

Social and other JDM has co-evolved with the routines and rituals of scientific inference. Novices (or individuals with short memories) tend to think that the process of scientific hypothesis testing and inference is mechanized and mathematized to the extent that the computational apparatus can do all the work. Human judgment is not needed anymore. Nothing could be farther from the truth. Even if some conventions have become so calcified that the human judge does not experience any freedom of choice, the origins of these conventions, their acceptance and perpetuation, are social phenomena. The p value typically deemed sufficiently low for the rejection of the null hypothesis is the most obvious example, but others abound. Some analytical preferences are social in that they are widely shared and are critical for the publication success of a submitted research paper. In the social psychological literature, mediation models are *de rigueur*, bested by moderated mediation, and soon eclipsed by hierarchical linear modeling. With the current trend favoring more complex data analytic methods, the number of assumptions embedded in the analysis increases sharply, and the transparency of theoretically relevant inferences suffers. In other words, more depends on faith and authority.

This is a troubling development. Of course, the "official" interpretation is that more complex statistics are more reliable and valid than simpler ones, and that they reduce the two types of error that will always be part of the induction enterprise: accepting false claims and failing to accept true ones. The trouble comes from the possibility that researchers, much like the research participants they study, are led astray by heuristic thinking (Dawes & Mulford, 1996). They may conform to current theoretical and statistical trends, yield to authority, and fail to intervene when called upon (e.g., fail to risk their reputation to protest or rebut deficient or frivolous research). Likewise, they may yield to the temptation of accepting their own tools of research design and data analysis as models of mind (Gigerenzer, 1991). If analysis of variance is *the* way to make inductive inferences, then the rational person must surely run some analog of it in her mind. Of course, this itself is an inductive (or rather analogical) way of thinking that cannot be logically justified. David Hume remains correct on this one.

Several chapters in this volume explore areas in which researchers' methodological intuitions and choices critically affect what is learned about ordinary people's judgments and decisions. The overall tenor of these chapters is a plea for simplicity. Cutting to the most fundamental issues of response scaling and measurement, Blanton and Jaccard (Chapter 5) review the metrics typically used to study social JDM, and they reveal the many pitfalls awaiting the unwary researcher, the result often being unwarranted charges of irrationality. Jussim, Stevens, and Salib (Chapter 6) reject the popular notion that categorical inferences regarding inaccuracy or bias are drawn from significance tests. As an alternative, they introduce a general-purpose index that scales accuracy versus error relative to their maximally possible values. Fiedler and Krueger (Chapter 10) are concerned with bivariate distributions and the proper interpretation of regression effects. They argue that, as an omnipresent phenomenon, regression to the mean offers many opportunities to reinterpret well-established JDM phenomena and predict new ones. Ullrich (Chapter 7) addresses multivariate scenarios of the type that are becoming increasingly popular. New techniques enable researchers to revisit classic JDM phenomena and question conventional interpretations. Ullrich's unpacking of attitudinal ambivalence is a case in point.

Years ago, the incomparable Paul Meehl asserted that "mathematics is hard, sociology is easy" (Meehl, 1990, p. 234). He insisted that a thorough methodological education is a healthy thing for psychologists, and that armchair analysis will not do. I don't know if he meant to insult the field of sociology, when it is well-known that many sociologists are masters of statistical technique and creative methodological innovators. From within the field of sociology, Theo Harder (1974), then professor at the University of Bielefeld, expressed a similar sentiment, referring to the use of methodological tools in empirical social science as "*Knochenarbeit*."°

Sampling observations and knowing when to stop is part of that *Knochenarbeit*. Size and selectivity are critical features of samples. Gilovich, Cone, and Rosenzweig (Chapter 1) explore how the mind samples relevant material that is associated with a stimulus to generate a space in which J and DM can occur. P. Fischer, Aydin, J. Fischer, Frey, and Lea (Chapter 2) review and integrate research on selectivity. They propose a simple general model of selectivity that cuts through the traditional distinction of cognition and motivation, thus offering a new understanding of many empirical results. Denrell and Le Mens (Chapter 9) show how valence-based asymmetries in the stopping rule can create many of the JDM phenomena conventionally attributed to biases in information *processing* (as opposed to information *sampling*). Finally, Todd, Place, and Bowers (Chapter 11) explore the adaptiveness of sequential sampling in the context of mate selection. Like some of the other contributors, these authors conclude that simple heuristics do quite well even in complex ecologies (but see DeScioli & Kurzban, Chapter 12).

° *Knochenarbeit*, literally "bone labor," or more aptly "bone-crushing labor," is a German colloquialism.

The mission of the present volume is to explore JDM through a social lens. It is my hope that the traditional disciplines of social psychology and JDM psychology benefit from this enterprise. That is why, in my framing of this mission, I relied on Paccioli's game, which is the closest thing we have to a creation myth. Among other things, the problem of points illustrates how even seemingly abstract reasoning problems are shot through with a social dimension.

Pascal, after having solved the problem of points (with Fermat), experienced a conversion to mystical Christianity but he continued to cogitate. In his *Pensées*, he turned his formidable talents on the question of how he might rationalize his belief in God. The result was a radical departure from the traditional attempts to *prove* the existence of God. All these attempts failed (Dawkins, 2006). Pascal asked how he should *decide* whether to live in accordance with religious demands (thereby forego-ing earthly gratifications) or not (thereby risking eternal damnation). The result was what is now known as the standard decision-theoretic paradigm, which evaluates a choice between options (e.g., what to do) in light of two true states of nature (God does or does not exist) by integrating their respective probabilities and values and by comparing the results (Swets, Dawes, & Monahan, 2000). Most of the issues regarding the accuracy of and bias in social JDM follow from this foundational arrangement.

Yet, Pascal's wager, and hence decision analysis, is still a simple affair because it assumes that God, if He exists, will unfailingly reward the faithful and punish all oth-ers. The idea of perfect justice entails this assumption. When the possibility of divine mercy (God pardons some of the wicked) or divine oversight (God fails to reward some of the virtuous) is introduced, Pascal's wager, and thus decision theory, goes stochastic and gets more complicated. And it gets better. God not only responds to Pascal's actions, but also to his intentions, and if Pascal can predict, or thinks he can predict, how God will evaluate his action or whether God is able to see through his tactical behavior, then the problem is one of interpersonal strategy (Brams, 1994). This dynamical aspect of social JDM, that is, its embeddedness in mutual perception, prediction, and outguessing, is the ultimate frontier of the field.

While struggling with these conceptual issues and the empirical challenges they entail, the social psychology of judgment and decision making must also seek to contribute to human welfare. I trust that the reader will find many useful insights and recommendations in the present volume. From the personal to the interper-sonal and on to the policy related, social JDM provides tools for living rationally and socially responsibly.

Joachim I. Krueger
Department of Cognitive, Linguistic, and Psychological Sciences
Brown University, Box 1853
190 Thayer Street
Providence, RI 02912
Phone: (401) 863-2503
Fax: (401) 863-1300
E-mail: Joachim_Krueger@Brown.edu
Web: http://research.brown.edu/research/profile.php?id=10378

REFERENCES

Bernstein, P. L. (1996). *Against the gods: The remarkable story of risk*. New York: Wiley.

Brams, S. J. (1994). *Theory of moves*. New York: Cambridge University Press.

David, F. N. (1962). *Games, gods, and gambling: A history of probability and statistical ideas*. London: Charles Griffin & Co.

Dawes, R. M. (1988). *Rational choice in an uncertain world*. San Diego: Harcourt Brace Jovanovich Publishers.

Dawes, R. M., & Mulford M. (1996). The false consensus effect and overconfidence: Flaws in judgment or flaws in how we study judgment? *Organizational Behavior and Human Decision Processes, 65*, 201–211.

Dawkins, R. (2006). *The God delusion*. New York: Houghton Mifflin.

Gigerenzer, G. (1991). From tools to theories: A heuristic of discovery in cognitive psychology. *Psychological Review, 98*, 254–267.

Gilovich, T., & Griffin, D. T. (2010). Judgment and decision making. In S. T. Fiske, D. T. Gilbert, & G. Lindzey (Eds.), *Handbook of social psychology*, 5th ed. (Vol. 1, pp. 542–588). Hoboken, NJ: Wiley.

Harder, T. (1974). *Werkzeug der Sozialforschung*. München: Wilhelm Fink.

Hastie, R., & Dawes, R. M. (2010). *Rational choice in an uncertain world: The psychology of judgment and decision making* (2nd ed.). Thousand Oaks, CA: Sage.

Helmholtz, H. (1867). *Handbuch der physiologischen Optik*. Leipzig: Leopold Voss.

Krueger, J. (2000). Distributive judgments under uncertainty: Paccioli's game revisited. *Journal of Experimental Psychology: General, 129*, 546–558.

Meehl, P. E. (1990). Why summaries of research on psychological theories are often uninterpretable. *Psychological Reports, 66*, 195–244.

Rock, I. (1983). *The logic of perception*. Cambridge, MA: MIT Press.

Swets, J. A., Dawes, R. M., & Monahan, J. (2000). Psychological science can improve diagnostic decision. *Psychological Science in the Public Interest, 1*, 1–26.

Tversky, A., & Kahneman, D. (1974). Judgments under uncertainty: Heuristics and biases. *Science, 185*, 1124–1131.

Editor

Joachim I. Krueger, PhD, is a professor of psychology at Brown University. He is a fellow of the Association for Psychological Science and the recipient of an Alexander-von-Humboldt research prize. His scientific interests center around inductive reasoning in social context. His work includes studies on social categorization, stereotyping, self-perception, as well as judgment and decision making. Rather than write a book himself, Dr. Krueger enjoys editing. Prior to the present volume, he edited *The Self in Social Judgment* (with M. Alicke & D. Dunning, 2005) and *Rationality and Social Responsibility* (a festschrift for Robyn Dawes, 2008). Both appeared with Psychology Press. Some of his heterodox views on a variety of psychological topics can be found on his blog "One among many": http://blogs.psychologytoday.com/blog/one-among-many.

Contributors

Nilüfer Aydin
University of Munich (LMU)
Munich, Germany

Jonathan Baron
University of Pennsylvania
Philadelphia, Pennsylvania

Max H. Bazerman
Harvard University
Cambridge, Massachusetts

Hart Blanton
University of Connecticut
Storrs, Connecticut

Robert I. Bowers
Indiana University
Bloomington, Indiana

Jeremy Cone
Cornell University
Ithaca, New York

Jerker Denrell
University of Oxford
Oxford, United Kingdom

Peter DeScioli
Brandeis University
Waltham, Massachusetts

Klaus Fiedler
University of Heidelberg
Heidelberg, Germany

Julia Fischer
University of Munich (LMU)
Munich, Germany

Peter Fischer
University of Regensburg
Regensburg, Germany

Dieter Frey
University of Munich (LMU)
Munich, Germany

Thomas Gilovich
Cornell University
Ithaca, New York

Ralph Hertwig
University of Basel
Basel, Switzerland

Ulrich Hoffrage
University of Lausanne
Lausanne, Switzerland

Jazmin L. Brown Iannuzzi
University of North Carolina
Chapel Hill, North Carolina

James Jaccard
Florida International University
Miami, Florida

Lee Jussim
Rutgers University
New Brunswick, New Jersey

Robert Kurzban
University of Pennsylvania
Philadelphia, Pennsylvania

Richard P. Larrick
Duke University
Durham, North Carolina

Stephen E. G. Lea
University of Exeter
Exeter, United Kingdom

Gaël Le Mens
Universitat Pompeu Fabra and
    Barcelona GS
Barcelona, Spain

Albert E. Mannes
Carnegie Mellon University
Pittsburgh, Pennsylvania

B. Keith Payne
University of North Carolina
Chapel Hill, North Carolina

Skyler S. Place
Indiana University
Bloomington, Indiana

Emily Rosenzweig
Cornell University
Ithaca, New York

Elizabeth R. Salib
Rutgers University
New Brunswick, New Jersey

Lisa L. Shu
Harvard University
Cambridge, Massachusetts

Jack B. Soll
Duke University
Durham, North Carolina

Sean T. Stevens
Rutgers University
New Brunswick, New Jersey

Peter M. Todd
Indiana University
Bloomington, Indiana

Chia-Jung Tsay
Harvard University
Cambridge, Massachusetts

Johannes Ullrich
Goethe University
Frankfurt, Germany

Section *I*

The Processes of Judgment and Decision Making

1

Where the Mind Goes
The Influence of Endogenous Priming on Thought and Behavior

THOMAS GILOVICH, JEREMY CONE,
and EMILY ROSENZWEIG

T hirty years ago, a group of political science students was asked what actions they would recommend to deal with a country that seemed poised to invade a less powerful neighbor. Substantial segments of the population of the threatened country were getting out of harm's way by setting out in small boats off the coast to neutral countries. The students' recommendations were quite varied, but on the whole they were much less interventionist than those of another group of students who were given the same information but told that the threatened people were fleeing in boxcars on freight trains. The difference in mode of transportation—small boats versus boxcars—was designed, along with other incidental features of the crisis, to remind the students either of Vietnam or World War II. Students reminded of World War II were expected to recommend stronger measures to deal with the crisis than those reminded of Vietnam—and they did (Gilovich, 1981).

Today, such an experiment would be called a priming study. Information outside the crisis situation itself—knowledge about Vietnam or World War II—was activated and brought to bear on the students' recommendations of what to do about the situation described. But it is an atypical priming study. In a typical priming experiment, the information that activates the construct in question stands apart from the entity being evaluated. Sentences are unscrambled, words are searched in a grid of letters, or stimuli are presented subliminally, and the effect of this prior activation on a subsequent, unrelated task is measured (Bargh, Chen, & Burrows, 1996; Epley & Gilovich, 1999; Ferguson, 2008; Higgins, Rholes, & Jones, 1977; Lammers & Stapel, 2009). Here, in contrast, it is information embedded in the to-be-evaluated-situation itself that primes the concept in question.

Both types of priming effects have their parallels in daily life. An encounter with a hostile colleague in the supermarket parking lot influences how friendly the clerk at the checkout line seems. A group of somber-looking people dressed formally in black induces the sedate behavior characteristic of a funeral. The former example constitutes a real-life version of a standard priming effect or what might be called *exogenous priming*. The latter represents an instance of what might be called *endogenous priming*. In exogenous priming, the stimuli that trigger the relevant top-down processing lie outside the information being evaluated; with endogenous priming, the triggering stimuli—the cues that activate the particular construct or schema in question—are part of the to-be-evaluated information itself.

Note that both types of priming can help or hinder accurate judgment. An exogenous or endogenous prime can connect directly to the essence of the information being evaluated and thereby facilitate the processing of that information. But both can also lead a person off-track. Exogenously priming a person with an image of a spider can make it harder for that person to identify an ice-cream cone as something delicious. Similarly, a superficial feature of a given geopolitical crisis that reminds people of Vietnam can make it harder to recommend intervention when intervention may be required.

We contend that psychologists' near-exclusive focus on exogenous priming has limited our understanding of how existing knowledge guides people's judgments and decisions in the complex situations they encounter in daily life—a limitation that can be overcome by considering the operation and impact of endogenous priming. We elaborate that contention by proposing that an understanding of endogenous priming can be advanced by considering "where the mind goes" when one confronts information. Whenever one confronts a stimulus, contemplates a question, or considers a prospect, the mind automatically goes somewhere. And where it goes has consequences. Even if it goes there only briefly, it tends to leave some tracks, channeling subsequent information processing.

This notion of the mind "going somewhere" is, of course, what priming is all about. Priming pulls the mind toward a given concept, which results in new information being evaluated with that information "in mind." Thirty years of priming research therefore gives a partial answer to the question of where the mind goes. First and foremost, it goes to recently visited places. Most priming studies are demonstrations that recently activated information has a disproportionate influence on the evaluation of new stimuli (Ford & Kruglanski, 1995; Higgins, Rholes, & Jones, 1977; Stapel & Koomen, 2000; Todorov & Bargh, 2002). The mind also goes to frequently visited places. That is, a number of experiments have shown that constructs and schemas that individuals use frequently tend to be activated quite readily, thereby influencing how newly encountered stimuli are evaluated (Andersen, Glassman, Chen, & Cole, 1995; Higgins, King, & Mavin, 1982).

In this chapter, we aim to examine other places the mind goes upon encountering new information, and to what effect. In particular, we argue that the mind often goes to (1) extreme exemplars; (2) to what one hopes, intends, or fears will happen; (3) to counterfactuals and descriptive norms; and (4) to moral considerations and prescriptive norms. In each case, we wish to explore how the information people encounter and the contexts in which they encounter it sends the mind to a particular location in one's storehouse of knowledge and how the accessibility of that information influences people's judgments and decisions (Hastie & Dawes, 2010; Morewedge & Kahneman, 2010). By focusing on these four domains, we hope to illustrate that endogenous priming has both motivational (hopes, fears, and moral considerations) and purely cognitive origins (extremity and some counterfactuals and descriptive norms). We consider this short list to be merely illustrative; there surely are other broad determinants of where the mind reflexively goes that also merit further analysis and empirical investigation.

GOING TO EXTREMES

Commuters waiting on a subway platform were asked to recall a time when they missed their train and had to wait for another. Some were asked just that ("a time"), whereas others were asked to recall the time they missed their train and suffered the worst consequences. Both groups were then asked to rate how troublesome it would be if they missed their train that day. Notably, those who were asked to think of a time they had missed their train recalled an instance that was every bit as bothersome as those asked to think of the worst time they had missed their train. When asked to think of a time they missed their train, in other words, respondents spontaneously accessed the most extreme instance. And doing so colored their assessments of how bad it would be if they missed their train that day, with participants asked to think of "a time" they missed their train indicating that they thought such a fate would be every bit as troublesome as those asked to recall the worst time they missed their train (Morewedge, Gilbert, & Wilson, 2005).

As this example makes clear, we often represent categories not by a typical exemplar but by an extreme exemplar (Barsalou, 1983, 1985; Frederickson & Kahneman, 1993; Kittur, Hummel, & Holyoak, 2006). The experience of missing a train is an experience of annoyance and inconvenience and so it stands to reason that people might spontaneously access a particularly annoying or inconvenient episode, not a typical episode of annoyance or inconvenience. Epley and Gilovich (2010) obtained analogous results in a series of studies in which people were asked to imagine how they would be rated by observers in the wake of a public triumph or public failure. Those simply asked to estimate how observers would judge them after a personal failure anticipated ratings that were every bit as critical as participants asked to estimate how the harshest members of the audience would judge them. And participants asked to estimate how observers would judge them after a personal triumph anticipated ratings that were every bit as positive as participants asked to estimate how the most charitable members of the audience would judge them. Again, the episodes participants were asked to imagine were all about personal failure or success and so it stands to reason that they would imagine the greatest success and the deepest failure that those situations permit. The tendency to spontaneously access the worst possible negative outcome (as opposed to a run-of-the-mill negative outcome) is one reason that many people have such pronounced social phobias (Fenigstein & Vanable, 1992; Leary & Kowalski, 1995), such as a debilitating fear of public speaking (Savitsky & Gilovich, 2003; Stein, Walker, & Forde, 1996).

This tendency to quickly access an extreme exemplar can also shed light on the well-documented above-average effect or the tendency of most people to rate themselves as above average on most traits and abilities (Alicke, Klotz, Breitenbecher, Yurak, & Vredenburg, 1995; Dunning, Heath, & Suls, 2004; Dunning, Meyerowitz, & Holzberg, 1989; Guenther & Alicke, 2010; Svenson, 1981). That is, when asked about their standing on a given trait or ability dimension, the information most likely to spring to mind for most people is their best past performance or their highest manifestation of a given trait. After all, their best is precisely what people are striving for and so it is likely to occupy a great deal of their attention and hence be particularly accessible. When assessing someone else's standing, in contrast, what is most likely to spring to mind is what that person is like on average. Assessing others is tantamount to assessing what they are like "in general" or "on average," and so representations of their personal bests are much less privileged. Note that any such difference in where the mind goes when thinking about the self and others almost guarantees an above-average effect.

Williams and Gilovich (2010) obtained support for this difference in what springs to mind and then serves as the basis of self-assessment and the assessment of others. In one study, one group of participants was asked to specify a range representing their own or an acquaintance's highest or lowest possible percentile standing on a number of traits—that is, to provide the equivalent of a confidence interval for their own or an acquaintance's true standing. A second group simply gave a point estimate of their own or an acquaintance's standing on these traits. As can be seen in Figure 1.1, participants' point estimates of their own standing tended to coincide with the upper end of the intervals provided by the first group of participants, but their point estimates of the acquaintances' standing tended to lie near the middle of the intervals. When assessing their own performance, in other words, what comes to mind is what they are like at their best; when assessing others, in contrast, what comes to mind is what others are like on average. A follow-up study directly examined this self-other asymmetry in the weight people assign to personal bests by asking participants whether their own or someone else's worst efforts, average efforts, or best efforts would give an observer the most accurate impression of the individual in question (self or other). Participants were more likely to say that a personal best would be most informative to an observer when asked about their own standing, and they were more likely to say that a personal average would be most informative when asked about someone else's standing.

Parents and teachers often tell children that they should try to judge individuals by the best that they have to offer. It appears that this lesson is easier to apply when it comes to evaluating the self than when it comes to evaluating others. People often evaluate themselves in terms of who they are at their best, but they typically evaluate someone else by what that person is like on average.

HOPE AND FEAR

Much of mental life is a battle for supremacy between our hopes and fears. Sometimes our hopes and intentions spring to mind automatically, dominate our

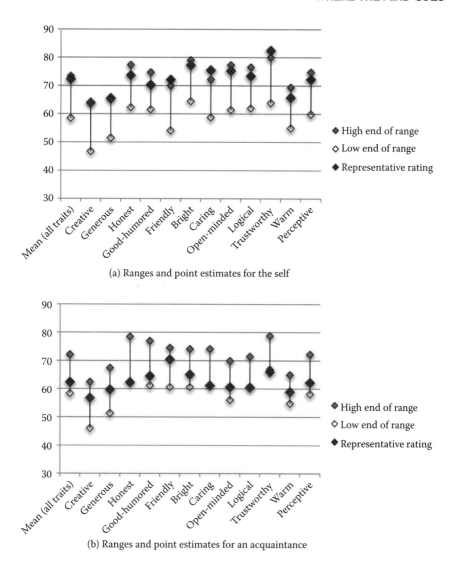

Figure 1.1 Participants' point estimates ("representative ratings") and upper and lower bounds on their standing on 12 traits and a composite of all 12. (a) Ranges and point estimates for the self. (b) Ranges and point estimates for an acquaintance. (From Williams, E., & Gilovich, T., 2010, *Stacking the Deck: Self Other Differences in the Basis of Self-Assessment*, Manuscript under review.)

thinking, and lead us to be optimistic about our prospects. At other times our minds run right to our fears and suspicions, fostering a disquieting pessimism. Happily, the former seems to occur more often for most people than the latter, as the vast literature on various optimistic biases attests (Dunning, Heath, & Suls, 2004; Taylor & Brown, 1988). A consideration of "where the mind goes" can provide some insight into when people's hopes and intentions are most likely to spring to mind and when their fears are likely to be more accessible—and therefore when people are likely to be predictably optimistic or pessimistic.

Part of the reason that optimism is so rampant is that people have ready access to their hopes and their intentions (Gilovich, Epley, & Hanko, 2005). When people consider what they might achieve, their minds go immediately to their hopes and intentions—in essence self-priming themselves for optimism and anticipated success. Evidence of people's ready access to their intentions, and its influence on social judgment, comes from several sources. Koehler and Poon (2006) found that participants' predictions of their future behavior were strongly tied to their intentions, but relatively insensitive to the presence or absence of various situational elements that make the behavior in question more or less likely. Kruger and Gilovich (2004) directly tied people's focus on their own intentions to the above-average effect, showing that people give considerable weight to their own intentions when assessing where they stand on various traits and abilities, but do not do so when assessing where others stand.

Because people typically aim to realize their potential, their sense of their own potential is also likely to spring to mind when assessing their current abilities. Consistent with this idea, Williams, Gilovich, and Dunning (2010) had participants engage in several rounds of a novel task and gave them feedback about their actual performance and an estimate of their long-term potential after each round. They found that participants tended to look disproportionately at the information conveying their potential. This was not the case when participants watched the performances and feedback given to others; they tended to look disproportionately at the information about others' actual performance not their long-term potential. This asymmetry in how readily information about a person's potential springs to mind led to a rather intriguing result in another study. Tennis players were asked whether they could think of anyone who regularly beat them but whom they nevertheless thought was not as good a tennis player as they were themselves. Most players had no trouble doing so and could think of significantly more such players than the complement—that is, players they regularly defeated but whom they nonetheless thought were better players. It appears, then, that people have ready access to their own goals and intentions and tend to think of themselves as "headed somewhere" (Williams & Gilovich, 2008). Where they are headed, in turn, springs to mind rapidly and effortlessly when assessing who they are. People have less knowledge about others' goals and intentions, and so the assessment of others draws more exclusively on what they have done in the past, rather than what they might do, or what they are capable of, in the future. Once again, rather flattering and optimistic self-assessments are the nearly inevitable result of these twin tendencies.

Pessimistic Assessments

Although the bulk of the psychological literature, at least the non-clinical literature, has focused on people's optimistic biases, everyday experience makes it clear that people are not always so sanguine about their attributes, abilities, or prospects for the future. Self-doubt and self-criticism are common. Indeed, attempts to document the existence of robust wishful thinking, defined as the tendency for the desirability of an outcome to causally influence its perceived likelihood, have not met with much success (Bar-Hillel & Budescu, 1995; Krizan & Windschitl, 2007; McKenna, 1993). Although there is plenty of evidence for various sorts of optimistic biases, such as self-enhancement (Alicke, 1985; Brown, 1986; Crary, 1966), unrealistic optimism (Armor & Taylor, 2002; Weinstein, 1980), and exaggerated perceptions of personal control over outcomes (Langer, 1975; Langer & Roth, 1975), people tend not to be overly optimistic that events outside their control are likely to turn out in their favor.

An analysis of where the mind goes helps to understand why. When a person can exert some control over an upcoming outcome, the mind naturally goes to what can be done to bring about the desired result. A person's thoughts about plans, contingencies, and intentions essentially serve as endogenous primes of success. In these contexts, then, optimism is common (Alicke, 1985). In contrast, when outcomes are thought by individuals to be beyond their control, thoughts about how to bring about the desired result are futile and so the mind tends not to go there. Instead, being adaptive creatures, people tend to think about what they can do to deal with or cope with a negative outcome should it occur (e.g., Cantor & Norem, 1989; Goodhart, 1986; Showers, 1992). "Bracing for failure," in other words, essentially primes failure, and therefore, in these contexts, pessimism can be quite common.

Consider the following thought experiment. You're in the middle of writing up a manuscript when a colleague asks how likely you think it is that it will be accepted for publication by the journal to which you plan to submit it. It seems likely that such a question would lead you to think of everything you plan to do to perfect the write-up and maximize its chances of acceptance—provide a compelling summary of the irresistible force of your findings, highlight a set of intriguing connections to important real-world problems, and specify a number of unanswered questions raised by the research that the field will race to address. With thoughts like these at the forefront of your mind, a successful passage through the editorial process can seem assured. But now imagine that you've already submitted the manuscript months ago and you receive an email from the journal to which it was submitted with the manuscript number in the subject heading ("Decision on Ms 10-0045"). How confident would you be in this circumstance? Because there is nothing you can do at this point to engineer a positive outcome, the mind is likely to race to how you might manage the receipt of bad news. And having primed yourself with the prospect of failure, the chances of success can seem very remote.

Support for this sort of pessimism for outcomes beyond a person's control receives support from several sources. First, people's optimism about all sorts of outcomes—those both within and outside their control—tends to decline the closer they get to the time the outcome will be decided (Gilovich, Kerr, & Medvec, 1993; Shepperd, Ouellette, & Fernandez, 1996). Because opportunities for effective instrumental action often decline as the moment of truth draws near, people are often left with little to do except brace for possible failure. With the thought of failure so clearly in the mind, it is hard to overcome those thoughts and remain confident about success. This can lead to outright pessimism, whereby people's assessments of their chances of success are lower than their objective odds (Shepperd, Findley-Klein, Kwavnick, Walker, & Perez, 2000).

Other evidence of pessimistic expectations for outcomes outside of one's control comes from research on the experience of surprise (Teigen & Keren, 2002). In one study, participants were told about an individual who was receiving treatment for heart disease. Half the participants were told the treatment had an initial 40% chance of success and that it turned out to be effective; the other half were told the treatment had an initial 60% chance of success and that it turned out to be ineffective. For both groups, then, an outcome with a 40% chance was realized. Despite the equivalence in how well the outcome mapped on to prior expectations, participants told that the outcome was positive rated what happened as substantially more surprising than those told that the outcome was negative. The authors argue that for these sorts of outcomes that are beyond the participant's control, bracing for failure is common, and so a negative outcome is not experienced as surprising—it has already been rehearsed.

The tendency to brace for failure, of course, is likely to be more pronounced the more consequential the outcome—the more there is something to brace for. Thus, the more negative the feared outcome, the more likely it can seem. A particularly interesting manifestation of this pattern of thought is the widespread belief that negative outcomes are more likely if one has done something to "tempt fate" (Risen & Gilovich, 2007, 2008). Baseball players, for example, believe it is bad luck to comment on a no-hitter in progress and, more generally, people believe that calling attention to success will make the success short-lived (Risen, Gilovich, Kruger, & Savitsky, 2010). People also believe that students are more likely to be called on by the teacher if they have not done the assigned reading than if they have (Risen & Gilovich, 2008), that those who celebrate prematurely will have nothing to celebrate (Risen & Gilovich, 2008), and that those who decline an opportunity to purchase insurance will end up needing it (Tykocinski, 2008).

In each of these examples, the possible negative outcome in question—the opposing team getting a hit, being called on in class, or suffering an accident—is something that is likely to elicit some bracing under any circumstances. But people know that they would feel even worse if they had done something that (superstitiously) would make such an outcome more likely (Miller & Taylor, 1995). The extra negativity of such an outcome elicits more bracing, which, in essence, primes still more negative thoughts and feelings that elicit more of a foreboding sense that a bad outcome will, in fact, occur.

Evidence of the mind automatically going to a negative outcome after actions that tempt fate comes from studies that examine the recognition latency for negative outcomes. More specifically, participants read a number of narratives in which the protagonist did or did not tempt fate, and ended up experiencing a positive or negative outcome. In one narrative, for example, an individual who hopes to be admitted to Stanford's PhD program receives a Stanford t-shirt from his mother. In one version of the narrative, he dons the T-shirt, thus tempting fate; in the other version, he stuffs the shirt at the bottom of his drawer. The time it took participants to read and understand the denouement of the narrative (e.g., "John was denied admission to Stanford") was recorded. Participants were much faster to process a negative ending if the protagonist had earlier tempted fate. The actions that tempted fate sent the participants' minds to the very negative outcomes one might fear and, having already considered those outcomes, participants had an easier time processing them (Risen & Gilovich, 2008).

COUNTERFACTUALS, NORMS, AND SOCIAL COMPARISONS

After a grueling race, two Olympic swimmers touch the wall and look up to see their times. One finishes two-hundredths of a second behind the winner, taking the silver medal. The other finishes two-hundredths of a second ahead of the fourth-place swimmer, earning the bronze. Medvec, Madey, and Gilovich (1995) demonstrated that the mind tends to go to very different places for athletes who find themselves in these situations. One is likely to focus upward, on almost having won the gold; the other is likely to focus downward, on almost failing to make it to the medal stand. And where the minds of silver and bronze medalists tend to go has profound consequences for their affective experience and sense of accomplishment. In three studies that examined high-level athletic competitions—the summer Olympics and the Empire State Games—silver medalists were found to be less happy than the bronze medalists they had just outcompeted, as evidenced by facial reactions both immediately after the competition and later on while on the medal stand, as well as in interviews with the news media after the event and in explicit self-reports (see also Matsumoto & Willingham, 2006; Medvec & Savitsky, 1997).

Findings such as these highlight the central theme of Kahneman and Miller's *norm theory* (1986)—that "each stimulus selectively recruits its own alternatives … and is interpreted in a rich context of remembered and constructed representations of what it could have been, might have been, or should have been" (p. 136). Events, in other words, regularly recruit alternatives that serve as salient comparisons that influence people's emotional reactions to what they have experienced. They also serve as endogenous primes that color the very meaning of the events that triggered them. Thoughts about almost receiving a gold medal can change what would otherwise be a satisfying success into a frustrating failure. Norm theory lays out a range of factors that determine when our minds are likely to be drawn to such counterfactual alternatives, including whether an event departs from an ideal, represents an exception to a routine, or is thought of as an effect rather than a cause.

Like priming effects generally, the counterfactual alternatives that serve as endogenous primes can, depending on the circumstances, have either assimilative or contrastive effects on people's judgments, decisions, and emotional reactions. Consider a study by McMullen and Markman (2000) in which participants were asked to imagine that they had money invested in an account and then saw the putative performance history of that investment. At one point, their investment had come close to, but had not fallen below, a critical value that determined whether the participants would have lost half the money in the account. The participants were encouraged to make a downward comparison that would lead either to assimilation (thinking about how bad it would have been if that critical value had been breached) or contrast (thinking about what they currently had and how it compared to what could have happened). Participants who generated assimilative downward counterfactuals subsequently indicated that they would have chosen to divest their money from the market at a substantially higher rate (63%) than those who generated contrastive downward counterfactuals (6%).

In related work, Markman, McMullen, and Elizaga (2008) provide evidence that upward counterfactuals that focus on the gap between one's own performance and a target performance lead to greater persistence and success on subsequent tasks. Similarly, Smallman and Roese (2009) report that generating counterfactuals to a negative outcome facilitates the formation of detailed behavioral intentions designed to achieve better outcomes in the future. Thus, both the direction and nature of the counterfactuals that spring to mind can have substantial impact on people's behavior. Note, furthermore, that counterfactuals need not pertain to an individual's own outcomes to have significant consequences for thought, feeling, and behavior. The generation of counterfactuals to others' outcomes has been shown to influence people's understanding of the causal structure of events (Wells & Gavanski, 1989), as well as such assessments as how generously crime victims should be compensated (Miller & McFarland, 1986), whether coincidences are seen as suspicious (Miller, Turnbull, & McFarland, 1989), and whether academic tests are seen as fair (Miller & Gunasegaram, 1990).

Social Comparison

Another place the mind often goes when contemplating an outcome or potential outcome—in fact, a close cousin of the counterfactual comparisons that people so often entertain—is to thoughts about what other people have achieved or are likely to achieve. Indeed, the thoughts entertained by disgruntled silver medalists are likely to be a mixture of (1) counterfactual ideation of themselves pictured on a box of Wheaties as the world's best in their sport and (2) envious thoughts about the actual gold-medal winners who bested them. Counterfactual comparisons blend together with social comparisons. There is, of course, a long and distinguished history in social psychology demonstrating that social comparisons have a powerful impact on people's emotional reactions and subsequent behavior (Festinger, 1954; Kruglanski & Mayseless, 1990; Mussweiler, 2003; Suls, Martin, & Wheeler, 2002; Suls & Wheeler, 2000). The bulk of this work has focused on the mind's tendency to focus on other people and their outcomes when evaluating one's own fate. For example, when the doctor tells us our cholesterol is dangerously high, our minds reflexively turn to a friend who eats bacon and eggs each morning, salami at lunch, and steak for dinner—and has yet to receive such grim news. An extensive program of research by Mussweiler and colleagues has delineated just how reflexively the mind accesses relevant social comparisons when people contemplate their own standing and outcomes (Mussweiler, 2003; Mussweiler, Rüter, & Epstude, 2004). In one study, participants who were asked to evaluate themselves on a series of personality attributes were faster to respond (relative to suitable controls) to the name of their best friend in a lexical decision task (Mussweiler & Rüter, 2003).

Thus, people's minds automatically go to a common standard of comparison—their best friends—when making assessments about the self.

Note that this process works in reverse as well, when others' outcomes make us think right away about our own. When a colleague announces that she just got an article accepted in *Science,* there probably are few scientists whose minds do not immediately race to their own publication records. The tendency to spontaneously access one's own standing on a given attribute when thinking about others has been examined systematically by Dunning and Hayes (1996) who argue that people tend to use their own performance as a standard when evaluating others. In one study, they first asked participants to read a set of scenarios describing a target person and to make trait judgments about the target. In a subsequent task, the participants were asked to make yes or no judgments about themselves on a series of trait dimensions and to complete a survey outlining the degree to which they possessed each of the traits in question. Response latencies for the yes or no self-judgments were faster for traits they had considered when evaluating the target, and those participants who showed greater levels of self-activation—who described their own behaviors more quickly—were the ones who evaluated the target most egocentrically. The authors concluded that people automatically turn to themselves when evaluating others, measuring others against the yardstick of the self.

PRESCRIPTIVE NORMS AND THE IMMEDIACY OF MORAL ASSESSMENTS

Anyone who has ever heard a young child scream, "That's not fair!" (that is, anyone who has ever been around young children) understands that the mind does not jump only to descriptive norms. Prescriptive norms also command attention and powerfully influence evaluation. Coming to grips with an event—understanding what *is*—is closely tied to thinking about what *should be.* Much of the recent research in moral psychology has demonstrated just how automatically moral considerations and prescriptive norms spring to mind when evaluating our own and others' actions (Greene & Haidt, 2002; Haidt, 2001, 2007).

This may be most apparent when it comes to considerations of equity and fairness. It is hard to have a sense that an outcome is unfair in the absence of any representation of what a fair outcome would be. Consider the ultimatum game, in which one participant is asked to propose a split of, say, $10 with another participant who can either accept or reject the proposal. If it is rejected, neither participant receives anything; if it is accepted, each receives the amount proposed. According to the standard economic analysis that posits rational, self-interested participants, proposers should make very asymmetric offers (say, $9 for themselves and $1 for the other participant) and the responders should accept (because $1 is more than $0). In reality, however, 50–50 splits are commonly proposed and proposals that depart notably from 50–50 tend to be rejected (Bolton & Zwick, 1995; Thaler, 1988). It is hard to imagine the minds of proposers or responders not going right away to a 50–50 split before deciding what to do in these studies. Responders' quick comparisons between the offers made and a 50–50 split, furthermore, result in some very strong, and very immediate, gut reactions. In one study (Chapman, Kim, Susskind, & Anderson, 2009), participants played 20 rounds of the ultimatum game with a series of confederates who were coached to vary the proposed split, from $5 each to $9–$1. Participants did so, furthermore, while their physiological responses were recorded electromyographically (EMG). Activation of the levator labii muscle—which commonly occurs when exposed to foul odors and bitter tastes and is associated with the subjective experience of disgust—was directly proportional to the unfairness of the offer with which participants were presented. Levator labii activation was significantly greater upon receipt of especially unfair offers ($9–$1) than either fair offers ($5–$5) or moderately unfair offers ($7–$3) and the more activation observed, the more participants reported being disgusted with the offer. The mind thus appears to compute unfairness—which involves a comparison of what is with what should be—very quickly, unleashing a facial signature that unfolds largely automatically.

Evidence that the mind automatically seizes on a fair outcome when presented with evidence of unfairness can also be seen far from the psychological laboratory. It sometimes happens in professional basketball that players are awarded foul shots they do not deserve. That is, a foul is called on an opposing player when it is obvious to everyone, the player benefitting from the call included, that no foul was actually committed. What happens when these players go to the free-throw line and attempt their foul shots? It seems that their minds are preoccupied with the injustice because, as shown in Figure 1.2, their performance suffers. On the first free-throw taken after benefitting from an unjust call, NBA players make a significantly lower percentage of their shots than the league-wide average percentage for first free-throws and their own season-long free-throw percentage

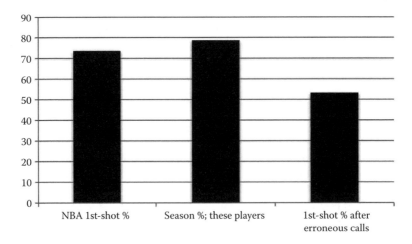

Figure 1.2   Free-throw shooting accuracy of NBA players on the first shot taken after going to the free-throw line after an incorrect call, compared to the league average for all first free-throw attempts and the overall free-throw percentage for these players. (From Haynes, G., & Gilovich, T., 2010, "The Ball Don't Lie": How Inequity Aversion Can Undermine Performance, *Journal of Experimental Social Psychology, 46*(6), 1148–1150.)

(Haynes & Gilovich, 2010). It is unclear whether this effect stems from players simply being distracted by their concern with fairness or whether they, however consciously or automatically, are "trying" to set things right by being less likely to make their shots. But in either case, it is clear that their minds are occupied with what is fair.

METAPHOR, FRAMEWORK, OR THEORY?

Greg Maddux, who pitched for the Cubs, Braves, Dodgers, and Padres during his 23 years in the major leagues, is probably the best pitcher anyone reading this chapter has ever seen. He won the eighth most games of anyone in the history of the sport and of the seven pitchers who won more, only one pitched a single inning after 1950. He won the Cy Young Award as the league's best pitcher four times, the most of anyone not accused of having artificially pumped himself up on steroids. He also won the Rawlings Gold Glove Award as the best fielder at his position a staggering 18 times in the last 19 years of his career. Maddux accomplished all of this, furthermore, without being an especially imposing physical specimen, at 6 feet and 180 pounds. He excelled, in other words, using intelligence, guile, and craft, attributes presumably highly prized by academic psychologists.

Psychologists, then, might be particularly interested in his response to the question of what constitutes the key to success as a pitcher: "To throw balls that look like they're going to be strikes; and to throw strikes that look like they're going to be balls." With these comments, Maddux offers what is essentially a theory of pitching, one that accomplishes one of the most important things scientists expect from a theory: It changes how we view the phenomenon in question. We suspect that for most readers, thinking of pitching in this way changes how they think about—indeed, what they *see*—in the contest between pitcher and batter.

We offer the present analysis of endogenous priming—of where the mind goes—as an attempt to provide a similar sort of theory. Theories come in many flavors. Some are very literal; others are metaphoric. Some are largely explanatory; others are largely heuristic. Maddux's theory is not particularly explanatory; after all, he doesn't specify *how* to throw balls that look they are going to be strikes. Our account is not very explanatory either; we do not specify *why* the mind tends to go where it does in the contexts we have outlined. But we hope that our theory (or our framework, or metaphor even) offers some of the same value as Maddux's theory of pitching. We hope that it changes the way one thinks about the phenomena we have outlined, and tried to integrate, in this chapter. The above-average effect, the tendency to brace for possible failure, counterfactual thinking, and the other phenomena we have discussed in this chapter can all seem different when understood in terms of the common thread of the mind automatically seizing on particular representations when contemplating a question, confronting a stimulus, or considering a prospect.

At first blush, our account of endogenous priming might seem less like priming than, well, thinking. That is, what the mind attends to and what representations are accessed and processed is precisely what thinking is all about. How is our analysis anything other than some musings about what people think about when contemplating such things as where they stand among their peers on various traits, whether it makes sense to tempt fate, and so on?

What we have presented, we believe, is more than a haphazard collection of some elements of what thinking *is*; it is a structured account of where thinking *starts*. As we have tried to make clear, the mind automatically goes somewhere when we encounter stimuli or contemplate propositions, and where it goes situates, and hence powerfully affects, all other thinking that is brought to bear on the subject. By considering the triggers and operations of endogenous priming, in other words, we can apply all that our field has learned about exogenous priming to help us understand how social cognition gets channeled, and how people end up making the judgments and decisions that they do. That is, by understanding where the mind goes initially and reflexively, we can get a much better handle on where it ends up deliberatively.

REFERENCES

Alicke, M. D. (1985). Global self-evaluation as determined by the desirability and controllability of trait adjectives. *Journal of Personality and Social Psychology, 49*, 1621–1630.

Alicke, M. D., Klotz, M. L., Breitenbecher, D. L., Yurak, T. J., & Vredenburg, D. S. (1995). Personal contact, individuation, and the better-than-average effect. *Journal of Personality and Social Psychology, 68*, 804–825.

Andersen, S. M., Glassman, N. S., Chen, S., & Cole, S. W. (1995). Transference in social perception: Chronic accessibility in significant-other representations. *Journal of Personality and Social Psychology, 69*, 41–57.

Armor, D. A., & Taylor, S. E. (2002). When predictions fail: The dilemma of unrealistic optimism. In T. Gilovich, D. W. Griffin, & D. Kahneman (Eds.), *Heuristics and biases: The psychology of intuitive judgment* (pp. 334–347). New York: Cambridge University Press.

Bar-Hillel, M., & Budescu, D. (1995). The elusive wishful thinking effect. *Thinking and Reasoning, 1*, 71–103.

Bargh, J. A., Chen, M., & Burrows, L. (1996). Automaticity and social behavior: Direct effects of trait construct and stereotype activation. *Journal of Personality and Social Psychology, 71*, 230–244.

Barsalou, L. W. (1983). Ad hoc categories. *Memory & Cognition, 11*, 211–227.

Barsalou, L. W. (1985). Ideals, central tendency, and frequency of instantiation as determinants of graded structure in categories. *Journal of Experimental Psychology: Learning, Memory, and Cognition, 11*, 629–654.

Bolton, G. E., & Zwick, R. (1995). Anonymity versus punishment in ultimatum bargaining. *Games and Economic Behavior, 10*, 95–121.

Brown, J. D. (1986). Evaluations of self and others: Self-enhancement biases in social judgments. *Social Cognition, 4*, 353–376.

Cantor, N., & Norem, J. K. (1989). Defensive pessimism and stress and coping. *Social Cognition, 7*, 92–112.

Chapman, H. A., Kim, D. A., Susskind, J. M., & Anderson, A. K. (2009). In bad taste: Evidence for the oral origins of moral disgust. *Science, 323*, 1222–1226.

Crary, W. G. (1966). Reactions to incongruent self-experiences. *Journal of Consulting Psychology, 30*, 246–252.

Dunning, D., & Hayes, A. F. (1996). Evidence for egocentric comparison in social judgment. *Journal of Personality and Social Psychology, 71*, 213–229.

Dunning, D., Heath, C., & Suls, J. M. (2004). Flawed self-assessment: Implications for health, education, and the workplace. *Psychological Science in the Public Interest, 5*, 69–106.

Dunning, D., Meyerowitz, J. A., & Holzberg, A. D. (1989). Ambiguity and self-evaluation: The role of idiosyncratic trait definitions in self-serving assessments of others. *Journal of Personality and Social Psychology, 57*, 1082–1090.

Epley, N., & Gilovich, T. (1999). Just going along: Nonconscious priming and conformity to social pressure. *Journal of Experimental Social Psychology, 35*, 578–589.

Epley, N., & Gilovich, T. (2010). *Going to extremes: Imagining atypical audiences when anticipating others' evaluations of the self.* Manuscript in preparation.

Fenigstein, A., & Vanable, P. A. (1992). Paranoia and self-consciousness. *Journal of Personality and Social Psychology, 62*, 129–138.

Ferguson, M.J. (2008). On becoming ready to pursue a goal you don't know you have: Effects of nonconscious goals on evaluative readiness. *Journal of Personality and Social Psychology, 95*, 1268–1294.

Festinger, L. (1954). A theory of social comparison processes. *Human Relations, 7*(2), 117–140.

Ford, T. E., & Kruglanski, A. (1995). Effects of epistemic motivations on the use of momentarily accessible constructs in social judgment. *Personality and Social Psychology Bulletin, 21*, 950–962.

Fredrickson, B. L., & Kahneman, D. (1993). Duration neglect in retrospective evaluations of affective episodes. *Journal of Personality and Social Psychology, 65*, 45–55.

Gilovich, T. (1981). Seeing the past in the present: The effect of associations to familiar events on judgments and decisions. *Journal of Personality and Social Psychology, 40*, 797–808.

Gilovich, T., Epley, N., & Hanko, K. (2005). Shallow thoughts on the self: The automatic elements of self-assessment. In M. Alicke, D. Dunning, & J. Krueger (Eds.), *The self in social judgment* (pp. 67–84). New York: Psychology Press.

Gilovich, T., Kerr, M., & Medvec, V. H. (1993). Effect of temporal perspective on subjective confidence. *Journal of Personality & Social Psychology, 64*, 552–560.

Goodhart, D. E. (1986). The effects of positive and negative thinking on performance in an achievement situation. *Journal of Personality and Social Psychology, 51*, 117–124.

Greene, J., & Haidt, J. (2002). How (and where) does moral judgment work? *Trends in Cognitive Sciences, 6*(12), 517–523.

Guenther, C. L., & Alicke, M. D. (2010). Deconstructing the better-than-average effect. *Journal of Personality and Social Psychology, 99*, 755–770.

Haidt, J. (2001). The emotional dog and its rational tail. *Psychological Review, 108*, 814–834.

Haidt, J. (2007). The new synthesis in moral psychology. *Science, 316*, 998–1002.

Hastie, R. K., & Dawes, R. M. (2010). *Rational choice in an uncertain world: The psychology of judgment and decision making* (2nd ed.). Thousand Oaks, CA: Sage.

Haynes, G., & Gilovich, T. (2010). "The ball don't lie": How inequity aversion can undermine performance. *Journal of Experimental Social Psychology, 46*(6), 1148–1150.

Higgins, E. T., King, G. A., & Mavin, G. H. (1982). Individual construct accessibility and subjective impressions and recall. *Journal of Personality and Social Psychology, 43*, 35–47.

Higgins, E. T., Rholes, W. S., & Jones, C. R. (1977). Category accessibility and impression formation. *Journal of Experimental Social Psychology, 13*, 141–154.

Kahneman, D. T., & Miller, D. (1986). Norm theory: Comparing reality to its alternatives. *Psychological Review, 93*, 136–153.

Kittur, A., Hummel, J. E., & Holyoak, K. J. (2006). Ideals aren't always typical: Dissociating goodness-of-exemplar from typicality judgment. In R. Sun & N. Miyake (Eds.), *Proceedings of the 28th Annual Conference of the Cognitive Science Society*. Mahwah, NJ: Erlbaum.

Koehler, D. J., & Poon, C. S. K. (2006). Self-predictions overweight strength of current intentions. *Journal of Experimental Social Psychology, 42*, 517–524.

Krizan, Z., & Windschitl, P. D. (2007). The influence of outcome desirability on optimism. *Psychological Bulletin, 133*, 95–121.

Kruger, J., & Gilovich, T. (2004). Actions, intentions, and trait assessment: The road to self-enhancement is paved with good intentions. *Personality and Social Psychology Bulletin, 30*, 328–339.

Kruglanski, A. W., & Mayseless, O. (1990). Classic and current social comparison research: Expanding the perspective. *Psychological Bulletin, 108*(2), 626–630.

Lammers, J., & Stapel, D. A. (2009). How power influences moral thinking. *Journal of Personality and Social Psychology, 97*, 279–289.

Langer, E. J. (1975). The illusion of control. *Journal of Personality and Social Psychology, 32*(2), 311–328.

Langer, E. J., & Roth, J. (1975). Heads I win, tails it's chance: The illusion of control as a function of the sequence of outcomes in a purely chance task. *Journal of Personality and Social Psychology, 32*, 951–955.

Leary, M. R., & Kowalski, R. M. (1995). *Social anxiety.* New York: Guilford.

Markman, K. D., McMullen, M. N., & Elizaga, R. A. (2008). Counterfactual thinking, persistence, and performance: A test of the reflection and evaluation model. *Journal of Experimental Social Psychology, 44*, 421–428.

Matsumoto, D., & Willingham, B. (2006). The thrill of victory and the agony of defeat: Spontaneous expression of medal winners of the 2004 Athens Olympic games. *Journal of Personality and Social Psychology, 91*, 568–581.

McKenna, F. P. (1993). It won't happen to me: Unrealistic optimism or illusion of control? *British Journal of Psychology, 84*, 39–50.

McMullen, M. N., & Markman, K. D. (2000). Downward counterfactuals and motivation: The wake-up call and the pangloss effect. *Personality and Social Psychology Bulletin, 26*, 575–584.

Medvec, V. H., Madey, S. H., & Gilovich, T. (1995). When less is more: Counterfactual thinking and satisfaction among Olympic medalists. *Journal of Personality and Social Psychology, 69*, 603–610.

Medvec, V. H., & Savitsky, K. (1997). When doing better means feeling worse: The effects of categorical cutoff points on counterfactual thinking and satisfaction. *Journal of Personality and Social Psychology, 72*, 1284–1296.

Miller, D. T., & Gunasegaram, S. (1990). Temporal order and the perceived mutability of events: Implications for blame assignment. *Journal of Personality and Social Psychology, 59*, 1111–1118.

Miller, D. T., & McFarland, C. (1986). Counterfactual thinking and victim compensation: A test of *norm theory. Personality and Social Psychology Bulletin, 12*, 513–519.

Miller, D. T., & Taylor, B. R. (1995). Counterfactual thought, regret, and superstition: How to avoid kicking yourself. In N. J. Roese & J. M. Olson (Eds.), *What might have been: The social psychology of counterfactual thinking* (pp. 305–332). Mahwah, NJ: Erlbaum.

Miller, D. T., Turnbull, W., & McFarland, C. (1989). When a coincidence is suspicious: The role of mental simulation. *Journal of Personality and Social Psychology, 57*(4), 581–589.

Morewedge, C. K., Gilbert, D. T., & Wilson, T. D. (2005). The least likely of times: How remembering the past biases forecasts of the future. *Psychological Science, 16,* 626–630.

Morewedge, C. K., & Kahneman, D. (2010). Associative processes in intuitive judgment. *Trends in Cognitive Sciences, 14,* 435–440.

Mussweiler, T. (2003). Comparison processes in social judgment: Mechanisms and consequences. *Psychological Review, 110,* 472–489.

Mussweiler, T., & Rüter, K. (2003). What friends are for! The use of routine standards in social comparison. *Journal of Personality and Social Psychology, 85,* 467–481.

Mussweiler, T., Rüter, K., & Epstude, K. (2004). The ups and downs of social comparison: Mechanisms of assimilation and contrast. *Journal of Experimental Social Psychology, 87,* 832–844.

Risen, J. L., & Gilovich, T. (2007). Another look at why people are reluctant to exchange lottery tickets. *Journal of Personality and Social Psychology, 93,* 12–22.

Risen, J. L., & Gilovich, T. (2008). Why people are reluctant to tempt fate. *Journal of Personality and Social Psychology, 95,* 293–307.

Risen, J. L., Gilovich, T., Kruger, J., & Savitsky, K. (2010). *Why people are reluctant to comment on success.* Unpublished manuscript.

Savitsky, K., & Gilovich, T. (2003). The illusion of transparency and the alleviation of speech anxiety. *Journal of Experimental Social Psychology, 39,* 618–625.

Shepperd, J. A., Findley-Klein, C., Kwavnick, K. D., Walker, D., & Perez, S. (2000). Bracing for loss. *Journal of Personality and Social Psychology, 78,* 620–634.

Shepperd, J. A., Ouellette, J. A., & Fernandez, J. K. (1996). Abandoning unrealistic optimism: Performance estimates and the temporal proximity of self-relevant feedback. *Journal of Personality and Social Psychology, 70,* 844–855.

Showers, C. (1992). The motivation and emotional consequences of considering positive or negative possibilities for an upcoming event. *Journal of Personality and Social Psychology, 63,* 474–484.

Smallman, R., & Roese, N.J. (2009). Counterfactual thinking facilitates behavioral intentions. *Journal of Experimental Social Psychology, 45,* 845–852.

Stapel, D. A., & Koomen, W. (2000). How far do we go beyond the information given? The impact of knowledge activation on interpretation and inference. *Journal of Personality and Social Psychology, 78,* 19–37.

Stein, M. B., Walker, J. R., & Forde, D. R. (1996). Public-speaking fears in a community sample: Prevalence, impact on functioning, and diagnostic classification. *Archives of General Psychiatry, 53,* 169–174.

Suls, J., Martin, R., & Wheeler, L. (2002). Social comparison: Why, with whom and with what effect? *Current Directions in Psychological Science, 11*(5), 159–163.

Suls, J., & Wheeler, L. (2000). A selective history of classic and neo-social comparison theory. In J. Suhls & L. Wheeler (Eds.), *Handbook of social comparison* (pp. 3–19). New York: Kluwer Academic/Plenum Publishers.

Svenson, O. (1981). Are we all less risky and more skillful than our fellow drivers? *Acta Psychologica, 47,* 143–148.

Taylor, S. E., & Brown, J. (1988). Illusion and well-being: A social psychological perspective on mental health. *Psychological Bulletin, 103,* 193–210.

Teigen, K. H., & Keren, G. (2002). When are successes more surprising than failures? *Cognition and Emotion, 16,* 245–268.

Thaler, R. H. (1988). Anomalies: The ultimatum game. *Journal of Economic Perspectives, 2*(4), 195–206.

Todorov, A., & Bargh, J. A. (2002). Automatic sources of aggression. *Aggression and Violent Behavior, 7,* 53–68.

Tykocinski, O. E. (2008). Insurance, risk, and magical thinking. *Personality and Social Psychology Bulletin, 34*, 1346–1356.

Weinstein, N. (1980). Unrealistic optimism about future life events. *Journal of Personality and Social Psychology, 39*, 806–820.

Wells, G. L., & Gavanski, I. (1989). Mental simulation of causality. *Journal of Personality and Social Psychology, 56*(2), 161–169.

Williams, E. F., & Gilovich, T. (2008). Conceptions of the self and others across time. *Personality and Social Psychology Bulletin, 34*, 1037–1046.

Williams, E., & Gilovich, T. (2010). *Stacking the deck: Self other differences in the basis of self-assessment.* Manuscript submitted for publication.

Williams, E., Gilovich, T., & Dunning, D. (2010). *Weighting potential in assessment of the self and others.* Manuscript submitted for publication.

2

The Cognitive Economy Model of Selective Exposure

Integrating Motivational and Cognitive Accounts of Confirmatory Information Search

PETER FISCHER, NILÜFER AYDIN, JULIA FISCHER,
DIETER FREY, and STEPHEN E. G. LEA

Doubt is not a pleasant condition, but certainty is absurd.

Voltaire (1694–1778)

*I*n context of the U.S. invasion of Iraq in 2003, former U.S. President George W. Bush and most of his political and military advisors had a strong belief that Iraq was hiding weapons of mass destruction (WMDs). This strong belief led to a process that emphasized information supporting the invasion, while downplaying information doubting the existence of WMD (U.S. Select Senate Committee on Intelligence, 2004). After the invasion, it became clear that Iraq never possessed WMDs, and the original reason for the invasion was incorrect.

Besides this example, a great number of historical, political, and technological disasters have been caused by the human tendency to systematically prefer standpoint-consistent information (for example, groupthink leading to the *Bay of Pigs* invasion in Cuba; [Janis, 1982]). This tendency is called *selective exposure* to supporting (or consistent) information (Festinger, 1957; Fischer, Greitemeyer, & Frey, 2008; Frey, 1986; Hart et al., 2009; Jonas, Schulz-Hardt, Frey, & Thelen, 2001), it often leads to poor decision outcomes (Greitemeyer & Schulz-Hardt, 2003; Kray & Galinski, 2003), and it occurs in both individual (Fischer, Greitemeyer, & Frey,

2008; Frey, 1986; Jonas et al., 2001) and group decision making (Schulz-Hardt, Frey, Lüthgens, & Moscovici, 2000; Schulz-Hardt, Jochims, & Frey, 2002), as well as in stereotyping (Johnston, 1996) and attitude (Lundgren & Prislin, 1998) research.

Most theoretical explanations of selective exposure can be classified as either motivational or cognitive accounts. Motivational approaches stress that individuals prefer standpoint-consistent information, and neglect inconsistent information because they wish to defend their perspectives (Festinger, 1957; Frey, 1986; Hart et al., 2009; Olson & Stone, 2005). It has also been argued that selective exposure reduces cognitive dissonance (Festinger, 1957; Frey, 1986), threats to self-esteem (Pyszczynski & Greenberg, 1987), and the complexity of information processing (Ditto & Lopez, 1992; Ditto, Scepansky, Munro, Apanovitch, & Lockhart, 1998). Motivational approaches also note that selective exposure alleviates negative mood states (Jonas, Graupmann, & Frey, 2006).

Cognitive explanations for selective exposure are focused on biases in information processing, such as asymmetric attention to standpoint-relevant a priori information (Fischer, Schulz-Hardt, & Frey, 2008; Schulz-Hardt, Fischer, & Frey, 2009) or preferential assimilation of such information (Lord, Ross, & Lepper, 1979). Conversely, standpoint-inconsistent evidence is subjected to more elaborate testing than is confirmatory evidence (Ditto & Lopez, 1992; Ditto et al., 1998; Fischer, Jonas, Frey, & Schulz-Hardt, 2005). Other lines of research have explored factors such as the inadequate integration of base rates into judgment processes (for example, Fiedler, Brinkmann, Betsch, & Wild, 2000), positive testing strategies (for example, Klayman & Ha, 1987; Snyder & Swann, 1978), and option-oriented versus attribute-oriented information search (for example, Payne, Bettman, & Johnson, 1993). However, these latter lines of study have not been conducted within the classic selective exposure paradigm.

Previous models of selective exposure have drawn a sharp distinction between motivational or cognitive processes, and focused on either one of these. This distinction is often criticized as being too simplistic; consequently, the new model we propose in this chapter no longer separates cognitive and motivational processes. Instead, it explains selective exposure effects through a metacognitive process related to subjectively experienced decision certainty. The model assumes that decision makers are boundedly rational (Simon, 1976), and that selective exposure is a function of a reasonably economic way of thinking. If decision makers are certain that their position is correct, it makes little sense for them to look for information that may be contradictory, since it is unlikely that their position will be changed. Therefore, it is economic to *reduce* the amount of inconsistent information sought, since it is harder to cognitively process than consistent information. In contrast, if decision makers are unsure of the validity of their position, it makes sense to *increase* processing effort, thus searching for potentially disconfirming information that can prevent faulty decisions from being made (cf. Greitemeyer & Schulz-Hardt, 2003; Kray & Galinski, 2003). Uncertainty about the validity of the decision maker's positions may be induced by metacognitions about the decision context, such as cues that remind the decision maker of potential losses in case of poor decision making, low applicable decision-relevant knowledge, accuracy cues, or other warning signs. Metacognitions related to experienced decision certainty can be determined by a variety of personal and situational factors (for example, Fischer, Jonas, Frey, & Kastenmüller, 2008) including a priori knowledge about the decision context or cues in the decision situation (e.g., reminders of failure or loss cues). Fischer, Jonas et al. (2008) found that loss-framed decision scenarios led to lower levels of certainty (and thus fewer confirmatory tendencies in information search) than gain-framed decision scenarios (see also Kastenmüller et al., 2010, for similar findings).

In summary, personal and situational cues that reduce subjectively experienced decisions certainty decrease selective exposure effects. The more certain decision makers are of the validity of their choices, the less cautious they will be in processing decision-relevant information, which leads to a systematic preference for easy-to-process, standpoint-consistent information. In contrast, low decision certainty leads to a more cautious processing approach and results in a greater quantity of inconsistent information being sought, despite the comparative difficulty it poses for cognitive processing. In the following sections, this model will be explained theoretically, and its assumptions supported via (a) a review of previous relevant research on selective exposure and (b) a series of new studies designed to test its veracity.

PREVIOUS RESEARCH ON SELECTIVE EXPOSURE

Empirical investigations on selective exposure have typically been conducted within the framework of dissonance theory (Festinger, 1957; Frey, 1981a, 1981b, 1981c, 1986; Jonas et al., 2001). The theory assumes that when individuals are close to making a decision, they experience unpleasant psychological arousal because of the potentially negative ramifications of their choice and the potentially positive outcomes associated with foregone alternatives (Festinger, 1957; Frey, 1986). One way of reducing dissonance is through selective exposure, by displaying a systematic preference for evidence that supports one's decisions or standpoints, and in turn, neglecting conflicting information (Frey, 1986; Jonas et al., 2001). The extent to which people prefer consistent to inconsistent information is called *confirmation bias*, and represents the single, classic indicator of the strength of selective exposure effects (Fischer, Greitemeyer, & Frey, 2008; Frey, 1986; Hart et al., 2009; Jonas et al., 2001; Schulz-Hardt et al., 2000).

Other lines of inquiry not directly associated with classic selective exposure research have investigated its processes from alternative theoretical perspectives, such as positive testing strategies (Klayman & Ha, 1987; Snyder & Swann, 1978), inadequate integration of base rates into judgment processes (Fiedler et al., 2000), or option-oriented versus attribute-oriented information search (Payne et al., 1993). The research paradigms used in these areas of study differ significantly from the one used in classic selective exposure research.

In the classic paradigm (see Fischer et al., 2005; Frey, 1981a, 1981b, 1981c, 1986; Jonas et al., 2001), participants know in advance whether a specific piece of information will be consistent or inconsistent with their decision preference: participants are asked to work on a decision problem that requires them to choose between two competing decision alternatives and to make a tentative decision (such as whether a manager's contract should be extended). This decision can be revised after the information search task based on relevant information. Once this selection is made, participants can search for new pieces of information, typically received as short statements indicating clearly the standpoints of particular newspaper articles, experts, or former participants. From these statements, the information seeker learns the crux of the author's argument, and their resulting recommendation regarding the decision case (e.g., "The manager successfully developed new products. Thus, his contract should be prolonged."). Regardless of the participants' primary decision, half of the new pieces of information will support it, and half will conflict with it. Participants are asked to indicate the pieces of information that they would like to read in more detail later, with selective exposure occurring if more decision-consistent than -inconsistent pieces of information are selected (Fischer, Greitemeyer, & Frey, 2008; Frey, 1986; Jonas et al., 2001).

A broad variety of situational variables have been identified that increase the likelihood of selective exposure, such as restricted access to additional information (Fischer et al., 2005); decision irreversibility (Frey, 1981a); high commitment to a position (Brock & Balloun, 1967; Schwarz, Frey, & Kumpf, 1980; Sweeney & Gruber, 1984); gain-framed (compared to loss-framed) decision problems (Fischer, Jonas et al., 2008); gain-framed information search instructions (Kastenmüller et al., 2010); freedom of choice (Frey & Wicklund, 1978); increasing levels of dissonance arousal (Rhine, 1967; for an overview, see Frey, 1986), and negative affective states (Jonas, Graupmann, & Frey, 2006).

DEBATES ABOUT UNDERLYING PSYCHOLOGICAL PROCESSES

Research on the psychological processes underlying the selective exposure effect is fragmented and ambiguous. Some researchers explain selective exposure solely through motivational processes, such as dissonance reduction (Festinger, 1957, 1964; Frey, 1981a, 1981b, 1981c, 1986) or defense motivation suggesting that individuals seek standpoint-consistent information to protect their positions (Jonas et al., 2001, 2006; see also Hart et al., 2009, for a recent meta-analysis).

Other recent research has explored the selective exposure effect from a more cognitive angle. This line of inquiry suggests that selective exposure is an "unintended by-product" (Schulz-Hardt et al., 2009) of striving for accuracy (and thus, wanting to hold an accurate position; see also Simon, 1976). According to this approach, individuals seek confirmatory information because they systematically overestimate its quality in comparison to inconsistent information. This bias perceptual is the result of two tendencies. First, the quality of inconsistent information tends to be tested more critically than that of consistent information (Ditto & Lopez, 1992; Ditto et al., 1998); so it is more likely that its flaws will be detected. Second, skewed decision-relevant knowledge is often used as a reference point (Fischer et al., 2005; Fischer, Schulz-Hardt et al., 2008). For example, decision makers may store more supportive than conflicting information regarding their standpoints, which helps them to argue against and diminish inconsistent information (Schulz-Hardt et al., 2009; see also Betsch, Haberstroh, Glöckner, Haar, & Fiedler, 2001; Kunda, 1990; Raju, Lonial, & Mangold, 1995). Schulz-Hardt et al. (2009) have shown that perceived information quality is a strong predictor of selective exposure. When searching for the best pieces of information, decision makers tend to prefer that which is standpoint consistent (see also Fischer et al., 2005; Fischer, Schulz-Hardt et al., 2008).

This new model tries to overcome the strict distinction between motivational and cognitive processes in the context of selective exposure. In contrast to previous dual-process explanations, the new model assumes a single process that integrates cognitive and motivational accounts of selective exposure. It is based on evolutionary, functional, and economic assumptions. In the following sections, these assumptions will be outlined. Figure 2.1 presents an overview of the model.

Basic Assumption 1: Economic Use of Cognitive Resources

In general, individuals tend to be economic regarding their engagement in cognitive elaboration and prefer to make less (rather than more) effort as cognitive resources are limited and can be exhausted by use (Muraven & Baumeister, 2000; Vohs, Baumeister, & Ciarocco, 2005). Thus, cognitive resources can be considered self-regulating. Research by Baumeister and colleagues has shown that depleting these resources leads to a variety of reductions in psychological and physical functioning; therefore, it is functional to conserve these resources, part of which entails employing them only when truly necessary.

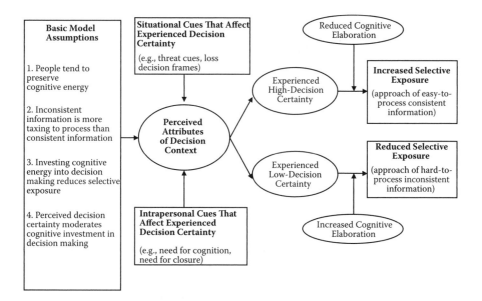

Figure 2.1   The cognitive economy model of selective exposure.

Basic Assumption 2: Processing Differences Between Consistent and Inconsistent Information

Standpoint-inconsistent information requires more effort to cognitively process than consistent information, as it is more difficult to integrate inconsistent information into the existing knowledge structure (Ditto & Lopez, 1992; Ditto et al., 1998; Schulz-Hardt et al., 2009). This is so because individuals typically store more consistent than inconsistent information—otherwise, they would not actually have a standpoint (Kunda, 1990; Schulz-Hardt et al., 2009). In addition, a motivational perspective would observe that inconsistent information leads to increased levels of dissonance (Festinger, 1957; Frey, 1986); threatens the individual's self-esteem (Pyszczynski & Greenberg, 1987), and elicits negative affect (Kruglanski & Klar, 1987). All these processes require increased amounts of cognitive and self-regulatory resources to cope with (Fischer, Greitemeyer, & Frey, 2008). Therefore, both cognitive and motivational perspectives view seeking and processing inconsistent information as laborious, effortful, and joyless tasks that are thought to consume considerable amounts of cognitive resources (i.e., self-regulation; Fischer, Greitemeyer, & Frey, 2008; Schmeichel, Vohs, & Baumeister, 2003).

Basic Assumption 3: Investing Cognitive Energy Reduces Selective Exposure

Increased use of cognitive resources generally results in lower levels of selective exposure. It follows from assumption 2 that if decision makers are willing to invest increased amounts of cognitive energy in the decision and information search process, they will probably exhibit lower levels of selective exposure (for example, Fischer, Jonas et al., 2008).

Basic Assumption 4: Metacognitions Related to Decision Certainty Moderate the Selective Exposure Effect

Subjectively experienced decision certainty is an indicator that signals whether the amount of cognitive elaboration upon standpoint-relevant information should be increased or decreased (Fischer, Jonas et al., 2008). In the context of decision making and information processing, individuals tend to invest cognitive resources only when it is functional to do so to prevent faulty choices. Therefore, subjectively experienced decision certainty is a cue that indicates whether an individual should invest extra or fewer cognitive resources to prevent suboptimal decision outcomes. Whereas low certainty indicates that it is necessary to invest more resources to help prevent mistakes, high certainty signals that it is not necessary to make this investment. Since the individual's current standpoint is usually well established and has high levels of subjectively experienced reliability, it is economic to preserve cognitive resources for the analysis of standpoints that are less established and leave more at stake.

Given the assumptions that individuals are cognitive economists (Assumption 1) and that inconsistent information takes more effort to process than consistent information (Assumption 2), it is proposed that perceptions of low decision certainty serve as a metacognitive cue, which acts to signal potential threats to decision validity (Assumption 4). Consequently, it is functional for individuals to invest cognitive resources in validating their current standpoints by seeking inconsistent information (Assumption 3)—even though it is more laborious to process than consistent information. In contrast, high decision certainty serves as a metacognitive indication that everything is fine, epistemologically speaking, and that the validity of the decision maker's perspective is not at stake. Therefore, there is no need to change anything. As a result, decision makers will act as cognitive economists and will save their mental resources. One way of doing this is to reduce the proportion of hard-to-process inconsistent information analyzed and to rely on easily digested consistent information instead.

Summary: Processes Assumed by the Cognitive Economy Model of Selective Exposure

Given the four assumptions, it is easy to predict and interpret selective exposure effects. Given the existence of situational (e.g., social influence, such as the presence of other decision makers who hold the same standpoints) or personal cues (e.g., prior experience with the specific decision context) that indicate the validity of an individual's decision preference, the amount of cognitive resources employed in the information search process will be reduced, leading to a preference for decision-consistent information. In this instance, the decision is perceived as a sure thing and one that does not require the consideration of potentially conflicting material, leading to increased levels of selective exposure effects.

In contrast, if threats to the validity of the individual's decision preference are present (induced by situational or personal variables, such as holding a minority position or having little experience with the current decision context), decision makers opt to invest more cognitive energy during information search and thus approach a significantly larger amount of decision inconsistent information. Therefore, it can be hypothesized that these decision makers will show lower levels of selective exposure effects (see Figure 2.1). The critical theoretical innovation of the model is that it can explain and predict the intensity of selective exposure effects via a simple, one-process assumption related to subjectively experienced decision certainty.

EMPIRICAL EVIDENCE FOR THE PROPOSED COGNITIVE ECONOMY MODEL OF SELECTIVE EXPOSURE

In this section, empirical evidence for the cognitive economy model of selective exposure is presented. First, the results of recent studies from different laboratories will be reviewed. Classic dissonance studies on selective exposure will then be reinterpreted in light of the new model, before the implications of more recent findings are discussed. Finally, the results of research that has directly tested the model's main assumptions will be briefly presented.

Direct Evidence From Previous Selective Exposure Research for the Basic Assumptions of the Proposed Cognitive Economy Model of Selective Exposure

The most direct evidence for the moderating role of decision certainty is provided by Fischer, Jonas et al. (2008) who investigated the impact of equivalent gain versus loss decision frames (Kahneman & Tversky, 1979) on selective exposure. A series of three studies showed that selective exposure was stronger after gain-framed (i.e., the potential positive outcomes of a decision alternative is highlighted) than loss-framed decision problems (i.e., the potential negative outcomes of a decision alternative is highlighted), with the effect being mediated by different levels of subjectively experienced decision certainty. Specifically, loss frames were associated with lower levels of certainty than gain frames (Studies 1 and 2). The authors explained this effect by arguing that loss frames remind decision makers of potential threats to the quality of their choices, and thus make them more cautious when processing decision-relevant information. This tendency is reflected in reduced levels of decision certainty, and leads to decision makers to invest more cognitive resources in information search and to consider both decision-consistent and contradictory information (Study 3).

The propositions that (a) negative (or loss) cues in a decision context increase the cognitive elaboration of decision-relevant information and that (b) decision certainty is a crucial mediating variable in regulating the amount of cognitive resources invested are also supported by research. Ditto et al. (1998) showed that decision makers perform more cognitive analyses when exposed to negative, unfavorable decision prospects. Similarly, Dawson, Gilovich, and Regan (2002) found that participants with critical mindsets (induced by having them consider threatening task rules) were less likely to exhibit a confirmation bias on a Wason deductive reasoning task. Moreover, Kastenmüller et al. (2010) found that decision makers exhibited less selective exposure in an information search task that was framed negatively (i.e., participants having to decide which pieces of information they did *not* want to read) than in a task that was positively framed (participants deciding which pieces of information they *wanted* to read). Finally, Fischer, Crelley, Frey, and Köppl (2009) showed that other types of threat also decrease confirmatory tendencies in information search. High threat (including decision, terrorist, and social forms) leads to reduced experienced decision certainty and in turn to reduced levels of selective exposure.

To summarize, a variety of studies directly supports the assumption that individuals respond to threat cues in decision contexts by having reduced certainty in the validity of their selection. This reduced certainty leads to greater investments of cognitive resources in decision and information search tasks. Moreover, the research supports the assumption that decision certainty is positively associated with selective exposure. The more certain decision makers are that their stance is correct, the less cognitive effort and analysis they invest, and the more they tend to neglect decision-inconsistent information. In the next section, the results of classic dissonance studies on selective exposure will be reinterpreted in light of the new model.

REINTERPRETATION OF CLASSIC DISSONANCE RESULTS IN LIGHT OF THE COGNITIVE ECONOMY MODEL OF SELECTIVE EXPOSURE

Reversibility of Decisions

Frey (1981b) showed that nonreversible (final) decisions led to higher levels of selective exposure than those that were reversible (or tentative).[1] This result was originally explained by dissonance theory suggesting that tentative decisions arouse less dissonance than irreversible ones because they permit a change of mind. The cognitive economy model of selective exposure, however, can also explain this effect. Arguably, participants asked to make a final decision invest more cognitive effort in the decision-making process because the costs of a poor choice are higher than when the decision is only preliminary. Hence, individuals making irreversible decisions should be more convinced that they've made a good judgment (due to feeling that they have invested more cognitive resources than preliminary decision makers) and should thus be surer about the validity of their decision preference. Moreover, after making a final decision, investing too many cognitive resources in an additional information search is not rational or economic, since the decision is already made and cannot be changed. In contrast, participants who have made only a preliminary choice may have invested less effort in doing so because the option of changing their minds is still available. As a consequence, participants in the preliminary decision condition feel less certain about the validity of their selection, invest more cognitive resources during information search, and exhibit lower levels of selective exposure compared to final decision makers.

Commitment

The classic commitment effect in selective exposure research is an increased affective binding toward one's own decisions, attitudes, standpoints, or opinions (Kiesler, 1971). This effect can be reinterpreted in terms of metacognitions about experienced decision certainty. Established manipulations of commitment used in classic dissonance studies—such as explanations of the participant's own standpoint (Schwarz et al., 1980), public compliance with attitude-inconsistent behavior (Carlsmith, Collins, & Helmreich, 1966; Frey & Stahlberg, 1986), or a priori "natural" affiliation to a group with a specific type of attitude or behavior (Brock & Balloun, 1967; Sweeney & Gruber, 1984)—have been shown to increase selective exposure. So far, the commitment effect has been predominantly explained by dissonance processes, underpinned by the notion that cognitive dissonance is particularly likely to occur when people feel attached to (and responsible for) a specific decision, opinion, or behavior (Cooper & Fazio, 1984; Festinger, 1964). Since dissonance arousal is an aversive state that motivates its own reduction, conditions of high commitment increase the systematic preference for supporting information or the systematic neglect of inconsistent information (Brock & Balloun, 1967; Schwarz et al., 1980; Sweeney & Gruber, 1984).

Using the cognitive economy model of selective exposure, most of the commonly employed commitment manipulations can be simply viewed as alterations in decision certainty. For example, Schwarz et al. (1980) manipulated commitment by asking participants to write standpoint-consistent or standpoint-neutral essays. They could subsequently select additional information that supported or questioned their views. It was found that individuals who wrote an attitude-consistent essay exhibited a stronger confirmation bias in information search than participants who wrote a neutral essay (for similar commitment manipulations, see Behling, 1971; Jonas et al., 2001). According to the new model, it should be clear that individuals who have written an essay that supports their standpoint should be more confident in its validity than participants who have written a neutral one (see also research on the "explanation effect"; Koehler, 1991; and research on the impact of "ease-of-retrieval" as a metacognition on individuals' self-assessments; for example, Schwarz et al., 1991). In order to actually *write* the supportive essay, they will have needed to reflect on their standpoint, consider arguments favoring it, and demonstrate more overall elaboration on it. Thus, it is likely that subjectively experienced decision certainty will be increased and that selective exposure will therefore increase as a means of saving cognitive resources. In the last section of this review we will provide data that directly shows the link between standpoint (counter)explanations, decision certainty, and selective exposure (see Study 3).

Choice

Choice is another classic dissonance variable that can be reinterpreted by the cognitive economy model of selective exposure. Early studies showed that selective exposure mainly occurs when participants have a high degree of choice in obtaining a specific position or decision preference (Cotton & Hieser, 1980; Frey, 1986; Frey & Wicklund, 1978). For example, Cotton and Hieser (1980) showed that participants who had high levels of choice in writing an attitude-inconsistent essay exhibited more selective exposure than participants with little choice. From a dissonance perspective, a high degree of choice is considered a fundamental requirement in ensuring that individuals feel responsible for a specific behavior; thus experiencing a need to justify said behavior (which they can do through selective exposure).

The cognitive economy model of selective exposure can handily account for the choice effect. Under high-choice conditions, people invest cognitive resources in making a decision (under low-choice conditions, this is unnecessary or even impossible). Thus, high levels of choice should encourage people to feel more strongly about the decision being their own, which should make them more certain of the validity of their decision preference compared to individuals with low levels of choice. In contrast, individuals with little or no choice are less certain about the validity of their standpoint and will exhibit more cognitive effort in information search, leading to greater balance in information selection (including higher proportions of inconsistent information).

Degree of Dissonance

The final effect the new model will reevaluate is the impact of different degrees of dissonance on selective exposure. Studies in this area have shown a curvilinear relationship between the two factors. For example, Rhine (1967) manipulated degrees of dissonance by varying the amounts of standpoint-consistent and -inconsistent information (on politics). Low levels of dissonance should be aroused when participants are exposed to a large quantity of consistent information and only a small amount of inconsistent information, with high levels of dissonance occurring if the proportions are reversed. A curvilinear association between dissonance arousal and selective exposure was found, for as the number of pieces of standpoint-inconsistent information increased, selective exposure also increased. However, this only happened up to a certain point, after which further exposure to inconsistent information led to less confirmatory bias during periods of information search.

Although Rhine (1967) explained this inverted-U function via dissonance processes, the cognitive economy model of selective exposure offers a new interpretation. The model suggests that when participants are exposed only to low levels of standpoint-inconsistent information, they feel confident about the validity of their stance. This then leads to a reduction in cognitive effort through a selective preference for easy-to-process, standpoint-consistent information over hard-to-process, conflicting information. After a point, however, the quantity of conflicting information becomes overwhelming and participants start having more doubts and critical thoughts about the validity of their standpoint. As a consequence, they decide to invest more cognitive effort in information processing and approach the formerly dismissed inconsistent information more often.

Frey (1982) also found a curvilinear relationship between (assumed) dissonance arousal and selective exposure. He induced different degrees of dissonance by varying the gains and losses participants were to expect in a game. Participants who experienced neither gains nor losses (a medium level of dissonance) exhibited the highest levels of selective exposure, whereas participants who experienced reduced gains or increased losses showed the lowest levels. The cognitive economy model of selective exposure suggests that reduced gains and increased losses serve as a warning sign that something is going wrong in the game. Participants increase the cognitive effort they devote to game-relevant information processing and thus become more balanced in their information search. For participants who do not have these experiences, confidence in the current behavior's correctness increases, leading to less energy being expended in analyzing relevant information, increased search for easy-to-process consistent information, and finally increased levels of selective exposure.

Conclusion

Most of the classic explanations of selective exposure effects—including facets such as reversibility, commitment, choice, and degree of dissonance—can be reinterpreted by the cognitive economy model. Having provided direct evidence from the authors' own studies in addition to that from other researchers, the next section will examine more recent and more cognitively interpreted research on selective exposure, and demonstrate that most of it can also be reexplored in light of the new model.

REINTERPRETATION OF RECENT SELECTIVE EXPOSURE RESULTS IN LIGHT OF THE COGNITIVE ECONOMY MODEL OF SELECTIVE EXPOSURE

Information Search Mode

Jonas et al. (2001) found that decision makers exhibit higher levels of confirmatory information search when they are exposed to decision-consistent and -inconsistent information sequentially (as opposed to viewing them simultaneously). The effect emerged because participants in the sequential condition compared every new piece of information with the tentative decision they had made before, which resulted in increased commitment, which in turn intensified selective exposure. In contrast, when participants received a simultaneous overview of all the information, selective exposure was reduced in this condition: participants compared the pieces of information to each other, instead of comparing each isolated piece with the initial decision. As a consequence, the simultaneous presentation of information prevents commitment to the initial decision from rising and hinders a confirmatory information search with it.

Alternatively, the cognitive economy model of selective exposure suggests that the sequential presentation of information increases subjectively experienced decision certainty, because each new piece prompts the reconsideration (and reinforcement) of the initial decision. This leads to more cognitive energy being invested in validating this decision (the recognition heuristic; Goldstein & Gigerenzer, 2002), causing higher levels of perceived decision validity, less cognitive effort being applied to the analysis of subsequent information, and increased levels of selective exposure. Participants who are shown all of the new information simultaneously invest more cognitive energy in processing the additional information (in order to make a good decision and feel increased decision certainty) and show reduced levels of selective exposure.

Information Quantity

Fischer, Schulz-Hardt et al. (2008) provided participants with either two pieces of decision-relevant information (one consistent and one inconsistent with their initial decision) or ten additional pieces of decision-relevant information (five consistent and five inconsistent). Participants were allowed to select exactly one piece of information for further inspection. The authors found that exposure to two pieces of information led to a balanced (or even nonconfirmatory) search, whereas exposure to ten pieces led to increased levels of selective exposure. The authors explained this effect via participants' use of different selection criteria: in the two-pieces-of-information condition, participants focused on the *direction* of the additional pieces of information (and predominantly selected the inconsistent one in order to appear balanced in their information processing; illusion of objectivity; Pyszczynski & Greenberg, 1987). In contrast, participants in the ten-pieces-of-information condition focused on information quality (in order to find the highest quality pieces), and thus predominantly selected that information which was consistent.

The new model can explain this effect. Participants who received two pieces of information assume that the quantity of available decision-relevant information is low. This might lead them to believe that the decision topic is still unexplored, making them more cautious in information processing and leading to less selective exposure. In contrast, participants with ten pieces of information condition know that there are at least five consistent pieces available, which makes them more confident that there is enough available evidence to support their initial opinion. Hence, decision makers presented with ten pieces of information have more confidence in the validity of their initial decision, and thus exhibit higher levels of selective exposure.

Self-Regulation Resources

Fischer, Greitemeyer, and Frey (2008) manipulated participants' available self-regulation resources by using ego-depletion tasks (such as the e-crossing task, where participants must find specific letters in a text under easy or difficult rules; Baumeister, Bratlavsky, Muraven, & Tice, 1998). As expected, ego-depleted participants exhibited higher levels of selective exposure than those who were nondepleted. The authors explained the effect in terms of increased decision-relevant commitment: In one experiment, individuals with reduced self-regulatory resources clung to their standpoint more strongly and were thus more confirmatory in their information search.

This line of research is important for two of the main assumptions of the cognitive economy model of selective exposure. First, the research shows that participants who are cognitively and motivationally exhausted (ego-depleted) tend to avoid the increased cognitive effort required in searching for (and processing) inconsistent information. Second, it shows that an increased affiliation toward one's personal standpoint is associated with increased levels of selective exposure. It follows that it is not necessary to differentiate between the motivational concept of commitment and the more cognitive concept of decision certainty, since both ideas are more or less interchangeable in the context of selective exposure; after all, it is likely that individuals will feel committed to positions they feel are highly valid. Conversely, one should feel sure that a position is valid when one feels a strong emotional attachment toward it.

Group Decision Making and Selective Exposure

The cognitive economy model can also explain selective exposure effects in groups. Schulz-Hardt et al. (2000) found that homogeneous groups (i.e., groups in which all members have the same tentative decision preference) exhibited more selective exposure than heterogeneous groups (which comprise more diverse tentative decision preferences). Once more, this result fits with the predictions of the cognitive economy model: Homogeneous groups are more likely to be sure that their decision preference is correct and thus see no need to increase cognitive effort in order to search for hard-to-process, inconsistent pieces of decision-relevant information, leading in increased selective exposure. In contrast, when group members recognize that other individuals in the in-group have different decision preferences, they become cautious and uncertain about the validity of their own selection. This uncertainty leads to the investment of more cognitive energy in processing additional decision-inconsistent information and thus to reduced selective exposure (see also Greitemeyer & Schulz-Hardt, 2003).

Conclusion

Most of the recent studies on selective exposure can be interpreted in terms of the proposed single-process cognitive economy model. The model can account for the differential impact of sequential versus simultaneous information search procedures (Jonas et al., 2001); the impact of different quantities of information on selective exposure (Fischer, Schulz-Hardt et al., 2008); the effects of reduced self-regulation resources on confirmatory information processing (Fischer, Greitemeyer, & Frey, 2008), and group decision processes and selective exposure (Schulz-Hardt et al., 2000).

GENERAL DISCUSSION

The present theory and research began with questioning why findings in selective exposure research are so frequently inconsistent, ambiguous, and fragmented. Due to this inconsistent picture, a multitude of psychological explanations for the effect have emerged. In contrast to the multitude of prior selective exposure accounts, the new cognitive economy model of selective exposure (see Figure 2.1) can predict whether decision makers will show selective exposure and when they will be balanced, and when they search for and select additional pieces of decision-relevant information. The model is parsimonious because it makes few simple assumptions about cognitive economy. If decision makers perceive threats to decision quality (and thus perceive reduced levels of decision certainty), they will increase the cognitive effort they devote to information search in order to prevent decision failure leading to more balanced information search (Fischer, Jonas et al., 2008), as hard-to-process inconsistent information will be approached more frequently. In contrast, a lack of threats to decision quality (reflected by increased levels of decision certainty) leads to the reduced investment of cognitive effort in information search (because the decision situation appears rather clear) and thus to a preference for consistent information or a reduced approach to inconsistent information (in order to save cognitive energy, which the individual does not perceive the situation as requiring). By employing these simple assumptions about cognitive economy, the results of both the motivational and cognitive fields in classic selective exposure research can be explained. Also, most of the authors' own published research supports the cognitive economy model of selective exposure; with three new studies directly testing and supporting its basic assumptions and predictions.

The main theoretical advance of the proposed model is that it resolves many problems arising from its previous accounts, which differentiated between cognitive and motivational psychological processes. This differentiation is not viewed as leading to a unified model of selective exposure. The advantage of the new model is that it does not require any distinction between these processes, as all of its levels and assumptions permit both to work at the same time and thus do not lead to conflicting results. For this model, it does not matter whether decision threats and associated subjectively experienced decision certainty stem from cognitive or motivational processes: comparatively low levels of decision certainty lead to less selective exposure than comparatively higher levels, independent of whether they are induced by motivational (defense) or cognitive (informational) cues. With regard to informational cues, associated accuracy motivation can lead to both reduced (Hart et al., 2009) and increased intensities in selective exposure effects (see Fischer et al., 2005, Fischer, Schulz-Hardt et al., 2008). From the new perspective, the direction of the effect depends on metacognitions about subjectively experienced decision certainty.

In contrast to previous models of selective exposure (for example, Frey, 1986), the cognitive economy model is believed to be the first "real" one-process form in the field of selective exposure research: If individuals feel uncertain about their decision, they decide to invest increased amounts of cognitive resources and thus search for new information in a balanced way. In contrast, if they feel that their decision is a sure thing, they opt to save cognitive energy by principally approaching easy-to-process, decision-consistent information.

The cognitive economy model presents a unique perspective on the *functionality* of selective exposure by suggesting that both balanced and selective forms of exposure have their own particular advantages. If decision quality is under threat (which can be signaled by loss framing, threat cues, or the existence of disconfirming information), it is functional for the decision maker to invest cognitive energy and to be less reluctant to approach hard-to-process inconsistent information. This leads to increased subjectively experienced decision certainty and it lowers the likelihood of a poor decision outcome (a physical or material benefit). In contrast, when subjectively experienced decision certainty is already high (signaled by the absence of decision threat cues), it is functional for the individual to save cognitive energy by mainly approaching easy-to-process consistent information. In sum, the presented model resolves the ambiguity in the discussion about the functionality of selective exposure, assuming that both balanced and selective forms of exposure have functional aspects, which are dependent on the decision context and associated subjectively experienced decision certainty.

AUTHOR NOTE

Please direct all correspondence to: Professor Dr. Peter Fischer, University of Regensburg, Department of Experimental Psychology, Social and Organizational

Psychology, Universitätsstrasse 31, 93053 Regensburg; e-mail: peter.fischer@psychologie.uni-regensburg.de/.

NOTE

1. In the context of tentative decisions, participants make a preliminary decision, afterward search for additional decision-consistent and -inconsistent information, and finally have the chance to make a final decision. Participants in final-decision scenarios only make one decision in the beginning, which cannot be revised after the subsequent information search.
2. A short version of the presented model will be published elsewhere.

REFERENCES

Baumeister, R. F., Bratlavsky, E., Muraven, M., & Tice, D. M. (1998). Ego depletion: Is the active self a limited resource? *Journal of Personality and Social Psychology, 74,* 1252–1265.

Behling, C. F. (1971). Effects of commitment and certainty upon exposure to supportive and nonsupportive information. *Journal of Personality and Social Psychology, 19,* 152–159.

Betsch, T., Haberstroh, S., Glöckner, A., Haar, T., & Fiedler, K. (2001). The effects of routine strength on adaption and information search in recurrent decision making. *Organizational Behavior and Human Decision Processes, 84,* 23–53.

Brock, T. C., & Balloun, J. C. (1967). Behavioral receptivity to dissonant information. *Journal of Personality and Social Psychology, 6,* 413–428.

Carlsmith, J. M., Collins, B. E., & Helmreich, R. L. (1966). Studies in forced compliance: The effect of pressure for compliance on attitude change produced by face-to-face role playing and anonymous essay writing. *Journal of Personality and Social Psychology, 4,* 1–13.

Cooper, J., & Fazio, R. H. (1984). A new look at dissonance theory. *Advances in Experimental Social Psychology, 17,* 229–265.

Cotton, J. L., & Hieser, R. A. (1980). Selective exposure to information and cognitive dissonance. *Journal of Research in Personality, 14,* 518–527.

Dawson, E., Gilovich, T., & Regan, D. T. (2002). Motivated reasoning and performance on the Wason selection task. *Personality and Social Psychology Bulletin, 28,* 1379–1387.

Ditto, P. H., & Lopez, D. F. (1992). Motivated skepticism: Use of differential decision criteria for preferred and non-preferred conclusions. *Journal of Personality and Social Psychology, 63,* 568–584.

Ditto, P. H., Scepansky, J. A., Munro, G. D., Apanovitch, A. M., & Lockhart, L. K. (1998). Motivated sensitivity to preference-inconsistent information. *Journal of Personality and Social Psychology, 75,* 53–69.

Festinger, L. (1957). *A theory of cognitive dissonance.* Stanford, CA: Stanford University Press.

Festinger, L. (1964). *Conflict, decision, and dissonance.* Stanford, CA: Stanford University Press.

Fiedler, K., Brinkmann, B., Betsch, T., & Wild, B. (2000). Sampling approach to biases in conditional probability judgments: Beyond base rate neglect and statistical format. *Journal of Experimental Psychology: General, 129,* 399–418.

Fischer, P., Crelley, D., Frey, D., & Köppl, J. (2009). *The impact of perceived threat on confirmatory information processing.* Manuscript in preparation.

Fischer, P., Greitemeyer, T., & Frey, D. (2008). Self-regulation and selective exposure: The impact of depleted self-regulation resources on confirmatory information processing. *Journal of Personality and Social Psychology, 94,* 382–395.

Fischer, P., Jonas, E., Frey, D., & Kastenmüller, A. (2008). Selective exposure and decision framing: The impact of gain and loss framing on biased information seeking after decisions. *Journal of Experimental Social Psychology, 44*, 312–320.

Fischer, P., Jonas, E., Frey, D., & Schulz-Hardt, S. (2005). Selective exposure to information: The impact of information limits. *European Journal of Social Psychology, 35*, 469–492.

Fischer, P., Schulz-Hardt, S., & Frey, D. (2008). Selective exposure and information quantity: How different information quantities moderate decision makers' preference for consistent and inconsistent information. *Journal of Personality and Social Psychology, 94*, 231–244.

Frey, D. (1981a). Postdecisional preference for decision-relevant information as a function of the competence of its source and the degree of familiarity with this information. *Journal of Experimental Social Psychology, 17*, 51–67.

Frey, D. (1981b). Reversible and irreversible decisions: Preference for consonant information as a function of attractiveness of decision alternatives. *Personality and Social Psychology Bulletin, 7*, 621–626.

Frey, D. (1981c). The effect of negative feedback about oneself and cost of information on preferences for information about the source of this feedback. *Journal of Experimental Social Psychology, 17*, 42–50.

Frey, D. (1982). Different levels of cognitive dissonance, information seeking, and information avoidance. *Journal of Personality and Social Psychology, 43*, 1175–1183.

Frey, D. (1986). Recent research on selective exposure to information. In L. Berkowitz (Ed.), *Advances in experimental social psychology* (Vol. 19, pp. 41–80). New York: Academic Press.

Frey, D., & Stahlberg, D. (1986). Selection of information after receiving more or less reliable self-threatening information. *Personality and Social Psychology Bulletin, 12*, 434–441.

Frey, D., & Wicklund, R. A. (1978). A clarification of selective exposure: The impact of choice. *Journal of Experimental Social Psychology, 14*, 132–139.

Goldstein, D. G., & Gigerenzer, G. (2002). Models of ecological rationality: The recognition heuristic. *Psychological Review, 109*, 75–90.

Greitemeyer, T., & Schulz-Hardt, S. (2003). Preference-consistent evaluation of information in the hidden profile paradigm: Beyond group-level explanations for the dominance of shared information in group decisions. *Journal of Personality and Social Psychology, 84*, 322–339.

Hart, W., Albarracin, D., Eagly, A. H., Brechan, I., Lindberg, M. J., & Merrill, L. (2009). Feeling validated versus being correct: A meta-analysis of selective exposure to information. *Psychological Bulletin, 135*, 555–88.

Janis, I. L. (1982) *Groupthink*. Boston, MA: Houghton Mifflin Company.

Johnston, L. (1996). Resisting change: Information-seeking and stereotype change. *European Journal of Social Psychology, 26*, 799–825.

Jonas, E., Graupmann, V., & Frey, D. (2006). The influence of mood on the search for supporting versus conflicting information. *Personality and Social Psychology Bulletin, 32*, 3–15.

Jonas, E., Schulz-Hardt, S., Frey, D., & Thelen, N. (2001). Confirmation bias in sequential information search after preliminary decisions: An expansion of dissonance theoretical research on "selective exposure to information." *Journal of Personality and Social Psychology, 80*, 557–571.

Kahneman, D., & Tversky, A. (1979). Prospect theory: An analysis of decision under risk. *Econometrica, 47*, 263–291.

Kastenmüller, A., Fischer, P., Jonas, E., Greitemeyer, T., Frey, D., Aydin, N., & Köppl, J. (2010). Selective exposure: The impact of framing information search instructions as gains and losses. *European Journal of Social Psychology, 40*(5), 837–846.

Kiesler, C. A. (1971). *The psychology of commitment.* New York, NY: Academic Press.

Klayman, J., & Ha, Y. W. (1987). Confirmation, disconfirmation, and information in hypothesis testing. *Psychological Review, 94,* 211–228.

Koehler, D. J. (1991). Explanation, imagination, and confidence in judgment. *Psychological Bulletin, 110,* 499–519.

Kray, L. J., & Galinsky, A. D. (2003). The debiasing effect of counterfactual mindsets: Increasing the search for disconfirmatory information in group decisions. *Organizational Behavior and Human Decision Processes, 36,* 362–377.

Kruglanski, A. W., & Klar, Y. (1987). A view from a bridge: Synthesizing the consistency and attribution paradigms from a lay epistemic perspective. *European Journal of Social Psychology, 17,* 211–241.

Kunda, Z. (1990). The case for motivated reasoning. *Psychological Bulletin, 108,* 480–498.

Lord, C., Ross, L., & Lepper, M. (1979). Biased assimilation and attitude polarization: The effects of prior theories on subsequently considered evidence. *Journal of Personality and Social Psychology, 37,* 2098–2109.

Lundgren, S. R., & Prislin, R. (1998). Motivated cognitive processing and attitude change. *Personality and Social Psychology Bulletin, 24,* 715–726.

Muraven, M., & Baumeister, R. F. (2000). Self-regulation and depletion of limited resources: Does self-control resemble a muscle? *Psychological Bulletin, 126,* 247–259.

Olson, J. M., & Stone, J. (2005). The influence of behavior on attitudes. In D. Albarracin, B. T. Johnson, & M. P. Zanna (Eds.), *The handbook of attitudes* (pp. 223–271). Hillsdale, NJ: Erlbaum.

Payne, J. W., Bettman, J. R., & Johnson, E. J. (1993). *The adaptive decision maker.* Cambridge, UK: Cambridge University Press.

Pyszczynski, T., & Greenberg, J. (1987). Toward an integration of cognitive and motivational perspectives on social inference: A biased hypothesis-testing model. In L. Berkowitz (Ed.), *Advances in experimental social psychology* (Vol. 20, pp. 297–340). New York: Academic Press.

Raju, P. S., Lonial, S. C., & Mangold, W. G. (1995). Differential effects of subjective knowledge, objective knowledge, and usage experience on decision making: An exploratory investigation, *Journal of Consumer Psychology, 4,* 153–180.

Rhine, R. J. (1967). The 1964 presidential election and curves of information seeking and avoiding. *Journal of Personality and Social Psychology, 5,* 416–423.

Schmeichel, J. S., Vohs, K. D., & Baumeister, R. F. (2003). Intellectual performance and ego depletion: Role of the self in logical reasoning and other information processing. *Journal of Personality and Social Psychology, 85,* 33–46.

Schulz-Hardt, S., Fischer, P., & Frey, D. (2009). *Confirmation bias in accuracy-motivated decision making: A cognitive explanation for biased information seeking.* Manuscript in preparation.

Schulz-Hardt, S., Frey, D., Lüthgens, C., & Moscovici, S. (2000). Biased information search in group decision making. *Journal of Personality and Social Psychology, 78,* 655–669.

Schulz-Hardt, S., Jochims, M., & Frey, D. (2002). Productive conflict in group decision making: Genuine and contrived dissent as strategies to counteract biased information seeking. *Organizational Behavior and Human Decision Processes, 88,* 563–586.

Schwarz, N., Bless, H., Strack, F., Klumpp, G., Rittenauer-Schatka, H., & Simons, A. (1991). Ease of retrieval as information: Another look at the availability heuristic. *Journal of Personality and Social Psychology, 61,* 195–202.

Schwarz, N., Frey, D., & Kumpf, M. (1980). Interactive effects of writing and reading a persuasive essay on attitude change and selective exposure. *Journal of Experimental Social Psychology, 16,* 1–17.

Simon, H. (1976). *Administrative behavior* (3rd ed.). New York: The Free Press.

Snyder, M., & Swann, W. B. (1978). Behavioral confirmation in social interaction: From social perception to social reality. *Journal of Experimental Social Psychology, 14,* 148–162.

Sweeney, P. D., & Gruber, K. L. (1984). Selective exposure: Voter information preferences and the Watergate affair. *Journal of Personality and Social Psychology, 46,* 1208–1221.

U.S. Select Senate Committee on Intelligence. (2004, July 9). *Report on the U.S. intelligence community's prewar intelligence assessments on Iraq.* Retrieved from http://intelligence.senate.gov

Vohs, K. D., Baumeister, R. F., & Ciarocco, N. J. (2005). Self-regulation and self-presentation: Regulatory resource depletion impairs impression management and effortful self-presentation depletes regulatory resources. *Journal of Personality and Social Psychology, 88,* 632–657.

3

Automatic and Controlled Decision Making
A Process Dissociation Perspective

B. KEITH PAYNE and JAZMIN L. BROWN IANNUZZI

*T*here was a time when a psychologist interested in unconscious processes had to struggle against the overwhelming weight of received opinion that the human mind made decisions by deliberately computing costs and benefits, and methodically weighting them by their likelihood. That time is past.

The last two decades have revealed dozens of ways that decisions can be shaped by unconscious, unintended, or unwanted influences. Although such findings are sometimes controversial, there is little reason left to argue about such basic questions as whether unconscious processes can drive decisions. The time has come to ask a next generation of questions about exactly how unconscious and automatic processes interact with conscious, deliberate reasoning. This chapter describes a process dissociation approach to decision making that addresses these second-generation questions. In particular, we will address such questions as: To what extent was a given decision influenced by automatic versus intentionally controlled processes? How do automatic and controlled processes interact? And, when automatic and controlled processes are in conflict, which one wins the day? Along the way, we hope to shed light on questions of accuracy and bias in human decision making.

AUTOMATIC INFLUENCES IN DECISION MAKING

When Simon (1955) and Kahneman and Tversky (1973) fired the opening salvos against expected utility theory as a psychological theory of how humans decide, few would have guessed how far their charge would lead. Whereas they showed that people sometimes *satisfice* and use heuristics, later authors have gone much further, sometimes suggesting that conscious deliberation plays a minimal role in people's decisions (Bargh & Chartrand, 1999; Wegner, 2002). Is such a conclusion warranted? We believe that taking a quantitative approach to separating automatic and controlled contributions can put the issue in greater perspective. Before describing how, we selectively review some key pieces of evidence supporting the importance of automatic decision making.

The psychology literature is full of demonstrations that unconscious, unintended, and unwanted thought processes influence decisions. Some of these findings are based in the fact that seemingly minor, logically irrelevant cues can alter people's behaviors in ways that are startling, not only to us readers, but also to the people doing the behaving. For example, a researcher exposing subjects to words related to "hostility" might cause them to judge an ambiguous target person as more hostile (Srull & Wyer, 1979), behave with more hostility themselves (Bargh, Chen, & Burrows, 1996), and even become motivated to actively seek an opportunity to aggress against someone (Todorov & Bargh, 2002; see Gilovich, Cone, & Rosenzweig, this volume, Chapter 1).

Decisions, however, are not simply about what concepts are salient but also about how people value their options. A number of studies have shown that the process of valuation also has important automatic aspects. In one study, Winkielman, Berridge, and Wilbarger (2005) subliminally presented photos of happy or angry faces as subjects were trying a novel beverage. Happy faces led subjects to drink more and be willing to pay more for the drink. Additional evidence comes from a study in which subjects completed an instrumental conditioning task with subliminal reward cues (Pessiglione et al., 2008). Each trial presented a masked image of a coin to indicate that they could win money if they pressed a key, or a coin with a bar through it to indicate that they could lose money if they pressed the key. After each decision they received feedback about whether they had won or lost money. Even though subjects could not report what the cue image was, their key-press decisions showed that they learned to respond adaptively over a few dozen trials. Priming research thus demonstrates that subtle cues can shape some components of the decision-making process.

Other research suggests that when making complex choices it is advantageous to rely on unconscious processes as opposed to conscious processes. Dijksterhuis and colleagues (Dijksterhuis, 2004; Dijksterhuis & Nordgren, 2006) compared the decisions people made when they were instructed to think about the decision, with the decisions they made when their attention was directed elsewhere for a few minutes. They found that decisions were higher in quality when they were distracted, and this was especially true for more complex decisions (see also Wilson & Schooler, 1991).

There has been controversy over the sophistication of unconscious decision making. Some research has demonstrated that conscious thought processes among subjects who made decisions at their own pace performed just as well or better than those in the unconscious condition (Payne, Samper, Bettman, & Luce, 2008; see also González-Vallejo & Phillips, 2010). This controversy extends an older controversy on the "incubation effect"—the finding that problem solving is often aided by shifting conscious attention away from the problem for a while (Wallas, 1926). The debate concerns whether distraction has its effects through an active, unconscious thought process or by simply removing impediments such as getting stuck on wrong solutions, overweighting nondiagnostic information, forgetting distracting information, or spending more time than is needed to make a decision (Acker, 2008; Payne et al., 2008; Shanks, 2006; Vul & Pashler, 2007). The debates currently underway are likely to yield a more focused picture of exactly when and how unconscious thought aids decision making and when it does not. But this is not the only paradigm that suggests a powerful role for the unconscious in driving decisions.

Some researchers have suggested that unconscious processes are not merely one aspect of decision making, but that decisions are made unconsciously, and consciousness comes in only after the fact to claim credit. Libet, Gleason, Wright, and Pearl's (1983) seminal research showed that the experience of consciously making a decision was preceded in time by unconscious neural activity. Recent research using functional magnetic resonance imaging (fMRI) has found that decision outcomes can be predicted by as much as 7 seconds before the subject's behavioral response (Soon, Brass, Heinze, & Haynes, 2008). In reviewing this and other research, Wegner (2002) proposed that the experience of consciously willing an act is an illusion. According to Wegner's theory, unconscious thought processes produce both actions and the thoughts that accompany them. Because the thoughts and the actions reliably happen together, we mistakenly infer that our thought caused the action. Not all theories go so far as to claim that consciously willed aspects of decisions are an illusion, of course. In the next section we consider some theories that have been developed to explain the joint contributions of automatic and consciously controlled cognition.

DUAL PROCESS THEORIES AS INTEGRATIVE EXPLANATIONS

A variety of dual process (or dual system) theories have been proposed to account for the automatic-controlled distinction (Chaiken & Trope, 1999). For example, Strack and Deutsch (2004) distinguish between reflective and impulsive bases for behavior. Sloman (1996) distinguishes between rule-based and association-based reasoning. Smith and DeCoster (2000) link social psychology research on automatic and controlled processing with implicit and explicit memory systems. Gawronski and Bodenhausen (2006) focus on the distinction between associative and propositional processes, and Evans, Clibbens, Cattani, Harris, and Dennis (2003) on the distinction between implicit and explicit processes. Recognizing the similarities across these models, Stanovich and West (2000) proposed the more general terms *System 1* and *System 2* to describe automatic and controlled thought processes.

These models all differentiate the conditions when automatic versus controlled processes are most likely to influence decisions and behavior. These conditions are closely tied to the definitions of automatic and controlled processes. Because automatic processes are efficient and effortless, whereas controlled processes are slow and effortful, it is clear when each kind of process is likely to matter. When conditions allow people to think slowly and carefully, controlled processes are likely to dictate behavior. But when they are unmotivated or unable to think carefully, automatic responses will be important.

Although they differ in their particulars, these theories converge on the general idea that automatic (or implicit, associative, etc.) and consciously controlled (or explicit, propositional, etc.) processes contribute to judgment, decisions, and behavior. The convergence between theories is encouraging, in that it suggests that they are revealing a basic duality about human psychology (but see Keren & Schul, 2009). The trouble with dual-process theories is that many findings might be just as easily predicted or explained by one dual-process theory as another. For example, when making a decision influenced by a subliminal prime, is the decision based on implicit rather than explicit processes? Impulsive rather than reflective systems? Associative rather than propositional reasoning? Choosing one theory over another can be difficult (Meehl, 1990).

Although verbal theories are useful for organizing thinking about the processes underlying behavior, quantitative theories are sometimes necessary for the greater rigor and detail they can provide. One way that quantitative theories offer greater specificity is by requiring researchers to specify the relations between processes. For example, when choosing how to vote do citizens go with the first thoughts that come to mind by default, and only reconsider their choice if their initial ideas are suppressed? Or do automatic impulses only drive choices when more controlled efforts fall apart? Or do automatic and controlled influences have additive effects in a tug-of-war for control of action? Most dual-process theories do not distinguish between such process accounts at this level of detail, and consequently increases in one process cannot be disentangled from decreases in the other. To answer these questions, we need to pose a more formal model that makes assumptions about the relations between processes, and then test those assumptions against experimental data. The process dissociation procedure provides a means of doing so.

THE PROCESS DISSOCIATION PROCEDURE

Larry Jacoby developed the process dissociation procedure to separate controlled and automatic uses of memory (Jacoby, 1991; Jacoby, Toth, & Yonelinas, 1993). Prior research had relied on the comparison of explicit and implicit memory tests. For example, researchers might use a cued recall test to measure explicit memory and a word fragment completion test to measure implicit memory. Comparisons of this kind assume that implicit tests purely reflect automatic memory processes, and that explicit tests purely reflect controlled memory processes. However, as Jacoby and others argued, subjects sometimes used controlled memory retrieval to complete implicit tests, and automatic influences sometimes influenced explicit tests. Implicit and explicit tests could thus be contaminated, so neither was likely to provide a process-pure measure of underlying processes. The process dissociation procedure provided an experimental paradigm, along with simple equations, for separating underlying processes.

The ability to disentangle the influence of control and automatic processes relies on pitting these processes against one another. By setting up an experiment that includes congruent conditions, in which automatic and controlled processes work in concert, and incongruent conditions, in which automatic and controlled processes work in opposition to one another, we can estimate the contributions of control and automatic processes (Jacoby, 1991; Jacoby et al., 1993). Process dissociation defines control over behavior by whether an act is consistent with intentions. Automatic responses are those made regardless of intentions (Jacoby, 1991).

As process dissociation has been discussed in the context of memory elsewhere (Kelley & Jacoby, 2000; Yonelinas, 2002), we focus in this chapter on decision making and social cognition research. We will first describe the use of process dissociation in social cognition research, where it has been applied widely in recent years. Then we describe new applications to studies of decision making in the tradition of research on judgments under uncertainty.

Process Dissociation in Social Cognition

Process dissociation has been used increasingly in recent years to disentangle the cognitive processes underlying social judgments and behavior. Research into unintended aspects of prejudice and stereotyping was stimulated by the widely publicized death of Amadou Diallo, who was mistakenly shot by New York City police officers who mistook the wallet in his hand for a gun. Because Diallo was unarmed and Black, some observers alleged that the officers' use of force was biased by race. Following this incident, we wanted to study whether people in general tended to assume that objects associated with Black men were weapons (Payne, 2001). We developed a task in which a picture of a Black or White individual was quickly flashed on a computer screen followed by a picture of either a gun or a tool. The task is to ignore the face and press one key for "gun" and another for "tool." This task arranges the situation so that successful control of responses can be estimated using process dissociation's C parameter, and automatic influences of stereotypes can be estimated with the A parameter, as follows.

When a Black face precedes a gun, unintended race biases and the intended gun response both lead to the same behavior (a congruent trial). In contrast, when a Black face precedes a tool, the unintended race bias favors the gun response, whereas carrying out the intended identification process favors the tool response (an incongruent trial). When both sources of information favor the same response, then correct responses could result from either controlled responding (C) or automatic bias (A) given the failure of control (1 − C). This relationship may be expressed mathematically in the equation

$$P(\text{correct}|\text{congruent}) = C + A \times (1 - C) \tag{3.1}$$

That is, when a Black face was paired with a gun, the correct response (gun) could be consistently achieved in two ways. The first way was by successfully controlling the response. The second was by unintentionally responding gun because of the race prime, even when unable to implement the response based on the actual target. On incongruent trials, the two processes were set in opposition to one another. As an example, consider the trials in which a Black face was paired with a tool. If control failed and a participant was influenced by activated stereotypes, then he or she would incorrectly respond gun. When cognitive control and stereotypic automatic bias were opposed to one another, false alarms would occur when an automatic bias (A) operated in the absence of control $(1 - C)$. Mathematically, this can be written as:

$$P(\text{stereotypic error}|\text{incongruent}) = A \times (1 - C) \tag{3.2}$$

Notice that the term $A \times (1 - C)$ is common to Equations 3.1 and 3.2. On the assumption that A and C operate independently, one can solve algebraically for estimates of controlled responding (C) and automatic bias (A). The estimate of controlled responding is the difference between responding gun on congruent and incongruent trials:

$$C = P(\text{correct}|\text{congruent}) - P(\text{stereotypic error}|\text{incongruent}) \tag{3.3}$$

Conceptually, this reflects the idea that on congruent trials, one can achieve the correct response by either controlling one's response or relying on automatic influences in the absence of control. However, stereotypic errors in the incongruent trials are posited to result only from automatic influences in the absence of control. Subtracting these terms allows researchers to identify how well participants exerted control over their responses. Once the degree of control has been estimated, it can be used to further solve for estimates of automatic influence. Stereotypical errors in the incongruent trials are posited to reflect automatic bias in the absence of control. Dividing the rate of stereotypical errors by $(1 - C)$ allows researchers to estimate the degree of automatic bias independent of control failures.

$$A = P(\text{stereotypic error}|\text{incongruent})/(1 - C) \tag{3.4}$$

Applying this model produces two parameters (C and A). C represents the probability that controlled processes contribute to a response, and A represents the probability that automatic processes contribute to responding. More concretely, the C parameter reflects how well participants successfully distinguish between guns and tools as they intend to do. The A parameter reflects influences of race stereotypes, which bias responses when control over behavior fails.

The results of the study showed that subjects were indeed biased by the race primes, as subjects were more likely to mistake a tool for a gun when it was primed with a Black face than a White face (see also Correll, Park, Judd, & Wittenbrink, 2002, 2007; Greenwald, Oakes, & Hoffman, 2003; Plant & Peruche, 2005). The process dissociation estimates showed that automatic and controlled processes played distinct roles in driving responses. Requiring subjects to respond quickly reduced the controlled component. But the controlled component was unaffected by the race primes. In contrast, the race primes affected the automatic component, but response speed did not.

The weapons task has been used to estimate automatic and controlled processes that can predict other meaningful behaviors. In one study, after completing the weapons task, subjects formed an impression of a new Black person from a vignette about a typical day in this person's life (Payne, 2005; see Srull & Wyer, 1980). Although the behaviors in the vignette were identical for all subjects, the kinds of impressions they formed varied widely. Subjects who showed the most stereotypical automatic biases in the weapons task liked the Black character less. Moreover, the impact of automatic bias depended on how much control subjects exerted over their behaviors. For subjects who displayed high control estimates in the weapons task, automatic stereotyping was not associated with more negative impressions. This suggests that the automatic and controlled estimates in the weapons task are not bound only to performance of that particular task. Instead, the automatic component is informative about an individual's propensity to engage in automatic stereotyping across tasks, and the control estimate is informative about the individual's ability to supersede automatic processing with controlled processing.

Taking these insights about individual differences in automatic and controlled processing a step further, Stewart, von Hippel, and Radvansky (2009) studied age differences in racial bias using the Implicit Association Task (IAT; Greenwald, McGhee, & Schwartz, 1998). Many studies have documented greater prejudice among older adults as compared to younger adults. Two explanations have often been offered to explain these differences. The first is that generational differences lead to greater prejudice among the elderly because they experienced times when prejudice was more widespread; the second is that older adults have deficits in cognitive control, and thus cannot filter the expression of prejudice as well as the young.

These compatible and incompatible trials on the IAT are analogous to "inclusion" and "exclusion" conditions of the process dissociation procedure. Using accuracy data rather than response times in the IAT, Stewart and colleagues found that older adults showed lower control estimates than younger adults, but the groups did not differ in their automatic biases. Only the automatic component of responses distinguished the racial groups. So, both race and age influenced the amount of bias displayed on the IAT, but they did so through different processes. White Americans showed more bias because they had more biased automatic impulses. Older adults showed more bias because they lacked control.

Process Dissociation in Judgment and Decision Making

Process dissociation has been used to understand several classic judgment and decision-making situations where controlled deliberation seems to fail. Ferreira, Garcia-Marques, Sherman, and Sherman (2006) applied the process dissociation principles to separate rule-based reasoning from heuristic reasoning. They set up problems that either pitted these two types of reasoning against each other or allowed them to work in concert. The study used three types of classic decision-making problems to create congruent and incongruent conditions: ratio bias problems, base-rate problems, and conjunction problems. The ratio bias problems investigated the phenomenon that people generally use a heuristic that weighs absolute numbers more heavily than proportional numbers (Kirkpatrick & Epstein, 1992). For example, when choosing odds at winning the lottery, an individual might choose 19 out of 100 chances to win rather than 2 out of 10 because of a heuristic to favor larger absolute numbers. The base-rate problems operated on the principle that people tend to neglect base rates and weigh salient information more heavily when making judgments (Kahneman & Tversky, 1973).

The conjunction problems were created to investigate the heuristic that the likelihood of a salient event is greater than the likelihood of a larger class of events that include the salient event. For example, people tend to think a woman described as bright, outspoken, and concerned with social justice is more likely to be a feminist bank teller than simply a bank teller (Tversky & Kahneman, 1983).

Ferreira and colleagues created versions of each problem in which the heuristic-based and rule-based solutions would be the same (congruent conditions) and versions in which they would conflict (incongruent conditions). Using these conditions, Ferreira and colleagues (2006) were able to separately estimate controlled and automatic components of decision making. The data revealed that instructions to complete the problems in a rational (versus intuitive) way increased the estimate of rule-based reasoning, whereas having participants perform a distracting secondary task reduced the estimate of rule-based reasoning. Both manipulations left estimates of heuristic processing unchanged. In contrast, priming participants to complete problems using heuristic strategies selectively increased estimates of heuristic processing.

Bishara (2005) expanded the use of process dissociation to understand the anchoring and adjustment heuristic (Tversky & Kahneman, 1974). This mental shortcut leads people to bias their responses toward an initial anchor. To test the dual process model of anchoring and adjustment, participants were given time to study correct answers before starting the experiment, which allowed them to use controlled processing in the form of memory retrieval. Therefore, if participants remembered the answer, they could use controlled processing, but if control failed (e.g., they forgot the information) they would rely on the automatic accessibility of the anchor. Studying the answers beforehand increased the estimated parameter of control but did not change the estimated parameter of automatic processes. In contrast, a manipulation of whether the numerical anchors were relevant for the question influenced only the automatic estimate. Related anchors, but not unrelated anchors, increased the automatic anchoring estimate.

Process dissociation has recently been used to investigate how repetition influences agreement with persuasive messages (Moons, Mackie, & Garcia-Marques, 2009). Previous research has shown that repeated statements are considered more valid than novel statements (Begg, Armour, & Kerr, 1985; Hasher, Goldstein, & Toppino, 1977). Moons and colleagues (2009) asked participants to listen to strong and weak arguments advocating for comprehensive exit exams in universities. Some arguments were presented repeatedly, whereas other arguments were only presented once. Participants were asked to rate the extent to which they agreed with each argument. This fully crossed design created conditions in which controlled processing of argument quality and presumably automatic influences of repetition were placed in concert and in opposition. In addition to these manipulations, half of the participants were asked to judge whether they agreed with the implementation of comprehensive exams in *their* school, and the other half was asked about agreement for another distant university. The results revealed that participants in the low-relevance condition engaged in less controlled processing than participants in the high-relevance condition, with no effects of relevance on the automatic estimate. In contrast, the automatic estimate was increased by repeated presentation of the arguments. These findings suggest that agreement with a message may be automatically influenced by repetition of the message, but that this is most likely to affect attitudes under conditions of low elaboration.

WHEN AUTOMATICITY FAILS

The experiments described thus far all applied a version of the process dissociation procedure, which assumes that automatic processing only drives responses when control fails. But in fact, Jacoby developed two complementary forms of the model. The second form assumes that control processes only drive responses in the absence of an automatic influence. This model was originally developed for use in the color/word Stroop task (Lindsay & Jacoby, 1994). In the Stroop task, automatic word-reading processes were hypothesized to dominate performance unless they are overridden by controlled color naming. Figure 3.1 displays the two models for comparison. We refer to the first model as a control-dominant model because according to this model, if automatic and controlled processes conflict, the control process dominates the response. In contrast, we describe the second model as an automatic-dominant model because the automatic process dominates responses when they conflict.

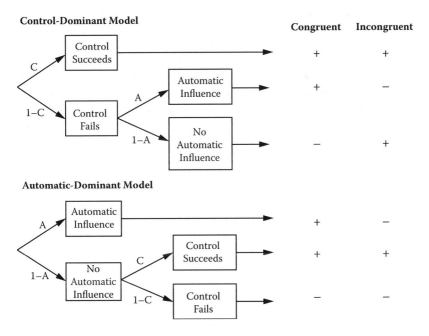

Figure 3.1 Two variants of the process dissociation model. In the control-dominant model, controlled responding drives responses whenever it is active. Automatic processing drives responding only when control fails. Thus, control dominates whenever the processes conflict. In the automatic-dominant model, automatic influences drive responses whenever they are active. Controlled processes drive responses only in the absence of automaticity. Thus, automatic influences dominate when both are active.

Importantly, these models do not imply any temporal order. It is well known that controlled processes typically take longer to operate than automatic processes, and this difference in speed is frequently used as a defining characteristic of automatic versus controlled processing (Bargh, 1994). It is therefore a mistake to interpret these models as claiming that one process comes "first" in a temporal sequence. To illustrate why this is so, consider Figure 3.2, which displays an algebraically equivalent version of the control-dominant model. As in the original depiction, whenever control is active, responses are correct. Only when control fails do automatic processes drive responses. Notice that this depiction, though algebraically equivalent to the control-dominant model in Figure 3.1, appears more consistent with two-stage dual-process models that are common in social psychology (Chaiken & Trope, 1999). Both control-dominant and automatic-dominant models are consistent with the idea that automatic thoughts, feelings, and impulses spring quickly to mind and that controlled monitoring and deliberation unfold only slowly, with effort and concentration. The feature that differentiates the two models is which processes "wins" when they are in conflict.[1]

Process dissociation models provide powerful tools for testing hypotheses about how automatic and controlled processes interact. They do not, however, make a priori predictions about whether automatic or controlled processes are likely to be dominant. Researchers must rely on substantive theories about the domain in question. The models provide a means of testing such hypotheses by comparing the fit of competing models. However, the theoretical interpretations of the models and a priori predictions will depend on the topic of study.

The control-dominant model has been used much more commonly than the automatic-dominant model. In many cases in which both models have been compared, the control-dominant model has often provided a superior fit to data. For example, Bishara and Payne (2009) examined four studies using the weapon identification task and found that the control-dominant model provided the best fit

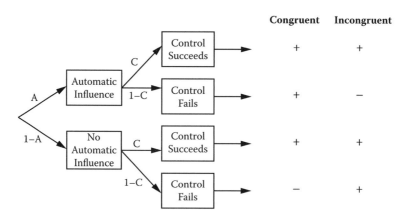

Figure 3.2 An algebraically equivalent representation of the control-dominant model. Placing control to the right of automatic influence fits with intuitive notions of temporal order. The fact that this model and the control-dominant model in Figure 3.1 are equivalent illustrates that the models have no temporal order.

to the data. However, in some cases the automatic-dominant model better explains the data. As alluded to earlier, the automatic-dominant model provides a good description of the Stroop task (Lindsay & Jacoby, 1994). A recent set of studies suggests that the automatic-dominant model also provides a good description of the illusory truth effect (Fazio, Marsh, & Payne, 2009).

The illusory truth effect is the finding that when a statement is repeated it becomes rated as more true. In deciding whether a particular statement is true, people might deliberately retrieve whatever they know about the topic and use that information to assess the truth value of the new statement. Alternatively, they might simply respond based on an intuitive feeling of familiarity, assuming that if it seemed familiar it is likely to be true. Fazio and colleagues presented participants with facts that were easy (e.g., the short pleated skirt that Scottish men wear is called a kilt) and facts that were hard (e.g., the Tiber River runs through Rome) along with matched false statements (e.g., the short pleated skirt that Scottish men wear is called a sari). In an initial phase the statements were either presented or not, under the guise of having participants rate how interesting they were. Later, participants read each statement and decided whether it was true or false. Consistent with other research on the illusory truth effect, participants were more likely to call a statement true if it was repeated than if it was novel. This happened not only for the hard facts, which most participants did not know, but also for easy ones, that they already knew. These results suggest that participants did not always retrieve the statements from memory, but in some cases responded on the information that came easily to mind.

How did deliberate retrieval and spontaneous familiarity processes interact? In this case, the automatic-dominant model provided a good fit to the data, whereas the control-dominant model did not. When the outcomes of automatic familiarity and controlled retrieval processes conflicted, the automatic process won. If the control-dominant model described these findings, it would mean that familiar ideas only seemed true whenever people are unable to retrieve the fact from memory. Instead, the results imply that when a fact came automatically to mind, participants did not bother to retrieve the fact from memory but simply assumed that the fact was true. This finding has interesting implications for political propaganda and advertising, in which claims are often repeated extensively. This suggests that the power of "staying on message" is twofold. Not only does repeating a message make it seem true, it also makes people less likely to think critically about it.

EXTENSIONS OF PROCESS DISSOCIATION LOGIC IN NEW MODELS

We have described two versions of process dissociation models—the control-dominant and automatic-dominant models—that instantiate what Jacoby (1991) described as the logic of opposition. Both models rely on placing automatic and controlled processes in opposition, as well as in concert, to estimate their unique contributions. That basic logic has been extended in recent research to estimate the contributions of other processes as well.

Conrey, Sherman, Gawronski, Hugenberg, and Groom (2005) proposed the quadruple process model as a means of distinguishing four processes. Two of the processes are similar to the automatic and controlled parameters in the original process dissociation model. The quad model's detection parameter reflects the ability to discriminate between correct and incorrect responses (as does the control parameter in process dissociation) and the association activation parameter reflects automatic influences of implicit associations (similar to process dissociation's automatic parameter). The model also includes a general guessing parameter that captures whether participants tend to guess with one response rather than another. Guessing parameters can be practically useful because they can represent responses that are driven neither by controlled nor automatic processes, such as mindless guessing or random responding. The guessing parameter does not strongly distinguish the two models at a theoretical level, however, because process dissociation has also been implemented at times with a guessing parameter (Buchner, Erdfelder, & Vaterrodt-Plünnecke, 1995; Yonelinas & Jacoby, 1996).

The parameter that seems to distinguish between models is called "overcoming bias." This parameter has been interpreted as a kind of inhibitory control, in which participants suppress automatic responses and respond instead based on their detection of the correct answer. More concretely, the parameter indicates which process drives responses when detection and association activation are in conflict.

We discussed earlier how comparing control-dominant and automatic-dominant models could reveal which process "wins" when they are in conflict. The approach taken by the quad model shares important similarities with these model comparisons. Bishara and Payne (2009) provided a proof that when the quad model's overcoming bias parameter equals zero, the quad model reduces to the automatic-dominating process dissociation model (with a guessing parameter). And when the overcoming bias parameter equals one, the quad model reduces to the control-dominant model. In other words, estimating the quad model and comparing automatic-dominant versus control-dominant models accomplish largely the same goal. The difference is that in the quad model, the likelihood that automatic or controlled processes dominate is estimated by the overcoming bias parameter; in our studies comparing models, it is estimated by model fit statistics. The convergence between models is an encouraging sign that researchers beginning with different assumptions have found common processes underlying a variety of different tasks.

ACCURACY AND BIAS

The studies reviewed illustrate how process estimates can clarify the processes underlying many sources of error and bias, as well as sources of accuracy. Contemporary psychology research has been critiqued as focusing too heavily on errors and biases, and too little on how often perceivers get things right (Krueger & Funder, 2004). Although the purpose of the process dissociation procedure is to separate intentional and unintentional contributions to behavior, in some cases it has the fortunate side effect of quantifying the degree of accuracy and bias in responses at the same time.

Process dissociation is not inherently tied to accuracy; it is inherently tied to intent. The procedure defines control as responding based on intent, and it defines automatic processing as responding independent of intent. Yet in many cases, accurately responding on a task that requires a lot of cognitive control provides a good way to measure control. As an example, consider tasks that are used to measure executive control, such as working memory, flanker, and Stroop tasks. In each of these tasks there is one source of diagnostic information on which subjects are instructed to respond (target items in working memory and flanker tasks, and color names in the Stroop). There is also a source of irrelevant information that interferes with intentional responding (intervening operations in working memory tasks, flankers in the flanker, and color words in the Stroop). In executive control tasks such as these, responding based on the target items leads to accuracy, and accuracy is used as a measure of executive control.

In process dissociation studies of memory, intentionally retrieving a conscious memory of an episode will lead to accurate responding, even under exclusion instructions. And in tasks such as the weapon identification task, carrying out the intention to distinguish between guns and tools will lead to high accuracy. To be sure, cognitive control is not the same thing as accuracy, and automatic processing is not the same as bias. Nonetheless, accuracy and bias are often good ways to operationally measure intended and unintended responses.

When process dissociation is applied in a task using accuracy to measure control, process dissociation parameters can be interpreted as estimates of accuracy and bias. Thinking about decision tasks from this perspective reframes the question of whether people are accurate or biased. Studies documenting the use of heuristics in decision making are sometimes interpreted as showing that people's reasoning is terribly flawed. Studies showing effects of stereotypes on judgment are sometimes interpreted as showing that people are hopelessly unfair. Yet, studies using process dissociation typically find that people are relatively good at responding based on relevant information (Dawes, 1979; Jussim, 1991; Kunda & Thagard, 1996).

First, control estimates are often quite high. And second, studies across many domains (though not all) have found that a control-dominant model better explains the data than an automatic-dominant model. In cases where controlled processes dominate and automatic processes drive responses only when control fails, it is difficult to argue that automatic processing has an overwhelming effect on behavior. Bargh (1999) described automatic social cognition as a "cognitive monster" that cannot often be constrained by efforts at controlled thought. Kihlstrom (2006) criticized this view, describing instead an "automaticity juggernaut" that threatened to overrun social psychology research with a one-sided emphasis on automatic thought. Questions about the scope of automatic and controlled processes in everyday life cannot easily be resolved with a few empirical studies. However, the process dissociation approach provides a tool for researchers to study the relative dominance of each kind of processing, one behavior at a time. An accumulated database of such studies might eventually provide a basis for making broader claims about the dominance of automaticity (for an extended discussion, see Payne & Bishara, 2009).

Process dissociation highlights that accuracy and bias coexist in the same task and within the same person. Like signal detection analyses, the procedure assumes that accuracy and bias are independent of each other (see also Swets, Dawes, & Monahan, 2000). Finding evidence of bias does not imply, therefore, that the person's judgment is inaccurate. Thinking of accuracy and bias as independent components of decision making advances the question about human accuracy and bias. Rather than asking whether people are accurate or biased in their decisions, it underscores that many processes contribute to accuracy and bias, even within a single person making a single decision.

CONCLUSION

We began this chapter by reviewing a number of exciting findings about the ways that unconscious and automatic processes influence decision making. Dual-process theories provide useful frameworks for thinking about automatic and controlled processes in general, but they do not provide the specificity needed to identify how automatic and controlled processes interact to drive a particular decision. Formal models such as process dissociation provide that specificity. After decades of demonstrations that decisions are driven by unconscious, impulsive, and unintended influences as well as deliberate reasoning, new research is beginning to ask a next generation of questions. Process dissociation provides a set of tools to study how unobservable automatic and controlled processes relate to decisions and to each other.

NOTE

1. Although the models are agnostic with respect to temporal order, estimates derived from the models may be used to answer questions about the time course of processing. As an example, McElree, Dolan, and Jacoby (1999) asked participants to complete a recognition memory test while responding to each item as soon as they received a signal to respond. By varying the timing of the signal they derived a speed-accuracy trade-off function. Moreover, they estimated automatic and controlled contributions at each time interval using process dissociation analyses. These analyses showed that automatic influences developed very early (i.e., within milliseconds), whereas controlled processes came online much more slowly (i.e., over the course of a few seconds). Temporal sequencing is thus an empirical question that is likely to have different answers for different tasks. Quantitative models provide a tool to help identify answers

ACKNOWLEDGMENT

B. Keith Payne acknowledges funding from the National Science Foundation Grant No. 0924252.

REFERENCES

Acker, F. (2008). New findings on unconscious versus conscious thought in decision making: Additional empirical data and meta-analysis. *Judgment and Decision Making, 3,* 292–303.

Bargh, J. A. (1994). The four horsemen of automaticity: Awareness, intention, efficiency, and control in social cognition. In R. S. Wyer & T. K. Srull (Eds.), *Handbook of social cognition* (pp. 1–40). Hillsdale, NJ: Erlbaum.

Bargh, J. (1999). The cognitive monster: The case against the controllability of automatic stereotype effects. In S. Chaiken & Y. Trope (Eds.), *Dual-process theories in social psychology* (pp. 361–382). New York: Guilford Press.

Bargh, J. A., & Chartrand, T. L. (1999). The unbearable automaticity of being. *American Psychologist, 54*(7), 462–479.

Bargh, J. A., Chen, M., & Burrows, L. (1996). Automaticity of social behavior: Direct effects of trait construct and stereotype activation on action. *Journal of Personality and Social Psychology, 71,* 230–244.

Begg, I., Armour, V., & Kerr, T. (1985). On believing what we remember. *Canadian Journal of Behavioral Science, 17,* 199–214.

Bishara, A. J. (2005). *Control and accessibility bias in single and multiple anchoring effects.* Unpublished doctoral dissertation, Washington University, St. Louis, MO.

Bishara, A. J., & Payne, B. K. (2009). Multinomial process tree models of control and automaticity in weapon misidentification. *Journal of Experimental Social Psychology, 45,* 524–534.

Buchner, A., Erdfelder, E., & Vaterrodt-Plünnecke, B. (1995). Toward unbiased measurement of conscious and unconscious memory processes within the process dissociation framework. *Journal of Experimental Psychology: General, 124,* 137–160.

Chaiken, S., & Trope, Y. (1999). *Dual-process theories in social psychology.* New York: Guilford Press.

Conrey, F. R., Sherman, J. W., Gawronski, B., Hugenberg, K., & Groom, C. (2005). Separating multiple processes in implicit social cognition: The quad-model of implicit task performance. *Journal of Personality and Social Psychology, 89,* 469–487.

Correll, J., Park, B., Judd, C., & Wittenbrink, B. (2002). The police officer's dilemma: Using ethnicity to disambiguate potentially threatening individuals. *Journal of Personality and Social Psychology, 83,* 1314–1329.

Correll, J., Park, B., Judd, C., & Wittenbrink, B. (2007). The influence of stereotypes on decisions to shoot. *European Journal of Social Psychology, 37,* 1102–1117.

Dawes, R. M. (1979). The robust beauty of improper linear models in decision making. *American Psychologist, 34,* 571–582.

Dijksterhuis, A. (2004). Think different: The merits of unconscious thought in preference development and decision making. *Journal of Personality and Social Psychology, 87,* 586–598.

Dijksterhuis, A., & Nordgren, L. (2006). A theory of unconscious thought. *Perspectives on Psychological Science, 1,* 95–109.

Evans, J., Clibbens, J., Cattani, A., Harris, A., & Dennis, I. (2003). Explicit and implicit processes in multicue judgment. *Memory & Cognition, 31,* 608–618.

Fazio, L. K., Marsh, E. J., & Payne, B. K. (2009, November 19–22). *Prior knowledge does not protect against illusory truth effects.* Paper presented at the 2009 meeting of the Psychonomic Society, Boston, MA.

Ferreira, M. B., Garcia-Marques, L., Sherman, S. J., & Sherman, J. W. (2006). Automatic and controlled components of judgment and decision making. *Journal of Personality and Social Psychology, 91,* 797–813.

Gawronski, B., & Bodenhausen, G. (2006). Associative and propositional processes in evaluation: An integrative review of implicit and explicit attitude change. *Psychological Bulletin, 132,* 692–731.

González-Vallejo, C., & Phillips, N. (2010). Predicting soccer matches: A reassessment of the benefit of unconscious thinking. *Judgment and Decision Making, 5,* 200–206.

Greenwald, A., McGhee, D., & Schwartz, J. (1998). Measuring individual differences in implicit cognition: The implicit association test. *Journal of Personality and Social Psychology, 74,* 1464–1480.

Greenwald, A., Oakes, M., & Hoffman, H. (2003). Targets of discrimination: Effects of race on responses to weapons holders. *Journal of Experimental Social Psychology, 39,* 399–405.

Hasher, L., Goldstein, D., & Toppino, T. (1977). Frequency and the conference of referential validity. *Journal of Verbal Learning and Verbal Behavior, 16,* 107–112.

Jacoby, L. L. (1991). A process dissociation framework: Separating automatic from intentional uses of memory. *Journal of Memory and Language, 30,* 513–541.

Jacoby, L. L., Toth, J. P., & Yonelinas, A. P. (1993). Separating conscious and unconscious influences of memory: Measuring recollection. *Journal of Experimental Psychology: General, 122,* 139–154.

Jussim, L. (1991). Social perception and social reality: A reflection-construction model. *Psychological Review, 98,* 54–73.

Kahneman, D., & Tversky, A. (1973). On the psychology of prediction. *Psychological Review, 80,* 237–251.

Kelley, C. M., & Jacoby, L. L. (2000). Recollection and familiarity: Process-dissociation. In E. E. Tulving, E. Fergus, & I. M. Craik (Eds.), *The Oxford handbook of memory* (pp. 215–228). New York: Oxford University Press.

Keren, G., & Schul, Y. (2009). Two is not always better than one: A critical evaluation of two-system theories. *Perspectives on Psychological Science, 4,* 533–550.

Kihlstrom, J. F. (2006). The automaticity juggernaut. In J. Baer, J. C. Kaufman, & R. F. Baumeister (Eds.), *Psychology and free will* (pp. 155–180). New York: Oxford University Press.

Kirkpatrick, L. A., & Epstein, S. (1992). Cognitive-experiential self theory and subjective probability: Further evidence for two conceptual systems. *Journal of Personality and Social Psychology, 63,* 534–544.

Krueger, J., & Funder, D. (2004). Toward a balanced social psychology: Causes, consequences, and cures for the problem-seeking approach to social behavior and cognition. *Behavioral and Brain Sciences, 27,* 313–327.

Kunda, Z., & Thagard, P. (1996). Forming impressions from stereotypes, traits, and behaviors: A parallel-constraint-satisfaction theory. *Psychological Review, 103,* 284–308.

Libet, B., Gleason, C. A., Wright, E. W., and Pearl, D. K. (1983). Time of conscious intention to act in relation to onset of cerebral activity (readiness-potential). The unconscious initiation of a freely voluntary act. *Brain, 106,* 623–642.

Lindsay, D., & Jacoby, L. (1994). Stroop process dissociations: The relationship between facilitation and interference. *Journal of Experimental Psychology: Human Perception and Performance, 20,* 219–234.

McElree, B., Dolan, P. O., & Jacoby, L. L. (1999). Isolating the contributions of familiarity and source information to item recognition: A time course analysis. *Journal of Experimental Psychology: Learning, Memory, and Cognition, 25,* 563–582.

Meehl, P. E. (1990). Appraising and amending theories: The strategy of Lakatosian defense and two principles that warrant it. *Psychological Inquiry, 1,* 108–141.

Moons, W. G., Mackie, D. M., & Garcia-Marques, T. (2009). The impact of repetition-induced familiarity on agreement with weak and strong arguments. *Journal of Personality and Social Psychology, 96*, 32–44.

Payne, B. K. (2001). Prejudice and perception: The role of automatic and controlled processes in misperceiving a weapon. *Journal of Personality and Social Psychology, 81*, 181–192.

Payne, B. K. (2005). Conceptualizing control in social cognition: How executive control modulates the expression of automatic stereotyping. *Journal of Personality and Social Psychology, 89*, 488–503.

Payne, B. K., & Bishara, A. J. (2009). An integrative review of process dissociation and related models in social cognition. *European Review of Social Psychology, 20*, 272–314.

Payne, J. W., Samper, A., Bettman, J. R., & Luce, M. F. (2008). Boundary conditions on unconscious thought in complex decision making. *Psychological Science, 19*, 1118–1123.

Pessiglione, M., Petrovic, P., Daunizeau, J., Palminteri, S., Dolan, R. J., & Frith, C. D. (2008). Subliminal instrumental conditioning demonstrated in the human brain. *Neuron, 59*, 525–527.

Plant, E., & Peruche, B. (2005). The consequences of race for police officers' responses to criminal suspects. *Psychological Science, 16*, 180–183.

Shanks, D. R. (2006). Complex choices better made unconsciously? *Science, 313*(5788), 760–761.

Simon, H. A. (1955). A behavioral model of rational choice. *Quarterly Journal of Economics, 69*, 99–118.

Sloman, S. (1996). The empirical case for two systems of reasoning. *Psychological Bulletin, 119*, 3–22.

Smith, E., & DeCoster, J. (2000). Dual-process models in social and cognitive psychology: Conceptual integration and links to underlying memory systems. *Personality and Social Psychology Review, 4*, 108–131.

Soon, C., Brass, M., Heinze, H., & Haynes, J. (2008). Unconscious determinants of free decisions in the human brain. *Nature Neuroscience, 11*, 543–545.

Srull, T. K., & Wyer, S. (1979). The role of category accessibility in the interpretation of information about persons: Some determinants and implications. *Journal of Personality and Social Psychology, 37*, 1660–1672.

Srull, T., & Wyer, R. (1980). Category accessibility and social perception: Some implications for the study of person memory and interpersonal judgments. *Journal of Personality and Social Psychology, 38*, 841–856.

Stanovich, K., & West, R. (2000). Individual differences in reasoning: Implications for the rationality debate? *Behavioral and Brain Sciences, 23*, 645–665.

Stewart, B., von Hippel, W., & Radvansky, G. (2009). Age, race, and implicit prejudice: Using process dissociation to separate the underlying components. *Psychological Science, 20*, 164–168.

Strack, F., & Deutsch, R. (2004). Reflective and impulsive determinants of social behavior. *Personality and Social Psychology Review, 8*, 220–247.

Swets, J. A., Dawes, R. M., & Monahan, J. (2000). Psychological science can improve diagnostic decisions. *Psychological Science in the Public Interest, 1*, 1–26.

Todorov, A., & Bargh, A. (2002). Automatic sources of aggression. *Aggression and Violent Behavior, 7*, 53–68.

Tversky, A., & Kahneman, D. (1974). Judgment under uncertainty: Heuristics and biases. *Science, 185*, 1124–1131.

Tversky, A., & Kahneman, D. (1983). Extensional versus intuitive reasoning: The conjunction fallacy in probability judgment. *Psychological Review, 90*, 293–315.

Vul, E., & Pashler, H. (2007). Incubation benefits only after people have been misdirected. *Memory & Cognition, 35,* 701–710.

Wallas, G. (1926). *The art of thought.* London: Jonathan Cape.

Wegner, D. (2002). *The illusion of conscious will.* Cambridge, MA: MIT Press.

Wilson, T., & Schooler, J. (1991). Thinking too much: Introspection can reduce the quality of preferences and decisions. *Journal of Personality and Social Psychology, 60,* 181–192.

Winkielman, P., Berridge, K., & Wilbarger, J. (2005). Unconscious affective reactions to masked happy versus angry faces influence consumption behavior and judgments of value. *Personality and Social Psychology Bulletin, 31,* 121–135.

Yonelinas, A. P. (2002). The nature of recollection and familiarity: A review of 30 years of research. *Journal of Memory and Language, 46,* 441–517.

Yonelinas, A., & Jacoby, L. (1996). Response bias and the process-dissociation procedure. *Journal of Experimental Psychology: General, 125,* 422–434.

4

The (Ir)rationality Project in Social Psychology
A Review and Assessment

JOACHIM I. KRUEGER

Formulas are crutches. If we were logical, we wouldn't need them.

Professor Theo Harder, University of Bielefeld

S cientific psychologists have been sitting in judgment over the rationality of ordinary people. They have asked how well people fare executing everyday tasks of estimation, prediction, and inference. Reviewing the ebb and flow of these judgments throughout the 20th century, Zajonc (1999) found more ebb than flow. Of 33 influential social psychologists, Zajonc classified 23 as irrationalists, 7 as rationalists, and remaining undecided on 3. Had he included himself, the tally might have been even more skewed.

Zajonc (1999) doubted that social psychology had reached its goal of becoming a cumulative science. Were it cumulative, there should be growing consensus on the defining issues of the field. The lack of consensus on an issue as central as rationality suggests "a schism in our conceptions about the basic nature of the individual [and a difference in] a major premise about [the] rationality of behavior" (pp. 201–202). According to Zajonc, rationalists believe that human behavior involves "voluntary and willful reason," whereas irrational behavior is guided by "forces of nature and biological dispositions, often unconscious and uncontrollable" (p. 202). Crediting Mark Lepper with the idea, Zajonc listed four sources of irrationality: cognitive or logical inadequacies, biological causes (e.g., instincts), social pressure, and personal values.

Zajonc (1999) classified Freud, Sherif, Festinger, Milgram, and Tajfel as irrationalists, whose theories and findings illustrate varieties of irrationality. Freud

59

argued that unconscious forces residing in the id and the super ego control most human behavior. Sherif showed that people yield to social influence even when that influence is not based on valid information. Festinger found that people change their attitudes without sufficient reason. Milgram demonstrated that he could get ordinary people to (presumably) shock a fellow person to death simply on the grounds of obedience. Finally, Tajfel showed that the threshold for intergroup discrimination is intolerably low. On the other side of the divide, Zajonc listed Bandura as the clearest exemplar of rationalism for his tireless efforts to document the role of deliberative reasoning in human agency.

Some of Zajonc's classifications can be questioned, and his list is hardly complete. For example, Asch's work on normative social influence and Darley and Latané's work on the bystander effect had a strong irrationalist bent (cf. Krueger & Massey, 2009). Conversely, Kelley's (1967) attribution theory credited ordinary people with rational scientific minds, and so did Fishbein and Ajzen's (1975) theory of reasoned action.[1]

Quibbles aside, Zajonc's argument has great force. Since its beginning, social psychology has grappled with the yin of rationality and the yang of irrationality. Mostly, the yang carried the day without a fight, but during the last decade, the debate has become more open (for example, Barbey & Sloman, 2007; Krueger & Funder, 2004). An emerging theme is a careful consideration of the criteria by which rationality is evaluated, the contexts in which research participants make their judgments and decisions, and the type of rationality at stake (e.g., coherence or correspondence; Krueger, 2009a; Todd, Gigerenzer, & the ABC Research Group, in press).

With new theoretical models of rationality emerging and progressive empirical research programs taking shape, the next phase of scientific work will yield a more subtle and textured picture of what people do well, under what kinds of conditions they succeed, and how and when they fail. Rationality should no longer be a straw man null hypothesis; it deserves to be restored to its proper status as a hypothesis that may become less or more credible given relevant empirical evidence.

HOMO IDIOTICUS, OR THE TALE OF THE FAILED SCIENTIST

During the 1960s, the idea that ordinary people can be modeled as competent, if naïve, scientists enjoyed a honeymoon. The researchers who studied them believed that the general rational actor model prevailing in other social sciences could be applied to social psychology. The model assumes that people have access to a wealth of information relevant to the judgments they need to make, that they are willing and able to process this information without bias, and that they are conversant in the art of hypothesis testing (Kelley, 1967; Peterson & Beach, 1967). The model of the naïve scientist was an ideal, and hence vulnerable to attack. Notwithstanding the scientists' own failure to reach consensus on how scientific inferences are to be drawn (Gallistel, 2009; Krueger, 2001), they soon presented data suggesting that people systematically violate the precepts of logic and probability. In an influential essay, Ross (1977) declared that naïve scientists are best characterized not by their triumphs but by their shortcomings.

Soon after, Nisbett and Ross (1980) published their monograph *Human Inference* as a catalog of errors, illusions, and fallacies. The list was long and depressing; the naïve scientist had devolved into *homo idioticus*. Going beyond cataloguing, Nisbett and Ross argued that a handful of judgmental heuristics can explain most errors. They followed Tversky and Kahneman (1974), who had introduced "representativeness," "availability," and "anchoring (with insufficient adjustment)" as the Big Three heuristics. According to the heuristics-and-biases view, people base judgments of categorization mainly on the similarity between instance and category (i.e., representativeness), while neglecting the relative size of the category (i.e., base rates). The result is systematic categorization errors. Judgments of frequency and probability depend mainly on the ease with which relevant instances come to mind (i.e., availability). This heuristic also guarantees systematic error. Although it is reasonable to think that an instance can be recalled if its frequency in the environment is high, it is not necessarily true that an instance is frequent if it can be recalled. Finally, estimates of absolute value (e.g., number) can be contaminated by other, arbitrary values that happened to be under consideration prior to the estimation task (i.e., anchoring). Here, the bias lies in the inability to ignore information that is recognized as irrelevant.

The heart of Nisbett and Ross's (1980) argument was that many of the familiar social irrationalities could be reframed as the results of a few simple habits of mind. The signature bias in the field of social cognition is the "fundamental attribution error" (Ross, 1977), also known as "correspondence bias" (Jones & Harris, 1967). The error consists of overattributing behavior to the person and underattributing it to the situation. One concern about the heuristics-and-biases interpretation is that each of the Big Three heuristics offers a plausible explanation. When a behavior is observed, it seems to be representative of the person, not the situation; the person is more available in memory than the situation; the person attribution forms an anchor because it is an automatic inference, whereas a situation attribution can only be made by laborious adjustment.

Nisbett and Ross's (1980) framework not only assimilated past social-psychological findings into a common irrationalist paradigm, it also created new opportunities to extend the list of fallacies. Hence, it had the hallmarks of a scientific revolution (Kuhn, 1962). Journals soon teemed with demonstrations of cognitive and behavioral problems, and the psychology of ordinary people threatened to devolve into a litany of foul-ups. Krueger and Funder (2004) drew up a partial list of 42 biases (from "asymmetric insight illusion" to "vulnerability bias"). A more recent check of Wikipedia's "List of cognitive biases" (n.d.) yielded a list of 43 "decision-making and behavioral biases," 29 "biases in probability and belief," 20 "social biases," and 11 "memory errors." For those hungry for more, the site provides 14 "see also" links (e.g., "list of fallacies," "self-deception").

More is not always better. The original promise of the heuristics-and-biases paradigm was not to prove that humans are stupid, but to use their failures as a window into the architecture of mind. Clearly, an exclusively irrational mind is an untenable premise. People succeed at many tasks. To say that these successes are not interesting is to define social psychology as the psychopathology of everyday life. To avoid such an unappetizing reduction, it is necessary to claim that the study of failures is more informative than the study of successes. This argument is usually made by analogy. Much as perceptual illusions reveal how the mind reconstructs physical reality, cognitive illusions are supposed to reveal how the mind reconstructs social reality. Typically, this analogy is not probed, just asserted.

The idea that judgmental errors, biases, and fallacies might be the footprints of an adapted mind has not fully taken hold. Instead, these findings are often portrayed as serious problems in need of remedy rather than exciting signals of the mind's well-honed inner workings.[2] By suggesting that if people were more rational the world would be a better place, the irrationalist project implies an attitude of *meliorism*. Early on, Kahneman and Tversky (1979; cited in Makridakis, Hogarth, & Gaba, 2009, p. 197) declared that "man [*sic*] suffers from mental astigmatism as well as myopia, and any corrective prescription should fit the diagnosis."

The meliorist project found a natural theoretical frame within the dual-process models that began to emerge during the 1990s (Chaiken & Trope, 1999). Although each model has unique attributes, there are significant commonalities. They all assume that one process or system of processes (System 1) is characterized by fast, parallel, and easy information processing. This system operates automatically, reflexively, and associatively. The other process or system of processes (System 2) has limited resources, and its workings are laborious. This system operates reflectively in a controlled fashion, and it follows rules (Stanovich & West, 2000). Most dual-systems models are "default-interventionist," which means they assume that System 2 is engaged only when System 1 fails (Kahneman, 2003). "Parallel-competitive" models (for example, Epstein, 1994; Payne & Brown Iannuzzi, this volume, Chapter 3) offer an interesting alternative, as they do not assume that the two systems act in sequence (see also Kruglanski & Orehek, 2007).

The elaboration-likelihood model of persuasion (ELM) is an early example of a dual-systems model (Petty & Cacioppo, 1986). The ELM assumes that capable people who are properly motivated carefully consider attempts of persuasion by covertly arguing and counterarguing. Depending on the outcome of this internal review, they adopt an attitude consistent with the best available evidence. This reason-based attitude change is called the "central route," where *central* is another term for rational. All other forms of persuasion, that is, attitude change without prior argument elaboration, take the "peripheral route," which includes the application of various heuristics, such as yielding to persuasion attempts that include many arguments, repeated arguments, associations with charismatic communicators, or the presence of pleasant odors.[3]

The ELM foreshadowed some of the problems that plague dual-systems models today. One problem is the asymmetry between the two systems. Gilovich and Griffin (2010) note that "System 1 is almost certainly not as unitary as System 2" (p. 569). Most definitional efforts address the question of what System 2 is, so that System 1 ends up containing all psychological activity not included in System 2. System 1 is defined by exclusion—by what System 2 is not. This method of categorization renders System 1 unwieldy and incoherent, held together only by the faintest ties of family resemblance (Keren & Schul, 2009). Evans (2008) speculated that over evolutionary time many kinds of implicit-reasoning systems have been differentiated.

The asymmetry between the two systems vitiates any clear mapping of irrationality and rationality on System 1 and System 2, respectively. Many heuristics make rational sense (Fiedler & Wänke, 2009; Hertwig & Herzog, 2009). Within the context of the ELM, weighting a persuasive message by the communicator's expertise need not be the logical fallacy of "appeal to authority." Instead, it can be seen as good Bayesian practice to integrate a prior probability (that the expert is credible) with the weight of the evidence (the merits of the arguments). To ignore the communicator's expertise would be an instance of the much-bemoaned base-rate fallacy. Conversely, some effortful cogitation performed by System 2 is more rationalizing than rational. "System 2 is often used for the confabulation of explanations for these [System 1] behaviors" (Evans, 2008, p. 258). There is no guarantee that deliberate and rule-oriented cogitation applies the very rules endorsed by logicians or statisticians (Dawes, 1976).

The dominant view remains meliorist; it holds that biased judgments and erroneous decisions result from the quick and dirty operations of System 1. The task of System 2 is to come to the rescue by identifying instances where System 1 has gone astray and then correcting them. In Tversky and Kahneman's (1982, pp. 82, 89) words, System 2 acts like a benevolent editor, who retains "what is useful and valid in intuitive judgment while correcting the errors and biases to which it is prone."

Dawes (1988) assigned a more radical role to System 2. Expecting System 1 to not only miss the mark but to sometimes lead a person in the direction opposite to truth or survival, he argued that System 2 must actively and effortfully impose rationality against the resistance of System 1. Consider his analogy from the swimming pool. When children first go into the water they instinctively take an upright position to keep their heads in the air. Yet, a vertical orientation makes drowning more likely. To overcome this dangerous impulse, they have to learn to take a horizontal position and to keep their heads in the water while intermittently coming up for air.

The natatorial analogy is optimistic. It assumes that the simple inference system produces the wrong response and that the more complex system provides the correct response, which, with practice can be routinized. The analogy is not generally valid, however, because System 2 does not always provide the correct response. The conventional view is that errors and biases stem from limited psychological capacity, and that people fall back on simple heuristics that do not require extensive mental resources. Ironically, it is the resource-consuming System 2 that is characterized by limited capacity (e.g., attention span, short-term memory capacity), which raises the question of how a limited-capacity system can correct mistakes that result from limited capacity in the first place? Dawes (1976) noticed this problem in his prophetic essay on "shallow psychology." He wrote, "Conscious judgment—as opposed to automatic processing based on vast experience—is feeble. Yet it is precisely this sort of feeble conscious processing on which most people rely when attempting to solve most interpersonal and intrapersonal problems. This feebleness alone—without the help of motivational factors—may account for many of our disasters" (p. 11).

Let two examples illustrate the troubles of System 2.

Discounting. Hyperbolic discounting in intertemporal choice entails preference reversals (Ainslie, 1991). A person may prefer an immediate small reward (e.g., $100 today) over a larger future reward ($120 next week), yet also prefer the larger reward over the smaller one if both are delayed by the same interval (e.g., prefer receiving $120 in 53 weeks over receiving $100 in 52 weeks). This pattern is incoherent because the person both chooses and rejects the same reward depending on a condition (the delay) that does not discriminate between the options.

What is System 2 to do? One way to regain coherence is to always choose the smaller reward. In the delayed version of the example, however, it may seem silly to reject a 2% additional wait for a 20% increase in payout. Alternatively, one could always choose the larger reward. Yet, to ask a person to always override temptation seems more reflective of a moralistic norm of self-restraint than of a reasoned search for rational choice.[4] Yet, the equation of rational choice with resistance to temptation (Baumeister & Vohs, 2004) breaks down when the delay becomes very long. From an evolutionary perspective, some discounting is judicious because a reward (or the organism itself) might vanish while waiting (Haselton et al., 2009). Recognizing the visceral lure of immediate rewards (Loewenstein, 1996), Wang and Dvorak (2010) conclude that hyperbolic discounting can be "an adaptive mechanism linking human decision making to metabolic cues, indicating environmental scarcity on a micro level" (p. 186). It is an interesting hypothesis that such adaptations regarding food consumption generalized to how people think about money or other symbolic rewards (Briers, Pandelaere, Dewitte, & Warlop, 2006).

Resisting temptation is not always best. Aizer and Dal Bó (2010) suggested that a battered woman's desire to alert the authorities is strongest immediately after a beating incident. In locations where the law does not allow charges of abuse to be dropped, fewer women kill their abusers. If a battered woman's first impulse is the rational one, the task of System 2 is turned on its head. Now the system needs to protect the first response from dissipating instead of override it.

Framing. Another well-studied irrationality arises from the framing of prospects (Tversky & Kahneman, 1981). People tend to be risk averse when outcomes are described as gains, and risk seeking when they are described as losses. Whereas most people prefer a certain gain of $100 to the prospect of gaining $200 with a probability of .5, few people who have received an endowment of $200 give up $100 rather than risk a possible loss of $200. As a change in the reference point can reframe any gain as a loss, and vice versa, preference reversals violate the invariance criterion of rationality.

What is System 2 to do? A person encountering one frame has no incentive to simulate the problem in the other frame, and then to vow that the choice would be the same in the other frame *if anyone asked*. If both frames were presented (which they usually are not), the person might become aware of the inconsistency and remove it. Kahneman and Tversky (1984, p. 346) doubted, however, that the ordinary mind is "adequate to perform the task of recoding the two versions ... into a common abstract form." The real problem, however, is that the gambles selected for study typically involve prospects with very similar, if not identical, expected values (Levin, Schneider, & Gaeth, 1998). Indeed, if the expected values were drastically different, framing effects would disappear.

If there is no good reason to prefer the (un)certain outcome, indifference is the only reasonable attitude. Indifferent individuals may choose randomly, but it would be odd to see rational choice devolve into random choice. Ironically, no one would be accused of being irrational for choosing the (un)certain prospect half the time, as long as choice did not covary with frame. If there is covariation, it must be assessed over multiple problems and tested for statistical significance. For a person responding only to one problem in two frames, there is no way to tell if the framing effect arose from random responding or systematic bias.

Rules of Engagement

Adding to the troubles of the limited-capacity System 2 is the question of how it knows when to engage. If many heuristics yield adequate results much of the time, brute replacement of heuristic with systematic inference is inefficient. System 2 must be called upon selectively. The ELM addresses this problem by introducing motivation. The central, "less traveled," route is chosen when an important ego-involving issue is at stake. In a typical study, the merit of the arguments (strong versus weak) is orthogonal to the heuristic cue (e.g., the communicator's expertise). Therefore, systematic message elaboration improves overall performance.

In contexts outside of experiments, many of the cues favored by System 1 have such high validity that elaboration yields little or no incremental benefit (Gigerenzer & Brighton, 2009). The best use of System 2 would be to know when heuristics return a poor judgment and then to correct it. System 2 would have to have "both the inclination to monitor initial impressions and the ability to reason accurately" (Kahneman & Frederick, 2006, p. 46). Reflecting the default-interventionist perspective, Camerer, Loewenstein, and Prelec (2005) likened System 2 to a kind of mental fire department. "Controlled processes occur at special moments when automatic processes become interrupted, which happens when a person encounters unexpected events, experiences strong visceral states, or is presented with some kind of explicit challenge in the form of a novel decision or other type of problem" (p. 18), and they anticipated Kahneman and Frederick's position by suggesting that the two systems work like an "agency model in which a controller only steps in when an extreme state of the system (or unusual event) requires controlled processes to override automatic ones" (p. 56).[5]

Consider the implications of this view with an example from research on persuasion. Suppose an expert offers eight opinions, that, when compared with nature, fall into four categories: three true positives (expert yes, nature yes), three true negatives (expert no, nature no), one false positive (expert yes, nature no), and one false negative (expert no, nature yes). To always follow the expert yields reasonably high accuracy; $\Phi = .5$. If System 2 were activated to revisit each issue, the correlation between judgment and truth would become 1. This, however, is a costly strategy, which begs the question of why System 1 reliance on the expert should be run in the first place. It does not help to claim that System 2 already knows when and where the expert errs. If System 2 already knew where the errors lay, the question of why this system was brought in to help would be begged. In short, the decision of whether to activate System 2 cannot be made by System 2 itself (or by System 1).

A third possibility exists if the validity of expert judgment and the cost of additional thinking are known. Now System 2 can choose the optimal number of randomly selected issues to be audited. In the example, the probability p of the heuristic response to be correct is .75. If one issue is randomly selected for review, the probability of correcting an error is $1 - p = .25$. If a correction occurs, the overall probability of being correct increases to .875. More generally, the postcorrection probability of being correct is $p + (1 - p)k/n$, where k is the sample size, and n is the set size. Assuming that the cost of reviewing a sample is k/n, sampling becomes unattractive (irrational) when the ratio of cost to benefit exceeds 1. Psychophysical logic suggests that the perceived benefit of any additional numerically constant increment in the overall probability correct will diminish exponentially (i.e., $[(1 - p)k/n]^e$, where $e < 1$). Once decision makers know how much they care about improving the accuracy of their judgments, they can find the optimal number of items to be reviewed. If $e = .2$, for example, samples of 5 and 6 items are, respectively, worthwhile and too costly.

The solution is a general one for any heuristic cue that is known to be valid ($r > 0$) but imperfectly so ($r < 1$). In the absence of other information, perfect reliance on the one valid cue is the optimal strategy. When additional information must be bought, buying should stop when the cost exceeds the benefit.

The example makes the simple assumption that the cost of cognition depends only on a proportion of judgments reviewed. Another assumption is that System 2 is perfectly able to repair a judgment. The cost of repair for a single judgment can vary dramatically, however. Some tasks are so easy that they are only of interest in a developmental context. For example, it is intuitive that if 8 out of 10 events are hits, the probability of a hit is .8. Fewer people can predict joint outcomes. What is the probability that there will be at least two hits if there are three independent operators that each produces a hit with a probability of .8? A savvy person knows about the binomial expansion and how to use a spreadsheet. No one knows offhand what the probability of producing a hit should be for an individual operator so that the probability of having at least two hits is .8. No amount of glucose (Masicampo & Baumeister, 2008) can generate enough energy to overcome the lack of capacity. The savvy person suspends judgment and consults a mathematician.[6]

It makes no sense to blame irrational judgment on limited cognitive capacity. To demand unlimited capacity and to blame humans for not having it is frivolous. The only meaningful framework of the study of rationality is an ecological one that studies human performance at the intersection of cognitive capabilities and tasks with characteristics suited to these capabilities (Gigerenzer, 2008; Simon, 1990). No one asks a rat to do calculus. Asking humans for a derivative is unfair and a waste of scientific effort. Viewed in this light, efforts to abandon the dual-systems framework for a unified model seem promising (Kruglanski & Gigerenzer, 2011).

THE RETURN OF RATIONALITY

As the tide of irrationalism washed over social and cognitive psychology, the case for rationality was never dead. Critics questioned some of the assumptions and implications of the heuristics-and-biases paradigm (Cohen, 1981; Funder, 1987; Lopes, 1991), and proponents of rational models continued their work (Ajzen, 1985; Bandura, 1982; Funder, 1995). Over time there was a revival of interest in rationality. Only a small part of this revival can be attributed to efforts of the meliorist variety. The meliorist paradigm seeks to improve judgment and decision making through "debiasing." Strategy-based errors can be fought by raising "the cost of using a suboptimal judgment strategy" (Arkes, 1991, p. 492) or by increasing the benefits of attaining greater accuracy. Association-based errors, however, tend to resist incentive-based methods. Instead, they will motivate subjects to "perform the suboptimal behavior more enthusiastically" (Arkes, 1991, p. 493).[7]

Rationality has returned to the scene, in part, because of three developments, all of which suggest that the heuristic inference system performs rather well. First, some formerly accepted *criteria* of rational judgment have become questionable. Upon reformulation, former errors and biases have taken on a more rational mien. Second, some of the *contexts* in which judgments seemed irrational turned out to be rather abstract, arcane, or artificial. In more appropriate, accessible, or ecologically valid contexts, judgments make more sense. Third, study designs allowing investigators to see the long-term or across-domain effects of judgments reveal remarkably good *correspondence* with criteria.

Criteria

Consider three examples for changing the criteria of rationality. The fundamental attribution error (Ross, 1977), the false consensus effect (Ross, Greene, & House, 1977), and self-enhancement (the better-than-average effect; Alicke, 1985) were long considered the three signature biases of social judgment. All three shrink under scrutiny.

The charge that person attributions are fundamentally erroneous when situations affect behavior turned out to be erroneous itself. Person and situation effects can be conceptualized in a common framework without assuming that an increase in one effect entails a reduction in the other (Krueger, 2009b). Moreover, the notion of the fundamental attribution error involves a self-referential paradox because it is itself a person attribution (Krueger & Funder, 2004). The actor–observer effect, an offshoot of the fundamental attribution error, expired unceremoniously in a meta-analysis (Malle, 2006; see also Gawronski, 2004).

The false consensus effect is not all that false. People who have no information about others may expect them to be similar to themselves. By using their own preferences, traits, or behaviors as sample observations, they can form rational Bayesian beliefs about the likely characteristics of others. The predictions made with this projection strategy are more accurate than predictions made by guessing (Dawes, 1989). When people are interdependent, projection can improve outcomes. In the

prisoner's dilemma, and other games in which positive coordination is socially efficient, the expected value of cooperation increases inasmuch as participants expect
others to make their choices the way they themselves do (Krueger, 2007).

Even self-enhancement is not necessarily a cognitive illusion. The principal difficulty with this effect is that there are too many ways of measuring it. They all seek
to solve the problem of separating a self-image that is too positive from one that
is just positive. These measures tend to correlate positively with one another, but
they reflect different theoretical premises, none of which has been able to claim
supremacy (Krueger & Wright, 2011). Current research seeks to gain a deeper
understanding of the role of regression effects (Moore & Small, 2007, 2008; see
also Fiedler & Krueger, this volume, Chapter 10), information sampling (Denrell &
Le Mens, this volume, Chapter 9), and the relation between self-enhancement and
overconfidence (Larrick, Burson, & Soll, 2007; Moore & Healy, 2008).

Context

Now consider two examples of the role of context. Wason (1960) famously showed
that people fail to use *modus tollens* when testing the truth of a conditional proposition. Presented with cards that had a letter (A or B) on one side and an even or
odd number on the other side, they were asked to test the rule "If there is an A
on one side there is an even number on the other." Few participants turned over a
card showing an odd number. The Wason task assumes that abstract reasoning is
the proper domain of rationality. Hence, the violation of an abstract rule of deductive logic is probative for the lack of rationality.

An alternative view is that most everyday reasoning problems are embedded
in socially meaningful contexts. With this view, performance on abstract tasks says
little about how well people generally do. Cosmides (1989) rewrote the Wason task
to represent a social rule (e.g., "If a person is under 21 years of age, he or she does
not drink alcohol"). Here, a test of the rule becomes a challenge to detect a breach
of a social or legal rule. Consequently, many participants know the value of investigating the age of individuals who are known to drink.

Oaksford and Chater (1994) recast the Wason task in the context of inductive
reasoning, showing that when evaluating the proposition "if p, then q," it makes
good sense to examine the associates of p, q, $-q$, and $-p$ in that order. Indeed, when
both p and q are rare occurrences (e.g., eating tripe and getting sick), asking if a
sick person (q) had eaten tripe (p) yields more useful information than asking if a
well person ($-q$) has eaten tripe (see also Klayman & Ha, 1987).

The other example regarding the role of context is learning how to exploit a
probabilistic environment. Having observed, for example, that foraging for food in
the left patch turns up edibles with a probability of .7, whereas foraging in the right
patch is rewarded with a probability of .3, the rational strategy is to consistently
forage on the left. Yet, humans and some other animals tend to select each option
with the probability with which it has been rewarded (Tversky & Edwards, 1966).
Such probability matching means that people fail to maximize their payoffs.

Hastie and Dawes (2010) suggest that a desire to control the uncontrollable
lies at the root of probability matching. People "cannot bring themselves to believe

that the situation is one in which they *cannot* predict" (p. 323). In contrast, Shanks, Tunney, and McCarthy (2002) showed that in an optimal learning context, most individuals learn to maximize. These authors offered large financial incentives, concrete performance feedback, and long periods of training. Whether such contexts are ecologically valid, is arguable; but the research demonstrates that probability matching is not an impenetrable cognitive illusion.

There is, however, a more radical explanation for why organisms tend to match probabilities. Tversky and Edwards (1966) observed that participants distributed their responses even more broadly when they were told to expect changes in the relative reward probabilities. Because the reward probabilities were stationary in the experiment, performance suffered. Had there been changes (as promised), however, participants would have been more likely to detect them. If nonlaboratory environments are not perfectly stable, organisms do well if they balance the exploitation of currently productive patches with the exploration of emerging alternatives (Steyvers, Lee, & Wagenmakers, 2009).

An organism that tries to balance exploration with exploitation faces an immensely difficult task; the derivation of an optimal rule must be nontrivial, to say the least, especially if the rate of possible environmental change is unknown. In a situation that is computationally intractable, heuristics do best, and probability matching is relatively simple and robust (and because of that perhaps innate; Gallistel et al., 2007).[8]

Correspondence

The idea that "in general, these heuristics are quite useful, but sometimes they lead to severe and systematic errors" (Tversky & Kahneman, 1974, p. 1124) has had a strong if imbalanced impact on research on judgment and decision making. Many investigators took the first clause of this claim to be self-evident. Concentrating their efforts on shedding light on the second clause, they could construe their research as challenging detective work. If heuristics generally work well, snooping out "severe and systematic errors" seems like risky research. When the null hypothesis of rationality has a high prior probability of being true, its rejection yields the greatest advance in knowledge. The theoretical advances derived from error detection have not, however, lived up to their promise; they have done little to explain why heuristics generally work.

A different school of researchers has taken on the task of systematically studying the correspondence between heuristic judgments and external criteria; that is, of exploring the first clause of the Tversky–Kahneman claim (Hastie & Rasinski, 1987). A good 20 years of work in this research program has shown that many heuristics perform well and often better than more complex and resource-consuming inference strategies (Hertwig & Herzog, 2009; see also Jussim, Stevens, & Salib, this volume, Chapter 6).

To illustrate how the correspondence issue was initially misconstrued, consider the idea that judgment by heuristic amounts to an overweighting bias (Kahneman, 2003; Morewedge & Kahneman, 2010). The way a heuristic works can be represented in the lens model (Brunswik, 1952). In the case of the "recognition heuristic"

(Goldstein & Gigerenzer, 2002), for example, items (e.g., cities) vary on some criterion (e.g., size) and some dimension (e.g., presence in the media). The association between the distal criterion and the proximal cue is the "ecological correlation." When the criterion is not directly observable, judges may infer it from the cue. The association between their judgments and the cue values is the "surrogate correlation."

The measure of success is the "accuracy correlation," that is, the correlation between judgments and criterion values. The heuristic works if both the ecological and the surrogate correlation are positive, but the judges can only affect the latter. If they assume the cues are valid and if no other information is at hand, their best strategy is to act as if the cues were perfectly valid. Then the accuracy correlation will be equal to the ecological correlation. As cue utilization (i.e., the surrogate correlation) becomes weaker, the accuracy correlation will attenuate because the expected value of the accuracy correlation is the product of the ecological and the surrogate correlation. In other words, a pure case of heuristic judgment, which involves a single cue of some validity, most likely entails an underweighting bias instead of an overweighting bias. Accuracy (correspondence) would increase if people reasoned heuristically in a more principled way. When there are multiple valid cues, summed unit weights outperform optimal regression weights in cross-validation (Dana, 2008; Dawes, 1979).[9]

CONSCIOUSNESS AND FREE WILL

The tendency (or temptation) to see rationality bound up with consciousness and free will is strong. Baumeister (2008, p. 71) cited John Searle (2001) for the claim that "theories of rationality almost inevitably presuppose some degree of free will." The views expressed by Hastie and Dawes (2010) and Zajonc (1999) are no exceptions. The frequent mapping of rational thinking onto System 2 thinking, which was critically reviewed earlier, may be responsible here. System 2 thinking is assumed to be controlled, and controlled thinking is assumed to be conscious and free. This line of reasoning—perhaps ironically—appears to be rather associative and illogical.

Perhaps it is best to resist the temptation to view issues of rationality through the prism of consciousness and free will. It is hard enough to define and measure rationality in terms of coherence or correspondence. Both criteria operate on judgments and decisions and how they relate to one another (coherence) or how they relate to external benchmarks (correspondence). They do *not* involve a person's subjective experience while making these judgments or decisions. Once this is understood, we can evaluate the rationality of nonhuman animals in contexts appropriate to their species without being embarrassed. An added benefit of this strategy is that one need not worry that the eventual victory of the determinists over the free willers will spell the demise of rationality.

AUTHOR NOTE

This chapter is an expansion and elaboration of a brief article titled "Rationality Restored" (Krueger, 2009c). I thank Hannah Ertl, Andra Geana, and Mika MacInnis for discussion and comments. Correspondence should be addressed to: Joachim I. Krueger, Department of Cognitive, Linguistic, and Psychological Sciences, Brown University, Box 1853, Providence, RI 02912. Electronic mail may be sent to: Joachim_Krueger@Brown.edu.

NOTES

1. Fishbein and Ajzen are noted in the text but not included in the list of theorists.
2. For arguments of how errors reveal more fundamental adaptations, see Arkes (1991) or Kenrick et al. (2009).
3. Note that these labels could be reversed. So-called central-route processes may actually be peripheral because they are mediated by elaborative reasoning, and thus indirect; so-called peripheral processes may actually be central because they are unmediated and thus direct.
4. In defense of humans, it may be said that nonhuman animals have much steeper discounting functions (Stevens & Hauser, 2004).
5. The agency model entails that when an error occurs, both systems have failed. "Biased judgment […] represents a joint failure of System 1 and System 2: System 1 generates a biased impression and System 2 fails to correct it" (Morewedge & Kahneman, 2010, p. 437).
6. Hence, I respectfully disagree with my teacher Theo Harder (quoted in the introduction). We can be logical and use formulas. Indeed, we can be logical *because* we use formulas (Dawes, 1979).
7. Arkes's (1991) analysis is profound and subtle. Strategy-based errors can be avoided by using more cues, considering other evidence, or by making counterfactual comparisons. Avoiding association-based errors requires the suppression of automatically activated ideas, which is difficult by definition. Arkes was guardedly optimistic that a third type of error, which is psychophysically based, can also be reduced by bringing overlooked costs to mind. Framing effects fall into this category.
8. The implications of this analysis for mate search and choice remain to be studied. In this context, "exploration" (or "foraging" for mates) may generate different additional costs and benefits for the two sexes.
9. The accuracy-enhancing logic of social projection can also be cast in a lens model (Hoch, 1987), but the probability-matching heuristic cannot.

REFERENCES

Ainslie, G. (1991). Derivation of "rational" economic behavior from hyperbolic discount curves. *The American Economic Review, 81*, 334–340.

Aizer, A., & Dal Bó, P. (2010). Love, hate, and murder: Commitment devices in violent relationships. *Journal of Public Economics, 93*, 412–428.

Ajzen, I. (1985). From intentions to actions: A theory of planned behavior. In J. Kuhl & J. Beckman (eds.), *Action-control: From cognition to behavior* (pp. 11–39). Heidelberg, Germany: Springer.

Alicke, M. D. (1985). Global self-evaluation as determined by the desirability and controllability of trait adjectives. *Journal of Personality and Social Psychology, 49*, 1621–1630.

Arkes, H. R. (1991). Costs and benefits of judgment errors: Implications for debiasing. *Psychological Bulletin, 110*, 486–498.

Bandura, A. (1982). Self-efficacy mechanism in human agency. *American Psychologist, 37*, 122–147.

Barbey, A. K., & Sloman, S. A. (2007). Base-rate respect: From ecological rationality to dual processes. *Behavioral and Brain Sciences, 30*, 241–297.

Baumeister, R. F. (2008). Free will, consciousness, and cultural animals. In J. Baer, J. C. Kaufman, & R. F. Baumeister (Eds.), *Are we free? Psychology and free will* (pp. 65–85). New York: Oxford University Press.

Baumeister, R. F., & Vohs, K. D. (2004). *Self-regulation: Research, theory, and applications.* New York: Guilford.

Briers, B., Pandelaere, M., Dewitte, S., & Warlop, L. (2006). Hungry for money: The desire for caloric resources increases the desire for financial resources and vice versa. *Psychological Science, 17*, 939–943.

Brunswik, E. (1952). *The conceptual framework of psychology.* Chicago: Chicago University Press.

Camerer, C., Loewenstein, G., & Prelec, D. (2005). Neuroeconomics: How neuroscience can inform economics. *Journal of Economic Literature, 43*, 9–64.

Chaiken, S., & Trope, Y. (1999). *Dual-process theories in social psychology.* New York: Guilford.

Cohen, L. J. (1981). Can human irrationality be experimentally demonstrated? *Behavioral and Brain Sciences, 4*, 317–331.

Cosmides, L. (1989). The logic of social exchange: Has natural selection shaped how humans reason? Studies with the Wason selection task. *Cognition, 31*, 187–276.

Dana, J. (2008). What makes improper linear models tick? In J. I. Krueger (Ed.), *Rationality and social responsibility: Essays in honor of Robyn Mason Dawes* (pp. 71–89). New York: Psychology Press.

Dawes, R. M. (1976). Shallow psychology. In J. S. Carroll, & J. E. Payne (Eds.), *Cognition and social behavior* (pp. 3–11). Hillsdale, NJ: Erlbaum.

Dawes, R. M. (1979). The robust beauty of improper linear models in decision making. *American Psychologist, 81*, 571–582.

Dawes, R. M. (1988). *Rational choice in an uncertain world.* San Diego, CA: Harcourt Brace Jovanovich.

Dawes, R. M. (1989). Statistical criteria for establishing a truly false consensus effect. *Journal of Experimental Social Psychology, 25*, 1–17.

Epstein, S. (1994). Integrating the cognitive and the psychodynamic unconscious. *American Psychologist, 49*, 709–724.

Evans, J. St. B. T. (2008). Dual-processing accounts of reasoning, judgment, and social cognition. *Annual Review of Psychology, 59*, 255–278.

Fiedler, K., & Wänke, M. (2009). The cognitive-ecological approach to rationality in social psychology. *Social Cognition, 27*, 699–732.

Fishbein, M., & Ajzen, I. (1975). *Belief, attitude, intention, and behavior: An introduction to theory and research.* Reading, MA: Addison-Wesley.

Funder, D. C. (1987). Errors and mistakes: Evaluating the accuracy of social judgment. *Psychological Bulletin, 101*, 75–90.

Funder, D. C. (1995). On the accuracy of personality judgment: A realistic approach. *Psychological Review, 102*, 652–670.

Gallistel, C. R., (2009). The importance of proving the null. *Psychological Review, 116*, 439–453.

Gallistel, C. R., King, A. P., Gottlieb, D., Balci, F., Papachristos, E. B., Szalecki, M., & Carbone, K. S. (2007). Is matching innate? *Journal of the Experimental Analysis of Behavior, 87*, 161–199.

Gawronski, B. (2004). Theory-based bias correction in dispositional inference: The fundamental attribution error is dead, long live the correspondence bias. *European Review of Social Psychology, 15*, 183–217.

Gigerenzer, G. (2008). *Rationality for mortals.* New York, NY: Oxford University Press.

Gigerenzer, G., & Brighton, H. (2009). Homo heuristicus: Why biased minds make better inferences. *Topics in Cognitive Science, 1*, 107–143.

Gilovich, T., & Griffin, D. T. (2010). Judgment and decision making. In S. T. Fiske, D. T. Gilbert, & G. Lindzey (Eds.), *Handbook of social psychology* (5th ed., Vol. 1, pp. 542–588). Hoboken, NJ: Wiley.

Goldstein, D. G., & Gigerenzer, G. (2002). Models of ecological rationality: The recognition heuristic. *Psychological Review, 101*, 75–90.

Haselton, M. G., Bryant, G. A., Wilke, A., Frederick, D. A., Galperin, A., Frankenhuis, W. E., & Moore, T. (2009). Adaptive rationality: An evolutionary perspective on cognitive bias. *Social Cognition, 27*, 733–763.

Hastie, R., & Dawes, R. M. (2010). *Rational choice in an uncertain world: The psychology of judgment and decision making* (2nd ed.). Thousand Oaks, CA: Sage.

Hastie, R., & Rasinski, K. (1987). The concept of accuracy in social judgment. In D. Bar-Tal & A. Kruglanski (Eds.), *The social psychology of knowledge* (pp. 193–208). Cambridge, UK: Cambridge University Press.

Hertwig, R., & Herzog, S. M. (2009). Fast and frugal heuristics: Tools of social rationality. *Social Cognition, 27*, 661–698.

Hoch, S. J. (1987). Perceived consensus and predictive accuracy: The pros and cons of projection. *Journal of Personality and Social Psychology, 53*, 221–234.

Jones, E. E., & Harris, V. A. (1967). The attribution of attitudes. *Journal of Experimental Social Psychology, 3*, 1–24.

Kahneman, D. (2003). A perspective on judgment and choice: mapping bounded rationality. *American Psychologist, 58*, 697–720.

Kahneman, D., & Frederick, S. (2006). Frames and brains: Elicitation and control of response tendencies. *Trends in Cognitive Sciences, 11*, 45–46.

Kahneman, D., & Tversky, A. (1979). Intuitive prediction: Biases and protective procedures. *TIMS Studies in Management Sciences, 12*, 313–327.

Kahneman, D., & Tversky, A. (1984). Choices, values, and frames. *American Psychologist, 39*, 341–350.

Kelley, H. H. (1967). Attribution theory in social psychology. In D. Levine (Ed.), *Nebraska symposium on motivation* (Vol. 15, pp. 192–240). Lincoln, NE: University of Nebraska Press.

Kenrick, D. T., Griskevicius, V., Sundie, J. M., Li, N. P., Li, Y. J., & Neuberg, S. L. (2009). Deep rationality: The evolutionary economics of decision making. *Social Cognition, 27*, 764–785.

Keren, G., & Schul, Y. (2009). Two is not always better than one: A critical evaluation of two-system theories. *Perspectives on Psychological Science, 4*, 533–550.

Klayman, J., & Ha, Y. (1987). Confirmation, disconfirmation, and information in hypothesis testing. *Psychological Review, 94*, 211–228.

Krueger, J. (2001). Null hypothesis significance testing: On the survival of a flawed method. *American Psychologist, 56*, 16–26. doi:10.1037/0003-066X.56.1.16.

Krueger, J. I. (2007). From social projection to social behaviour. *European Review of Social Psychology, 18*, 1–35.

Krueger, J. I. (2009a). Rationality restored: Introduction to the special issue on rationality in social psychology. *Social Cognition, 27*, 635–638.

Krueger, J. I. (2009b). A componential model of situation effects, person effects and situation-by-person interaction effects on social behavior. *Journal of Research in Personality, 43*, 127–136.

Krueger, J. I. (2009c). Rationality restored: Introduction to the special issue on rationality in social psychology. *Social Cognition, 27*, 635–638.

Krueger, J. I., & Funder, D. C. (2004). Toward a balanced social psychology: Causes, consequences and cures for the problem-seeking approach to social behavior and cognition. *Behavioral and Brain Sciences, 27*, 313–376.

Krueger, J. I., & Massey, A. L. (2009). A rational reconstruction of misbehavior. *Social Cognition, 27*, 785–810.

Krueger, J. I., & Wright, J. C. (2011). Measurement of self-enhancement (and self-protection). In M. D. Alicke & C. Sedikides (Eds.), *Handbook of self-enhancement and self-protection* (pp. 472–494). New York: Guilford.

Kruglanski, A. W., & Gigerenzer, G. (2011). Intuitive and deliberative judgments are based on common principles. *Psychological Review, 118,* 97–109.

Kruglanski, A. W., & Orehek, E. (2007). Partitioning the domain of social inference: Dual mode and systems models and their alternatives. *Annual Review of Psychology, 58,* 291–316.

Kuhn, T. S. (1962). *The structure of scientific revolutions.* Chicago: University of Chicago Press.

Larrick, R. P., Burson, K. A., & Soll, J. B. (2007). Social comparison and confidence: When thinking you're better than average predicts overconfidence (and when it does not). *Organizational Behavior & Human Decision Processes, 102,* 76–94.

Levin, I. P., Schneider, S. L., & Gaeth, G. J. (1998). All frames are not created equal: A topology and critical analysis of framing effect. *Organizational Behavior and Human Decision Processes, 76,* 149–188.

List of cognitive biases. (n.d.) In *Wikipedia.* Retrieved February, 13, 2011, from http://en.wikipedia.org/wiki/List_of_cognitive_biases.

Loewenstein, G. F. (1996). Out of control: Visceral influences on behavior. *Organizational Behavior and Human Decision Processes, 65,* 272–292.

Lopes, L. A. (1991). The rhetoric of irrationality. *Theory and Psychology, 1,* 65–82.

Makridakis, S., Hogarth, R., & Gaba, A. (2009). *Dance with chance: Making luck work for you.* Oxford, UK: Oneworld.

Malle, B. F. (2006). The actor-observer asymmetry in attribution: A (surprising) meta-analysis. *Psychological Bulletin, 132,* 895–919.

Masicampo, E. J., & Baumeister, R. F. (2008). Toward a physiology of dual-process reasoning and judgment. *Psychological Science, 19,* 255–260.

Moore, D. A., & Healy, P J. (2008). The trouble with overconfidence. *Psychological Review, 115,* 102–117.

Moore, D. A., & Small, D. A. (2007). Error and bias in comparative judgment: On being both better and worse than we think we are. *Journal of Personality and Social Psychology, 92,* 972–989.

Moore, D. A., & Small, D. A. (2008). When it is rational for the majority to believe that they are better than average. In J. I. Krueger (Ed.), *Rationality and social responsibility: Essays in honor of Robyn M. Dawes* (pp. 141–174). New York: Psychology Press.

Morewedge, C. K., & Kahneman, D. (2010). Associative processes in intuitive judgment. *Trends in Cognitive Sciences, 14,* 435–440.

Nisbett, R., & Ross, L. (1980). *Human inference: Strategies and shortcomings of social judgment.* Englewood Cliffs, NJ: Prentice-Hall.

Oaksford, M., & Chater, N. (1994). A rational analysis of the card selection task as optimal data selection. *Psychological Review, 101,* 608–631.

Peterson, C. R., & Beach, L. R. (1967). Man as an intuitive statistician. *Psychological Bulletin, 68,* 29–46.

Petty, R. E., & Cacioppo, J. T. (1986). The elaboration likelihood model of persuasion. In L. Berkowitz (Ed.), *Advances in experimental social psychology* (Vol. 19, pp. 123–205). New York: Academic Press.

Ross, L. (1977). The intuitive psychologist and his shortcomings: Distortions in the attribution process. In L. Berkowitz (Ed.), *Advances in experimental social psychology* (Vol. 10, pp. 174–221). New York: Academic Press.

Ross, L., Greene, D., & House, P. (1977). The false consensus effect: An egocentric bias in social perception and attribution processes. *Journal of Experimental Social Psychology, 13*, 279–301.

Searle, J. R. (2001). *Rationality in action*. Cambridge, MA: MIT Press.

Shanks, D. R., Tunney, R. J., & McCarthy, J. D. (2002). A re-examination of probability matching and rational choice. *Journal of Behavioral Decision Making, 15*, 233–250.

Simon, H. A. (1990). Invariants of human behavior. *Annual Review of Psychology, 41*, 1–19.

Stanovich, K. E., & West, R. F. (2000). Individual differences in reasoning: Implications for the rationality debate? *Behavioral and Brain Sciences, 23*, 645–726.

Stevens, J. R., & Hauser, M. D. (2004). Why be nice? Psychological constraints on the evolution of cooperation. *Trends in Cognitive Sciences, 8*, 60–65.

Steyvers, M., Lee, M. D., & Wagenmakers, E. J. (2009). A Bayesian analysis of human decision-making on bandit problems. *Journal of Mathematical Psychology, 53*, 168–179.

Todd, P. M., Gigerenzer, G., & the ABC Research Group (Eds.). (in press). *Ecological rationality: Intelligence in the world*. New York: Oxford University Press.

Tversky, A., & Edwards, W. (1966). Information versus reward in binary choice. *Journal of Experimental Psychology, 71*, 680–683.

Tversky, A., & Kahneman, D. (1974). Judgments under uncertainty: Heuristics and biases. *Science, 185*, 1124–1131.

Tversky, A., & Kahneman, D. (1981). The framing of decisions and the psychology of choice. *Science, 211*, 453–458.

Tversky, A., & Kahneman, D. (1982). Judgments of and by representativeness. In D. Kahneman, P. Slovic, & A. Tversky (Eds.), *Judgments under uncertainty: Heuristics and biases* (pp. 84–98). Cambridge, UK: Cambridge University Press.

Wang, X. T., & Dvorak, R. D. (2010). Sweet future: Fluctuating blood glucose levels affect future discounting. *Psychological Science*. Online publication. doi: 10.1177/095679760935809.

Wason, P. C. (1960). On the failure to eliminate hypotheses in a conceptual task. *Quarterly Journal of Experimental Psychology, 12*, 129–140.

Zajonc, R. B. (1999). One hundred years of rationality assumptions in social psychology. In A. Rodrigues & R. V. Levine (Eds.), *Reflections on 100 years of experimental social psychology* (pp. 200–214). New York: Basic Books.

Section *II*

Measurement Issues

5

Irrational Numbers
Quantifying Accuracy and Error

HART BLANTON and JAMES JACCARD

I will send you the chapter in two weeks.

Hart Blanton in an e-mail to Joachim Krueger, 8 weeks too soon

INTRODUCTION

*E*xperimental psychologists thrive on deficiencies. Consider just a handful of shortcomings that interest them: judgmental overconfidence, the better-than-average effect, correspondence bias, the fundamental attribution error, confirmation bias, the planning fallacy, gambler's fallacy, hindsight bias, egocentric bias, the sunk-costs fallacy, the illusion of control, omission bias, neglect bias, and on and on (see Jussim, Stevens, & Salib, this volume, Chapter 6; Krueger, this volume, Chapter 4). These phenomena differ from one another in substantive regards, but they share an important quality. Each points to ways in which social judgments can be systematically distorted away from a criterion of "accuracy" or "rationality" that is held up as an ideal in a theoretical model of human cognition. Such comparisons between actual judgments and idealized judgments pervade the psychological literature. At times, the idealized model has been explicated as the response that should be observed when people adhere to rational thought processes (for example, Jones & Davis, 1965; Kelley, 1967). Other times, it is adapted from statistical or mathematical models (for example, Tversky & Kahneman, 1971). Still other times, the ideal is so obviously the "correct" response that researchers merely appeal to the counterintuitive nature of a response (Prentice & Miller, 1992).

Most research examining the limitations and errors in human judgment has been carried out in the psychological laboratory, where are revealed when participants respond to experimental stimuli in a manner inconsistent with the idealized, rational model. Consider "gambler's fallacy" as an example. Through application of Bayes's theorem, psychologists know that the results of separate tosses of a fair coin will be statistically independent of one another, such that each toss will yield a 50% likelihood of generating heads as opposed to tails. Experimental psychologists have shown, however, that by manipulating information about the results of prior coin tosses that research participants act as if independent coin tosses are causally linked (Gold & Hester, 2008; Tversky & Kahneman, 1971). A string of heads is thought to increase the probability of tails and a string of tails is thought to increase the probability of heads. It is because this response pattern departs from a known statistical model that the "gambler's fallacy" is not labeled "gambler's preference" or "gambler's tendency." It is a *fallacy*.

Measuring Accuracy, Quantifying Error

It often seems to students of psychology that it would be a straightforward task to apply the same logic of accuracy criteria when measuring the accuracy of human judgments. Such a pursuit might take a variety of forms: labeling specific judgments as "correct" or "incorrect," quantifying the prevalence of errors in a group of respondents, or estimating the average magnitude of the errors expected in a given group. After all, there are models that convey right and wrong answers in the "real world"—just as there are rational criteria to apply in the laboratory. Consider for purposes of illustration a college student who makes a prediction about her grade on a final exam. If she believes she will get a score of 100 out of 100 and she only gets a 65, then she has made an error. If a researcher collected similar data from a sample of students taking this same course, it seems easy enough to measure the magnitude and prevalence of errors in the classroom by comparing group predictions to group reality.

Despite the intuitive appeal of such inferences, the quantification of errors has proven to be an unusually difficult task. For one thing, many of the perceptions psychologists study cannot be easily linked to "rational" models. This is illustrated in the documented tendency for many adults to view positive traits as more self-descriptive than negative traits (Alicke, 1985). This tendency might reveal the presence of an "error" or "illusion," one that leads individuals to see themselves in overly positive terms (Taylor & Brown, 1988). However, who is to say that any given response pattern is inaccurate, and how would one ever quantify the number of positive traits a person *should* endorse? Thus, although it is easy enough to generate examples in which a precise judgment can be compared to an obvious reality, many consequential social judgments occupy a conceptual space that cannot be so easily quantified.

Even with a seemingly straightforward judgment—like the test-prediction example—an unusually complex array of issues must be considered to quantify error. Consider a study that had college students estimate the time it would take them to finish their senior theses (Buehler, Griffin, & Ross, 1994). The average estimate was 33.9 days but the actual completion time was 55.5 days. This clear demonstration of the "planning fallacy" calls to mind instances we all have experienced, ones in which we expect one outcome and experience another. Certainly, it is reasonable to state that there is a mean tendency toward "error." However, it is precisely the methodological convention used in this study that we wish to scrutinize and often challenge with this chapter. Our thesis is that even when the criterion for evaluating a judgment seems clear, the strategy of comparing a measured perception to a rational criterion can be misleading.

An Informal Take on Formal Models

The perspective we adopt draws heavily on classic methodological work documenting the measurement hurdles standing in the way of researchers who wish to measure the accuracy of perceptions (Anderson, 1981; Cronbach, 1955; Hastorf & Bender, 1952). The effect of these works was that they all but shut down early interest in measuring the accuracy of human judgments, and this was perhaps one of the reasons researchers moved into the research laboratory, where experimental control permitted stronger statements about error. Unfortunately, these seminal critiques are rarely examined in graduate methods classes, and each draws on formal mathematical models that are hard for many students and scholars to digest. We think that as a result there has been a drift in some areas of the judgment literature that place trust in simple criterion comparisons, violating the spirit of these seminal works. Our goal is to present some of the concerns in these papers through informal examples and often hypothetical data sets. We begin by discussing four psychometric criteria that have relevance to the accuracy question, giving particular attention to the measurement of overconfidence.

PSYCHOMETRIC HURDLES: QUANTIFYING OVERCONFIDENCE

By most any reasonable definition, individuals who think that they know things that they do not are overconfident. This logic has driven many of the analyses of overconfidence. For instance, one common technique for measuring this type of error has individuals answer knowledge questions and then estimate the probability that they have answered each question correctly. If respondents' mean confidence scores are higher than their mean accuracy scores, this is treated as evidence of overconfidence (Fischhoff, Slovic, & Lichtenstein, 1977). The difficulty of such an approach can be revealed by first considering an obviously inadequate measurement strategy.

A Limited Measure

Psychologists quite often rely on measures that assess perceptions using numeric response formats, made meaningful with semantic anchors. Suppose that a researcher followed this strategy and administered the following question to a student, prior to a final:

How well do you think you will perform on the final?

Not at all 0 1 2 3 4 5 6 7 8 9 10 *Extremely Well*

The student circles the number 8 and later receives a grade of 74 out of 100 on the final exam. Can we say that this student committed an error with respect to her judged ability to do well on the exam? Certainly not.

A variety of issues prevent psychologists from inferring that this student's knowledge perception was in any way faulty. First, it is not at all clear what level of perceived knowledge is conveyed by an 8. It seems possible that the student perceived her knowledge to be high, because she circled a number that was at the upper end of the response metric. Perhaps, however, this rating conveyed a perceived ability to do satisfactory work and if so, the student's perception seems accurate—as she exhibited satisfactory performance on the final exam. Alternatively, the student may have given only cursory thought to how her knowledge might translate into a test performance when she circled an 8, and if so, comparisons between her rating and exam grade are of dubious value.

This example illustrates how documentation of a seemingly straightforward bias can elude researchers who employ measures that are not up to the task. We now introduce refinements to this measure to improve accuracy estimation and in the process review four measurement dimensions that speak to the utility of psychometric measures in psychological research.

Valid Versus Invalid Measures

The student in our example was asked to rate her knowledge using a metric that ranged from 0 to 10. This numbering system can be useful for researchers interested in examining the causes and consequences of perceived knowledge. Such researchers are not concerned with quantifying accuracy or error. Instead, they are interested in testing psychological theories that speak to the underlying processes that might influence judgment outcomes. These processes might promote more accurate judgments in some contexts and less accurate judgments in others, but no attempt is made to assess the overall accuracy of any given judgment, in any given context. In research enterprises such as this, investigators do not need measures that can gauge accuracy. They simply need measures that are valid.

In the way we use it here, validity refers to the extent to which variation in an observed measure is related to variation in the construct that the measure is intended to reflect. Our 0 to 10 measure of perceived knowledge is valid by this definition to the extent that the respondents who feel less knowledgeable circle lower numbers than those who feel more knowledgeable. Researchers need not know the absolute level of perceived knowledge that is reflected by an 8, as compared to a 7 or 9, for it to be valid. They only need to know that respondents who circle 8 are, on average, higher in confidence than those who circle 7 and lower than those who circle 9, and that the variation in the observed measure is linked to variation in the underlying dimension being measured.

To illustrate, suppose that a researcher measured perceived knowledge on a valid 0-to-10 metric in order to test the theory that perceived knowledge is causally influenced by actual knowledge. Table 5.1 presents two data sets that might be generated in a class of five students, and the theoretical conclusions they would support. Notice that the first data set shows that perceived knowledge has a perfect correlation with exam performance ($r = 1.00$), whereas in the second data set,

TABLE 5.1   Knowledge Estimation

	Data Set 1			Data Set 2	
Student	Perceived Knowledge	Exam Grade	Student	Perceived Knowledge	Exam Grade
1	5	64	1	5	64
2	6	69	2	6	69
3	7	74	3	7	74
4	8	79	4	8	79
5	9	84	5	9	84
Mean	7	74	Mean	7	74
	$r = 1.00$			$r = -0.10$	

the correlation is near zero ($r = -.10$). The first data set suggests that perceived knowledge is driven entirely by actual knowledge (at least as measured by exam performance). In contrast, the second data set suggests that perceived and actual knowledge are independent of one another. Thus, although the researcher cannot determine whether the student who circled an 8 in either data set was overconfident or if either sample was showing signs of systematic error or bias, statements can be made about the theoretical link between perception and reality. For instance, a number of studies investigating the links between perceived and actual knowledge suggest that the dynamic represented by Data Set 2 often occurs. In many content domains, measures of perceived knowledge appear to be valid estimates of what people think they know, even though what people think they know seems to be independent of what they actually know (for example, Lichtenstein & Fischhoff, 1977). Such findings suggest that people often base their confidence estimates on information they should not, but in no way does it quantify the prevalence or magnitude of error.

Meaningful Versus Arbitrary Metrics   At times, investigators seek knowledge of a metric's meaning. Typically, this occurs in applied settings, where practitioners want to make accurate inferences about the absolute standing of an individual or group of individuals on the psychological dimension of interest. For instance, clinicians working with depressed populations want to know which of their clients are at a high as opposed to low risk of suicide. It is not enough for them to know that the depression inventory given to a set of clients shows a correlation with suicide risk (suggestive of validity). They also want to know which scores reveal an unacceptable risk of suicide and which scores suggest little reason for concern.

The example of clinical assessment points to the need for psychological inventories that have meaningful, as opposed to arbitrary, metrics. It is important to keep in mind that a measure can be valid yet still have an arbitrary metric. For example, weight as measured in kilograms is a valid measure of weight, but most people in the United States have no idea how much a person weighs when told the individual weighs 60 kilos. For people in the United States, the metric system of weights represents an arbitrary (but valid) metric. Blanton & Jaccard (2006a) define metrics as arbitrary "when it is not known where a given score locates an individual on the underlying psychological dimension or how a one-unit change on the observed score reflects the magnitude of change on the underlying dimension" (p. 28). The perceived knowledge scale we examined earlier had an arbitrary metric by this definition, even though it can be useful (valid) tool for testing a causal theory about the relationship between perceived and actual knowledge.

To move beyond mere validity, a researcher must empirically link scores on the metric to other perceptions or benchmarks to get some sense of what different numbers mean (Blanton & Jaccard, 2006b). Suppose, for instance, that a researcher uses an arbitrary 0-to-10 scale to measure perceived knowledge of psychology in a sample of 1,000 introductory psychology students, and further collects detailed information on grade expectations. Through careful analysis, the researcher learns that students who circle 8 on the confidence rating most typically report an expectation of getting a B in the course, students who circle 8 or lower report feeling satisfied with a B or higher on the final, and those who circle 9 or higher report feeling dissatisfied with any grade other than an A. From these data, the number 8 begins to take on meaning. This hypothetical data pattern suggests that a rating of 8 reveals an expectation of B-level performance.

Of course this fictitious study is not realistic, but many arbitrary metrics do become meaningful when their real-world implications are detailed. Consider measures of IQ. Tests of IQ have been used to such an extent that many educational psychologists have a reasonable sense of what to expect from students with IQ scores of 90, and they know how they would likely differ from those with IQ scores of 120. IQ tests rely on a metric that, however imperfect, has become less arbitrary over time.

Verifiable Versus Indefinite Metrics To go beyond absolute inferences and estimate accuracy, the score generated by a respondent must be compared to some external criterion of "truth." To this end, psychologists often measure judgments on the same metric as some accuracy criteria. For instance, to determine if the student was too confident in her ability to do well on an exam, one might ask her what score she expected out of 100: What grade do you think you will get on the final exam (0–100)? Use of this 0–100 metric gives an investigator the ability to state whether the student made an error in judgment. If she predicted an 85 on the final exam and received a 74, then she made a mistake. By moving from a 0–10 rating scale to a 0–100 rating scale, the researcher seems to have shifted from a metric with indefinite meaning to one that can be mapped directly onto a verifiable criterion. That is, it appears that the accuracy of the rating can now be assessed.

Again, however, the thesis of our chapter calls verifiability into question when logic such as this is employed. This point is introduced by two hypothetical data sets in Table 5.2. Notice that with each data set, the students overestimated their exam grades by an average of 11 points. However, the dynamics underlying this identical average grade overestimation differed dramatically in the two data sets. In the first data set, all of the students overestimated their grades, but the students who made the highest predictions performed the best on the exam and those who made the lowest predictions performed the worst. In the second data set, each of the students again overestimated their own grades, but there was little relationship

TABLE 5.2 Grade Estimation

| | Data Set 1 | | | Data Set 2 | |
| | Grade | | | Grade | |
Student	Predicted	Actual	Student	Predicted	Actual
1	75	64	1	75	69
2	80	69	2	80	74
3	85	74	3	85	84
4	90	79	4	90	79
5	95	84	5	95	64
Mean	85	74	Mean	85	74
	$r = 1.00$			$r = -0.10$	

between predicted grade and actual grade. Is it reasonable to say that the students in the first data set are biased in their ratings or that their ratings reveal an error when this group seems strongly attuned to true relative standing in the classroom? Is it reasonable to use the same term to describe the grade overestimation tendencies in these two data sets?

Before answering, note that these two data sets were designed to have the same underlying psychological dynamics as the two data sets in Table 5.1. Specifically, the correlation between perceived and actual knowledge in the first data set is $r = 1.00$ and in the second data set is $r = -.10$. Recall that in Table 5.1, the dynamics in the first data set were used to support the theory that respondents showed a degree of insight into their true competencies, whereas the data from the second were used to argue against that perspective. Because the data sets in Table 5.2 employed a metric that seems meaningful as opposed to arbitrary (in the sense that it reflects a percent correct) and because it seems verifiable as opposed to indefinite (in the sense that the 0–100 metric is also employed in the accuracy standard), then a data pattern that suggested knowledge and insight in Table 5.1 seems to suggest bias and error in Table 5.2. This is problematic.

We suggest that if researchers adopt new interpretations of the same data pattern simply because of a change in the metric, then perhaps too much faith is being placed in numeric rating systems. The arbitrary nature of the first metric focuses attention on the correlation pattern, whereas the seemingly verifiable nature of the second metric focuses attention on mean differences. This shift is expected if researchers mistakenly assume they have shifted from metric indeterminacy to metric transparency.

Transparent Versus Indeterminate Metrics   People often say what they mean and mean what they say. If a student says she will ace an exam, then it seems fair to assume that she thinks she will receive an A for her grade. If she then fails the exam, it also seems fair to infer that she was overconfident. At times, however, the meaning of a communication is not so clear and the inferences that follow are indeterminate, given such ambiguity. If a student says she will thrash or annihilate an exam, the meanings of her utterances are not fully clear. These words need to be translated before their truth value can be determined.

In many research settings, the meaning of ratings is clear and transparent, and in others it is indeterminate or fuzzy. When a researcher poses a question to a respondent for purposes of obtaining a rating, the researcher has a set of thoughts that this investigator wants to convey to the respondent, in the context of the question. For the researcher to communicate those thoughts, the researcher must convert each thought into an external symbol system and then convey these symbols to the respondent. In turn, the respondent must then decode—that is, interpret—this system and extract meaning from it. Ideally, the respondent will infer the meaning that was intended by the researcher. However, should the symbolic expressions evoke a different thought in the respondent than what the researcher intended, a miscommunication will occur, and the underlying meanings ascribed to the symbols will differ from the researcher's intent.

From this framework, we define a measure as *transparent* when the underlying meanings intended to be conveyed by the researcher are the same as the underlying meanings extracted by the respondent. Transparency by this definition is related to validity, because validity occurs to the extent that there is correspondence between the underlying meaning intended by the researcher and extracted by the respondent. We introduce transparency as a distinct quality, however, for two reasons. First, we wish to draw attention to the communication process occurring between questioner and respondent. Second, and more specifically, we wish to highlight the communication gaps that can occur when experimenters allow their own interest in measuring accuracy drive their interpretations of a question. Although researchers may think that by adopting a metric that can be verified that the metric has transparent meaning, at times this strategy can cause researchers to interpret questions in ways that respondents will not. Common interpretations of probability ratings provide an example of this.

When incorporated into formal mathematical models, the meaning of probability units is known and understood. If a coin has a 50% chance of landing on heads, then the expected number of heads in a sample of 1,000 coin tosses is 500. But consider the meaning that percentage scales convey when used to quantify psychological experiences. If someone says she is 99.9% sure that she will have a date on Friday, she probably is not invoking the metric of percentages to communicate that if she were to randomly sample 1,000 future Fridays from the population of possible Fridays like the upcoming one, that she would expect to stay home on 1 of these nights. Rather, she is probably using this metric to communicate subjective certainty that a date will occur.

Of course psychologists typically avoid casual utterances in favor of formal ratings scales, and they do this partly to move to a shared meaning system. The move to structured ratings has great value in improving the psychometric properties of questions, but there will always be a potential for gaps of interpretations. The use of structured probability rating scales provides one such example. Only a few specialized populations—gamblers and weather forecasters, for instance—have extensive experience using percentage estimates to make formal predictions. Members of other populations communicate in percentage terms only rarely and may be unable or unwilling to use these scales in a way that comports with the meaning in formal probability models.

Consider as another example a structured response scale that is routinely employed to document a cognitive error. This is the perception of unique invulnerability (Weinstein, 1980). The typical question that might be used to reveal this bias is as follows:

What is the likelihood that you, relative to other same-sex college students, will fall and break a bone?

−3	−2	−1	0	1	2	3
Much Less Likely			*Same Likelihood*			*Much More Likely*

The pattern of results typically observed is for respondents, on average, to rate their own likelihood of experiencing negative events (like falling and breaking a bone) as lower than that of comparable others. Because it is not possible for everyone to have lower odds of experiencing misfortune than everyone else, a negative mean score on this scale seems to reveal the presence of a collective error. But is it appropriate to use such a label?

By following this convention, researchers must explicitly assert or implicitly assume transparent meaning. More specifically, they must assume that the value of zero on this metric has a clear interpretation and provides a meaningful dividing line between two distinct psychological states, one that indicates a collective error toward unique vulnerability and another that indicates a collective error toward invulnerability. Although this interpretation follows if the scale means precisely what it looks like it means, to our knowledge, the transparency assumption of this metric and zero-point hypotheses have never been tested. And there is reason to think that if such research were conducted that it would not be supportive. Various investigators have studied the properties of comparative ratings scales such as this one and their results suggest that, although respondents are asked to estimate *relative* probabilities, the ratings participants give are driven more by their perceptions of their own, *absolute* probabilities (for example, Kruger, 1999). Thus, although it appears that the negative mean for individuals reveals false belief in unique invulnerability, perhaps it just reveals a (mostly correct) view that most negative events are unlikely.

The problem of transparency points to the need to test for the presence of errors empirically, rather than through conceptual or logic-based assertions. To illustrate, suppose a researcher administers a 100-item, multiple-choice test of knowledge to a sample of 1,000 individuals. After each question, and following common practices in the overconfidence field, he asks participants to rate the likelihood that they will get each question correct. He finds that when he averages the confidence ratings for each question, participants tend to overestimate their performance by 10 points. Thus, on average, students who get 50% of the questions correct on the test report an average confidence rating across the 100 items of 60%. Students who get 60% of the questions right on the test report an average confidence rating across the 100 items of 70%. And so on. If we view probability ratings as a nonarbitrary subjective estimate of performance and if we view actual test scores as a nonarbitrary objective estimate of test performance, then the estimate of the sample can be verified relative to the normative standard and it is fair to say that participants exhibited an overconfidence effect.

But is the psychology underlying these ratings transparent? We might ask, what does a 70% mean to a participant who makes this rating? How does it differ from a 50%? Perhaps many of the students who indicate 70% are simply conveying a subjective sense that there is a "pretty good chance" of getting a question right. How might one determine if the ratings of 50% or 60% or 70% are faulty in a psychological sense? One way to get traction on these ratings would be to abandon assertions about the meaning of probability numbers in the minds of respondents and instead seek to identify through empirical research the real-world consequences of different numeric ratings. Suppose, for instance, a researcher looks past the 10-point difference in true and estimated probabilities to see if participants are acting like a group that has overestimated its knowledge. To this end, the researcher asks participants if they are willing to enter into a bet for each item on the test, with varying payoffs for each question. By random lottery, the payoffs for a given question will range from 9:1 to 1:9, with each point representing the exchange of 10 cents. If a participant is given 7 to 3 odds for a given question, this means that a correct answer will yield 70 cents and an incorrect response 30 cents. If someone is given 2 to 8 odds, this means then a correct answer will yield 20 cents and an incorrect response 80 cents. With such a setup, the researcher can empirically examine what risks people will take at the different levels of confidence they generate. If a participant truly believes that her chances of being correct on a given item are 60%, then she should enter into any bet that gives better than 4 to 6 odds. Over the long haul at 60%, she will win money with those odds if her estimate is accurate. If the participant is consistently overestimating her probability of knowing, she should enter into wagers that do not favor her and over the long haul lose money.

This study would require sophisticated experimental controls and even then the effects would be open to multiple interpretations, as factors other than knowledge confidence, like the tendency toward "risk taking," can influence gambling decision. These and other obvious limitations would need to be examined, but we introduce this example to convey the spirit of quantifying error based on the *consequences* of judgments rather than strict and literal interpretations of numeric ratings. As we show shortly, this approach provides one of two methods we advance for gaining traction on accuracy and error.

Summary of Four Properties

We have examined four qualities of a response metric and related them to the study of error: validity, meaningfulness, verifiability, and transparency. We argued that researchers should not assume that metrics, however valid, reveal what they intuitively seem to reveal, especially for the purpose of asserting an error. A participant who answers questions about absolute or relative probability might not be communicating probability estimates in a fashion consistent with formal probability models, and so deviation from rational models might reflect poor measurement translation rather than cognitive miscalculation. Further complicating matters, the meaning of a single scale metric might shift from one judgment to the next (Schwarz, 1996). For instance, when psychology majors rate their knowledge of psychology, they might use the scale to convey how their mastery of psychology compares to their mastery of other topic areas (see Marsh, 1986). When the same group rates the knowledge of other psychology majors at their school using the same metric, they might use the scale to convey how psychology majors at their own institution compare to psychology majors at comparable institutions (see Biernat & Crandall, 1996). If researchers do not consider the shifting meaning of a seemingly identical metric from one question to the next, they might draw faulty inference when they make direct comparisons between them.

We think misplaced faith in transparency is one reason many judgment problems are framed in terms of probabilities. Many times, when human judgments are measured using precise mathematical language, the correct answer can often be unerringly determined. But the transparent meaning of percentages when conveying the true likelihood of a criterion does not necessarily hold when this metric is imported to psychological judgments. In fact, there is considerable evidence that the natural metric of human probability judgments is not one of probabilities (for example, Windschitl & Wells, 1996). We thus see some irony in the faith that judgment researchers place in their measures, in light of their conclusions. The judgment and decision literature has focused attention on the human tendency to make faulty judgments of odds and probabilities, but such conclusions only follow if one also embraces strong assumptions about the human capacity to accurately and precisely report this same information.

STRATEGIES FOR STUDYING ACCURACY AND ERROR

We propose two strategies that avoid such strong assumptions. The first "pragmatic approach" focuses on the consequences of accurate versus inaccurate judgments. The second "process approach" focuses on the psychological mechanisms surrounding accuracy and error, rather than accuracy per se.

The Pragmatic Approach: Measuring Mistakes

Our hypothetical betting example illustrated a pragmatic approach to measuring error. In that study, the meaning of a seemingly transparent metric was deduced empirically (but imperfectly) through research that linked observed values to meaningful, real-world events. Elsewhere, we have discussed how this approach can bring meaning to arbitrary metrics that measure racial bias (Blanton & Jaccard, 2006b). In the current chapter, we extend the logic to consider the task of making meaningful statements about errors. Our review shows that it is one thing to define errors through analytic conventions but quite another to determine meaning by linking numeric ratings to daily outcomes.

The pragmatic approach to errors calls on researchers to operationalize judgmental shortcomings, independent of the numeric rating system they adopt (for example, Dawes & Mulford, 1996; Moore & Small, 2008). Researchers can then empirically link ratings to judgments in order to identify cut points and critical regions on the response metric that they find to be associated with the tendency to make errors of judgment. For instance, one might define overconfidence in betting as the tendency to lose money. With this definition chosen beforehand, one could then determine the magnitude of discrepancy between perceived and true probabilities (if any) that leads to an error. Perhaps the error will be linked to the tendency to overestimate true odds by 10 points. Perhaps it will be linked to the tendency to underestimate true odds by 10 points. Regardless, the meaning assigned on any given rating discrepancy is established empirically, not by definitional fiat.

Pragmatic meaning has parallels in treatments of human judgment pointing to the need to link empirical findings to contexts of interest (Brunswick, 1956; Todd & Gigerenzer, 2007). Funder (1987) focused discussion of this issue around a distinction he makes between "errors" (responses that deviate from normative models of correctness) and "mistakes" (maladaptive responding in daily life rooted in faulty perceptions). In a sense, the pragmatic approach we are suggesting shifts attention away from research strategies that seek to quantify errors to alternative strategies that seek to quantify mistakes.

To illustrate, consider again the example of the student who mistakenly predicted her grade to be an A. Her prediction did not correspond to her actual grade, and so she did make an error. But was this a mistake? If the student hopes to be admitted to a selective college, if she believed that she needed to obtain an A in the course to remain competitive, and if she stopped studying based on her belief that she had learned enough to get an A on the final, then she made a mistake. If her prediction had no discernible effect on her studying behavior or her emotional reaction to the grade, then no mistake was made. A similar analysis can be applied to the illusion of invulnerability, discussed earlier. If researchers can document that groups shift from adaptive to maladaptive behavior as they move from positive to negative ratings, then the current convention for scoring an error has pragmatic value for measuring mistakes. If the zero-point is not a dividing line, the convention is called into question.

Quantification of shortcomings in terms of consequences will not always be easy or straightforward. In any given research context, researchers must seek consensus around a definition of a "mistake" to link observable events to specific points on the scale metric (see Blanton & Jaccard, 2006a, 2006b). This will move researchers away from clean, universal definitions of inaccuracy and irrationality that can follow from logical definitions to a multitude of operationalizations, each rooted in the consequences of cognition. The reason is that the consequences of a given judgment depend on the specific environments where thought translates into action (Berg & Gigerenzer, 2010). Further complicating matters, a given judgment or judgmental process might be deemed adaptive when it is evaluated in relation to one of its outcome and maladaptive when it is evaluated in relation to another. Suppose, for instance, that a particular cognitive style is linked to both economic gain and hedonic loss (Quoidbach, Dunn, Petrides, & Mikolajczak, 2010). Whether this tendency reveals a "mistake" in daily life depends on the criterion of interest. Importantly, the multitude of criteria that might be used to evaluate cognition must be expressed *a priori* and applied consistently across a program of study.

The reason is that most positive outcomes will come with some attendant negatives, and so it will be easy for researchers to seize on the "bad news" to highlight human tendencies toward irrationality, after the fact (Krueger & Acevedo, 2007; Mazzocco, Alicke, & Davis, 2004).

These complexities aside, a pragmatic approach can light a bright path for those who wish to understand the meaning of the phenomena they study. Overconfidence takes on meaning when a researcher identifies the points on the scale metric where measured hubris is linked to unacceptably high risks of teen pregnancy or drunk driving or budget overruns. In each case, interest in real-world outcomes pulls a researcher's attention away from numbers and toward everyday life. It thereby adds a new twist to traditional debates over whether commonly measured forms of "irrationality" are adaptive (Taylor & Brown, 1988) or maladaptive (Colvin & Block, 1994), as it inextricably binds the assessment of rationality to its measureable effects.

The Process Approach: Quantifying Erroneous Influences, Not Errors

The psychometric hurdles reviewed here are only of concern when researchers wish to estimate accuracy and error. These can be circumvented, however, if a researcher instead focuses on modeling the antecedents and consequences of irrational thought process. This alternate approach is consistent with common uses of laboratory experimentation. Recall that experimental psychologists document errors by determining how experimental stimuli influence responses in ways not accounted for by idealized rational models. The same logic can be incorporated into measurement enterprises. Researchers can model the factors that influence judgments, *after known rational influences have been statistically controlled*. The factors that operate independent of known, rational influences can then be interpreted as biasing factors—factors that distort judgments away from what would be predicted on the basis of the rational model.

For instance, in one idealized model, confidence in judgments will vary systematically as a function of the accuracy of these judgments (plus or minus random error). One can thereby identify factors that systematically bias judgmental confidence by modeling the variables that predict confidence ratings for a judgment or set of judgments, after judgmental accuracy has been statistically controlled. Blanton, Pelham, DeHart, and Carvallo (2001) deployed this approach in a study of judgmental overconfidence. They were interested in determining if egoistic factors exert irrational influences on judgmental confidence. The judgment task involved a blind taste test in which participants needed to discriminate between Coke and Pepsi placed in two separate cups. Although the ability to identify Coke from Pepsi is trivial in most senses, some individuals state strong preferences for one cola over the other. A stated "preference" implies a perceived ability to discriminate between the two colas on the basis of taste. Pilot testing for this study revealed, however, that many individuals are not able to distinguish between the two colas, even if they state a preference between them. Blanton et al. thus hypothesized that the stronger the stated preference for one cola over the other, the more confidence would become inflated, independent of judgmental accuracy. Further, because research suggests that self-affirmations ameliorate threats to the self (Steele, 1988), they predicted that a self-affirmation manipulation would diminish the nonrational influence of preference on confidence.

Results indicated that the relationship between judgmental confidence and accuracy was close to zero, $r = -.05$, suggesting that participants had little insight into their ability to perform the taste test. Further, participants expressed 78% confidence in their ability to label the two colas accurately, although only 73% of the participants were able to do this. The difference in these values was statistically significant ($p < .05$) and would traditionally be interpreted as evidence that the sample was about 5% overconfident. However, such an interpretation requires adoption of the questionable transparency assumption. To avoid this, confidence ratings were regressed on the two factors that were thought to exert irrational influences (preference and self-affirmation) and their cross-product, with judgmental accuracy statistically controlled. Results indicated that in the absence of an affirmation a stronger tendency to state a preference of one cola over the other was associated with a higher confidence rating, independent of judgmental accuracy. In the presence of an affirmation, however, this irrational influence was eliminated. This study thus provided evidence that motivation can exert influences on confidence levels that operate outside their effects on accuracy. The findings pointed to an irrational thought process that can promote error in some contexts, but error was not quantified by this research method.

This same logic can be used in studies designed to determine the *consequences* of irrational thought processes. This is done by examining the influence of a perception on some other outcome of interest, after controlling for all other factors highlighted by a rational model. Jaccard, Dodge, and Guilamo-Ramos (2005) examined sexual risk taking in over 8,000 female adolescents who participated, over two years, in two waves of a national survey on health-related cognitions and behavior. Jaccard and colleagues hypothesized that perceived knowledge of sexual risk factors would influence sexual health decisions, and they examined the influence of perceived knowledge on such decisions while controlling the influence of actual knowledge (measured with a knowledge test). By so doing, they modeled irrational influences of perceived knowledge on sexual risk taking.

Consistent with the cola preference study, this study showed that perceived knowledge was largely uncorrelated with actual knowledge, $r = .10$. Further, perceived knowledge of sexual risk taking predicted (unplanned) pregnancy occurrence when actual knowledge (and a large set of covariates) was controlled. The nature of the effect was that for every unit that perceived knowledge changed (on the five-category scale), the predicted odds of a pregnancy increased by a factor of 1.53, holding actual knowledge constant. Subsequent analyses suggested that this effect was due, in part, to the effects of perceived knowledge on sexual activity. Independent of actual knowledge, the perception of knowledge predicted greater sexual activity. Since perceived knowledge was unrelated to protective behavior, this increased sexual activity resulted in higher rates of pregnancy.

Together, these studies show how one might study irrational influences that can undermine accuracy and promote error. One approach involves studying factors that influence perceptions and beliefs after rational influences have been statistically controlled. Another involves studying the effects of perceptions and beliefs on outcomes of interest after the rational influences of these perceptions and beliefs have been statistically controlled. Both approaches can reveal psychological dynamics that depart from idealized rational models, but each avoids the many thorny measurement issues created by seeking to study accuracy or quantify error (although they leave many thorny issues related to establishing reliability and validity). By focusing on irrational processes of thought, rather than irrational content of thought, this analytic method can move researchers beyond the mere documentation of errors to understanding their effects (cf. Krueger & Funder, 2004).

CONCLUSION

We all make errors, and psychologists have a long tradition of studying the causes and consequences of these errors. This chapter was written with an eye for the many ways psychologists themselves might err by pursuing seemingly straightforward methods of quantifying error. We offered a pragmatic approach and a process approach as alternatives that at times will be less intuitive and straightforward, but that have the potential of helping researchers gain a better understanding of human decision making and its effects.

REFERENCES

Alicke, M. D. (1985). Global self-evaluation as determined by the desirability and controllability of trait adjectives. *Journal of Personality and Social Psychology, 49*, 1621–1630.

Anderson, N. H. (1981). *Foundation of information integration theory*. New York: Academic Press.

Berg, N., & Gigerenzer, G. (2010). As-if behavioral economics: Neoclassical economics in disguise? *History of Economic Ideas, 18*, 133–166.

Biernat, M., & Crandall, C. S. (1996). Creating stereotypes and capturing their content. *European Journal of Social Psychology, 26*, 867–898.

Blanton, H., & Jaccard, J. (2006a). Arbitrary metrics in psychology. *American Psychologist, 61*, 27–41.

Blanton, H., & Jaccard, J. (2006b). Arbitrary metrics redux. *American Psychologist, 61*, 62–71.

Blanton, H., Pelham, B., DeHart, T., & Carvallo, M. (2001). Overconfidence as dissonance reduction. *Journal of Experimental Social Psychology, 37*, 373–385.

Brunswick, E. (1956). *Perception and the representative design of experiments*. Berkeley: University of California Press.

Buehler, R., Griffin, D., & Ross, M. (1994). Exploring the "planning fallacy": Why people underestimate their task completion times. *Journal of Personality and Social Psychology, 67*, 366–381.

Colvin, C. R., & Block, J. (1994). Do positive illusions foster mental health? An examination of the Taylor and Brown formulation. *Psychological Bulletin, 116*, 3–20.

Cronbach, L. J. (1955). Processes affecting scores on "understanding of others" and "assumed similarity." *Psychological Bulletin, 52*, 177–193.

Dawes, R. M., & Mulford, M. (1996). The false consensus effect and overconfidence: Flaws in judgment or flaws in how we study judgment? *Organizational Behavior and Human Decision Processes, 65*, 201–211.

Fischhoff, B., Slovic, P., & Lichtenstein, S. (1977). Knowing with certainty: The appropriateness of extreme confidence. *Journal of Experimental Psychology: Human Perception and Performance, 3*, 552–564.

Funder, D. C. (1987). Errors and mistakes: Evaluating the accuracy of social judgment. *Psychological Bulletin, 101*, 75–90.

Gold, E., & Hester, G. (2008). The gambler's fallacy and the coin's memory. In J. I. Krueger (Ed.), *Rationality and social responsibility: Essays in honor of Robyn Mason Dawes* (pp. 21–46). New York: Psychology Press.

Hastorf, A. H., & Bender, I. E. (1952). A caution respecting the measurement of empathic ability. *Journal of Abnormal and Social Psychology, 47*, 574–576.

Jaccard, J., Dodge, T., & Guilamo-Ramos, V. (2005). Metacognition, risk behavior, and risk outcomes: The role of perceived intelligence and perceived knowledge. *Health Psychology, 24*, 161–170.

Jones, E. E., & Davis, K. E. (1965). From acts to dispositions: The attribution process in person perception. In L. Berkowitz (Ed.), *Advances in experimental social psychology* (Vol. 2, pp. 219–266). New York: Academic Press.

Kelley, H. H. (1967). Attribution theory in social psychology. In D. Levine (Ed.), *Nebraska symposium on motivation* (Vol. 15, pp. 192–240). Lincoln: University of Nebraska Press.

Krueger, J. I., & Acevedo, M. (2007). Perceptions of self and other in the prisoner's dilemma: Outcome bias and evidential reasoning. *American Journal of Psychology, 120*, 593–618.

Krueger, J. I., & Funder, D. (2004). Toward a balanced social psychology: Causes, consequences, and cures for the problem-seeking approach to social behavior and cognition. *Behavioral and Brain Sciences, 27*, 313–327.

Kruger, J. (1999). Lake Wobegon be gone! The "below-average effect" and the egocentric nature of comparative ability judgments. *Journal of Personality and Social Psychology, 77*, 221–232.

Lichtenstein, S., & Fischhoff, B. (1977). Do those who know more also know more about how much they know? *Organizational Behavior and Human Performance, 20*, 159–183.

Marsh, H. (1986). Global self-esteem: Its relation to specific facets of self-concept and their importance. *Journal of Personality and Social Psychology, 51*, 1224–1236.

Mazzocco, P. J., Alick, M. D., & Davis, T. L. (2004). On the robustness of outcome bias: No constraint by prior culpability. *Basic and Applied Social Psychology, 26*, 131–146.

Moore, D., & Small, D. (2008). When it is rational for the majority to believe that they are better than average. In J. I. Krueger (Ed.), *Rationality and social responsibility: Essays in honor of Robyn Mason Dawes* (pp. 141–174). New York: Psychology Press.

Prentice, D. A., & Miller, D. T. (1992). When small effects are impressive. *Psychological Bulletin, 112*, 160–164.

Quoidbach, J., Dunn, E. W., Petrides, K. V., & Mikolajczak, M. (2010). Money giveth, money taketh away: The dual effect of wealth on happiness. *Psychological Science, 21*, 759–763.

Steele, C. M. (1988). The psychology of self-affirmation: Sustaining the integrity of the self. In L. Berkowitz (Ed.), *Advances in experimental social psychology* (Vol. 21, pp. 261–302). New York: Academic Press.

Taylor, S. E., & Brown, J. D. (1988). Illusion and well-being—A social psychological perspective on mental health. Psychological Bulletin, 103(2), 193–210.

Schwarz, N. (1996). *Cognition and communication: Judgmental biases, research methods, and the logic of conversation.* Hillsdale, NJ: Erlbaum.

Todd, P., & Gigerenzer, G. (2007). Environments that make us smart: Ecological rationality. *Current Directions in Psychological Science, 16,* 167–171.

Tversky, A., & Kahneman, D. (1971). Belief in the law of small numbers. *Psychological Bulletin, 76,* 105–110.

Weinstein, N. (1980). Unrealistic optimism about future life events. *Journal of Personality and Social Psychology, 39,* 806–820.

Windschitl, P., & Wells, G. (1996). Measuring psychological uncertainty: Verbal versus numeric methods. *Journal of Experimental Psychology: Applied, 2,* 343–364.

6

The Strengths of Social Judgment
A Review Based on the Goodness of Judgment Index

LEE JUSSIM, SEAN T. STEVENS,
and ELIZABETH R. SALIB

INTRODUCTION

*H*ow good is normal human judgment? Much of the scholarship in psychology (especially social psychology) and related disciplines has long suggested that it is not very good at all. Perspectives emphasizing error, bias, and how social beliefs create social reality have dominated the literature on social cognition (for example, Fiske & Taylor, 1991; Kahneman & Tversky, 1973; Ross Lepper, & Ward, 2010). These views have created an image of a social perceiver whose misbegotten beliefs and flawed processes construct not only illusions of social reality in the perceiver's mind, but actual social reality through processes such as self-fulfilling prophecies. In this bleak view, the mind becomes primarily a product of cognitive shortcomings and distorted social interactions.

We doubt that one can find any psychologist who can be directly quoted as claiming that people are generally fools. Instead, what happens is far more subtle. First, the amount of time, energy, and journal space devoted to research on error and bias vastly exceeds that devoted to accuracy. Second, the receptacles of "received wisdom" in social psychology—handbook chapters, annual review chapters, and textbooks—consistently review and emphasize research demonstrating error and bias while typically ignoring or deemphasizing research on accuracy (for example, Dovidio & Gaertner, 2010; Myers, 2008; Ross et al., 2010).

The unflattering picture of normal human judgment painted by social psychology can be seen in several ways. Social cognition over the last 60 years has been largely a "bias-documenting" enterprise (see Jussim, in press; Krueger & Funder,

2004, for whole tables listing social cognitive biases). Or, consider the following quotes (see Jussim, in press, for a large collection of such quotes):

> "Social perception is a process dominated far more by what the judge brings to it than by what he takes in during it" (Gage & Cronbach, 1955, p. 420).

> "Self-fulfilling prophecies occur ... across a wide variety of situations. Although there are some circumstances that counter their occurrence, on the whole, biases in both the perceiver's and target's interpretations of the meaning of behavior and social norms for reciprocating behavior would seem to favor their development" (Fiske & Taylor, 1991, pp. 549–550).

There are good reasons to study bias. Biases can reveal the inner workings of the mind by revealing the processes underlying perception and judgment (see Funder, 1987). Similarly, bad and foolish behavior is inherently attention grabbing (Jussim, 2005; Krueger & Funder, 2004). Furthermore, identifying errors and sources of irrationality is often a first step toward improving human judgment. Nonetheless, the good reasons *to* study bias do not constitute good reasons *not* to study accuracy or to overstate the role of bias in human judgment. Our view is that, at least within social psychology, this emphasis on bias is greatly overstated. The next several sections of this chapter point the direction toward a much-needed correction in the big take-away message from research on human social judgment. Describing that correction and its implications for understanding prior research is the centerpiece of this chapter.

The Failure of Bias Research in Social Psychology to Estimate How Good People's Judgments Are

Obviously, if one acts as a "bias detective," then one will be unmotivated to assess how good people are. Assessing error and bias versus how well people make judgments requires very different research efforts. For example, consider Bob Smith, who plays tennis better on clay than grass. He has a clay "bias." This provides no information about how good Bob is. To do so, one would have to examine his won–lost record.

Furthermore, bias is usually assessed against an implicit comparison of perfection or as an unconfirmable null hypothesis (Krueger & Funder, 2004). For example, in stereotype research, when people judge two groups (or individuals from two different groups) differently, it is interpreted as bias (for example, Dovidio & Gaertner, 2010; Fiske & Neuberg, 1990). The implicit standard of perfection here is unbiased responding (i.e., judging the groups or individuals identically) and any deviation from this standard is interpreted as bias. Furthermore, unbiased responding—a nondifference between experimental conditions—is not "accuracy." It is an uninterpretable "null" result (see Krueger & Funder, 2004, for more on this topic). Finally, the *pièce de résistance* is that such studies almost never show how good people's judgments are or how close they come to unbiased responding; they only address the probability of the observed difference occurring under the null assumption of no difference between experimental conditions. If one is fortunate, one might find the effect size of bias reported, but rarely does one find an effect size for accuracy or unbiased responding.

Thus, in such studies, the only thing that is assessed is how bad people's judgments are, the implicit standard for comparison is perfection (zero bias), and there is no corresponding assessment of how good they are. One cannot reach conclusions about the extent and power of bias in human social perception unless accuracy or unbiased responding is also measured.

We Rarely Care About Perfection

There is one more inherent problem with research that uses perfection as its standard for comparison. We rarely care about perfection (Jussim, 2005, in press; Simon, 1956). There are exceptions. In planning a lunar landing or when constructing a skyscraper, measurements that are incorrect by a tiny percentage may lead to disaster. Most of the time, however, we do not aspire to perfection.

Perfection is so high a standard that researchers rarely apply it when testing their own models, theories, and hypotheses. Correspondence of theoretical predictions with empirical outcomes almost never needs to be the equivalent of a correlation of 1.0. Consider a statistically significant confirmation of some hypothesis, with a corresponding effect size of $r = .20$ (the average effect size in all of social psychology; see Richard, Bond, & Stokes-Zoota, 2003). This can be interpreted as meaning that the theory was confirmed for 60% of the responses and disconfirmed for 40% (for example, Rosenthal, 1991). It generally will not, however, stop a researcher from exclaiming, "Eureka, the data confirm my theory!" We see no justification for holding lay beliefs to a higher standard than the standard to which social scientists hold their own hypotheses.

It is important for researchers examining the quality of human social judgment to (1) have a clear standard for optimal judgment, and (2) provide information not only on the probability that people deviate from that optimal judgment but also on how close they come to optimal judgment. These issues have been widely recognized in cognitive psychology for some time (for example, Gigerenzer, 2002; Katsikopoulos, Schooler, & Hertwig, 2010; Koriat, Goldsmith, & Panksy, 2000); one goal of this chapter is to develop a simple statistical method for bringing this idea to social psychological studies of bias. Toward this end, we introduce the Goodness of Judgment Index.

THE GOODNESS OF JUDGMENT INDEX (GJI): WHAT IT IS AND HOW TO USE IT

Assessing people's deviations from perfection can be a valuable and important research enterprise, and nothing in this chapter suggests otherwise. Nonetheless, we argue that it is useful, even imperative, to develop procedures that assess not merely how bad people's judgments are but also how good their judgments are. Just as scientists consider their theories pretty good even if they do not perfectly capture reality, it seems reasonable to evaluate the quality of lay judgments not merely by their deviation from perfection but by how closely they capture reality.

Of course, there are both theoretical perspectives and empirical research in social psychology that address people's accuracy (for example, Brunswik, 1952; Funder, 1987; Jussim, 1991; Kenny, 1994). Such perspectives, however, typically require statistically sophisticated techniques (structural equation modeling; the Social Relations Model, signal detection analysis, etc.), methodologically complex forms of data collection, or both. This emphasis on complexity in assessing accuracy probably derives from Cronbach (1955), Kenny (1994), and Judd and Park's (1993) heavy emphasis on complex componential approaches to accuracy.

Nonetheless, there are many useful and constructive approaches to accuracy that do not require complex componential analyses (see Jussim, 2005). More important, complex approaches typically require very specific methods uniquely tailored to yield data that can be analyzed using those methods. Absent the "right" data, many of these methods cannot be used to assess accuracy, rationality, optimal judgment, and so forth.

An important contribution to understanding issues of accuracy, error, and bias, therefore, would be the development of a relatively simple and straightforward method of assessing accuracy, reasonableness, or unbiased responding, especially one that is widely applicable even when a study was not specifically designed to employ sophisticated accuracy assessments. Such a statistic could provide several significant contributions to understanding social perception and judgment:

1. It could put studies of bias into some context. How much bias do they really find? How large is bias relative to accuracy or unbiased responding? Psychologists should want to know answers to these questions if they want to reach broad and general conclusions about people's tendencies toward error and bias.
2. It could sometimes extract information about accuracy, rationality, and so forth, from studies that only assessed bias as deviation from perfection.
3. Therefore, it could also help provide a broader and more complete view of social judgment and perception than is provided by studies focused on bias. If such a statistic showed that studies of bias often provide abundant evidence of unbiased, accurate, or rational responding—evidence that was overlooked because researchers only provided tests of bias—it could constitute one useful antidote to overstatements of bias.

This chapter introduces the Goodness of Judgment Index (GJI). The GJI is a simple arithmetic formula (it can be viewed as a statistic in the sense of being a computational tool with a purpose, but it has no probabilistic properties as do, for example, correlations, F tests). Although the GJI can be used to address many different questions about accuracy, optimality, and goodness of judgment, it can most easily be used to address three common questions:

1. How close do people's judgments come to perfection?
2. How far are people's judgments from perfection?
3. How much do people's judgments improve over some alternative model of judgment?

We created the GJI for the purpose of filling several holes in social psychological research on bias. First, the GJI can be used to explicitly and operationally articulate a standard for accuracy, reasonableness, or rationality, even when the original authors did not. Second, it provides a way to assess how close people's judgments come to perfection, even when the original authors only assessed deviation from perfection. Thus, it is capable of extracting information about accuracy, reasonableness, or rationality from studies reporting only evidence of bias. Last, it is a relatively simple calculation that can be used alone or along with more sophisticated techniques (e.g., signal detection, Bayesian analysis).

The next sections, therefore, first describe this new statistic, then apply it to several studies of bias, and, finally, discuss the implications of the findings obtained for broad and general understandings of bias, rationality, and accuracy in social cognition and judgment.

Computing and Using the GJI

Most results in studies of judgment, decision making, and prediction can be readily translated into a 0–1 scale, because such studies often use frequencies or percentages as their basis for identifying error and bias. The GJI then becomes:

$$\text{(Maximum possible imperfection} - \text{Actual degree of imperfection)}/\text{Maximum possible imperfection}$$

Maximum possible imperfection is the most anyone could possibly be wrong under the circumstances. *Imperfection* can be operationally defined as errors, discrepancies from predicted values, disagreements, and so forth, depending on the type of data in any given context. The GJI ranges from 0 to 1 and, when used as described here, it indicates the proportion improvement of social judgment compared to complete error. Thus, it is simple and easy to use.

The basic ideas and computations can be illustrated with almost any concrete example, say, predicting the number of days in March that New York City (NYC) will have snowfall of at least 1 inch. Let us assume that NYC has only one such day. Fred, however, predicted three such days. Fred was "wrong." It did not snow three times in March. Fred has an "anti-snow bias." But, because a prediction of 3 days of snow in March also means 28 days of no snow, Fred's prediction is far closer to reality than is implied by the blunt declaration that Fred was wrong or that he possesses an anti-snow bias. Indeed, Fred's GJI shows quite precisely how close he is to perfection:

Maximal possible error: 30 (there are 31 days in March, it snows once, so the most Fred could be wrong is 30)
Actual error: 2
GJI = (30 − 2)/30 = 28/30 = .93

In general, GJI scores above .6 indicate that the judgment is closer to complete agreement or accuracy than to complete disagreement or error; scores below

.5 mean that the judgment is closer to complete error or bias than to complete lack of bias or accuracy. Scores between .5 and .6 mean that people's responses are correct about as frequently as would be predicted by blind guessing.[1]

Issues in the Choice of Comparison for Maximal Possible Error

In many situations, use of the GJI requires scientific judgment regarding the appropriate choice for *maximal possible error.* The simplest meaning for maximal error is maximal possible, no matter how unlikely. Indeed, that is how our March snow example was conducted.

Nonetheless, the GJI is flexible enough that it could be used to compare the quality of people's judgments to some standard other than maximal possible error. However, when doing so, researchers should be explicit that such usage no longer involves comparison to complete error, since this alters the interpretation of the GJI. For example, consider again the March snow example used previously. Let us assume that there never have been more than 10 days of snow in March in NYC. If the researcher wishes to assume that 10 is an upper bound for predictions of days of snow in March in NYC, the GJI could be computed using 9 (10 − 1) as maximal error, rather than as 30.

Of course, this is now a very different assumption; such a researcher is now accepting that, in fact, people have a great deal of knowledge about the relative rarity of snow in March in NYC. Use of the smaller term of maximal error does not, somehow, eliminate all that valuable, valid knowledge that people have. Using it does, however, allow the researcher to estimate how good people's judgments about snow in March are, *over and above some level of knowledge against which the researcher is interested in comparing people's judgments.* In this latter case, Fred's GJI would be computed as:

$$\text{Maximal error} = 10$$
$$\text{Actual error} = 2\,(3 - 1)$$
$$\text{GJI} = (10 - 2)/10 = .80$$

Fred is still shown to be doing quite well, even taking for granted that he should have information about general snowfall levels in NYC in March.

This issue will often be important when deciding between *maximal error* versus *random responding* as a baseline. Random responding may produce many accurate predictions, if the base rate of some outcome is high enough. For example, consider predicting the outcome of coin flips. If it is a balanced coin, on average, it will come up heads 50% of the time. So, someone who "successfully" predicted five of ten coin flips is right five times. The GJI here could be computed as (10 − 5)/10 = .5. But, even though there is evidence here that their predictions are better than maximal error, there is no evidence here that they are clairvoyant.

One could use the GJI to test the quality of predictions over and above random responding. The GJI formula remains the same, but its elements need to be computed slightly different to reflect the different purpose to which it is being put. When comparing improvement over random responding:

Maximal error = (Number of trials − Expected number of hits based on random responding)

and

Actual error = (Number of trials − Number of hits)

In the case of someone successfully predicting 5 of 10 coin flips, the GJI would be computed as

$$[(10-5)-(10-5)]/(10-5) = (5-5)/5 = 0$$

If the person got 9 of 10 right, the GJI would be computed as

$$[(10-5)-(10-9)]/(10-5) = (5-1)/5 = .8$$

which is interpretable as meaning people did 80% better than chance. Of course, in such situations, the GJI can be negative, that is, when people perform worse than chance.

Admittedly, one does not need the GJI to figure out how successful someone is at predicting coin flips. The next sections, therefore, use the GJI to revisit several studies of bias. The first several studies (Darley & Gross, 1983; Hastorf & Cantril, 1954; Rosenhan, 1973) were selected precisely because they are classics, highly cited cornerstones in social psychological perspectives on bias. The final study (Monin & Norton, 2002) was selected because it is more recent and it staunchly carries on the tradition of research that focuses almost entirely on bias while, in fact, yielding more evidence of accuracy or unbiased responding than it does of bias. Lest we be accused of cherry-picking, we have purposely included highly cited studies that have been widely interpreted (both by the original authors and by many of those citing them) as clear and strong demonstrations of bias. As shall be shown, even these classics show that bias is generally quite modest, something that occurs around the edges of the main pattern of social judgment, which is largely accurate and in touch with reality.

This review is not a comprehensive reinterpretation of the vast literature on bias. Instead, its intention is to illustrate the main themes of this chapter: (1) psychology, especially but not exclusively social psychology, has a long history of bias in favor of bias; and (2) bias has long led psychologists to, intentionally or not, create an unjustified impression that bias dominates accuracy, when, in fact, their own data—even the data of some of the most classic demonstrations of bias—show that people are, in fact, far more accurate or unbiased than they are biased.

USING THE GJI TO EXTRACT INFORMATION ABOUT THE GOODNESS OF JUDGMENTS FROM PRIOR STUDIES OF ERROR AND BIAS

Under the right conditions, the GJI can be used to extract information about accuracy and agreement from studies that have focused exclusively on demonstrating error and bias. Even when the original research focused exclusively on testing for deviations from perfection, under some conditions, the information necessary to compute the GJI can be uncovered. Several conditions need to be met:

1. The research needs to report its evidence of error or bias in some sort of quantitative terms; means, percentages, and so forth, will usually work fine; *if*
2. The scales of measurement are also reported (so that it is possible to figure out what maximal possible error would be); *or, at least,*
3. Maximal error can be plausibly estimated, even if not identified precisely.

In the next sections, therefore, we use the GJI to reinterpret several oft-cited empirical demonstrations of bias.

They Saw Nearly Identical Games: The GJI Applied to Hastorf and Cantril (1954)

The classic "They Saw a Game" study by Hastorf and Cantril (1954) has long been cited as a sort of testament to the power of subjectivity, distortion, and bias (for example, Ross et al., 2010; indeed, according to Google Scholar, as of April 19, 2010, the study had been cited nearly 500 times, and, although we have not read all 500 such articles, we have never seen it discussed as a testament to the validity or accuracy of social perception). Consider, for example, Ross et al.'s treatment of the study in the most recent *Handbook of Social Psychology:*

> The early classic study by Hastorf and Cantril (1954), on the differing perceptions of Dartmouth and Princeton students watching the same football game through the prisms of their rival partisanships, reflected a radical view of the "constructive" nature of perception that anticipated later discussions of naïve realism. (2010, p. 23)

This quote nicely captures the received wisdom regarding the message of the study. Next, therefore, we examine the study's actual results through the lens of the GJI.

In 1951, Dartmouth and Princeton played a hotly contested, aggressive football game. A Princeton player received a broken nose; a Dartmouth player broke his leg. Accusations flew in both directions: Dartmouth accused Princeton of playing a dirty game; Princeton accused Dartmouth of playing a dirty game.

Into this mix stepped Hastorf and Cantril (1954). They showed a film of the game to 48 Dartmouth students and 49 Princeton students, and had them rate the total number of infractions by each team. Dartmouth students saw both teams as committing slightly over four (on average) infractions. The Princeton students also saw the Princeton team as committing slightly over four infractions; but they saw the Dartmouth team as committing nearly 10 infractions.

Here are Hastorf and Cantril's conclusions:

> There is no such "thing" as a "game" existing "out there" in its own right which people merely "observe." ... The "thing" simply is not the same for different people. (1954, p. 133)

To the extent that we evaluate the Dartmouth and Princeton students' judgments according to an implicit criterion of perfection, they were clearly biased in a self-serving manner: Dartmouth students saw Dartmouth committing only 4 infractions whereas the Princeton students saw Dartmouth as committing 10 infractions. People's judgments were not identical to one another. They deviate from perfection. Thus the study has come to be viewed as a testament to the subjectivity of social perception.

An analysis based on the GJI, however, yields a very different perspective. First, let us consider judgments regarding Princeton. Both Princeton and Dartmouth students estimated that Princeton committed about four infractions. One does not even need the GJI for this. For fully half of the football game (the half involving Princeton) there was no bias at all. If we computed a GJI for these results, it would equal 1.0.

Note that the GJI here is being used to assess in-group *biased* versus *unbiased* responding. It is not being used to assess *accuracy* per se. Total bias is readily assessed simply by comparing the perceptions of the two groups. When those perceptions differ, one does not know whether one group or both groups were biased, but one does know the total degree of bias across the two groups; it is the difference in perceived infractions. In this sense, we are using the GJI in exactly the same manner as did Hastorf and Cantril (1954) when they performed their original analyses.

Next, we computed the GJI for Dartmouth. The Princeton students saw Dartmouth commit 10 infractions; Dartmouth students saw Dartmouth commit 4 infractions. To compute the GJI, however, we need to know the *maximal possible disagreement*. To do so, we will make several simplifying assumptions. First, we assume that people saw no more than one infraction per play per team (it is sufficiently rare in football for a team to commit two independent infractions on a single play that this assumption is worth making). Second, we need to know how many plays there were in the game. Unfortunately, although we have searched high and low for a full reporting of the game, we could not find one that reports exactly how many plays there were. Nonetheless, a typical college football game has 60 to 100 plays. Indeed, the 60 figure is extremely low. But let us work with this lower figure because use of the higher figure would lead to a conclusion of even more agreement than we actually find.

With 60 plays, the maximal possible disagreement is 60. The Dartmouth and Princeton students could have, at least hypothetically, disagreed on every play. Computation of the GJI then becomes very simple:

$$\text{Maximal possible disagreement} = 60$$
$$\text{Actual disagreement} = (10 - 4) = 6$$
$$\text{GJI} = (60 - 6)/60 = .90$$

That is, even for the half of the game (the Dartmouth players) on which there was the greatest amount of disagreement and bias, 90% of the time, the students were completely unbiased. The goodness of students' judgments were 1.0 regarding Princeton and .90 (or, more likely, higher because there were most likely more than 60 plays) regarding Dartmouth. Interpretations of this as some sort of testament to the power of the "constructive" nature of social perception would appear to reflect the constructive nature of social psychological theories and theorists far more than the constructive power of laypeople's social perceptions.

On Judging Insane People as Insane: The GJI Applied to Rosenhan (1973)

The value of assessing accuracy via the GJI is also apparent when applied to Rosenhan's 1973 "On Being Sane in Insane Places" study, which (according to Google Scholar) has been cited over 1,000 times, usually (within social psychology) as a classic example of the power of labels and expectations to bias judgment (for example, Darley & Gross, 1983; Ross et al., 2010). In this study, eight pseudo-patients (who had no history of mental illness) complaining of auditory hallucinations got themselves admitted to psychiatric hospitals. Upon admission, they immediately ceased exhibiting symptoms and acted as normally as possible under the (abnormal) conditions of the psychiatric hospital setting. Most were kept for about two weeks, although one was kept for 52 days. None were diagnosed as sane. Instead, all were released with a diagnosis of schizophrenia "in remission." Furthermore, staff sometimes interpreted reasonable behavior as symptomatic of pathology (e.g., pacing halls from boredom as anxiety). Rosenhan believed he had shown that "we cannot distinguish insanity from sanity" (1973, p. 257).

Although this study provides more evidence of reasonableness and rationality on the part of the doctors and staff than usually recognized (see Jussim, in press), the results are not readily represented by the GJI. Rosenhan (1973), however, performed a follow-up study that is amenable to our method. In that study, he identified a hospital whose staff doubted that they would misdiagnose patients' sanity. He then informed them that pseudo-patients would attempt to gain admission to their hospital during the upcoming three months. Psychiatrists were asked to rate the 193 new patients admitted during this period. Rosenhan (1973, p. 252) described his results this way: "Twenty-three [pseudo-patients] were considered suspect by at least one psychiatrist." There were, however, no pseudo-patients.

To compute the GJI, we gave Rosenhan the benefit of the doubt, and assumed that no psychiatrist judged any of these 23 to be sane. This is not likely to be true. Rosenhan's phrase, "at least one psychiatrist" strongly suggests that, at least sometimes, there were one or more psychiatrists who did not believe one or more of these 23 were fakers. Nonetheless, our assumption biases our computation of the GJI in favor of finding as much bias as possible. Given our simplifying assumptions, the GJI is

Maximum possible number of errors = 193
Actual number of errors = 23
GJI = (193 − 23)/193 = .88

The psychiatrists were right 88% of the time, based on our starting assumptions favoring bias and error. If we assume that only half of the time, rather than all of the time, psychiatrists identified these 23 patients as pseudo, the GJI goes up to .94. Neither Rosenhan's conclusion that the insane are indistinguishable from the sane, nor the longstanding interpretation of this study as a testament to the constructive power of labels, are justified. Instead, the results suggest that the psychiatrists and staff were nicely, though not perfectly, in touch with reality. They were, however, unable to recognize that the people claiming auditory hallucinations were faking. They also judged that a small percentage of those sincerely admitting themselves to mental institutions were, in fact, sane. It is not clear that even this judgment was factually incorrect. Such a small percentage of people could actually have been fundamentally sane (perhaps they misdiagnosed themselves; perhaps they were misdiagnosed by other psychiatrists; perhaps their insane families convinced them that they were the insane one; etc.).

Where Is the Bias? The GJI Applied to Darley and Gross (1983)

Darley and Gross (1983) examined the potentially biasing effects of social class stereotypes. Princeton students were led to believe that a fourth-grade girl came from either a middle-class suburban background, or an inner-city impoverished background. Some then estimated her ability in liberal arts, reading, and math. These students showed little or no tendency to favor the students from the middle-class background.

Others viewed a videotape of her taking a math test. All of these students saw the exact same tape of the exact same girl answering the exact same questions. Nonetheless, they rated her ability, cognitive skills, and motivation more highly when they believed she came from a middle-class background. They even claimed that the girl answered more questions correctly. Darley and Gross (1983) concluded that people's expectations bias their judgments when people feel they have clear evidence relevant to those expectations but not in the absence of such evidence. This study has (according to Google Scholar) been cited about 600 times, typically uncritically as a demonstration of bias.

Although Darley and Gross (1983) used several dependent variables, we limit our analysis to the one with an objective metric, namely, estimates of how many math questions the girl answered correctly. Unfortunately, Darley and Gross did not report how many questions the girl answered correctly, which means that we cannot use the GJI to estimate people's accuracy. Fortunately, however, they reported the average percent correct estimated by perceivers with high versus low social class expectations, for easy, moderate, and difficult questions. This means that we can use the GJI to estimate how biased people were. The high versus low social class estimates of the percent correct were 94% versus 79% for the easy questions, 69% versus 53% for the moderate questions, and 37% versus 36% for the difficult questions. Maximal bias in all cases is 100%, because the most extreme bias would involve people with a high social class expectation believing 100% was answered correctly and people with a low social class expectation believing 0% was answered correctly. This means that:

Easy questions:
    Maximal possible bias: 100%
    Actual bias: 15% = 94% − 79%
    GJI = (100% − 15%)/100% = .85

Moderate questions:
    Maximal possible bias: 100%
    Actual bias: 16% = 69% − 53%
    GJI = (100% − 16%)/100% = .84

Difficult questions:
    Maximal possible bias: 100%
    Actual bias: 1% = 37% − 36%
    GJI = (100% − 1%)/100% = .99

There are other issues surrounding this study, such as the fact that two attempts to replicate it failed (Baron, Albright, & Malloy, 1995). On its own terms, the study did indeed find that the social class expectations biased perceptions of how many questions the girl got right. And one could argue that any bias here is interesting and important, and we would agree. Nonetheless, whatever tendency there was for social class to bias perceptions, it constituted a tiny minority of what perceivers saw. There is bias here, but, mainly there is a healthy dose of reality.

The Consensus May Be False, But the Judgment Is (Mostly) True: The GJI Applied to Monin and Norton (2002)

The three studies thus far revisited using the GJI were classics, but all involved stereotypes (schizophrenia, social class) or intergroup relations (Princeton, Dartmouth). The final study is both similar and different. Much like the prior three studies, it is one that the authors interpreted almost entirely as a testament to the power of bias, but which, in fact, provides far more evidence of unbiased responding than of bias. It also differs from the first three studies. It is far more recent and addresses a very different type of bias—false consensus. We believe this is useful because it shows that the GJI is not restricted to reinterpreting dated classics, nor is it restricted to reinterpreting research on stereotypes or intergroup biases. First, therefore, we describe that study.

During a community water crisis, Princeton students were asked to stop showering for about two days (Monin & Norton, 2002). The researchers surveyed Princeton students, and asked them: (1) how many showers they took during the ban and (2) what percentage of other Princeton students showered during the ban. Although this study is not (yet) considered a classic, it is included here because (1) it has a respectable citation record (almost 70 citations according to Google Scholar) and (2) it addressed a different type of bias: false consensus.

We focus on two of their data points: Days 2 and 3 of the ban. The researchers did not collect data the first day and the ban ended on Day 3; they did, however, report data for several days after the ban ended, which, for space purposes, are not included here. On Day 2, 33% of the respondents admitted to taking showers. Bathers predicted 63% would take showers, and nonbathers predicted that 39% would take showers. This is clearly a "false consensus" effect in that people's estimates seemed to have been influenced in the direction of their own behavior (bathers estimating more bathing than did nonbathers). How big is the bias?

Bathers:
   Maximal possible bias: 67% = 100% – 33%
   Actual bias: 30% = 63% – 33%
   GJI = (67% – 30%)/67% = .55

The bathers were indeed not very good at estimating the rate of bathing. These estimates were about as accurate as guessing. What about the nonbathers?

Nonbathers:
   Maximal possible bias: 67% = 100% – 33%
   Actual bias: 6% = 39% – 33%
   GJI = (67% – 6%)/67% = .91

The nonbathers, by contrast, were quite good at estimating the rate of bathing.

   During Day 3, 47% of their respondents admitted to taking showers. Bathers predicted that 66% took showers; nonbathers predicted that 47% took showers. One does not even need the GJI for the nonbathers—their prediction of the proportion of bathers was perfectly accurate (47%), and their GJI would be 1.0. But even the predictions of the bathers were clearly sensitive to reality.

   Maximal possible bias: 53% = 100% – 47%
   Actual bias: 19% = 66% – 47%
   GJI = (53% – 19%)/53% = .64

So, even though the bathers did indeed show a substantial bias, they were still more accurate than inaccurate, and more accurate than they would have been had people blindly guessed (the expected value for the GJI is .52 when maximal possible bias is 53% and people blindly guess). The average GJI across the four estimates was .78, which is remarkably high for a study in which the discussion section (except for a footnote) did not even mention accuracy.

   In some ways, this study captures much of what is wrong with much social psychological research demonstrating bias. The authors are not oblivious to the bases for concluding that social projection (false consensus) is far more rational (Dawes, 1989) and more accurate (Krueger, 1998) than usually indicated. These references do appear—in a footnote. Thus, the authors could plausibly defend themselves against "accusations of bias in favor of bias" by pointing out that they acknowledged the evidence of accuracy and rationality. This would be literally true. Yet, in our view, as in so much other research in social psychology on social cognition, social judgment, and social perception, this claim, though literally true, does not exonerate the authors from an accusation of bias in favor of bias. Burying accuracy and rationality in the footnotes does not constitute a balanced treatment of their results or the phenomenon.

One could imagine a different bias. The authors could have noted the extraordinary accuracy and rationality of participants in this study, and buried the evidence of bias in the footnotes. Indeed, for the most part, one can only imagine such papers in social psychology, because so much research on bias so rarely acknowledges accuracy and rationality, except to minimize or trivialize it.

One could also imagine a more balanced social psychology. Monin and Norton (2002), like Hastorf and Cantril (1954), Rosenhan (1973), and Darley and Gross (1983) before them, could have interpreted their results as demonstrating some degree of bias, and also—in the main sections of the paper rather than the footnotes—a great deal of reasonableness, rationality, and responding that was nicely in touch with social reality. We are not denying the existence or importance of research on bias. We are simply calling for greater recognition of the demonstrable strengths of social judgment—*even among some of the research most heavily interpreted as demonstrating bias*—in perspectives on social cognition, social judgment, and social perception.

CONCLUSION

Strengths and Limitations to the GJI

The GJI is not intended to replace any of the tools and methods that already exist for assessing accuracy, rationality, agreement, and so forth. Often, a simple correlation or regression coefficient will suffice (Brunswik, 1952; Funder, 1987, 1995; Jussim, 1991, 2005, in press). Other times, methods such as signal detection theory (Green & Swets, 1966) or other componential models (for example, Cronbach, 1955; Judd & Park, 1993; Kenny, 1994) are needed. Yet other times, researchers develop sophisticated normative models that attempt to reflect ideal judgment processes and outcomes against which lay judgment may be compared (Kahneman & Tversky, 1973; Katsikopoulos et al., 2010).

All of these methods have advantages and disadvantages. Both signal detection analysis and most componential models require very specific types of data collection. When one has obtained such data, typically, one should perform one of these sophisticated accuracy assessment analyses because they provide far more information than does the GJI. However, because these methods require specific types of data, they cannot always be performed. Use the "wrong" method or collect the "wrong" type of data, and one cannot perform a signal detection analysis, a componential analysis, or a comparison to a Bayesian normative model.

Among the great advantages of the GJI are its simplicity and flexibility. It does not require very specific types of data or methods. It can be used in almost any situation where it is possible to calculate (1) how much people could disagree or how wrong or biased they could be, and (2) how much they actually disagreed or were wrong or biased. As such, the GJI is particularly useful for two purposes that cannot readily be accomplished by most of the existing more complex approaches, and these are discussed next.

One particular value of the GJI is that it is readily used to revisit and reinterpret existing, published studies of bias—especially when such studies reported no evidence that bears on accuracy, agreement, or unbiased responding. The GJI can often be used to extract information about agreement, accuracy, and unbiased responding from them. We would argue that this is a particularly important endeavor. As illustrated in the present chapter, doing so with classics of the bias literature may often demonstrate that people are more in touch with reality than once recognized.

Our use of the GJI to review and reinterpret four studies exclusively framed by their authors as testaments to bias provides case study evidence in support of the proposition that introduced this chapter—social psychology's scholarship has been so biased in favor of bias that it has likely created a largely distorted and invalid view of human (ir)rationality. Of course, a review of merely four studies cannot fully demonstrate that such a view is misplaced. Nonetheless, these four studies, three of which are highly cited classics of bias, all actually demonstrate far more evidence of agreement, unbiased responding, or accuracy than they do of error, disagreement, or bias. This raises the possibility that the general image of deeply flawed human functioning that has emerged from social psychological scholarship is largely unjustified.

Thus, we suggest that one good use to which the GJI should be put is to provide a more comprehensive and detailed review of classics of error and bias. If most, and not merely the four we have chosen here, show that people are generally far more in touch with reality than out of touch with it, it would suggest the need for a major change in the tone and tenor—and substance—of the conclusions routinely brought to the fore in many reviews of social perception and social cognition regarding error, bias, and accuracy.

Second, the GJI may prove a useful tool for future research. In contrast to much research in cognitive psychology (for example, Kahneman & Tversky, 1973; Katsikopoulos et al., 2010; Koriat et al., 2000), most social psychological studies of error and bias still have no standard for determining what is good, appropriate, or well-justified judgment. The GJI can be used to provide that standard in almost any type of study of error and bias: 1.0 = (Maximal error − 0)/Maximal error. Researchers framing their studies as tests of bias should routinely report the GJI, or some other alternative that provides information on how good people's judgments are and not merely how bad they are. That way, the rest of us would have some context for evaluating how much bias they actually found. Were people mostly biased? Somewhat biased? Statistically significantly more biased than zero, but, in fact, hardly biased at all? The GJI can answer questions such as these. If we want to reach conclusions about how error- and bias-prone people are, how irrational they are, we should be compelled to compare the evidence to how good and accurate people are. The GJI provides a method for accomplishing exactly that.

Human Rationality and Irrationality

The present chapter does not justify broad conclusions about the extent of human irrationality versus rationality. Then again, we would argue that nor are they justified by much of the existing social psychological evidence supposedly attesting to bias for several reasons. This chapter has highlighted one such basis for this latter claim: Even some of the most classic demonstrations of bias actually provided more evidence of accuracy, agreement, or unbiased responding than they provided of inaccuracy, disagreement, or biased responding. Taken together, the four studies reviewed here actually provided far more evidence of unbiased than of biased responding. The average GJI was about .86, which means the average deviation from perfection was a mere .14.

Of course, the claim that people are far less out of touch with reality than social psychology usually suggests is based on far more than the GJI. People's expectations typically predict other's behavior, accomplishments, and characteristics far more because those expectations are accurate than because they lead to biases or self-fulfilling prophecies (for example, Jussim, 1991, in press). In contrast to stereotypes' reputation as nearly unmitigated, exaggerated, irrational, and unjustified evils that are rigidly resistant to change, stereotype accuracy is one of the largest relationships in all of social psychology (Jussim, Cain, Crawford, Harber, & Cohen, 2009). And many of the slew of errors and biases that have served as some of the foundations of the view of human judgment or memory as deeply flawed have been found to be quite useful, functional, and valid in the real world (for example, Gigerenzer, 2002; Katsikopoulos et al., 2010; Koriat et al., 2000).

Thus, our claim is not that the evidence shows that people are mostly rational. It is more limited, and merely that although abundant evidence shows that bias is alive and well, people often do quite well anyway. Even though it is premature for broad claims about how irrational versus rational people are, one thing is clear: The overwhelming emphasis on bias—without a concomitant recognition that people's social beliefs are so often valid, rational, and in touch with reality—in much of the social psychological literature is not well justified.

There really is a reality out there, and far more often than social psychology seems to recognize, it is so obvious, that it bites through our sometimes dense intellectual "top down" "cognitive miserly" expectations and beliefs. Social psychologists have a long history of extolling the allegedly "constructive" nature of social cognition, that is, the extent to which people's beliefs, expectations, stereotypes, and so forth influence and distort both their own perceptions of social reality and, sometimes, even that reality itself (for example, Fiske & Taylor, 1991; Ross et al., 2010). This review, and the evidence provided herein, does not deny an influence of social cognition on perception and reality. The evidence provided by applying the GJI to several classic studies of bias, however, suggests that social psychological perspectives emphasizing the constructive nature of social cognition are doing far more "constructing" of social reality than are the lay beliefs those theories aspire to describe.

NOTE

1. The expected value (EV) of the GJI, if people are making random guesses varies from about .5 to .58. If the criterion is 0% or 100%, the EV of the GJI for random guesses is .50. However, the EV of the GJI for random guesses has peaks of .58 when the

criterion is either 25% or 75%. At these values, more than half the possible guesses will produce GJIs greater than .50. For example, let us say people are asked to predict how often Bob Smith, a baseball player, will get a hit. In fact, he gets a hit 25% of the time. Let us further assume our sample has no knowledge whatsoever about baseball. A guess of 0% produces a GJI of .67 (.75 − .25)/.75. GJIs increase from 0% up until the guess is perfect. A guess of 25% produces a GJI of 1.00 (.75 − 0)/.75. GJIs then head down but do not drop below .5 until the guess reaches 63%, which produces a GJI of .49 (.75 − .38)/.75. In other words, guesses from 0% to 62% all produce GJIs greater than .50, and the average GJI for all 101 possible guesses (0% to 100%) is .58.

REFERENCES

Baron, R. M., Albright, L., & Malloy, T. E. (1995).Effects of behavioral and social class information on social judgment. *Personality and Social Psychology Bulletin, 21*(4), 308–315.

Brunswik, E. (1952). *The conceptual framework of psychology*. Chicago: University of Chicago Press.

Cronbach, L. J. (1955). Processes affecting scores on "understanding of others" and "assumed similarity." *Psychological Bulletin, 52*(3), 177–193.

Darley, J. M., & Gross, P. H. (1983). A hypothesis-confirming bias in labeling effects. *Journal of Personality and Social Psychology, 44*(1), 20–33.

Dawes, R. M. (1989). Statistical criteria for establishing a truly false consensus effect. *Journal of Experimental Social Psychology, 25*(1), 1–17.

Dovidio, J. F., & Gaertner, S. L. (2010). Intergroup bias. In S. T. Fiske, D. Gilbert, & G. Lindzey (Eds.), *Handbook of social psychology* (5th ed., Vol. 2, pp. 1084–1121). Hoboken, NJ: Wiley.

Fiske, S. T., & Neuberg, S. L. (1990). A continuum of impression formation, from category-based to individuating processes: Influences of information and motivation on attention and interpretation. *Advances in Experimental Social Psychology, 23*, 1–74.

Fiske, S. T., & Taylor, S. E. (1991). *Social cognition* (2nd ed.). New York: McGraw-Hill.

Funder, D. C. (1987). Errors and mistakes: Evaluating the accuracy of social judgment. *Psychological Bulletin, 101*, 75–90.

Funder, D. C. (1995). On the accuracy of personality judgment: A realistic approach. *Psychological Review, 102*(4), 652–670.

Gigerenzer, G. (2002). *Adaptive thinking: Rationality in the real world*. New York: Oxford University.

Green, D. M., & Swets, J. A. (1966). *Signal detection theory and psychophysics*. New York: Wiley.

Hastorf, A. H., & Cantril, H. (1954). They saw a game: A case study. *Journal of Abnormal and Social Psychology, 47*, 129–143.

Judd, C. M., & Park, B. (1993). Definition and assessment of accuracy in social stereotypes. *Psychological Review, 100*, 109–128.

Jussim, L. (1991). Social perception and social reality: A reflection-construction model. *Psychological Review, 98*, 54–73.

Jussim, L. (2005). Accuracy: Criticisms, controversies, criteria, components, and cognitive processes. *Advances in Experimental Social Psychology, 37*, 1–93.

Jussim, L. (in press). *Social perception and social reality: Why accuracy dominates bias and self-fulfilling prophecy*. New York: Oxford University.

Jussim, L., Cain, T., Crawford, J., Harber, K., & Cohen, F. (2009). The unbearable accuracy of stereotypes. In T. Nelson (Ed.), *Handbook of prejudice, stereotyping, and discrimination* (pp. 199–227). Hillsdale, NJ: Erlbaum.

Kahneman, D., & Tversky, A. (1973). On the psychology of prediction. *Psychological Review, 80*, 237–251.

Katsikopoulos, K. V., Schooler, L. J., & Hertwig, R. (2010). The robust beauty of ordinary information. *Psychological Review, 117*, 1259–1266.

Kenny, D. A. (1994). *Interpersonal perception: A social relations analysis.* New York: Guilford.

Koriat, A., Goldsmith, M., & Panksy, A. (2000). Toward a psychology of memory accuracy. *Annual Review of Psychology, 51*, 481–537.

Krueger, J. (1998). Enhancement bias in descriptions of self and others. *Personality and Social Psychology Bulletin, 24*(5), 505–516.

Krueger, J., & Funder, D. C. (2004). Toward a balanced social psychology: Causes, consequences, and cures for the problem-seeking approach to social behavior and cognition. *Behavioral and Brain Sciences, 27*, 313–327.

Monin, B., & Norton, M. I. (2002). Perceptions of a fluid consensus: Uniqueness bias, false consensus, false polarization, and pluralistic ignorance in a water conservation crisis. *Personality and Social Psychology Bulletin, 29*, 559–567.

Myers, D. G. (2008). *Social psychology* (9th ed.). New York: McGraw-Hill.

Richard, F. D., Bond Jr., C. F., & Stokes-Zoota, J. J. (2003). One hundred years of social psychology quantitatively described. *Review of General Psychology, 7*, 331–363.

Rosenhan, D. L. (1973). On being sane in insane places. *Science, 179*, 250–258.

Rosenthal, D. L. (1991). *Meta-analytic procedures for social research* (2nd ed.). Newbury Park, CA: Sage.

Ross, L., Lepper, M., & Ward, A. (2010). History of social psychology: Insights, challenges, and contributions to theory and application. In S. T. Fiske, D. Gilbert, & G. Lindzey (Eds.), *Handbook of social psychology* (5th ed., Vol. 1, pp. 3–50). Hoboken, NJ: Wiley.

Simon, H. A. (1956). Rational choice and the structure of the environment. *Psychological Review, 63*, 129–138.

7

A Multivariate Approach to Ambivalence
It Is More Than Meets the IV

JOHANNES ULLRICH

W hen you put that chocolate bar in your cart standing in line in the gro-
cery store, when you chase away the honey bee circling over your ham
sandwich, or when you mimic the attractive other's nonverbal behavior,
you reveal your preferences, as the economists say. In the language of psychologists,
who are more confident in their ability to measure mental states, you express a
"tendency to evaluate an object," or attitude (Eagly & Chaiken, 2007). Despite their
differences in theoretical orientation, economists and psychologists would agree
that attitudes cause behaviors. Indeed, when attitudes and behaviors are measured
appropriately (Ajzen & Fishbein, 2005; Jaccard & Blanton, 2005), they are typically
highly correlated, allowing for predictions as to what people will do or decide based
on attitudinal measures, which Louis Thurstone (1954) used to call the "obverse
psychophysical problem." That is, perhaps, unless their attitudes are ambivalent.

In this chapter, I discuss theory and research on the ways that ambivalent
attitude structures may complicate people's lives. For increased drama, I begin
by sketching out a perspective on attitudes that highlights how smoothly animal
behavior is usually guided by attitudes were it not for ambivalence. In the remainder of this chapter I offer a critical review of the logic underlying the conceptual-
ization, measurement, and statistical analysis of ambivalence, inviting the reader to
explore ambivalence as a fundamental aspect of human existence.

ATTITUDES ARE FOR ACTING

With the exception of a few enlightened individuals, people constantly evaluate.
Every waking hour we encounter perceived or imagined objects that we evaluate

by integrating memory traces and situational features in a sometimes more and sometimes less automatic fashion (Ferguson & Bargh, 2003; Wilson & Hodges, 1992). The resulting summary evaluation, or attitude, varies on a continuum from negative (minus infinity) to positive (infinity). A positive attitude implies in a quite literal sense an inclination to approach the attitude object, whereas a negative attitude inclines us to avoid or move away from the attitude object. The reverse relationship also exists. That is, we tend to infer positive attitudes from approach-related motor behaviors, such as flexing our arm or nodding our head, and negative attitudes from avoidance-related motor behaviors, such as extending our arm or shaking our head (for example, Cacioppo, Priester, & Berntson, 1993; Krieglmeyer, Deutsch, de Houwer, & de Raedt, 2010; Wells & Petty, 1980).

Such evidence of attitude embodiment illustrates the old idea that the primary function of attitudes is to facilitate behavior, which is why Francis Galton (1884) considered measuring attitudes in terms of posture, or bodily orientations. In fact, the term *valence*, which is today mainly used to describe the positive or negative evaluative quality of attitudes, was originally used to describe the action-prompting properties of attitude objects. According to Colombetti (2005), the term *valence* entered the psychological literature when Tolman was unsure how to translate Kurt Lewin's *Aufforderungscharakter*, which literally means "invitation-character," and describes the force of objects to direct behavior in terms of approach or withdrawal.

Indeed, it appears that animal brains have evolved so as to optimally prepare action by ranking behavioral options in the common currency of pleasure (Cabanac, 1992). In other words, animals regularly convert seemingly incommensurate metrics into one another to make decisions that maximize pleasure. For humans we can equate pleasure with positive valence or affect, and for other animals we stipulate that pleasure "indicates something that is biologically useful" (Panksepp, 1998, p. 182). Foraging rats accept an unpleasant drop in temperature if it is matched by a pleasant increase in nutritional value of the food to be obtained in the colder areas. Humans master the algebra necessary to select a less rewarding activity when the cherished company of a friend outweighs the more rewarding activity that can only be done alone. Although choice anomalies exist, often rising to great fame in the social judgment literature, behavior generally approximates the matching law, whereby animals distribute their activities in proportion to their reinforcement value (Herrnstein, 1970).

AMBIVALENT ATTITUDES: NOT FOR ACTING?

Complications arise when reinforcements are of mixed valence. At least since Miller's (1944) studies on experimental neurosis, we know that objects that invite both approach and withdrawal can produce hesitancy, tension, vacillation, or complete blocking of behavior. Consider rats running down a runway for a daily reinforcement (cf. Ettenberg, 2004). Food, water, sex, amphetamine, or heroin used as reinforcers cause the rats to run faster each day to get the reinforcer. They discover something that ranks high in the currency of pleasure and their positive attitude is expressed in increasingly shorter running times. Not so with cocaine. Although cocaine quickly produces euphoria, it also slowly builds up anxiety, which then becomes associated with the drug injection area. Unlike his sex rats, Ettenberg's cocaine rats take progressively longer each day to reach the goal box, which is not due to slower running but to their tendency to stop, retreat, and approach the goal box again multiple times, which is characteristic of a typical approach–avoidance conflict. (If you feel pity for these rats, be assured that they get over it with a little amount of alcohol.)

Similar observations have been made with humans using a computer mouse to express their evaluations of a target person (Vallacher, Nowak, & Kaufman, 1994). Their task was to imagine a person for whom they had positive, negative, or mixed feelings, and express their moment-to-moment feelings by moving a representation of the self on the computer screen toward or away from a representation of the target. The characteristic observation in the mixed feelings condition was a type of mouse behavior that you might perform to check if your computer is still responding, that is, a high-frequency oscillation rendering the representations of self and target as spatially close together in one second and far apart in the next.

Obviously, such oscillating evaluations are difficult to translate into action. Empirical demonstrations of human behavior that would mirror the vacillation of rats discussed earlier do not exist (except in clinical case studies perhaps), but Miller (1944) mentioned the examples of a bashful lover or a timid man urged to demand a higher salary from his boss. It is not difficult to picture these characters as they walk down the hall to the boss's door, stop, retreat, approach again, but never knock, or as they sit next to the telephone and repeatedly dial their sweetheart's number only to hang up before the first ringtone.

The other three of Miller's (1944) major criteria of approach–avoidance conflicts, hesitancy, tension, and blocking of behavior, have indirectly found their way into current theory and research on attitude ambivalence. *Hesitancy* appears in studies measuring the latency of people's self-reports of their attitudes. Ambivalent attitude holders need to integrate a greater number of evaluatively inconsistent pieces of information, which retards responses to attitude queries (for example, Bassili, 1996; van Harreveld, van der Pligt, de Vries, Wenneker, & Verhue, 2004). *Tension* has been studied as "subjective" or "felt" ambivalence (for example, Newby-Clark, McGregor, & Zanna, 2002; Priester & Petty, 1996; Thompson, Zanna, & Griffin, 1995), and physiological arousal (for example, Maio, Greenland, Bernard, & Esses, 2001; van Harreveld, Rutjens, Rotteveel, Nordgren, & van der Pligt, 2009). Finally, ambivalence may lead people to avoid the object of ambivalence altogether (for example, Hänze, 2001), which can be viewed as an instance of *behavioral blocking*.

Inaction can be fatal in emergency situations. Janis and Mann (1977) famously describe several examples of defective modes of decision making resulting from strong decisional conflict. On a more optimistic note, ambivalent attitudes in everyday life may indeed be for *not* acting and serve to prevent premature action. It is interesting to note that the term *procrastination* used to have the connotation of "wise restraint" and only acquired its negative meaning during the Industrial Revolution (Steel, 2007).

Whether adaptive or maladaptive, all of these criteria suggest that ambivalent attitudes are not for acting. However, another theoretical focus suggests that ambivalence may not at all be in the way of action. Building on Freud's idea of reactive displacement, according to which energy from the erotic impulse can be added to the hostile one or vice versa, Katz's theory of response amplification (Katz, Glass, & Cohen, 1973; Katz, Wackenhut, & Glass, 1986) holds that ambivalence should be associated with more vigorous and extreme behavior, with the direction of behavior being contingent on relative cost and availability: "Once the direction of the response has been determined, however, its intensity will be greater if there was initial ambivalence than if there was not" (Carver, Gibbons, Stephan, Glass, & Katz, 1979, p. 50). Psychoanalysts are well aware of their patients' ambivalence toward them. In a famous joke, a patient concludes the last session of treatment by first expressing his utmost gratitude to the analyst and then pulling out a gun, saying "But you know too much!"

Besides making behavior more intense and extreme, ambivalence seems to share some of the features of strong attitudes, which are defined to be not only (1) more stable, (2) more predictive of behavior, and (3) more resistant to persuasion than weak attitudes, but (4) should also have a greater impact on information processing (Krosnick & Petty, 1995). Although ambivalence would seem to be indicative of weak attitudes according to the first three of these criteria, several studies have found increased systematic processing and greater elaboration of persuasive messages among participants with ambivalent attitudes (Clarkson, Tormala, & Rucker, 2008; Jonas, Diehl, & Brömer, 1997; Maio, Bell, & Esses, 1996; Nordgren, van Harreveld, & van der Pligt, 2006).

An in-depth reading of the ambivalence literature leaves one confused (if not ambivalent). Based on the empirical evidence, ambivalent attitudes could be characterized as strong or weak, and as favorable or unfavorable for the behavioral enactment of attitudes. McGuire's (1973) seventh koan, "The opposite of a great truth is also true," reminds us that Bubba already knows the results of psychological studies even if they contradict each other. But Bubba rarely knows when a result or its opposite will be obtained in a study, which is why she has to defer to psychologists. Lest we let Bubba down, we should not be indifferent about attitude ambivalence (Thompson et al., 1995), and we should begin by asking focused research questions.

ASKING FOCUSED VERSUS DIFFUSE QUESTIONS IN RESEARCH ON AMBIVALENCE

My central argument is that much of the confusion in the empirical literature on ambivalence is the result of asking diffuse research questions. I borrow this terminology from the literature on statistical contrasts (Rosenthal, Rosnow, & Rubin, 2000), because the problem is structurally similar. Their first example of a diffuse research question deals with the hypothesis of age-related development of motor skills. Having children from five age groups play a video game, a researcher might use analysis of variance (ANOVA) to test for a main effect of age on motor skills treating age as a nominal scale (i.e., several unordered categories). The underlying null hypothesis is that all age groups have the same mean. Such a test is diffuse because it includes a large subset of results that are highly implausible (for instance, a linear age decline of motor skills) and is not specifically sensitive to results that are more plausible *a priori* (e.g., a linear increase in motor skills; for a more detailed example of the misuse of ANOVA, see Hale, 1977).

The problem of asking diffuse questions in ambivalence research has two aspects: one related to experimental design and one to statistical analysis. I will first try to clarify conceptual distinctions relevant to study design by way of introducing the idea of bivariate evaluative space, and then give an empirical illustration of the statistical aspect of the problem in the next section.

Consider the hypothesis of response amplification: Behavior should be more intense "if there was initial ambivalence than if there was not" (Carver et al., 1979, p. 50). Even granting that the meaning of ambivalence is unequivocally understood as the presence of both positivity and negativity toward the attitude object, what exactly is the absence of ambivalence? To provide a context for ambivalent attitudes, it is useful to conceive of the bases or components of attitudes as defined by a bivariate evaluative plane (Cacioppo, Gardner, & Berntson, 1997).

Figure 7.1 illustrates the idea that positive and negative attitude components (e.g., beliefs about a behavior) do not have to be reciprocally related to each other, allowing for the existence of ambivalence. Consistent with the general definition of attitude as evaluative tendency (Eagly & Chaiken, 2007), the model of bivariate evaluative space implies that attitudes are the net difference of positivity minus negativity. Thus, along the coactivity axis, a range of different attitude structures (combinations of positivity and negativity) all implies the same neutral attitude. Attitudes near the minimum of underlying positivity and negativity may be called indifferent, and attitudes near the maximum of positivity and negativity may be

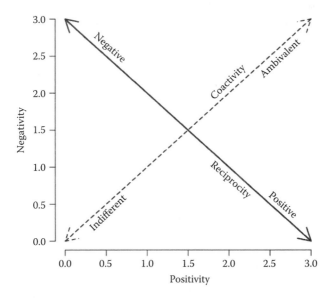

Figure 7.1   Model of a bivariate evaluative space.

called ambivalent (Kaplan, 1972). In contrast, moving along the reciprocity axis we find that different attitude structures are associated with different attitudes, varying from highly negative (top left) to highly positive (bottom right). Positivity and negativity are rarely perfectly reciprocally related (i.e., a correlation of −1), but their relationship naturally varies across attitude objects (see the empirical example in the next section).

Whenever positivity and negativity are to some extent independent, we can roughly divide our sample into four groups of people: those holding negative attitudes, positive attitudes, indifferent attitudes, and those holding ambivalent attitudes. If we want to demonstrate response amplification among ambivalent people, what should be the comparison group? A fair comparison would seem to consist of contrasting ambivalent people with indifferent people. It would be an interesting result to find quantitative differences in behavior between groups of people with the same net attitude. A bolder hypothesis would also contrast ambivalent people with positive and negative people. Perhaps the reactive displacement that is hypothesized to underlie response amplification is so strong that it increases the intensity of ambivalent behavior beyond the levels found among highly negative or highly positive people. In short, once we begin to sharpen the focus of a diffuse research question, several distinct hypotheses emerge that are more or less plausible or risky.

To date, most ambivalence research has not considered the full range of outcomes implied by a bivariate evaluative space. In response amplification studies, research questions are typically diffuse in that they contrast ambivalent people with unspecified "others" (for example, Bell & Esses, 2002) or construct experimental conditions in which the attitude object is presumably evaluated ambivalently or not (for example, a confederate belonging to a stigmatized or nonstigmatized group; Gibbons, Stephan, Stephenson, & Petty, 1980). Although it is interesting to learn that responses to stigmatized others are more extreme than responses to nonstigmatized others, results obtained from such study designs do not illuminate the nature of ambivalence. Are ambivalent people more extreme in their responses compared with indifferent people? Are they more extreme compared with positive people, or negative people, or both, or are they more extreme than all three other groups of people?

The greatest concern is that the difference between ambivalent and nonambivalent people could be a statistical artifact. This possibility can be seen more clearly if we closely examine the formulas underlying the two most frequently used indices for quantifying the amount of ambivalence associated with a given attitude structure. According to Kaplan's (1972) formula, which is usually referred to as the Conflicting Reactions Model (CRM), ambivalence corresponds to total affect (the sum of positivity and negativity) minus polarization (the absolute difference between positivity and negativity):

$$A_{CRM} = (P + N) - |P - N| \tag{7.1}$$

The CRM suggests that ambivalence is a positive function of the conflicting reaction (cf. Priester & Petty, 1996). When positivity is higher than negativity, ambivalence corresponds to (twice) the amount of negativity and vice versa. A variant of this formula recognizes a potential drawback of the CRM, namely, that it ignores how similar positivity and negativity are regardless of their intensity, although it could be argued that the greater the difference between positivity and negativity, the less problematic the evaluative conflict. Thus, the Similarity–Intensity Model (SIM) (Thompson et al., 1995) modifies Kaplan's (1972) formula as follows:

$$A_{SIM} = (P + N)/2 - |P - N| \tag{7.2}$$

The SIM suggests that ambivalence increases with the strength of the conflicting reaction and decreases (as a flatter function) with the strength of the dominant reaction (cf. Priester & Petty, 1996). For example, a person with $P = 3$ and $N = 1$ would be less ambivalent than a person with $P = 2$ and $N = 1$, reflecting the greater dissimilarity of positivity and negativity.

Table 7.1 shows the predicted values of ambivalence according to the CRM and the SIM, ranging from 0 (minimum of ambivalence) to 1 (maximum of ambivalence). By comparing the patterns predicted by the CRM and the SIM, we can verify that the SIM distinguishes between various attitude structures that are considered equivalent by the CRM. However, an important conclusion to draw from Table 7.1 is that both models predict the same value of ambivalence for multiple combinations of positivity and negativity. For instance, ambivalence is at its minimum when positivity is minimal and negativity is maximal, but also when negativity is minimal and positivity is maximal. Intuitively, this fact suggests that statistical relationships involving ambivalence as a single variable must be ambiguous with regard to the underlying pattern of positivity and negativity.

To appreciate the possibility of a statistical artifact being responsible for a prima facie response amplification effect, let us assume that the SIM formula (Equation 7.2) is used to classify people as ambivalent (above the median) or not. A demonstration of response amplification requires two experimental conditions. In one condition, we expect more negative responses (e.g., an unfavorable message

TABLE 7.1   Predicted Values of Ambivalence for Different Combinations of Positivity and Negativity

		Negativity			
	Positivity	0	1	2	3
Conflicting Reactions Model (CRM)	0	0	0	0	0
	1	0	.33	.33	.33
	2	0	.33	.67	.67
	3	0	.33	.67	1
Similarity–Intensity Model (SIM)	0	.33	.22	.11	0
	1	.22	.56	.44	.33
	2	.11	.44	.78	.67
	3	0	.33	.67	1

Note: Entries are scaled on a percent metric from 0 to 1 because the minima and maxima differ between the CRM and the SIM.

about an out-group is presented to participants), and in the other condition we expect more positive responses (e.g., a favorable message is presented). Will ambivalent participants be more negative in the negative condition and more positive in the positive condition compared with nonambivalent participants?

It can be shown (Ullrich, Schermelleh-Engel, & Böttcher, 2008, Equation 7) that this result is a statistical necessity when the negative behavior observed in the negative condition (of all participants, that is, not only the ambivalent ones) depends more strongly on negativity than on positivity, and when the positive behavior in the positive condition depends more strongly on positivity than on negativity, which is not implausible. When this condition is met, our results would not reveal anything about our ambivalent participants except that their positive and negative attitude components were above average to begin with. But the same could be said about participants with univalent positive attitudes in the positive condition and participants with univalent negative attitudes in the negative condition, which means that our test confounds overall ambivalence with its components.

If we allow for the possibility that positive and negative attitude components are not reciprocally related (as we should if the phenomenon of ambivalence is not a delusion), then we should design studies that isolate the components of ambivalence. In our fictitious example of a study on response amplification we might assume that positivity and negativity are defined as either low or high by experimental manipulations, so that four groups of participants can be distinguished who are positive, negative, ambivalent, or indifferent toward the attitude object (see Figure 7.1). We should then ask six focused research questions: Do ambivalent participants respond more positively to a favorable message, and more negatively to an unfavorable message, compared with positive, negative, and indifferent participants, respectively? In addition, we might test the assumption of the SIM that indifferent participants also show more extreme responses in both the positive and the negative message condition than positive or negative participants.

More generally, we should ask: Are responses in the negative condition more negative, and are responses in the positive condition more positive, the higher the conflicting reaction, whether it is positivity or negativity? If we sympathize with the idea that the similarity of positivity and negativity also contributes to ambivalent responding (as assumed by the SIM), we should also ask whether the dominant reactions reduce response extremity, whether positivity or negativity is dominant.

A MULTIVARIATE APPROACH TO DATA ANALYSIS IN AMBIVALENCE RESEARCH

The previous example of a response amplification study has revealed problems with study designs that represent ambivalence as a single independent variable. I have argued that designs that separate positivity and negativity enable us to avoid artifacts by asking focused research questions. However, a second problem that is frequently encountered in ambivalence research is that when interest lies in naturally occurring attitudes, ambivalence tends to be measured rather than manipulated. This is usually done by means of a split semantic differential procedure (Kaplan, 1972), in which participants are asked to separately rate the extent of their positivity and negativity toward an attitude object. It is bad practice to force such quantitative variables into the familiar ANOVA scheme by dichotomizing them on their central tendencies (MacCallum, Zhang, Preacher, & Rucker, 2002). Thus, an important question is how to ask focused research questions about the effects of ambivalence when its components are measured as continuous variables.

Recently, two independent methodological contributions have converged on similar solutions to this problem (Locke & Braun, 2009; Ullrich et al., 2008). Because the approach suggested by Locke and Braun (2009) is less general and does not model potential multiplicative effects of positivity and negativity, I will describe the multivariate approach that my colleagues and I have proposed. The empirical material I use is from an unpublished study on the bivariate attitude structures of several attitude objects, one of which was also used to measure subjective ambivalence. This brings us back to Miller's (1944) tension criterion of evaluative conflict and to the interesting question if social judges and decision-makers are unbiased perceivers of their own ambivalence.

In 2005, 148 German students at Philipps University, Marburg, Germany (122 women, median age = 21, range from 18 to 29), volunteered to complete an attitude questionnaire. Participants rated their positivity and negativity toward six attitude objects: Michael Jackson, women, Turks in Germany, homosexuals, your mother, your partner (single participants were instructed to rate their best friend instead). The order of positivity and negativity measures as well as the order of objects was varied, but no order effects were observed. Based on Kaplan (1972), when rating positivity, participants were instructed to ignore any negative qualities and rate how positive the positive qualities of the attitude object were on a scale from 0 (not at all) to 3 (very much). Similarly, when rating negativity, participants were instructed to ignore any positive qualities and rate how negative the negative qualities of the attitude object were (from 0 to 3). Positivity and negativity were measured with three items each (positive versus negative, pleasant versus unpleasant, worthy of love versus worthy of hatred). Cronbach's alphas for positivity and negativity toward Turks in Germany, the focus of the present empirical example, were both equal to .83.

Subjective ambivalence toward Turks in Germany was assessed by asking participants to indicate their level of agreement to the following statements on a 1 to 6 scale with the endpoints labeled *do not agree at all* and *agree completely*: (1) "With regard to the issue of 'Turks in Germany', I find it hard to be pro or con." (2) "I have mixed feelings toward Turks living in Germany." (3) "I feel conflicted toward Turks living in Germany." Cronbach's alpha was .77, the mean was 3.63 ($SD = 1.23$). Table 7.2 shows descriptive statistics of the measures of participants' positive and negative attitude components. Note that positivity and negativity were unrelated for most attitude objects, confirming the assumption underlying Cacioppo et al.'s (1997) model of evaluative space that positivity and negativity are not necessarily reciprocally related to each other. Reciprocity is approximated for the attitude objects "your mother" and "your partner," as might often be the case with important others (for example, people's spouses; Fincham & Linfield, 1997). Still, the correlation is far from being perfectly negative, which implies that a subset of participants might well have ambivalent attitude structures.

TABLE 7.2   Means (Standard Deviations) and
Intercorrelations of Positivity and Negativity

Attitude Object	Positivity	Negativity	r
Michael Jackson	1.12	1.83	−.06
	(.75)	(.77)	
Women	2.47	1.35	.02
	(.54)	(.69)	
Turks	1.75	1.56	.08
	(.69)	(.80)	
Homosexuals	1.90	.93	.09
	(.77)	(.72)	
Your mother	2.64	1.13	−.51
	(.53)	(.75)	
Your partner	2.72	1.06	−.41
	(.42)	(.67)	

Note: Positivity and negativity are scaled from 0 to 3.

Let us now consider the question of how positivity and negativity toward Turks, the largest ethnic minority group in Germany, relate to participants' subjective reports of ambivalence. The conventional approach would be to quantify ambivalence using the indices implied by the CRM or SIM (see earlier) and then calculate the sample correlation between ambivalence and subjective reports of ambivalence. In the present sample, ambivalence and subjective ambivalence are moderately to strongly correlated, if one adopts the usual verbal labels for correlational effect sizes ($r = .38$ for the SIM index and $r = .36$ for the CRM index), which is a typical result (Priester & Petty, 1996; Riketta, 2000). However, assuming that we are looking at two measures of the same psychological phenomenon, the correlations appear to be too low.

Given the theoretical and empirical hesitations about accepting these correlations as evidence that people can accurately report the amount of ambivalence inherent to their attitude structures, it is useful to explore the relationship between ambivalence and subjective ambivalence. To visualize the joint effect of two variables (positivity and negativity) on a third variable (subjective ambivalence) with as little information loss as possible, I translated the amount of subjective ambivalence into the size and color of points in a bivariate scatterplot. All panels of Figure 7.2 show the empirical scatterplot of positivity and negativity from the current data. Some random noise was added to each observation to avoid excessive overplotting. The larger and the darker a data point in the top left panel of Figure 7.2, the higher the subjective ambivalence (scaled on a percent metric) reported by this participant. The top right and bottom panels of Figure 7.2 display the amount of subjective ambivalence predicted by the SIM and CRM, respectively, for a given participant. Note that these two plots mainly differ with regard to the observations in the lower left corner. Points are smaller and lighter in the CRM plot because the CRM ignores the similarity of low-intensity attitude components.

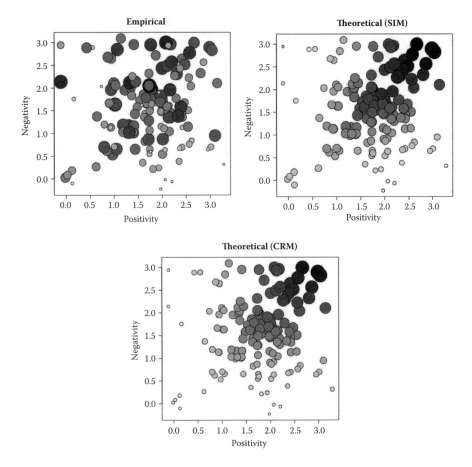

Figure 7.2   Observed and predicted ambivalence as a function of positivity and negativity.

Of course, a comparison of the top left panel in Figure 7.2 with the other panels quickly reveals that many observations strongly differ in size and darkness from the values predicted according to CRM or SIM. The question is are we looking at random or systematic deviations from the model. Upon closer inspection of the empirical plot it appears that subjective ambivalence is more strongly related to negativity than to positivity. As we move up from low negativity to high negativity, we find larger and darker points, whereas there appears to be no systematic change in size and darkness as we move right from low positivity to high positivity, except for smaller and lighter points when negativity is low, which resembles the lower portion of the top right panel (SIM). In other words, the symmetry of increasing subjective ambivalence along the coactivity axis in the theoretical plots does not reappear in the empirical plot.

The multivariate approach to ambivalence models (MAAM) (Ullrich et al., 2008) allows us to determine more precisely if and how the empirical relationships deviate from the predictions of the ambivalence models. For the case of ambivalence as a conceptual independent variable predicting an outcome variable, the MAAM estimates the following multiple regression equation:

$$Y = b_0 + b_1 P + b_2 N + b_3 W + b_4 PN + b_5 WP + b_6 WN + \varepsilon \qquad (7.3)$$

In Equation 7.3, Y refers to the dependent variable (i.e., subjective ambivalence in the present case); P and N refer to positivity and negativity, respectively; and W is a dummy variable that is set to 0 when $N < P$, to 1 when $P > N$, and that is randomly set to 0 or 1 when $P = N$. This dummy variable is important to determine W(hich) of positivity and negativity is the dominant or conflicting reaction. Finally, the terms PN, WP, and WN refer to products (interactions) of the aforementioned variables, and ε is a random error term. Note that for interpretational purposes, it is important to center (subtract the mean from) or standardize positivity and negativity before creating the product terms.

According to the MAAM, the assumptions of ambivalence models regarding how combinations of positivity and negativity give rise to ambivalence need to be translated into a pattern of predictions about regression coefficients. The coefficients b_1 and b_2 indicate the influence of positivity as a dominant reaction and negativity as a conflicting reaction, respectively, because we have coded W as 0 when negativity is smaller than positivity. All ambivalence models agree that ambivalence should increase with the strength of the conflicting reaction (Priester & Petty, 1996). Thus, as shown in Table 7.3, both the SIM and the CRM hypothesize the coefficient b_2 to be positive. In other words, when negativity is the conflicting

TABLE 7.3   Patterns of Regression Coefficients Implied by the Conceptual Hypothesis of a Positive Effect of Ambivalence on Subjective Reports of Ambivalence and Empirical Results

Coefficients	Hypotheses		Constraints		Empirical Results	
	CRM	SIM	CRM	SIM	b	SE
Intercept					.24	.17
$b_1 P$			$= 0$	$= -\dfrac{b_2}{3}$	$-.41°$	.16
$b_2 N$	> 0	> 0			$.59°°$	.18
$b_3 W$			$= 0$	$= 0$	$-.15$	.23
$b_4 PN$			$= 0$	$= 0$	.09	.09
$b_5 WP$			$= b_2$	$= \dfrac{4b_2}{3}$	$.48°$	.24
$b_6 WN$			$= b_2$	$= -\dfrac{4b_2}{3}$	$-.27$	.28

Note: The multiple correlation was $R = .5$. $°°\, p < .01$, $°\, p < .05$. CRM = Conflicting Reactions Model (Kaplan, 1972), SIM = Similarity–Intensity Model (Thompson et al., 1995). P and N refer to commensurate measures of positivity and negativity toward the attitude object; W is a dummy variable that equals 0 when $P > N$, that equals 1 when $P < N$, and that is randomly set to 1 or 0 when $P = N$. PN, WP, and WN refer to product terms representing interactions among the aforementioned variables.

reaction, subjective ambivalence should increase with increasing negativity. The models disagree with regard to the influence of the dominant reaction. According to the CRM, the coefficient b_1 should be zero. In other words, when positivity is the dominant reaction, changes in positivity should leave subjective ambivalence unaffected. In contrast, according to the SIM, when positivity is stronger than negativity, increases in positivity should reduce subjective ambivalence, which is reflected in the constraint $b_1 = -b_2/3$, meaning that the coefficient b_1 should be only a third of the size of b_2 and of opposite sign. (Note that the sign and expected relative size of the coefficients may be more easily understood by reexamining Table 7.1; for a more detailed derivation, see Ullrich et al., 2008).

For those participants whose positivity is smaller than their negativity, we derive the effects of the conflicting (i.e., positive) and dominant (i.e., negative) reactions by forming the sums of b_1 and b_2, respectively, and the corresponding interaction terms b_5 and b_6. That is, when positivity is the conflicting reaction, its influence is given by $b_1 + b_5$, and when negativity is the dominant reaction, its influence is given by $b_2 + b_6$. The constraints listed in Table 7.3 reflect the symmetry assumptions of the ambivalence models, which require, for example, that the effect of positivity as a conflicting reaction should be the same as the effect of negativity as a conflicting reaction $(b_1 + b_5 = b_2)$. Finally, the CRM and SIM make no assumptions regarding the effect of being more positive than negative about an attitude object (or vice versa), which implies that the coefficient b_3 is expected to be zero. Likewise, these models do not assume multiplicative effects of positivity and negativity, which implies that b_4 should be zero. It is important to model this interaction to obtain unbiased estimates of the other parameters (Yzerbyt, Muller, & Judd, 2004) and to explore the viability of another model of ambivalence, according to which ambivalence depends on the product of positivity and negativity (the cross-product model; for example, Hass, Katz, Rizzo, Bailey, & Moore, 1992).

The parameter estimates for Equation 7.3 as applied to the data on attitudes toward Turks in Germany are shown in the rightmost column of Table 7.3. Note that the dependent variable subjective ambivalence was rescaled to a range from 0 to 1 so that the unstandardized coefficients can be interpreted as percent change in subjective ambivalence, and positivity and negativity were standardized before the product terms were computed.

Starting with the influence of the conflicting reactions, we find that $b_2 = .59$, which indicates a significantly positive effect of negativity as conflicting reaction. When negativity is the conflicting reaction and is increased by 1 SD, subjective ambivalence increases by 59%, which is consistent with both the CRM and the SIM. However, the sum $b_1 + b_5$, indicating the influence of positivity as conflicting reaction, equals only .07, $t(141) = .47$, $p = .64$. Thus, only negativity as conflicting reaction seems to have the expected positive effect on subjective ambivalence.

Regarding the influence of the dominant reactions, we find that $b_1 = -.41$, which indicates a significantly negative effect of positivity as dominant reaction. Ignoring the additional requirement that the effect should be only a third of b_2 in absolute size, this effect is consistent with the SIM. However, the sum $b_2 + b_6$, indicating the influence of negativity as the dominant reaction, equals .32, $t(141) = 1.80$, $p = .07$.

Thus, only positivity as the dominant reaction seems to have the negative effect on subjective ambivalence expected by the SIM.

Another way of structuring these results is by positivity and negativity. Coefficient b_2 indicates a positive effect of negativity as conflicting reaction, but the nonsignificant coefficient b_6 indicates that this influence is not reduced to zero (cf. CRM) or below zero (cf. SIM) when the status of negativity changes from conflicting to dominant reaction. In line with the assumptions of the SIM, the coefficient b_1 indicates a negative effect of positivity as the dominant reaction and the interaction b_5 indicates that this effect is modified when the status of positivity changes from dominant to conflicting reaction. However, as we have seen before, the simple slope of positivity as conflicting reaction, which is given by the sum $b_1 + b_5$, is not different from zero.

In summary, the statistical analyses confirm the visual impression of asymmetrical effects of positivity and negativity (see the top left panel of Figure 7.2). The German sample studied here tends to report more subjective ambivalence about Turks, the higher their negativity toward Turks. Furthermore, for those who are more positive than negative about Turks, subjective ambivalence is lower, and the higher their positivity. Yet for those who are more negative than positive, positivity does not influence subjective ambivalence. Contrary to what the positive correlations between subjective ambivalence and the CRM and SIM index variables of ambivalence might have suggested, the results of the current application of the MAAM suggest that subjective ambivalence is not a function of the actual ambivalence existing in people's attitude structures. It seems that when people report "mixed feelings," they essentially express their negativity toward Turks. If such results turned out to be replicable, and they may well depend on cultural norms for interpreting the words *mixed* or *conflicted*, they would seem to caution us against using subjective measures of ambivalence to test theoretical predictions about the effects of ambivalence as long as a core assumption of ambivalence models is that its effects are driven by the conflicting reaction, *irrespective* of whether positivity or negativity is the conflicting reaction.

CONCLUSION

In this chapter I have fallen short of the implicit goal shared by all psychologists (cf. Gilbert, 2006), which is to write something that would allow me to finish the sentence "The human being is the only animal that …" Instead I have argued that it makes sense for ambivalence research to go back as far as Miller's rat models of conflict and use new approaches to examine old hypotheses such as the experience of tension. Humans may indeed turn out to be special with regard to their experience of ambivalence. For example, the Freudian idea of response amplification after reactive displacement might require a human unconscious. Alternatively, we might find that ambivalence works in much the same way for many different animals including humans, as seems to be the case for our broader attitudinal architecture. We will not find out, however, if we continue to ask diffuse research questions.

As a possible step forward, I have discussed a multivariate approach to ambivalence models, which is designed to answer focused questions about the effects of the positive and negative attitude components. In an empirical demonstration we have seen that subjective reports of ambivalence do not appear to be associated with ambivalent attitude structures but rather with more negative ones. However, recent theorizing suggests that ambivalent attitudes should especially be experienced as such when people confront a binary behavioral choice (Cunningham, Zelazo, Packer, & van Bavel, 2007; van Harreveld, van der Pligt, & de Liver, 2009). The multivariate model discussed earlier could easily be extended by introducing choice as a moderator variable. Furthermore, in hypotheses derived from the attitude strength perspective (Krosnick & Petty, 1995), ambivalence assumes the role of a moderator variable, and my colleagues and I have elsewhere presented a detailed exposition of statistical analyses that are useful in this scenario (Ullrich et al., 2008).

I began this chapter by noting that attitudes are for acting and that ambivalent attitudes may not be for acting. Animal models suggest that ambivalent attitudes may indeed be for not acting. Perhaps at last I should give in to the temptation of saying that the human being is the only animal who ... prefers the company of ambivalent others when he or she is ambivalent rather than indifferent (Ullrich & Krueger, 2010). Comparative psychologists, falsify that!

AUTHOR NOTE

Writing of this chapter was facilitated by Vacation Grant SON060810 from Wolfgang Ullrich.

REFERENCES

Ajzen, I., & Fishbein, M. (2005). The influence of attitudes on behavior. In D. Albarracín, B. T. Johnson, & M. P. Zanna (Eds.), *The handbook of attitudes* (pp. 173–221). Mahwah, NJ: Erlbaum.

Bassili, J. N. (1996). Meta-judgmental versus operative indexes of psychological attributes: The case of measures of attitude strength. *Journal of Personality and Social Psychology, 71,* 637–653.

Bell, D. W., & Esses, V. M. (2002). Ambivalence and response amplification: A motivational perspective. *Personality and Social Psychology Bulletin, 28,* 1143–1152.

Cabanac, M. (1992). Pleasure: The common currency. *Journal of Theoretical Biology, 155,* 173–200.

Cacioppo, J. T., Gardner, W.L., & Berntson, G.G. (1997). Beyond bipolar conceptualizations and measures: The case of attitudes and evaluative space. *Personality and Social Psychology Review, 1,* 3–25.

Cacioppo, J. T., Priester, J. R., & Berntson, G. G. (1993). Rudimentary determinants of attitudes. II: Arm flexion and extension have differential effects on attitudes. *Journal of Personality and Social Psychology, 65,* 5–17.

Carver, C. S., Gibbons, F. X., Stephan, W. G., Glass, D. C., & Katz, I. (1979). Ambivalence and evaluative response amplification. *Bulletin of the Psychonomic Society, 13,* 50–52.

Clarkson, J. J., Tormala, Z. L., & Rucker, D. D. (2008). A new look at the consequences of attitude certainty: The amplification hypothesis. *Journal of Personality and Social Psychology, 95,* 810–825.

Colombetti, G. (2005). Appraising valence. *Journal of Consciousness Studies, 12*, 103–126.

Cunningham, W. A., Zelazo, P. D., Packer, D. J., & van Bavel, J. J. (2007). The iterative reprocessing model: A multilevel framework for attitudes and evaluation. *Social Cognition, 25*, 736–760.

Eagly, A. H., & Chaiken, S. (2007). The advantages of an inclusive definition of attitude. *Social Cognition, 25*, 582–602.

Ettenberg, A. (2004). Opponent process properties of self-administered cocaine. *Neuroscience and Biobehavioral Reviews, 27*, 721–728.

Fazio, R. H. (1995). Attitudes as object-evaluation associations: Determinants, consequences, and correlates of attitude accessibility. In R. E. Petty, J. A. Krosnick (Eds.), *Attitude strength: Antecedents and consequences* (pp. 247–282). Hillsdale, NJ: Erlbaum.

Ferguson, M. J., & Bargh, J. A. (2003). The constructive nature of automatic evaluation. In J. Musch & K. C. Klauer (Eds.), *The psychology of evaluation: Affective processes in cognition and emotion* (pp. 169–188). Mahwah, NJ: Erlbaum.

Fincham, F. D., & Linfield, K. J. (1997). A new look at marital quality: Can spouses feel positive and negative about their marriage? *Journal of Family Psychology, 11*, 489–502.

Galton, F. (1884). Measurement of character. *Fortnightly Review, 42*, 179–185.

Gibbons, F. X., Stephan, W. G., Stephenson, B., & Petty, C. R. (1980). Reactions to stigmatized others: Response amplification vs. sympathy. *Journal of Experimental Social Psychology, 16*, 591–605.

Gilbert, D. T. (2006). *Stumbling on happiness*. New York: Knopf.

Hale, G. A. (1977). On use of ANOVA in developmental research. *Child Development, 43*, 1101–1106.

Hänze, M. (2001). Ambivalence, conflict, and decision making: Attitudes and feelings in Germany towards NATO's military intervention in the Kosovo war. *European Journal of Social Psychology, 31*, 693–706.

Hass, R. G., Katz, I., Rizzo, N., Bailey, J., & Moore, L. (1992). When racial ambivalence evokes negative affect, using a disguised measure of mood. *Personality and Social Psychology Bulletin, 18*, 786–797.

Herrnstein, R. J. (1970). On the law of effect. *Journal of the Experimental Analysis of Behavior, 13*, 243–266.

Jaccard, J., & Blanton, H. (2005). The origins and structure of behavior: Conceptualizing behavior in attitude research. In D. Albarracín, B. T. Johnson, & M. P. Zanna (Eds.), *The handbook of attitudes* (pp. 125–172). Mahwah, NJ: Erlbaum.

Janis, I. L., & Mann, L. (1977). *Decision making: A psychological analysis of conflict, choice and commitment*. New York, NY: Free Press.

Jonas, K., Diehl, M., & Brömer, P. (1997). Effects of attitudinal ambivalence on information processing and attitude-intention consistency. *Journal of Experimental Social Psychology, 33*, 190–210.

Kaplan, K. J. (1972). On the ambivalence-indifference problem in attitude theory and measurement: A suggested modification of the semantic differential technique. *Psychological Bulletin, 77*, 361–372.

Katz, I., Glass, D. C., & Cohen, S. (1973). Ambivalence, guilt, and the scapegoating of minority group victims. *Journal of Experimental Social Psychology, 9*, 423–436.

Katz, I., Wackenhut, J., & Glass, D. C. (1986). An ambivalence-amplification theory of behavior toward the stigmatized. In S. Worchel & W. G. Austin (Eds.), *Psychology of intergroup relations* (pp. 103–117). Chicago: Nelson-Hall.

Krieglmeyer, R., Deutsch, R., de Houwer, J., & de Raedt, R. (2010). Being moved: Valence activates approach-avoidance behavior independently of evaluation and approach-avoidance intentions. *Psychological Science, 21*, 607–613.

Krosnick, J. A., & Petty, R. E. (1995). Attitude strength: An overview. In R. E. Petty & J. A. Krosnick (Eds.), *Attitude strength: Antecedents and consequences* (pp. 1–24). Mahwah, NJ: Erlbaum.

Locke, K. D., & Braun, C. C. (2009). Ambivalence versus valence: Analyzing the effects of opposing attitudes. *Social Cognition, 27,* 89–104.

MacCallum, R. C., Zhang, S., Preacher, K. J., & Rucker, D. D. (2002). On the practice of dichotomization of quantitative variables. *Psychological Methods, 7,* 19–40.

Maio, G. R., Bell, D. W., & Esses, V. M. (1996). Ambivalence and persuasion: The processing of messages about immigrant groups. *Journal of Experimental Social Psychology, 32,* 513–536.

Maio, G. R., Greenland, K., Bernard, M., & Esses, V. M. (2001). Effects of intergroup ambivalence on information processing: The role of physiological arousal. *Group Processes and Intergroup Relations, 4,* 355–372.

McGuire, W. J. (1973). The yin and yang of progress in social psychology: Seven koan. *Journal of Personality and Social Psychology, 26,* 446–456.

Miller, N. E. (1944). Experimental studies of conflict behavior. In J. McV. Hunt (Ed.), *Personality and behavior disorders* (pp. 431–465). New York: Ronald Press.

Newby-Clark, I. R., McGregor, I., & Zanna, M. P. (2002). Thinking and caring about cognitive inconsistency: When and for whom does attitudinal ambivalence feel uncomfortable? *Journal of Personality and Social Psychology, 82,* 157–166.

Nordgren, L. F., van Harreveld, F., & van der Pligt, J. (2006). Ambivalence, discomfort, and motivated information processing. *Journal of Experimental Social Psychology, 42,* 252–258.

Panksepp, J. (1998). *Affective neuroscience.* Oxford, UK: Oxford University Press.

Priester, J. M., & Petty, R. E. (1996). The gradual threshold model of ambivalence: Relating the positive and negative bases of attitudes to subjective ambivalence. *Journal of Personality and Social Psychology, 71,* 431–449.

Riketta, M. (2000). Discriminative validation of numerical indices of attitude ambivalence. *Current Research in Social Psychology, 5,* 63–83.

Rosenthal, R., Rosnow, R. L., & Rubin, D. B. (2000). *Contrasts and effect sizes in behavioral research: A correlational approach.* Cambridge, UK: Cambridge University Press.

Steel, P. (2007). The nature of procrastination: A meta-analytic and theoretical review of quintessential self-regulatory failure. *Psychological Bulletin, 133,* 65–94.

Thompson, M. M., Zanna, M. P., & Griffin, D. W. (1995). Let's not be indifferent about (attitudinal) ambivalence. In R. E. Petty & J. A. Krosnick (Eds.), *Attitude strength: Antecedents and consequences* (pp. 361–386). Mahwah, NJ: Erlbaum.

Thurstone, L. L. (1954). The measurement of value. *Psychological Review, 61,* 47–58.

Ullrich, J., & Krueger, J. I. (2010). Interpersonal liking from bivariate attitude similarity. *Social Psychological and Personality Science, 1,* 214–221.

Ullrich, J., Schermelleh-Engel, K., & Böttcher, B. (2008). The moderator effect that wasn't there: Statistical problems in ambivalence research. *Journal of Personality and Social Psychology, 95,* 774–794.

Vallacher, R. R., Nowak, A., & Kaufman, J. (1994). Intrinsic dynamics of social judgment. *Journal of Personality and Social Psychology, 67,* 20–34.

van Harreveld, F., Rutjens, B. T., Rotteveel, M., Nordgren, L. F., & van der Pligt, J. (2009). Ambivalence and decisional conflict as a cause of psychological discomfort: Feeling tense before jumping off the fence. *Journal of Experimental Social Psychology, 45,* 167–173.

van Harreveld, F., van der Pligt, J., de Vries, N. K., Wenneker, C., & Verhue, D. (2004). Ambivalence and information integration in attitudinal judgment. *British Journal of Social Psychology, 43,* 431–447.

van Harreveld, F., van der Pligt, J., & de Liver, Y. N. (2009). The agony of ambivalence and ways to resolve it: Introducing the MAID model. *Personality and Social Psychology Review, 13*, 45–61.

Wells, G. L., & Petty, R. E. (1980). The effects of overt head movements on persuasion: Compatibility and incompatibility of responses. *Basic and Applied Social Psychology, 1*, 219–230.

Wilson, T. D., & Hodges, S. D. (1992). Attitudes as temporary constructions. In L. Martin & A. Tesser (Eds.), *The construction of social judgment* (pp. 37–65). Hillsdale, NJ: Erlbaum.

Yzerbyt, V. Y., Muller, D., & Judd, C. M. (2004). Adjusting researchers' approach to adjustment: On the use of covariates when testing interactions. *Journal of Experimental Social Psychology, 40*, 424–431.

Section III

Ecological Rationality

8

Simple Heuristics in a Complex Social World

ULRICH HOFFRAGE and RALPH HERTWIG

We have all had the experience. Agonizing over a difficult decision—be it a matter of the heart, a moral predicament, a risky financial proposition, or a grave medical decision—we have on occasion wished for ourselves a sage *consigliere* who would simply tell us the right thing to do. When Joseph Priestley, an eminent 18th-century scientist and discoverer of oxygen, faced a particularly difficult choice, he had no need to dream up a wise man—he knew one. It was Benjamin Franklin, 27 years his senior, one of the Founding Fathers of the United States, and a noted polymath. Asked for his counsel, Franklin did not tell Priestley what to do. Franklin (1772/1987) gave him a potentially even more precious piece of advice—a versatile decision tool that can be employed to decide which of two options to choose, whatever the options may be:

> In the Affair of so much Importance to you, wherein you ask my Advice, I cannot for want of sufficient Premises, advise you what to determine, but if you please I will tell you how. ... My Way is, to divide half a Sheet of Paper by a Line into two Columns, writing over the one *Pro*, and over the other *Con*. Then during three or four Days Consideration I put down under the different Heads short Hints of the different Motives that at different Times occur to me for or against the Measure. When I have thus got them all together in one View, I endeavour to estimate their respective Weights; and where I find two, one on each side, that seem equal, I strike them both out: If I find a Reason *pro* equal to some two Reasons *con*, I strike out the three. If I judge some two Reasons con equal to some three Reasons pro, I strike out the five; and thus proceeding I find at length where the Ballance lies; and if after a Day or two of farther Consideration nothing new that is of Importance occurs on either side, I come to a Determination accordingly. And tho' the Weight of Reasons cannot be taken with the Precision of Algebraic Quantities, yet when each is

> thus considered separately and comparatively, and the whole lies before me, I think I can judge better, and am less likely to take a rash Step; and in fact I have found great Advantage from this kind of Equation, in what may be called *Moral or Prudential* Algebra. (p. 878)

Franklin's decision tool is to search for all considerations, positive or negative, weight them with care, and tot them up to find out where the balance lies. Franklin's tool embodies "two commandments that are often taken as characteristic of rational judgment" (Gigerenzer & Goldstein, 1999, p. 83), namely, complete search and compensation. The first stipulates that all the available information should be found (or if not possible that search should be terminated when the cost of further search exceeds the search's benefit). The second stipulates that all pieces of information should be combined in one judgment. Modern descendants of Franklin's tool, also embodying the commandments of complete search and compensation, are, for instance, multiple linear regression and nonlinear Bayesian networks.

We pursue a different vision of rationality, one that challenges the commandments of complete search and compensation. Instead, the vision of bounded rationality proposes that in navigating a world full of uncertainty under the constraints of limited time and knowledge, people cannot help but resort to fast and frugal decision making (Gigerenzer, Todd, & the ABC Research Group, 1999). Counterintuitively, this kind of decision making of mere mortals can be as accurate as strategies that use all available information (complete search) and expensive computation (compensation).

The research program on fast and frugal heuristics (henceforth also referred to as simple heuristics) has instigated a considerable amount of debate over the past decade (see, for example, the commentaries and the reply following Todd & Gigerenzer, 2000, or Gigerenzer, Hertwig, & Pachur, 2011). Moreover, it has stimulated research that has focused on two key aspects. The first aspect is the *ecological rationality* of simple heuristics, and the second is their potential also to account for judgments and decisions in the social world. Some of the research concerned with ecological rationality is featured in Todd, Gigerenzer, and the ABC Research Group (in press), whereas some of the research investigating the use of simple heuristics in a social world is featured in Hertwig, Hoffrage, and the ABC Research Group (in press), and in Hertwig and Herzog (2009).

The present chapter reflects the major themes of the aforementioned three volumes on simple heuristics. First, we will explain how simple heuristics can be understood as models of bounded rationality. Second, we will introduce the notion of ecological rationality and explain when and why simple heuristics perform so well, both to describe the environment and to model behavior. Third, we will show how this research program can be extended to the social world; specifically, we will provide illustrations of heuristics that can be used in what Hertwig and Hoffrage (in press) have called *games against nature* and *social games*, and we will describe how research on simple heuristics investigates the *structures of social ecologies*.

SIMPLE HEURISTICS AS MODELS OF BOUNDED RATIONALITY

Our premise is that much of human reasoning and decision making in the physical and social world can be modeled by *simple heuristics* that enable organisms to make inferences and decisions under conditions of limited time, knowledge and computational capacity. They are models of *bounded rationality* (Simon, 1956, 1982). In contrast to strategies that aim at finding the optimal solution to a problem at hand, models of bounded rationality take human constraints into account when specifying the (cognitive) processes that lead to a *satisficing* solution to a given problem; that is, to a solution that is both *satis*fying and *suf*ficing (Gigerenzer et al., 1999, 2011). Moreover, boundedly rational strategies are the only alternative when real-world problems become computationally intractable; their solutions cannot be computed, neither by the most brilliant minds nor by the fastest computers. Unlike models of classic rationality such as probability theory, rational choice theory, or logic, heuristics are task specific, designed to solve a particular task (e.g., choice, estimation, categorization, cooperation, resource allocation). They cannot, however, solve tasks that they are not designed for. A hammer is perfect for driving a nail into the wall but try cutting wood with it. Indeed, the premise of task specificity is fundamental to the notion of the *adaptive toolbox* (Gigerenzer & Selten, 2001), the collection of heuristics that has evolved through phylogenetic, cultural, social, and individual learning, and that can be used by the human mind.

Although simple heuristics differ with respect to the problems they have been designed to solve, their architecture has common properties. In particular, they are composed of *building blocks*, which specify how information, be it stored in memory or externally presented, is searched for (*search rule*); when information search is stopped (*stopping rule*); and how a decision is made based on the information acquired (*decision rule*). Thus, unlike models that assume all information is already known to the decision maker and that are merely used to predict the outcome of the decision-making process, simple heuristics specify the cognitive processes, including those involved in information acquisition (for related programs that explicitly include information search, see Busemeyer & Townsend, 1993, and Payne, Bettman, & Johnson, 1993).

Heuristics can be fast for two reasons. First, they do not integrate the acquired information (e.g., probabilistic cues, reasons) in a complex and time-consuming way. In this respect, many heuristics of the adaptive toolbox are extremely simple because they do not combine pieces of information at all; instead, they search for only a single cue (*one-reason decision making*). Examples are the recognition and the fluency heuristics (Goldstein & Gigerenzer, 2002; Hertwig, Herzog, Schooler, & Reimer, 2008; Schooler & Hertwig, 2005). Second, they can be fast as a consequence of being frugal, that is, they stop searching for further information early in the process of information acquisition. Examples are the take-the-best heuristic (Gigerenzer & Goldstein, 1996), the elimination-by-aspects model (Tversky, 1972), and the priority heuristic (Brandstätter, Gigerenzer, & Hertwig, 2006).

Research on simple heuristics endorses a methodological pluralism. Across investigations researchers employ (a) computer simulations to explore the performance of the heuristics in a given environment, in particular in real-world environments (for example, Czerlinski, Gigerenzer, & Goldstein, 1999); (b) mathematical and analytical methods to explore when and why they fare well or poorly (for example, Martignon & Hoffrage, 2002); and (c) experimental and observational studies to explore whether and when people actually use these heuristics (for example, Bröder, in press; Rieskamp & Hoffrage, 2008). The most important finding from these studies is that simple heuristics can perform well, both as prescriptive models when predicting the environment and as descriptive models when fitting behavioral data (for example, Gigerenzer et al., 2011; Goldstein & Gigerenzer, 2002).

SIMPLE HEURISTICS AS MODELS OF ECOLOGICAL RATIONALITY

Tools, be they physical or cognitive, work well in one domain but may not work in others. A corollary of this general law is that different environments can give rise to different simple heuristics that succeed in exploiting their particular information structure. To the degree that a match between heuristics and informational structures exists, heuristics need not trade accuracy for speed and frugality. The importance of considering the environment when studying the human mind is best illustrated in Simon's analogy of a pair of scissors, with the mind and environment as the two blades: "Human rational behavior is shaped by a scissors whose blades are the structure of task environments and the computational capabilities of the actor" (Simon, 1990, p. 7). By restricting one's attention to one blade at the expense of the other, researchers will fail to fully understand how the mind works, and also how simple heuristics can perform surprisingly well by co-opting the environment as an ally. In other words, the study of bounded rationality is also the study of ecological rationality (Todd et al., in press).

For illustration, consider Woike, Hoffrage, and Petty's (2011) investigation of venture capitalists. The authors used computer simulations to determine the performance of various strategies that venture capitalists may use to sequentially decide whether to invest in a series of business plans. Highlighting the importance of ecological rationality, the authors found that the profit the decision strategies accrued depended on the cue importance structure in the environment. When all cues were equally predictive, a simple equal-weighing strategy (Dawes, 1979) achieved highest profits (even higher than those by logistic regression). In contrast, when the distribution of the cues' predictive power was highly skewed, a fast and frugal decision tree (ordering cues lexicographically) achieved the best results and even outperformed logistic regression.

Another important ecological property that is relevant for the performance of simple cue-based inference heuristics and complex inference strategies is the ratio of structure and noise. Robustness is the ability of an inference model only to extract relevant information from the past, and to disregard irrelevant information, which will not generalize to the future (Gigerenzer & Brighton, 2009). Fitting, in contrast, refers to the ability to explain or describe the past (i.e., data that are already known).

An excellent fit can be indicative of overfitting, that is, lack of robustness (for example, Mitchell, 1997; Myung, 2000; Roberts & Pashler, 2000). A strategy is said to overfit relative to another strategy if it is more accurate in fitting known data (hindsight) but less accurate in predicting new data (foresight). One can intuitively understand overfitting from the fact that past experience can be separated into two classes: the structure class comprises those aspects of the past that are relevant for predicting the future; the noise class includes those aspects that are vacuous with regard to the future. Everything else being equal, the more difficult a criterion is to predict (that is, the higher its uncertainty), the more noise exists in past information and needs to be ignored. An adaptive cognitive system operating in an uncertain world thus needs to ignore part of the information. Robustness can be enhanced by ignoring information and by exploiting evolved capacities such as the ability to forget (Schooler & Hertwig, 2005). The art is to ignore the right information. Heuristics embodying simplicity, such as one-reason decision making, have a good chance of focusing on the information that generalizes because they are—due to their simplicity—more "immune" to noise than complex strategies built to combine plenty of information. Heuristics are less likely to be "fooled by randomness," seeing "faces in the clouds" when there is no robust pattern. Complex strategies, in contrast, are more prone to overfitting due to their greater flexibility in fitting data, and—as an unavoidable byproduct—noise.

In sum, the research program on simple heuristics (Gigerenzer et al., 1999; Hertwig et al., in press; Todd et al., in press) rests on Simon's (1956, 1982) notion of bounded rationality. Strongly emphasizing and elaborating on the ecological intelligence of heuristics, it has proposed models of heuristics across a wide range of tasks and domains. A model of a heuristic encompasses search, stopping and decision rules, and aims to describe the actual process—not merely the outcome—of decision making. By taking advantage of environmental structures, they can achieve as high or even higher accuracy than much more complex models (Gigerenzer & Brighton, 2009). Due to their simplicity and frugality, they are less likely to fall prey to the risk of overfitting, relative to complex models. We now show by means of examples how the framework of simple heuristics can be extended to a social world.

SIMPLE HEURISTICS IN A SOCIAL WORLD

Should simple heuristics be expected to excel in the social world? One reason to believe that they may fail is complexity. The social world has been characterized as more complex, unpredictable, or challenging than nonsocial ones (for example, Byrne & Whiten, 1988), and people, the key agents in the social world, have been described as "unavoidably complex as targets of cognition" (Fiske & Taylor, 1984, p. 18). Humphrey (1976/1988, p. 19), for instance, argued that social systems have given rise to "calculating beings," who "must be able to calculate the consequence of their own behaviour, to calculate the likely behaviour of others, to calculate the balance of advantages and loss." He concluded that "here at last the intellectual faculties required are of the highest order" (p. 19). Similarly, the neuroscientists Seymour and Dolan (2008) argued that "choice in social interaction harbors a level of complexity that makes it unique among natural decision-making problems" and that renders "many social decision-making problems computationally intractable" (p. 667).

The argument that navigating complex social systems requires and has given rise to complex intellectual operations echoes the commandments of complete search and compensation. Indeed, many scholars of rationality believe that the more complex a problem is, the more complex the cognitive machinery of a successful problem solver needs to be (see Hertwig & Todd, 2003). The world's complexity thus licenses—in fact, even calls for—models of unbounded rationality.

This argument, however, overlooks the importance of robustness—the aforementioned key ability of successful strategies. If social environments are indeed more complex than nonsocial environments, robustness will prove to be even more important in the former and will give a competitive edge to those simple strategies that successfully generalize to the unknown by ignoring irrelevant information. In addition, the problems of intractability (Reddy, 1988) and multitude of goals and criteria in social environments collude and put optimization out of reach, probably even more so than in nonsocial environments. Optimization requires a single criterion to be maximized. One cannot maximize several criteria simultaneously, unless one combines them by, say, a linear function (which, in turn, calls for a justifiable rationale for how to weight those criteria). Social environments are notorious for their multitude of conflicting criteria and goals, including speed, accuracy, loyalty, accountability, transparency, trust, fairness, dependability, control, freedom, autonomy, honor, pride, face-saving, consent, equity, equality, and self-interest.

To the extent that the same selective forces that are likely to favor the evolution of simple strategies in nonsocial environments—such as the need for generalizable (robust), fast, and informationally modest (frugal) solutions—are also likely to be at work in social environments (Todd, Hertwig, & Hoffrage, 2005), there is good reason to assume that evolution also selects for simple heuristics in a social world. This does not mean, however, that there is no difference between simple heuristics in a nonsocial and in a social world. Just like simple heuristics in a nonsocial world, those used in a social world may consist of some of the same building blocks (e.g., ordered search, one-reason decision making, or aspiration levels), but they may also include genuinely social building blocks such as emotions and social norms.

When considering the applications of simple heuristics in a social world, it is useful to distinguish between two broad domains. We refer to them as games against nature and social games (Hertwig & Hoffrage, in press). Games against nature refer to situations in which one person needs to predict, infer, or outwit nature in order to achieve his or her ends (e.g., predicting the temperature to inform agricultural decisions). The person's outcome is determined jointly by his or her decision(s) and by the state of nature. A person can engage in games against nature using purely nonsocial information, but can also call upon social information (e.g., what most other people are doing or what the most successful people are doing), thus possibly fostering performance. In contrast, social games refer to situations involving social exchanges, in which other people create the most important aspects of an agent's "reactive" environment (Byrne & Whiten, 1988, p. 5). Simple heuristics enable the protagonists in these interactions to make adaptive decisions regarding, for instance, the allocation of tangible and intangible resources, the choice of allies and mates, and the deduction of others' intentions to name but a few of those decisions involving others.

Games Against Nature

When making inferences about states of the world, people may not only rely on physical cues but also use social information, that is, their knowledge of other's behaviors, attributes, intentions, and preferences. Consider, for instance, the task of predicting the magnitude of risks in one's environment (for example, Hertwig, Pachur, & Kurzenhäuser, 2005). Following the September 11, 2001, terrorist attacks, many people considered alternatives to flying and worried about the safety of various means of long-distance transportation. Lacking official statistics, one way to gauge which of two means of transportation, say, taking the train or taking a cross-country bus, involves a higher risk is to collect information distributed in one's social environment. One hypothesis about how people search for such information is the *social-circle heuristic* (Pachur, Hertwig, & Rieskamp, in press; Pachur, Rieskamp, & Hertwig, 2005). It embodies sequential search and one-reason decision making, but rather than retrieving probabilistic cues, it samples instances of the target events in question. The heuristic proceeds as follows:

Search rule—Search through social circles in order of their proximity to the decision maker, beginning with the "self" circle, followed by the "family," "friends," and "acquaintances" circles. Look up the instances of the class of events in question (e.g., experienced accidents involving trains versus cross-country buses) in the most proximate circle first, and tally them.

Stopping rule—If one class of events has a higher value (i.e., more instances) than the other, then stop search and proceed to the next step. Otherwise search the next circle. If the least proximate circle does not discriminate, guess.

One-reason decision making—Predict that the event with the higher tally has the higher value on the criterion (e.g., is more risky).

The social-circle heuristic suggests that the external hierarchical structure of a person's social network, measured in terms of degree of kin relationship (oneself, family; Hamilton, 1964) and reciprocal relationship (friends, acquaintances), guides the order of search for social information in the person's cognitive space. Such a search policy is adaptive because the individuals probed by the social-circle heuristic tend to be those about whom we have the most extensive, accessible, reliable, and veridical knowledge.

Like the availability heuristic (Tversky & Kahneman, 1973), the social-circle heuristic samples instances; unlike the former, however, this heuristic does so in a sequential and ordered way. The assumption that search starts with one's own experiences is consistent with the argument that the self acts as a superordinate schema facilitating encoding and subsequent retrieval of information (cf. Alicke, Dunning, & Krueger, 2005). There are now several studies that have analyzed the performance of the heuristic, relative to other heuristics and complex search models, and the conditions under which people use the social-circle heuristic (Pachur et al., 2005, in press).

Others not only provide useful information for our judgments or decisions, they can also help us to learn information that boosts the performance of our simple heuristics used for making inferences, predictions, and decisions. One example is the learning of good cue orderings, a problem considered notoriously difficult by many researchers (see Katsikopoulos, Schooler, & Hertwig, 2010). Cues on which people base inductive inferences are typically uncertain, and the individual learning of cue validities (i.e., the relative frequency with which they correctly predict the criterion), apart from being computationally taxing (Juslin & Persson, 2002), can be dangerous (Boyd & Richerson, 2005). Indeed, people are not very efficient learners of cue validities (for example, Todd & Dieckmann, in press; but see Katsikopoulos et al., 2010). However, when individual learners are allowed to actively exchange information about their experience, they learn good cue orderings faster and perform better than individuals prohibited from coopting their social environment (Garcia-Retamero, Takezawa, & Gigerenzer, 2009). In other words, social exchange can enable individuals to efficiently and quickly learn the information that fosters the performance of their heuristics.

There is still another way that can help individuals to perform better in games against nature. The heuristic of imitating the behavior of others allows individuals to learn about the environment without engaging in potentially hazardous learning trials or wasting a large amount of time and energy on exploration (for example, Henrich & McElreath, 2003; Laland, 2001; Todd, Place, & Bowers, this volume, Chapter 11). The imitation heuristic, a prime example of social intelligence, is particularly versatile in that it can be more nuanced than an unconditional "do-what-others-do" heuristic. Depending on situational cues and opportunities, the behavior copied may be that exhibited by the majority (Boyd & Richerson, 2005; for example, of two similar restaurants, patrons tend to choose the one with the longer waiting queue; Raz & Ert, 2008), by the most successful individuals (as in the earlier example; Boyd & Richerson, 2005), or by the nearest individual. The crucial point is that using any variant of imitation (or even simpler forms of social learning; see Noble & Todd, 2002) can speed up and foster decision making by reducing the need for direct experience and information gathering.

Another route through which social learning can occur is by actively seeking the advice of others (rather than by just probing socially distributed information, for instance, as the social-circle heuristic does) and by interpreting institutional arrangements as implicit recommendations (for example, policy defaults; McKenzie, Liersch, & Finkelstein, 2006; Thaler & Sunstein, 2008). Advice taking can be seen as an adaptive social decision-support system that compensates for an individual's blind spots (Yaniv & Milyavsky, 2007).

How helpful is advice, and what if the wisdom of others widely diverges from or conflicts with one's own opinion? Consider a fund manager trying to predict the profitability of an investment tool (a game against nature). After asking each of her colleagues for a profitability estimate, she ends up with a heterogeneous set of numbers. How should she make use of them? From a prescriptive viewpoint, averaging the estimates from different people (and even one's own; Herzog & Hertwig, 2009) taps into the "wisdom of crowds" (Surowiecki, 2004) and is an efficient heuristic that exploits the principle of error cancelation and works very well under a wide range of situations (for example, Armstrong, 2001; Clemen, 1989; Larrick, Mannes, & Soll, this volume, Chapter 3; Soll & Larrick, 2009; Yaniv, 2004).

Social Games

We now turn to social games, that is, to exchanges between two or more agents. As with games against nature, we suggest that much of the decision-making processes in social games can be described in terms of simple heuristics. We illustrate this thesis with two examples: the equity heuristic, and fast and frugal trees in the ultimatum game.

Equity Heuristic   The equity heuristic (sometimes called $1/N$ rule) is an example to support the conjecture that the cognitive processes of social intelligence may not be qualitatively different from the processes of nonsocial intelligence. This heuristic has been proposed to describe how people invest their resources in N options, with the options referring to either social (e.g., children) or nonsocial entities (e.g., saving options for retirement). Although dismissed by some behavioral economists as naïve (for example, Benartzi & Thaler, 2001), the heuristic competes well with optimizing strategies in environments with high uncertainty, a large number of assets, or with small learning samples. Such environmental properties impose a unique risk on complex strategies: Given environmental noise, complex strategies tend to overfit the data, which results in a lack of robustness (i.e., reduced accuracy) in predicting new data. DeMiguel, Garlappi, and Uppal (2009) compared the performance of the $1/N$ allocation heuristic with the performance of optimizing mean variance, and various Bayesian and non-Bayesian models. The striking result was that with 10 years of investment data, none of the optimization models could consistently beat the simple $1/N$ rule.

The equity heuristic also provides a model of how contemporary parents may allocate limited resources to their children (Hertwig, Davis, & Sulloway, 2002). Parental resources such as affection, time, and money (e.g., for education) are notoriously limited, and parents with more than one child need to constantly decide how to allocate their resources among their N children. Consistent with parents' expressed values in egalitarian societies, the heuristic predicts that parents attempt to split resources equally among all N children at any given investment period. This simple heuristic has several interesting properties. By implementing an equal ("fair") allocation of resources, it takes into account parents' inequality aversion (for example, Bolton & Ockenfels, 2000; Fehr & Schmidt, 1999; Hertwig et al., 2002). In addition, it permits parents to justify their allocation decisions to the "stakeholders" in the family: quarreling children and observant grandparents. Finally, it allows parents to (sometimes) hand over the actual implementation of the allocation to their children and invite them to make use of the time-honored heuristic, "I cut, you choose," in which one sibling divides the cake (or a chore) in two parts that she likes equally well, and the other one gets to pick the piece he prefers.[1] Yet, the equity heuristic is not a panacea. Although each single allocation decision is fair, the equity heuristic predicts inequalities on higher levels of aggregation.

As an illustration of how the equity heuristic works in the home, consider the allocation of parental time. Although the heuristic guarantees an equal distribution of parental time for any given period, the *cumulative* distribution will be unequal. Middleborns will receive less time than either first- and lastborns. Unlike their siblings, middleborns never enjoy a period of exclusive attention in the family. Such inequalities in resource distribution—although smaller in size—will continue to exist even if parents attempt to find a reasonable compromise between equity and children's age-specific needs (Hertwig et al., 2002, p. 741).

Fast and Frugal Trees

The ultimatum game has become a bogey for classic economists. A simple bilateral two-person strategic situation with perfect information produces robust behavior that is inconsistent with the classical economic prediction. The dominant response among those economists who accepted the reliability of the behavior was to assimilate it into the existing utility framework by modifying the utility function. Rather than retaining the universal utility calculus, however, one could heed Rubinstein's (2003) call and begin "to open the black box of decision making, and come up with some completely new and fresh modeling devices" (p. 1215). Hertwig, Fischbacher, and Bruhin (in press) did so by using the building blocks of simple heuristics to shed light on the processes in the ultimatum game. Focusing on mini-ultimatum games, in which the proposer chooses between two fixed-income distributions for both players (e.g., 3:5 versus 2:8) and the responder gets to accept or reject it, the authors modeled people's choice in terms of fast and frugal decision trees. A fast and frugal tree is defined as a tree that allows for a classification at each level of the tree (Martignon, Vitouch, Takezawa, & Forster, 2003). It consists of the same building blocks as the take-the-best heuristic: ordered search, one-reason stopping rule, and decision making on the basis of one reason.

To illustrate, the *priority tree*, one of four decision trees proposed by Hertwig et al. (in press), consists of three criteria for rejecting or accepting an allocation. The first criterion checks whether the offered allocation is larger than zero. If so, a homo economicus would accept it, regardless of its size. According to the status tree, however, a person now considers relative *status* as the second criterion. If the proposer selects the allocation in which the responder does, relative to the proposer, at least as well, the responder will accept it. No other reason enters the decision. If that is not the case (here: 2 < 8), she does not reflexively reject. Instead, she considers a third criterion that involves a comparison between the actual and the forgone allocation, the *kindness* criterion. If the responder does at least as well as in the forgone distribution (here yes: 3 > 2), she will accept the offered allocation. Only if the allocation also fails this test in kindness, will she reject.

Hertwig et al. (in press) described people in terms of fast and frugal trees involving one, two, three, or four criteria. Modeling responders' decisions in terms of fast and frugal trees enables tests of both decision and process. Recall that status trees assume a sequential process of examining up to three criteria. The more criteria are examined, the longer the decision will take. For instance, the status tree predicts that accepting an allocation based on the kindness criterion will take the longest. In Hertwig et al.'s study, people took significantly more time to accept allocations that failed the status test but passed the kindness test, relative to allocations that passed the status test. Explaining such differences in response times requires a process model and thus can hardly be accounted for by social preference models.

Models of heuristics are not new in studies of social games. The tit-for-tat strategy and its relatives such as "generous tit-for-tat" (Axelrod, 1984; Nowak & Sigmund, 1992), for instance, are among the famous strategies enabling and restoring mutual cooperation in social dilemmas (see also Howard, 1988; Johnson & Smirnov, in press; Rieskamp & Todd, 2006). Another class of simple heuristics in social games is based on the emotion of anticipated regret (Hart, 2005). Regret is an emotion that may result when we relate the outcome of a previous decision to what we would have obtained had we opted for the rejected alternative. Hart's *regret-matching heuristic* suggests that a person continues with the current action if she does not anticipate any regret. If she realizes that a particular option may lead to feelings of regret, she switches to the other action with a probability proportional to the amount of regret. Hart concluded from his analytical results that "simple and far-from rational behavior in the short run [based on regret avoidance] may well lead to fully rational outcomes in the long run" (p. 1415).

Structures of Social Ecologies

Simple heuristics in the social world not only affect outcomes for the decision makers or their interactants, but they often have far-reaching social consequences. Some macro consequences simply reflect people's strategies and preferences. If many people prefer to spend their summer vacation at the beach, beaches will be overcrowded during this holiday season, and, conversely, overcrowded beaches allow us to draw inferences about where people desire to spend their vacations. However, there are interesting exceptions: Schelling (1978) observed that macrolevel patterns do not necessarily reflect microlevel intentions, desires, or goals. In his classic model on neighborhood segregation that initiated a large and influential literature, individuals with no desire to be segregated from those who belong to other social groups, nevertheless, end up clustering with their own type. Most investigations of Schelling's model and extensions thereof have replicated this result. There is an important mismatch, however, between theory and observation, that has received relatively little attention. Whereas Schelling-type models predict large degrees of segregation starting from virtually any initial condition, the empirical literature documents considerable heterogeneity in actual levels of segregation. Berg, Hoffrage, and Abramczuk (2010; see also Berg, Abramczuk, & Hoffrage, in press) introduced a mechanism that can produce significantly higher levels of integration and, therefore, brings predicted distributions of segregation more in line with real-world observation.

As in the classic Schelling model, agents in a simulated world want to stay or move to a new location depending on the proportion of neighbors they judge to be acceptable. In contrast to the classic model, Berg et al. (2010; in press) augmented agents with memory. This allows these agents to use a very simple heuristic, the FACE-recognition heuristic, to classify their neighbors as acceptable or not. This heuristic builds on an evolved capacity, namely, recording faces into recognition memory. At the same time, the acronym FACE (for *Fast Acceptance by Common Experience*) refers to the insight that shared local experience can facilitate rapid formation of relationships that absolutely overrules the inference that would have been made by stereotyping based on group identity. The classic Schelling model appears to be a special case in the FACE-recognition model: When agents have no recognition memory, judgments about the acceptability of a prospective neighbor rely solely on his or her group type (as in the Schelling model). A very small amount of recognition memory, however, eventually leads to different classifications that, in turn, produce dramatic macrolevel effects resulting in significantly higher levels of integration. The model is intended to contribute substantively and constructively to policy analysis with a simple message, namely, that we can, relatively cheaply, design institutions that produce modest opportunities for face-to-face encounters with members of other groups. Then, to the extent that people use a simple acceptance rule based partially on recognition, random face-to-face intergroup mixing could potentially generate large and stable levels of integration even though they are ruled out by the vast majority of simulation studies based on Schelling's model.

CONCLUSION

Simon (1990) emphasized that almost any real-world problem is far too complex and requires too much computation to be solved by present or future computers. His paradigmatic case was chess. "Playing a perfect game of chess by using the game-theoretic minimaxing algorithm is one such infeasible computation, for it calls for the examination of more chess positions than there are molecules in the universe" (pp. 5–6). If a well-defined board game, which is limited to merely six different types of "players" (pieces) with exactly prescribed strategies and a space of 64 squares, is too complicated for calculating the optimal solution, then problems in a social world, involving potentially many more players and a wider range of strategies (including deception), will be even more computationally intractable. Although we do not doubt that the social world is complex—as has been emphasized by many theorists—we do not know whether it is any more complex than the physical one. Irrespective of this relative complexity issue, one strong conclusion from the social world's complexity is unwarranted in our view: the argument that successfully navigating the social world requires complex calculations, and that simple heuristics are therefore doomed to fail in social ecologies (a view that Sterelny, 2003, appears to advocate). Simon's conclusion from his premise that nearly all real-world problems are computationally intractable was what he called "one of the most important laws of qualitative structure applying to physical symbol systems, computers and the human brain included: *Because of the limits on their computing speeds and power, intelligent systems must use approximate methods to handle most tasks. Their rationality is bounded*" (p. 6; his emphasis). Following Simon, we believe that much of human reasoning and decision making in the physical and social world proceeds on the basis of simple heuristics. Not only do they permit organisms to make inferences and decisions without overtaxing their resources, they are also the mind's ace in the hole in the many real-word situations that defy optimal solutions.

AUTHOR NOTE

Parts of this text are based on Hoffrage and Reimer (2004), and Hertwig and Herzog (2009). Our thanks go to the publishers, the Rainer Hampp Verlag and Guilford Press, respectively, for granting the permission to use these parts, to Klaus Fiedler and Joachim Krueger for their helpful comments, and to Laura Wiles for editing the manuscript.

NOTE

1. According to Brams and Taylor (1996, p. 10), the origin of this heuristic goes back to antiquity: "The Greek gods, Prometheus and Zeus, had to divide a portion of meat. Prometheus began by placing the meat into two piles and Zeus selected one." Interestingly, in a simple two-person, zero-sum cake-cutting game the heuristic achieves the efficient (pareto-optimal) solution. That is, if the cutter cuts the cake as evenly as possible to minimize the maximum amount the chooser can get, thus avoiding the worst (von Neumann's, 1928, minimax theorem), there will be no allocation that is better for one person and at least as good for the other person.

REFERENCES

Alicke, M., Dunning, D., & Krueger, J. (Eds.) (2005). *The self and social judgment*. New York: Psychology Press.

Armstrong, J. S. (2001). Combining forecasts. In J. S. Armstrong (Ed.), *Principles of forecasting: A handbook for researchers and practitioners* (pp. 417–439). New York: Kluwer.

Axelrod, R. (1984). *The evolution of cooperation*. New York: Basic Books.

Benartzi, S., & Thaler, R. (2001). Naïve diversification strategies in defined contribution saving plans. *American Economic Review, 91*, 79–98.

Berg, N., Abramczuk, K., & Hoffrage, U. (in press). Fast Acceptance by Common Experience: Augmenting Schelling's neighborhood segregation model with FACE-recognition. In R. Hertwig, U. Hoffrage, & the ABC Research Group, *Simple heuristics in a social world*. New York: Oxford University Press.

Berg, N., Hoffrage, U., & Abramczuk, K. (2010). Fast acceptance by common experience: FACE-recognition in Schelling's model of neighborhood segregation. *Judgment and Decision Making, 5*, 391–419.

Bolton, G. E., & Ockenfels, A. (2000). Erc—A theory of equity, reciprocity and competition. *American Economic Review, 90*, 166–193.

Boyd, R., & Richerson, P. J. (2005). *The origin and evolution of cultures*. New York: Oxford University Press.

Brams, S. J., & Taylor, A. D. (1996). *Fair division: From cake-cutting to dispute resolution*. Cambridge, UK: Cambridge University Press.

Brandstätter, E., Gigerenzer, G., & Hertwig, R. (2006). The priority heuristic: Making choices without trade-offs. *Psychological Review, 113*, 409–431.

Bröder, A. (in press). The quest for take the best: Insights and outlooks from experimental research. In P. Todd, G. Gigerenzer, & the ABC Research Group, *Ecological rationality: Intelligence in the world*. New York: Oxford University Press.

Busemeyer, J. R., & Townsend, J. T. (1993). Decision field theory: A dynamic-cognitive approach to decision making in an uncertain environment. *Psychological Review, 100*, 432–459.

Byrne, R., & Whiten, A. (Eds.) (1988). *Machiavellian intelligence: Social expertise and the evolution of intellect in monkeys, apes and humans*. Oxford, UK: Clarendon.

Clemen, R. T. (1989). Combining forecasts: A review and annotated bibliography. *International Journal of Forecasting, 5*, 559–583.

Czerlinski, J., Gigerenzer, G., & Goldstein, D. G. (1999). How good are simple heuristics? In G. Gigerenzer, P. M. Todd, & the ABC Research Group, *Simple heuristics that make us smart* (pp. 97–118). New York: Oxford University Press.

Dawes, R. M. (1979). The robust beauty of improper linear models in decision making. *American Psychologist, 34*, 571–582.

DeMiguel, V., Garlappi, L., & Uppal, R. (2009). Optimal versus naive diversification: How inefficient is the 1/N portfolio strategy? *Review of Financial Studies, 22*(5), 1915–1953.

Fehr, E., & Schmidt, K. (1999). A theory of fairness, competition, and cooperation. *Quarterly Journal of Economics, 114,* 817–868.

Fiske, S., & Taylor, S. (1984). *Social cognition.* Reading, UK: Addison-Wesley.

Franklin, B. (1987). *Writings* (pp. 877–878). New York: The Library of America. (Original letter written September 19, 1772).

Garcia-Retamero, R., Takezawa, M., & Gigerenzer, G. (2009). Does imitation benefit cue order learning? *Experimental Psychology, 56,* 307–320.

Gigerenzer, G., & Brighton, H. J. (2009). Homo heuristicus: Why biased minds make better inferences. *Topics in Cognitive Science, 1,* 107–143.

Gigerenzer, G., & Goldstein, D. (1996). Reasoning the fast and frugal way: Models of bounded rationality. *Psychological Review, 103,* 650–669.

Gigerenzer, G., & Goldstein, D. G. (1999). Betting on one good reason: The Take the Best heuristic. In G. Gigerenzer, P. M. Todd, & the ABC Group, *Simple heuristics that make us smart* (pp. 75–95). New York: Oxford University Press.

Gigerenzer, R., Hertwig, R., & Pachur, T. (2011). *Heuristics: Foundations of adaptive behavior.* New York: Oxford University Press.

Gigerenzer, G., & Selten, R. (Eds.). (2001). *Bounded rationality: The adaptive toolbox.* Cambridge, MA: MIT Press.

Gigerenzer, G., Todd, P. M., & the ABC Research Group. (1999). *Simple heuristics that make us smart.* New York: Oxford University Press.

Goldstein, D. G., & Gigerenzer, G. (2002). Models of ecological rationality: The recognition heuristic. *Psychological Review, 109,* 75–90.

Hamilton, W. D. (1964). The genetical evolution of social behaviour I and II. *Journal of Theoretical Biology, 7,* 1–52.

Hart, S. (2005). Adaptive heuristics. *Econometrica, 73,* 1401–1430.

Henrich, J., & McElreath, R. (2003). The evolution of cultural evolution. *Evolutionary Anthropology, 12,* 123–135.

Hertwig, R., Davis, J. N., & Sulloway, F. J. (2002). Parental investment: How an equity motive can produce inequality. *Psychological Bulletin, 128,* 728–745.

Hertwig, R., Fischbacher, U., & Bruhin, A. (in press). Simple heuristics in a social game. In R. Hertwig, U. Hoffrage, & the ABC Research Group, *Simple heuristics in a social world.* New York: Oxford University Press.

Hertwig, R., & Herzog, S. M. (2009). Fast and frugal heuristics: Tools of social rationality. *Social Cognition, 27,* 661–698.

Hertwig, R., Herzog, S. M., Schooler, L. J., & Reimer, T. (2008). Fluency heuristic: A model of how the mind exploits a by-product of information retrieval. *Journal of Experimental Psychology: Learning, Memory, and Cognition, 34,* 1191–1206.

Hertwig, R., & Hoffrage, U. (in press). The ABC of social rationality: A research program. In R. Hertwig, U. Hoffrage, & the ABC Research Group, *Simple heuristics in a social world.* New York: Oxford University Press.

Hertwig, R., Hoffrage, U., & the ABC Research Group. (in press). *Simple heuristics in a social world.* New York: Oxford University Press.

Hertwig, R., Pachur, T., & Kurzenhäuser, S. (2005). Judgments of risk frequencies: Tests of possible cognitive mechanisms. *Journal of Experimental Psychology: Learning, Memory and Cognition, 35,* 621–642.

Hertwig, R., & Todd, P. M. (2003). More is not always better: The benefits of cognitive limits. In D. Hardman & L. Macchi (Eds.), *Thinking: Psychological perspectives on reasoning, judgment and decision making* (pp. 213–231). Chichester, UK: Wiley.

Herzog, S. M., & Hertwig, R. (2009). The wisdom of many in one mind: Improving individual judgments with dialectical bootstrapping. *Psychological Science, 20,* 231–7.

Hoffrage, U., & Reimer, T. (2004). Models of bounded rationality: The approach of fast and frugal heuristics. *Management Revue, 15,* 437–459.

Howard, J. V. (1988). Cooperation in the prisoner's dilemma. *Theory and Decision, 24*, 203–213.

Humphrey, N. K. (1988). The social function of intellect. In R. Byrne & A. Whiten (Eds.), *Machiavellian intelligence: Social expertise and the evolution of intellect in monkeys, apes and humans* (pp. 13–26). Oxford, UK: Clarendon. (Original work published 1976.)

Johnson, T., & Smirnov, O. (in press). Cooperate with equals: A simple heuristic for social exchange. In R. Hertwig, U. Hoffrage, & the ABC Research Group, *Simple heuristics in a social world*. New York: Oxford University Press.

Juslin, P., & Persson, M. (2002). PROBabilities from exemplars: A "lazy" algorithm for probabilistic inference from generic knowledge. *Cognitive Science, 26*, 563–607.

Katsikopoulos, K., Schooler, L., & Hertwig, R. (2010). The robust beauty of ordinary information. *Psychological Review, 117*, 1259–1266.

Laland, K. (2001). Imitation, social learning, and preparedness as mechanisms of bounded rationality. In G. Gigerenzer & R. Selten (Eds.), *Bounded rationality: The adaptive toolbox* (pp. 233–248). Cambridge, MA: MIT Press.

Martignon, L., & Hoffrage, U. (2002). Fast, frugal and fit: Simple heuristics for paired comparison. *Theory and Decision, 52*, 29–71.

Martignon, L., Vitouch, O., Takezawa, M., & Forster, M. R. (2003). Naive and yet enlightened: From natural frequencies to fast and frugal decision trees. In D. Hardman & L. Macchi (Eds.), *Thinking: Psychological perspective on reasoning, judgment, and decision making* (pp. 189–211). Chichester, UK: Wiley.

McKenzie, C. R. M., Liersch, M. J., & Finkelstein, S. R. (2006). Recommendations implicit in policy defaults. *Psychological Science, 17*, 414–420.

Mitchell, T. M. (1997). *Machine learning*. New York: McGraw-Hill.

Myung, I. J. (2000). The importance of complexity in model selection. *Journal of Mathematical Psychology, 44*, 190–204.

Noble, J., & Todd, P. M. (2002). Imitation or something simpler? Modelling simple mechanisms for social information processing. In K. Dautenhahn & C. Nehani (Eds.), *Imitation in animals and artifacts* (pp. 423–439). Cambridge, MA: MIT Press.

Nowak, M. A., & Sigmund, L. (1992). Tit for tat in heterogeneous populations. *Nature, 355*, 250–253.

Pachur, T., Hertwig, R., & Rieskamp, J. (in press). The mind as an intuitive pollster. In R. Hertwig, U. Hoffrage, & the ABC Research Group, *Simple heuristics in a social world*. New York: Oxford University Press.

Pachur, T., Rieskamp, J., & Hertwig, R. (2005). The social circle heuristic: Fast and frugal decisions based on small samples. In K. Forbus, D. Gentner, & T. Regier, *Proceedings of the 26th annual conference of the cognitive science society* (pp. 1077–1082). Mahwah, NJ: Erlbaum.

Payne, J. W., Bettman, J. R., & Johnson, E. J. (1993). *The adaptive decision maker*. New York: Cambridge University Press.

Raz, O., & Ert, E. (2008). *Size counts: The effect of queue length on choice between similar restaurants*. Manuscript submitted for publication.

Reddy, R. (1988). AAAI presidential address: Foundations and grand challenges of artificial intelligence. *AI Magazine, Winter 1988*, 9–21.

Rieskamp, J., & Hoffrage, U. (2008). Inferences under time pressure: How opportunity costs affect strategy selection. *Acta Psychologica, 127*, 258–276.

Rieskamp, J., & Todd, P. M. (2006). The evolution of cooperative strategies for asymmetric social interactions. *Theory and Decision, 60*, 69–111.

Roberts, S., & Pashler, H. (2000). How persuasive is a good fit? A comment on theory testing. *Psychological Review, 107*, 358–367.

Rubinstein, A. (2003). Economics and psychology? The case of hyperbolic discounting. *International Economic Review, 44*, 1207–1216.

Schelling, T. C. (1978). *Micromotives and macrobehavior*. New York: W. W. Norton & Company.

Schooler, L. J., & Hertwig, R. (2005). How forgetting aids heuristic inference. *Psychological Review, 112*(3), 610–628.

Seymour, B., & Dolan, R. (2008). Emotion, decision making, and the amygdala. *Neuron, 58*, 662–668.

Simon, H. A. (1956). Rational choice and the structure of environments. *Psychological Review, 63*, 129–138.

Simon, H. A. (1982). *Models of bounded rationality*. Cambridge, MA: MIT Press.

Simon, H. A. (1990). Invariants of human behavior. *Annual Review of Psychology, 41*, 1–19.

Soll, J. B., & Larrick, R. P. (2009). Strategies for revising judgment: How (and how well) people use others' opinions. *Journal of Experimental Psychology: Learning, Memory and Cognition, 35*, 780–805.

Sterelny, K. (2003). *Thought in a hostile world: The evolution of human cognition*. Malden, MA: Blackwell.

Surowiecki, J. (2004). *The wisdom of crowds*. New York, NY: Doubleday.

Thaler, R., & Sunstein, C. (2008). *Nudge: Improving decisions about health, wealth, and happiness*. New Haven, CT: Yale University Press.

Todd, P. M., & Dieckmann, A. (in press). Simple rules for ordering cues in one-reason decision making. In P. M. Todd, G. Gigerenzer, & the ABC Research Group *Ecological rationality: Intelligence in the world*. New York: Oxford University Press.

Todd, P. M., & Gigerenzer, G. (2000). Precis of simple heuristics that make us smart. *Behavioral and Brain Sciences, 23*, 727–780.

Todd, P. M., Gigerenzer, G., & the ABC Research Group (in press). *Ecological rationality: Intelligence in the world*. New York: Oxford University Press.

Todd, P. M., Hertwig, R., & Hoffrage, U. (2005). Evolutionary cognitive psychology. In D. M. Buss (Ed.), *The handbook of evolutionary psychology* (pp. 776–802). Hoboken, NJ: John Wiley & Sons.

Tversky, A. (1972). Elimination by aspects: A theory of choice. *Psychological Review, 79*, 281–299.

Tversky, A., & Kahneman, D. (1973). Availability: A heuristic for judging frequency and probability. *Cognitive Psychology, 5*, 207–232.

Von Neumann, J. (1928). Zur Theorie der Gesellschaftsspiele. *Mathemathische. Annalen, 100*, 295–320.

Woike, J., Hoffrage, U., & Petty, J. (2011). *Billions to invest, they must have a plan: A simulation of venture capital decision making*. Manuscript submitted for publication.

Yaniv, I. (2004). The benefit of additional opinions. *Current Directions in Psychological Science, 13*, 75–78.

Yaniv, I., & Milyavsky, M. (2007). Using advice from multiple sources to revise and improve judgments. *Organizational Behavior and Human Decision Processes, 103*, 104–120.

9

Social Judgments From Adaptive Samples

JERKER DENRELL AND GAËL LE MENS

Why is it that people sometimes believe "what is not so?"

Thomas Gilovich, 1991

A vast amount of research has documented the systematic judgment errors that people make. They use inaccurate stereotypes about those belonging to other groups, they develop superstitious beliefs, they are overconfident about their predictive abilities, and so on. Much of the existing social psychological literature suggests that such biases emerge because people process information inaccurately; they use flawed hypotheses tests and motivated reasoning, and rely on biased heuristics (for example, Fiske & Taylor, 2007; Tversky & Kahneman, 1974).

Recently, however, a number of scholars have challenged the perspective that fallible judgment is driven by flawed processing of information. Noting that the environment often produces unrepresentative samples of information, they have demonstrated that even if individuals process available information correctly, their judgments will be subject to systematic error patterns akin to those previously explained by invoking information-processing deficiencies (see Fiedler & Juslin, 2006, for a review). This sampling approach has, for example, produced alternative explanations for in-group bias, illusory correlation (Fiedler, 2000), and overconfidence (Juslin, Winman, & Hansson, 2007).

In this chapter, we argue that an important source of such information bias is *adaptive sampling*, defined here as the tendency of decision makers to select again, and thus continue to sample, activities that led to positive experiences but to avoid activities that led to poor experiences. Such a tendency is basic to most learning mechanisms.[1] It is *adaptive* because it ensures that decision makers avoid activities with consistently poor outcomes. Nevertheless, it generates a sample bias: The likelihood that an individual will take another sample and get more information about the outcome of an activity depends on past experiences with that alternative. In particular, the decision maker will stop learning about alternatives she (possibly mistakenly) evaluates negatively.

We argue that adaptive sampling can cast new light on several well-known judgment biases in social psychology, such as in-group bias in impression formation (Denrell, 2005), risk aversion (Denrell, 2007; Denrell & March, 2001), more positive assessments of popular alternatives (Denrell & Le Mens, 2011b; Le Mens & Denrell, 2011), illusory correlations (Denrell & Le Mens, 2011a), and social influence (Denrell & Le Mens, 2007).

Our perspective emphasizes an understudied interaction between two important aspects of belief formation. The first aspect pertains to the goal of the decision maker. People sometimes select alternatives or interact with other individuals just to learn about those. But, they often care about the immediate outcomes of their choices, and not just about the informational content of their experiences: their goal is often to ultimately have positive, enjoyable experiences. This desire for positive experiences is important because it provides the rationale for the adaptive selection of alternatives, based on past experiences used as predictors for future experiences. The second aspect is the role of the environment as a factor that constrains and enables access to information and thus indirectly influences decision making and judgment. Constrained access to information, combined with adaptive sampling, can explain what seem to be "irrational" judgments without assuming flawed information processing.

This chapter is organized as follows. We start by delineating what we mean by adaptive sampling and discussing its most basic implication: the tendency to underestimate the value of uncertain alternatives. Then, we illustrate how this tendency emerges using computer simulations of a simple learning model. We then discuss the role of access to information and describe the various biases that can be explained by our approach. Finally, we conclude the chapter by a discussion of the rationality of adaptive sampling.

ADAPTIVE SAMPLING IN DECISION MAKING AND JUDGMENT

What Is Adaptive Sampling?

To explain what we mean by adaptive sampling, consider the following restaurant review: "Not a happy dining experience. The service was absent minded, and the curry really wasn't up to very much. I won't be going here again" (Tim, *San Jose Mercury News*, December 15, 2005). Clearly, Tim's experience was poor. As a result, Tim's impression of the restaurant is negative and he has decided to avoid the restaurant in the future.

This is adaptive sampling at work; the probability that Tim will go to the restaurant again is low because his experience was poor and his impression negative. To avoid another poor experience, Tim avoids the restaurant in the future. If Tim's experience had been positive, however, Tim would probably have gone to the restaurant again and, doing so, would have had access to information about it. Thus, the probability that Tim will sample the restaurant again, go there and experience the food again, depends on Tim's previous experiences—positive experiences lead to further sampling, whereas negative experiences lead to avoidance.

More generally, we refer to the strategies that increase the probability of sampling alternatives with favorable past outcomes and reduce the probability of sampling alternatives with poor past outcomes as *adaptive sampling* schemes. These strategies are adaptive because they use information obtained from experience to adapt their behavior and to ultimately improve the average outcome obtained by those who adopt it. By changing the probability of sampling in response to past experiences, decision makers ensure that alternatives with consistently poor outcomes are avoided and that alternatives with consistently good outcomes are pursued.[2]

Adaptive sampling is basic to almost any experiential learning process because of this beneficial feature and is thus often observed. People tend to continue to interact with others with whom they have had good experiences and they tend to engage again in activities they have enjoyed. Conversely, people tend to avoid individuals with whom they did not get along well, and they tend to avoid activities they did not find enjoyable.

Adaptive Sampling Leads to a Negativity Bias

Despite the fact that adaptive sampling is both a sensible and a common sampling strategy, it generates a subtle sample bias that has systematic consequences for belief formation (Denrell & March, 2001; Gilovich, 1991; March, 1996).

The basic problem resides in the very nature of adaptive sampling: the likelihood that an individual will take another sample and get more information about the quality of an activity depends on the outcome of past experiences with that activity. As a result, the probability of sampling is not fixed, as in randomized experiments, but is contingent on the history of experiences with the alternative. Because the probability of sampling is higher for alternatives with good past outcomes, more information will be gained about such alternatives than about alternatives with poor past outcomes. It can be shown that this information asymmetry leads to a negativity bias, or systematic tendency to underestimate the value of uncertain alternatives (Denrell, 2005; Denrell & March, 2001).

To explain this, let us reflect on the consequences of Tim's initial experience at the restaurant. Following his poor experience, he will avoid the restaurant. And unless he obtains additional information about it in some other way, his negative impression will persist.

Suppose, by contrast, that Tim's initial experience with the restaurant was positive and that he leaves the restaurant with a positive impression. If he follows an adaptive sampling strategy, he is likely to go to that same restaurant again in the future. In information terms, Tim is likely to sample that alternative again. By doing so, Tim will gain additional information about the restaurant and will be able update his impression. If this second dinner is a really poor experience, Tim might develop an overall negative impression of the restaurant, despite his positive first experience.

The crucial aspect of this story is that a poor second experience can overcome a positive initial experience. By contrast, the opposite correction cannot occur. When the first experience is negative, there is simply no second experience, and thus there is no possibility for upward correction. This constraint implies that negative impressions are more stable than positive impressions. Overall, this process leads to a general tendency to underestimate the value of the restaurant.

Underestimation Versus Overestimation

Another way to explain this outcome is to note that due to adaptive sampling errors of *overestimation* are likely to be corrected, whereas errors of *underestimation* are likely to persist.

To explain this asymmetry, let us make Tim's restaurant story more specific. Suppose that 50% of the time the restaurant serves good meals and 50% of the time it serves bad meals. Tim gives good meals a 4 and bad meals a 2 on a 1 to 5 scale. Tim initially does not know anything about the quality of the restaurant.

When Tim experiences a good meal and gives it a 4, he overestimates the quality of the restaurant. Because he is likely to revisit the restaurant, however, he can experience a generally more representative set of outcomes and correct his error of overestimation. After a few meals, he might develop a rather accurate assessment of the quality of the restaurant. Formulated differently, his assessment of the quality of the restaurant is likely to "regress to the mean" (see Fiedler & Krueger, this volume, Chapter 10, for an overview of regression effects).

Contrast this to what happens if Tim initially experiences a bad meal. He gives the restaurant a 2, which corresponds to an underestimation of the quality of the restaurant. Because Tim is likely to avoid the restaurant in the future, he cannot experience a more representative set of outcomes and thus cannot correct his error of underestimation. As a result, his assessment will not regress to the mean after a negative experience.

Overall, this asymmetry in the probability of correcting errors of over- and underestimation implies that errors of underestimation will be more likely than errors of overestimation.

Errors in Social Perception and Adaptive Sampling

As we noted in the introduction, social psychologists have documented several errors and biases in social perception. Why do such errors occur and why are they not eventually corrected as social perceivers gain further information? Much research in social psychology is motivated by this question and several mechanisms have been discussed in the literature that could explain why erroneous perceptions persist (e.g., confirmation biases, self-fulfilling prophecies). Most existing explanations emphasize limitations of the mind of the social perceiver (but see Jussim, Stevens, & Salib, this volume, for an alternative interpretation of existing findings). As other scholars who have developed sampling-based explanations, we suggest that the source of errors might reside outside the mind of the decision maker. More precisely, we argue that adaptive sampling is a less explored but potentially important mechanism for why some errors are not corrected. Erroneous and negative perceptions might imply that social perceivers avoid further sampling and thus jeopardizes their chances to correct their errors.

There are obviously many exceptions to the adaptive sampling assumptions. We discuss them at a latter stage in this chapter but now turn to an illustration of the emergence of the negativity bias using computer simulations of a simple learning model.

A SIMULATION MODEL OF ADAPTIVE SAMPLING

Model

Consider an individual, T, who has to decide, repeatedly, whether to engage in an activity. For example, T may have to decide whether to go to a restaurant.

We assume the payoff from the activity is uncertain. For example, the quality of the meals served at a restaurant may vary from day to day or with variations of the quality of the ingredients. To model this variability, we assume that T's payoff from selecting the activity in period t, $X(t)$, is drawn from a normal distribution with mean 0 and standard deviation 1.

Every time T chooses the activity, T learns more about it and updates his impression of the activity. We use a simple model to capture this type of learning. We assume that the updated impression is a weighted average of the old impression and the experienced payoff (N. H. Anderson, 1981; Hogarth & Einhorn, 1992; Kashima & Kerekes, 1994). That is,

$$I(t) = (1 - b) I(t - 1) + bX(t),$$

where $I(t)$ is the impression of A at the end of period t and b is a parameter regulating the weight of the new experience. For most of the following simulations we will assume that $b = 0.5$.[3] We assume that T can only learn about the activity in periods when she chooses it. In periods when T does not choose the activity, we assume that T's impression remains the same:

$$I(t) = I(t - 1).$$

We assume that the initial impression is equal to 0. That is, the initial impression is unbiased—it is equal to the expected payoff of the activity.

The adaptive sampling assumption is implemented by assuming that the probability, $P(t)$, that T will choose the activity in period t is an increasing function of the impression. More precisely, we assume that $P(t)$ is a logistic function of the impression:

$$P(t) = \frac{1}{1 + \exp(-s * I(t-1))}.$$

This logistic choice rule has often been used to model choices under uncertainty (for example, Luce, 1959). Here, $s > 0$ is a parameter regulating how sensitive the choice probability is to the impression. If s is large then $P(t)$ is close to one whenever $I(t-1) > 0$ and close to zero whenever $I(t-1) < 0$. If s is close to zero then the choice probability is close to one half even for positive impressions. In the following simulations, we will assume that s equals 3 (see Denrell, 2005, for a discussion of the effect of varying s). Figure 9.1 plots how the choice probability, $P(t)$, varies with the impression, $I(t-1)$, when $s = 3$.

Negativity Bias

The aforementioned model implies that T's impression is a weighted average of all of T's experiences. Nevertheless, due to adaptive sampling, T's impression will be negatively biased, as illustrated in Figure 9.2. This figure plots the distribution of T's impression at the end of period 10 together with the normal distribution with mean zero and variance one. The distribution of the impressions is negatively skewed like in the restaurant example discussed earlier: Most impressions are

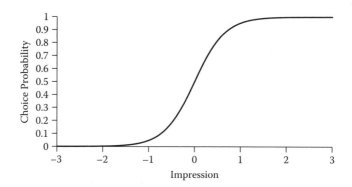

Figure 9.1   Plot of how the choice probability, $P(t)$, varies with the impression, $I(t-1)$.

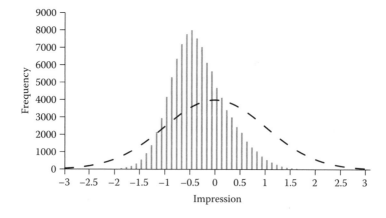

Figure 9.2   The distribution of T's impression after period 10 compared to the normal distribution of the payoff (based on 100,000 simulations).

negative. The average impression is also negative; it is –0.31. Moreover, in period 10, T chooses the activity in only 35% of the simulation runs.

The reason for this negativity bias is the asymmetry in error corrections discussed earlier. If T's impression is positive, and thus overestimates the expected payoff (0 in that case), then T is likely to choose the activity again and T's updated impression will be a weighted average of the previous impression and of the latest payoff. Because the expected payoff is zero, T's new impression will tend to decline toward zero (this is the well-known phenomenon of regression to the mean). Moreover, there is a chance that $X(t)$ is so negative that T's new impression will become negative. If T's impression is negative, T underestimates the expected payoff. In that case, T is unlikely to select the activity again and T's impression will not be updated, that is, it will remain negative. Stated differently, negative impressions tend to be stickier.

This reasoning suggests that an important condition for the negativity bias to emerge is that there is a possibility for errors in estimation of the quality of an alternative. If it were enough to select the alternative just once to fully know its value, the negativity bias would not emerge. Conversely, the negativity bias will be stronger the higher the likelihood and the amplitude of estimation errors. This line of reasoning leads us toward an important implication of adaptive sampling: the emergence of seemingly risk-averse behavior.

Risk-Averse Behavior

The model of adaptive sampling produces seemingly risk-averse behavior (Denrell, 2007; Denrell & March, 2001; March, 1996). That is, T is less likely to select the activity whenever its payoff distribution is more variable. To illustrate this, we simulated the learning model for different values of the standard deviation of the payoff distribution. Figure 9.3 shows that the probability that T will choose the activity in period 10 decreases when the standard deviation of the payoff distribution increases. In other words, T behaves as if he were *risk averse*.

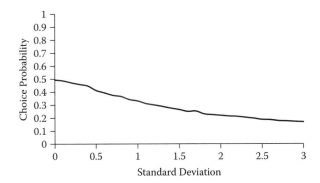

Figure 9.3   The probability that T will choose the object in the 10th period is decreasing with the standard deviation of the payoff distribution. Each point is the average of 10,000 simulations.

This effect occurs because a more variable payoff distribution tends to produce more extreme negative payoffs that lead to premature avoidance of the alternative. What matters is that the stronger the error of underestimation, the lower the likelihood that it will be corrected. Large errors of overestimation are less consequential because they will generally be quickly corrected (they lead to further selections of the alternative). Overall, this implies that both the choice probabilities and impressions tend to be lower for more variable alternatives than for less variable alternatives.

The aforementioned model shows how a tendency to choose a less variable alternative can be the result of learning. Thus, the model offers an explanation of seemingly risk-averse behavior that differs from explanations that attribute risk aversion to a concave utility function (Arrow, 1971) or to loss aversion (Kahneman & Tversky, 1979). In the aforementioned model, seemingly risk-averse behavior can emerge as a result of learning, even if the decision maker is formally *risk neutral*, that is, has a linear utility function and does not directly care about the variability of the outcomes. What happens in the model is that decision makers' impressions of the more variable alternatives will be lower. That is, decision makers learn to avoid a risky alternative because they have a poor impression of these alternatives. Denrell (2007) formally demonstrated that such risk-averse behavior emerges for a broad class of learning models.

INFORMATION ACCESS AND JUDGMENT

The most important implication of adaptive sampling is that it can explain why access to information can have a systematic effect on judgment and choice even if this information is unbiased. In this section, we discuss how this can be the case. And, in the next section, we will show that this can cast a new light on a number of judgment biases reported in social psychology and the decision-making and judgment literatures.

Why Access to Information Has a Systematic Effect on Judgment and Choice

The explanation of the negativity bias through adaptive sampling relied on the assumption that people obtain information about the quality of an alternative only if they actively select it. If they do not select the alternative, they do not get additional information and thus do not update their beliefs about it. But this condition does not always hold: sometimes people have access to information about an alternative even if they do not select it. For example, people might not control which individuals or activities they get exposed to. For example, people may have to continue to work with colleagues they find disagreeable or incompetent. In some other settings, people can get access to information about others without interacting with them. For example, you might learn about the achievement of one of your colleagues even if you do not interact with him or her. In this latter setting, even if you select or avoid activities and interactions based on past experience, access to information might not be fully determined by your adaptive sampling strategy. When this is the case, adaptive sampling does not lead to a negativity bias.

This simple observation has the following important implication: If people follow an adaptive sampling strategy, then estimates of the quality of an alternative are systematically and positively influenced by access to information. In particular, having access to one additional observation of the payoff distribution they are learning about tends to increase the tendency to evaluate this alternative positively. The reason is that such access to unbiased information eliminates the negativity bias that adaptive sampling otherwise would have led to. This is what is commonly known in the probability literature as regression to the mean (see also the chapter by Fiedler & Krueger, this volume, for an overview of regression effects in social psychology).

Simulation Model of the Impact of Information Access

To formally demonstrate this systematic effect of access to unbiased information, suppose we change the simulation model in the following way: In each period there is a probability r that T will be able to observe the payoff of the uncertain alternative even if T does not choose it (Denrell, 2005). The previous discussion of the effect of one more observation suggests that the higher the probability that T will be able to observe such "foregone" payoffs, the higher the probability that T will have a positive impression of the alternative. This intuition is confirmed by the simulation results reported on Figure 9.4, which plots the probability that T's impression is positive in period 10 as a function of r. When $r = 1$, T observes information about the uncertain alternative in every period, and T's impression is thus an unbiased estimate of the quality of the alternative. For lower values of r, there is some negativity bias, but with a lower magnitude than what happens when sampling is strictly adaptive as in the previous section. For example, if $r = 0.3$, the probability of a positive impression in period 10 is 37%, whereas it is 49% when $r = 0.8$.

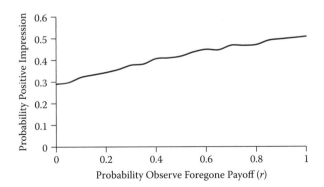

Figure 9.4   The probability that T's impression is positive in period 10 is increasing with r, the probability that T will be able to observe the payoff of the uncertain alternative even in period when T does not choose the uncertain alternative. Each point is the average of 10,000 simulations.

A similar effect would also have emerged if T had been forced to revisit the restaurant, when he would have avoided it on the basis of a negative impression. This type of situation might happen if other restaurants are closed and there is no other alternative for a meal. Alternatively, an individual might go to the restaurant with his or her friends. If your friends really want to go to that restaurant and the quality of your company matters more than the quality of your meal, you might still go. Regardless of the reason, such forced choice would lead to an information sample that is less affected by prior experiences than in the base case. If, at the limit, forced choice occurs whenever the decision maker would not have selected the alternative on the basis of his impression, the impression will be an unbiased estimate of the quality of the alternative.

Experimental Evidence

An experiment on attitude formation by Fazio, Eiser, and Shook (2004) illustrates how adaptive sampling can lead to a negativity bias and how access to information can eliminate it. Participants participated in a survival game, in which they had to eat beans with positive energy levels and avoid beans with negative energy levels in order to survive. Initially they did not know what type of beans generated positive energy levels, but they could learn from experience. They only learned from their own experience, that is, by choosing beans and experiencing their outcome. They did not learn about the energy value of the beans they avoided.

At the end of the game, participants were presented with beans of different types and asked to estimate if these beans were of the positive or negative type. The basic result was that a negativity bias emerged. Specifically, participants made more errors of underestimation than overestimation—they were more likely to mistake a positive bean for a negative than vice versa. The reason was that if they suspected, perhaps falsely, that a bean of a particular type was negative, they avoided these types of beans in the future. In contrast, if they suspected that a bean was positive, they continued to select this type of bean. In other words, they followed a strategy of adaptive sampling.

In one manipulation, Fazio and his colleagues changed the information structure so that participants also learned about the energy values of the beans they avoided. In this case, there was no negativity bias. Instead, participants were equally likely to make an error of under- or overestimation. We also obtained similar results in experimental investigations of variations of the multiarmed bandit setting (Le Mens & Denrell, 2010).

ADAPTIVE SAMPLING AND JUDGMENT BIASES

Now that we have explained the nature of adaptive sampling and its most basic implication for the role of information on belief formation and choices, we can illustrate how it can help explain several phenomena that have been viewed as puzzling and irrational, including in-group bias, social influence, or illusory correlations. The usual explanations of these phenomena attribute them to mental "flaws," such as inaccurate perception and biased information processing (Fiedler,

2000). In a series of articles (Denrell, 2005, 2007; Denrell & Le Mens, 2007, 2011; Le Mens & Denrell, 2011a), we have suggested that adaptive sampling may provide an alternative explanation.

In putting forward this alternative explanation, we do not want to suggest that existing accounts are incorrect. There is substantial experimental evidence that heuristic processing can give rise to some of the effects we describe next. Nevertheless, our work suggests an alternative, complementary explanation that may be important in settings where information is not provided to people but has to be actively sampled.

In-Group Bias in Impression Formation

Why do people develop more positive opinions of those close to them? College students have more positive opinions of their roommates than of other students (Festinger, Schachter, & Back, 1950; Segal, 1974) and members of ethnic groups have more positive opinions of their own groups (Dasgupta, 2004; Hewstone, Rubin, & Willis, 2002). Explanations for this tendency have focused on how flawed hypothesis testing, confirmation biases, motivated reasoning, or prior expectations can distort impressions (Wood, 2000).

Denrell (2005) suggested that adaptive sampling could provide an alternative explanation. Key to this explanation is the observation that more information is usually available about in-group members that one does not personally interact with, simply because one tends to be more connected to the in-group. In addition, people are more likely to continue to interact with in-group members they have a negative impression of than with out-group members they have a negative impression of. For example, Levin, van Laar, and Sidanius (2003) show that although individuals often avoid members of other groups if initial encounters are negative, they tend to continue to interact with in-group members. In some cases, it may also be difficult to avoid interacting with in-group members one dislikes, such as members of the same family or department.

This implies that the negativity bias generated by adaptive sampling will be eliminated or at least attenuated for in-group members. As previously shown, this leads to more positive evaluations of in-group members as compared to out-group members.

Denrell (2005) also showed that this explanation implies that evaluations of out-groups will be more positive for larger out-groups, simply because it is more likely that one will come into contact with them at work or in schools, for example. As shown by the recent meta-analysis of contact and prejudice by Pettigrew and Tropp (2006), there is substantial evidence for the underlying idea that contact leads to reduction in prejudice. Moreover, several studies have shown that larger out-groups, because of the increased probability of contact, lead to reductions in prejudice (see Denrell, 2005, for a review).

The explanation offered by adaptive sampling is clearly distinct from other perspectives. Rather than emphasizing flawed perception or preconceived notions, it stresses how access to information can give rise to negative stereotypes about out-groups. From a normative point of view this shift in perspective is important.

It demonstrates why debiasing individuals may not be enough. Rather, more even access to information, perhaps through more even access to formal and informal contacts, may be essential to the elimination of biased stereotypes.

Evidence from a recent natural experiment on the effect of additional interactions on racial attitudes is consistent with this suggestion. Shook and Fazio (2008) analyzed the evolution of automatically activated racial attitudes toward African Americans of White freshmen that were randomly assigned an African American roommate or a White roommate. The racial attitudes of those with an African American roommate became more positive after one quarter but the racial attitudes of those with a White roommate did not change. Although several interpretations are possible, this study suggests that additional exposure can help correct the negativity bias against out-group members.

A recent model by DiDonato, Ullrich, and Krueger (2011) also explains differences of perception between the in-group and the out-group by invoking differences in knowledge about the two groups. The mechanism they propose is different but also emphasizes differences in information access. DiDonato and colleagues suggests that people project their self to the in-group but not to the out-group. Because most people have a positive self-image, impressions of the in-group will be more favorable than impressions of the out-group. Adaptive sampling could complement this model by suggesting another mechanism for why people will end up with more favorable self-images.

Social Influence

Why do proximate others tend to develop similar attitudes? Previous explanations of such social influence have focused on why an individual would be motivated to agree with the opinions or beliefs of others (for example, Cialdini & Goldstein, 2004; Wood, 2000).

In Denrell and Le Mens (2007), we have shown that motivated reasoning and imperfect information processing are not necessary to explain social influence. Rather, a social influence effect can also emerge because of adaptive sampling. Our explanation focuses on how an individual, A, can indirectly influence the attitude of another individual, B, by affecting the activities that B samples and gets exposed to. Surprisingly, this effect emerges even if the outcomes experienced by B, when sampling an activity, are independent of A's experiences.

To explain how this mechanism works, consider two friends, A and B. Suppose that A likes a restaurant, whereas B does not. Usually, B would then avoid the restaurant. However, if B and A are friends, B may sometimes join A at the restaurant if B cares more about her friendship with A than about the food. By sampling the restaurant again, B gets new information, which might change her attitude from negative to positive, that is, closer to A's attitude. This would not have happened, however, if A also had a negative impression. In that case, they would have both avoided the restaurant.

As this example shows, influence over sampling can indirectly lead to influence over attitudes. B did not change her negative attitude to the restaurant simply because A had a positive attitude. Thus, A had no direct influence over B's attitude. But A had an indirect influence over B's attitude by changing B's sampling behavior. More generally, this social influence through interdependent sampling provides a novel mechanism for why public conformity in behavior might lead to private acceptance.

Denrell and Le Mens (2007) showed that this mechanism provides a simple account of existing findings in the literature. For example, it explains why beliefs tend to be influenced more in the direction of those of powerful people than in the direction of people with less power. The explanation, according to our mechanism, is that powerful people have more influence over what activities others get exposed to. And, in turn, they have more influence on their attitudes.

The explanation of social influence through interdependent sampling leads to novel empirical predictions. In particular, it implies an asymmetry in social influence. Consider, again, two individuals, A and B. The model of interdependent sampling implies that A's attitude is more influential if B's attitude is negative than if B's attitude is positive. The reason is that if B's attitude is negative, B is likely to avoid sampling and might only sample if A has a positive attitude. If B instead has a positive attitude, B might sample anyway, whether A's attitude is positive or not. We found that this asymmetric pattern of social influence is present in Newcomb's (1961) longitudinal data on students' attitudes toward each other.

Preference for Popular Alternatives

The systematic positive effect of additional information on impression formation also has interesting population-level implications. It suggests that there will be a sample bias that favors established and popular alternatives over novel and potentially superior alternatives.

The general idea is that the social environment tends to provide additional information about popular alternatives, even if the decision maker does not personally choose them. For example, popular restaurants get reviewed, and thus one can learn about those even if one does not attend them. But information about new or unpopular venues is harder to access, and one often has to go there to learn about the venue. If the decision maker avoids a popular restaurant following poor experiences, she might still learn about it by reading reviews and learn that it is not that bad. This might not happen for the unpopular restaurant. This asymmetry in terms of access to information can help explain why more popular alternatives are often more positively evaluated.

Popularity can also influence impression formation in a different way, through its effect on sampling. In some cases, people might feel compelled to try out popular alternatives, even if they do not believe they are of high quality. As a result of this additional incentive to sample, people may get more positive evaluations of the quality of popular alternatives.

One reason why people might want to sample popular alternatives, even if they do not believe that their quality is the highest, is that the payoff from adopting an alternative may increase with the number of others adopting the same alternative. For example, in evaluating an operating system for a personal computer people may care about both its reliability (i.e., quality) and the number of others who have chosen the same operating system. Ideally, they would like to choose an operating system with the highest quality, but such an operating system might be less useful if few others have adopted it because sharing programs with others is also important. Alternatively, people may decide to go along with the majority and select the most popular alternative to avoid being seen as deviant (Cialdini & Goldstein, 2004; Granovetter, 1978) or because of adverse reputation effects to receiving a poor outcome with an unusual alternative (Keynes, 1936).

Denrell and Le Mens (2011b) show that in the presence of such external influences on sampling, quality assessments of the alternatives will also be biased toward the popular alternative when people do not know the qualities of the alternatives but can only learn about them from their own experiences. When there are only two alternatives, most people will come to believe that the most popular alternative is also of superior quality, even when it is not.

The reason is that here popularity affects opportunities for error corrections: If an agent mistakenly believes that the most popular alternative is the worst, she is likely to discover her mistake. But if she mistakenly believes that the least popular alternative is the worst, she is unlikely to discover her mistake. To see why, suppose that Alternative 1 is the best. In addition, suppose that, by chance, most people have come to select Alternative 2. If an agent incorrectly believes that Alternative 1 is the worst, she is likely to avoid it, because it is also unpopular. As a result, her negative estimate of the quality of Alternative 1 remains unchallenged and therefore persists. Now, suppose that Alternative 1, rather than Alternative 2, is the most popular. If the agent incorrectly believes that Alternative 1 is the worst, she might still want to select it again to gain the benefit of coordination. Because she obtains some additional information about the quality of Alternative 1 when selecting it again, she might discover that it is not that bad, and even superior to Alternative 2. This asymmetry in error corrections leads to an overall tendency to underestimate the quality of unpopular alternatives.

Illusory Correlations

Adaptive sampling also suggests a novel explanation for the emergence of illusory correlations in person perception (Denrell & Le Mens, 2011a). In standard studies on illusory correlations, experimental participants observe a set of items each characterized by a pair of attribute values (X, Y). Existing theories explain illusory correlation by proposing that some observations receive more weight in the computation of the correlation than others (for example, Allan, 1993; Hamilton & Gifford, 1976). This assumption of differential weighing is not necessary to our explanation based on adaptive sampling.

To see how adaptive sampling can explain illusory correlations, consider the following example. Suppose you learn about two traits of individuals you meet at a swing dance venue. Suppose you learn, from experience, about whether the people you meet are good dancers and agreeable individuals.

Suppose that dancing skills and agreeableness are uncorrelated in the population. That is, an individual who is a good dancer is not more or less likely to be more agreeable than an individual who is not a good dancer. If you want to interact with people that are good on at least one of the two dimensions (i.e., good dancer and/or agreeable) you will end up perceiving the two attributes to be *positively* correlated.

The key to the emergence of this illusory correlation is that you may stop interacting with somebody depending on your assessment of her dancing skills and agreeableness. Suppose you believe a given individual, *i*, to be a poor dancer. If you find *i* disagreeable, you are unlikely to interact with her again, and thus your belief about her poor dancing skill will tend to persist even if she is in fact a good dancer. If, on the contrary, you believe *i* to be agreeable, you are likely to dance with her again. Doing so, you might discover that she is in fact a skilled dancer. Overall, this sequential process of belief formation and information sampling implies that the distribution of estimates will diverge from the distribution of attributes in the population of swing dancers. Because combinations of estimates that lead to avoidance (low-perceived dancing skills, low-perceived agreeableness) will be more stable than combinations of estimates that lead to further sampling (e.g., low-perceived dancing skills, high-perceived agreeableness), combinations of estimates that lead to avoidance will be overrepresented.

In this example, we assumed that you wanted to interact with others that were good on at least one of the two dimensions. Suppose that, instead, you only want to interact with those you perceive to be good dancers and agreeable. In this case, adaptive sampling will lead you to believe that the two attributes are negatively correlated in the population. The reason is that the only combinations of estimates that lead to further sampling are those with high values on both dancing skills and agreeableness. Because estimates that lead to further sampling are less stable than estimates that lead to avoidance, combinations consisting of high perceived dancing skills and high perceived agreeableness will be underrepresented in the distribution of final estimates relative to other types of combinations. It follows that unbalanced combinations (corresponding to a high value on one dimension and a low value of the other dimension) will tend to be overrepresented in the distribution of estimates relative to balanced combinations (both high values or both low values). Such an asymmetry corresponds to a negative correlation (Allan, 1993). More generally, the sign of the illusory correlation depends on how the decision maker combines estimates in making her sampling decisions (for further explanation and boundary conditions, see Denrell & Le Mens, 2011b).

This mechanism provides an alternative account of phenomena such as the halo effect in person perception or the documented tendency for people to like proximate others better than distant others. Again, these phenomena are shown to emerge from adaptive sampling—the key to the aforementioned results is how the attributes of others are sampled and when you stop sampling those.

CONCLUSION: THE RATIONALITY OF BIASED JUDGMENTS

Our argument so far has been that decision makers who follow well-known learning processes will end up making seemingly biased judgments because of the sample bias generated by adaptive sequential sampling. Would not a rational person, who understands the effect of sample bias, be able to correct for it and thus avoid the aforementioned judgment biases?

Interestingly, the answer is no. It can be demonstrated that several of the judgment biases continue to hold even if it is assumed that the decision maker is rational, follows Bayes's rule in updating beliefs, and is aware of the sample bias in the available data (Denrell, 2007; Le Mens & Denrell, 2011).

Consider first the basic negativity bias: Most decision makers end up under-estimating the uncertain alternative. One might suspect that this result emerges only when decision makers do not follow Bayes's rule in updating their estimates of the value of the uncertain alternative. As Denrell (2007) showed, however, the basic result continues to hold even if decision makers are rational and follow the optimal (expected payoff-maximizing) learning strategy. That is, decision makers follow Bayes's rule, they have an accurate prior, and they are able to compute the optimal amount of experimentation. Even under these conditions most decision makers will end up underestimating the uncertain alternative.

This conclusion sounds paradoxical: How can rational decision makers have a tendency to underestimate the value of the uncertain alternative? The key to resolving this paradox is first to realize that when outcomes matter, rational deci-sion makers will not prioritize accuracy at the cost of obtaining poor outcomes. In particular, if they have tried the uncertain alternative several times and payoffs have been negative, it is optimal to avoid that alternative and choose the known alternative instead. By doing so they will stop getting further information about the uncertain alternative and will not be able to correct errors of underestimation. As a result, errors of underestimation will be more likely than errors of overestima-tion as in the case when heuristic choice rules are used (like in our simulations). Nevertheless, when decision makers are rational, estimates are correct on average (the expected estimates of the alternatives, across decision makers, are unbiased). Thus, even if a rational decision maker is aware that she is more likely to underes-timate than overestimate the value of the uncertain alternative, she would have no incentive to change her estimate. There is nothing paradoxical about this; it simply reflects the fact that the distribution of estimates is unbiased as well as skewed (with most estimates being negative).

Consider, next, the effect of information access on beliefs and preferences. Le Mens and Denrell (2011) show that this effect also continues to hold even if decision makers are rational in the sense that they update their beliefs following Bayes's rule, they are aware of the possible sample bias, and they follow an optimal policy of experimentation (an optimal learning policy). Thus, even if decision mak-ers were rational they would end up being more likely to believe that an alternative for which information is more accessible is superior.

These results illustrate how adaptive sampling and constraints on information access can, without the further assumption of biased information processing, lead to biased judgments. In line with recent work on *rational analysis*, this suggests that what appears to be irrational behavior could possibly be a rational solution to a problem different from the one that the researcher had in mind (J. Anderson, 1990; Dawes & Mulford, 1996; Klayman & Ha, 1987; Oaksford & Chater, 1994).

In making this suggestion we are by no means claiming that cognitive biases are unimportant; there is conclusive evidence that they have substantial effects. Rather, our approach suggests alternative, complementary explanations that may be important in settings where information has to be sequentially sampled and people care about outcomes as well as accuracy. Our approach also has important normative implications. For example, to eliminate the in-group bias, it may not be enough to de-bias how people process social information. Rather, information about out-group members needs to be provided.

NOTES

1. It is the foundational principle of reinforcement learning algorithms (Sutton & Barto, 1998). See also the law of effect (Thorndike, 1911).
2. To be sure, such approach-avoidance strategies are adaptive only to the extent that past experiences are valid predictors for the qualities of future experiences, that is, to the extent that the environment is relatively stable.
3. The exact value of b does not qualitatively affect the results we discuss in this chapter, provided that b is higher than 0 and lower than 1. The value of b, however, affects the size of the effects and how quickly they unfold over time.

REFERENCES

Allan, L. G. (1993). Human contingency judgments: Rule based or associative? *Psychological Bulletin, 114*, 435–448.

Anderson, J. (1990). *The adaptive character of thought*. Hillsdale, NJ: Lawrence Erlbaum.

Anderson, N. H. (1981). *Foundations of information integration theory*. New York, NY: Academic Press.

Arrow, K. J. (1971). *Essays in the theory of risk bearing*. Chicago, IL: Markham.

Cialdini, R. B., & Goldstein, N. J. (2004). Social influence: Compliance and conformity. *Annual Review of Psychology, 55*, 591–621.

Dasgupta, N. (2004). Implicit ingroup favoritism, outgroup favoritism, and their behavioral manifestations. *Social Justice Research, 17*(2), 143–169.

Dawes, R., & Mulford, M., (1996). The false consensus effect and overconfidence: Flaws in judgment or flaws in how we study judgment? *Organizational Behavior and Human Decision Processes, 65*(3), 201–211.

Denrell, J. (2005). Why most people disapprove of me: Experience sampling in impression formation. *Psychological Review, 112*, 951–978.

Denrell, J. (2007). Adaptive learning and risk taking. *Psychological Review, 114*, 177–187.

Denrell, J. (2008). Indirect social influence. *Science, 321*(5885), 47–48.

Denrell, J., & Le Mens, G. (2007). Interdependent sampling and social influence. *Psychological Review, 114*(2), 398–422.

Denrell, J., & Le Mens, G. (2011a). Seeking positive experiences can produce illusory correlations. *Cognition, 119*(3), 313–324.

Denrell, J., & Le Mens, G. (2011b). *Learning to be satisfied with the status quo*. Unpublished manuscript.

Denrell, J., & March, J. G. (2001). Adaptation as information restriction: The hot stove effect. *Organization Science, 12*, 523–538.

DiDonato, T. E., Ullrich, J., & Krueger, J. I. (2011). Social perception as induction and inference: An integrative model of intergroup differentiation, ingroup favoritism, and differential accuracy. *Journal of Personality and Social Psychology, 100*, 66–83.

Fazio, R. H., Eiser, J. R., & Shook, N. J. (2004). Attitude formation through exploration: Valence asymmetries. *Journal of Personality and Social Psychology, 87*, 293–311.

Festinger, L., Schachter, S., & Back, K. W. (1950). *Social pressures in informal groups: A study of human factors in housing*. Stanford, CA: Stanford University Press.

Fiedler, K. (2000). Beware of samples! A cognitive-ecological sampling approach to judgment biases. *Psychological Review, 107*, 659–676.

Fiedler, K., & Juslin, P. (2006). Taking the interface between mind and environment seriously. In K. Fiedler & P. Juslin (Eds.), *Information sampling and adaptive cognition* (pp. 3–29). Cambridge, UK: Cambridge University Press.

Fiske, S. T., & Taylor, S. E. (2007). *Social cognition: From brains to culture* (3rd ed.). New York, NY: McGraw-Hill.

Gilovich, T. (1991). *How we know what isn't so: The fallibility of human reason in everyday life*. New York, NY: Free Press.

Granovetter, M. S. (1978). Threshold models of collective behavior. *American Journal of Sociology, 83*, 1420–1443.

Hamilton, D. L., & Gifford, R. K. (1976). Illusory correlation in interpersonal perception: A cognitive basis of stereotypic judgments. *Journal of Experimental Social Psychology, 12*, 392–407.

Hewstone, M., Rubin, M., & Willis, H. (2002). Intergroup bias. *Annual Review of Psychology, 53*(1), 575.

Hogarth, R. M., & Einhorn, H. J. (1992). Order effects in belief updating: The belief-adjustment model. *Cognitive Psychology, 24*, 1–55.

Juslin, P., Winman, A., & Hansson, P. (2007). The naive intuitive statistician: A naive sampling model of intuitive confidence intervals. *Psychological Review, 114*, 678–703.

Kahneman, D., & Tversky, A. (1979). Prospect theory: An analysis of decisions under risk. *Econometrica, 47*, 263–291.

Kashima, Y., & Kerekes, A. R. Z. (1994). A distributed memory model for averaging phenomena in person impression formation. *Journal of Experimental Social Psychology, 30*, 407–455.

Keynes, J. M. (1936). *General theory of employment interest and money*. London, UK: Macmillan.

Klayman, J., & Ha, Y.-W. (1987). Confirmation, disconfirmation, and information in hypothesis testing. *Psychological Review, 94*, 211–228.

Levin, S., van Laar, C., & Sidanius, J. (2003). The effects of ingroup and outgroup friendships on ethnic attitudes in college: A longitudinal study. *Group Processes & Intergroup Relations, 6*(1), 76–92.

Le Mens, G., & Denrell, J. (2010). *A systematic effect of access to information on impression formation*. Unpublished manuscript.

Le Mens, G., & Denrell, J. (2011). Rational learning and information sampling: On the "naivety" assumption in sampling explanations of judgment biases. *Psychological Review, 118*(2), 379–382.

Luce, R. D. (1959). *Individual choice behavior: A theoretical analysis*. New York, NY: Wiley.

March, J. G. (1996). Learning to be risk averse. *Psychological Review, 103*, 309–319.

Newcomb, T. M. (1961). *The acquaintance process*. New York, NY: Holt, Rinehart & Winston.

Oaksford, M., & Chater, N. (1994). A rational analysis of the selection task as optimal data selection. *Psychological Review, 101*(4), 608–630.

Pettigrew, T. F., & Tropp, L.R. (2006). A meta-analytic test of intergroup contact theory. *Journal of Personality and Social Psychology, 90*(5), 751–783.

Segal, M. W. (1974). Alphabet and attraction: An unobtrusive measure of the effect of propinquity in a field setting. *Journal of Personality and Social Psychology, 30*, 654–657.

Shook, N. J., & Fazio, R. H. (2008). Interracial roommate relationships: An experimental field test of the contact hypothesis. *Psychological Science, 19*, 717–723.

Sutton, R., & Barto, A. G. (1998). *Reinforcement learning*. Cambridge, MA: The MIT Press.

Thorndike, E. L. (1911). *Animal intelligence: Experimental studies*. Lewiston, NY: Macmillan.

Tversky, A., & Kahneman, D. (1974). Judgment under uncertainty: Heuristics and biases. *Science, 27,* 1124–1131.

Wood, W. (2000). Attitude change: Persuasion and social influence. *Annual Review of Psychology, 51,* 539–570.

10

More Than an Artifact
Regression as a Theoretical Construct

KLAUS FIEDLER AND JOACHIM I. KRUEGER

Regression to the mean is like the weather: Everybody talks about it, but few of us do anything about it. However, it is unlike the weather, because most of us fail to recognize it, even when it hits us in the nose.

Lewis R. Goldberg (1991, p. 181)

INTRODUCTION

*O*ne scientist's research finding is often another's artifact. Upon reflection, a presumed artifact can turn out to be of great scientific value. We explore this possibility with regard to phenomena of statistical regression. Regression effects pervade social science and especially the psychology of judgment and decision making. Yet, the typical response is to see these effects as threats to a study's internal validity (Campbell & Kenny, 1999) or to ignore them altogether. In contrast, we will show that regression can be a powerful explanatory construct with important theoretical implications.

Regression and the Phenomenology of Unusual Outcomes

Scientific Discoveries   Consider the common and rather distressing finding that empirical effects tend to weaken with replication (Jennions & Møller, 2002). When initial discoveries fail to replicate with their original strength, it is tempting to search for causal explanations, such as differences in the study design, the location of study, or the type of participant sample. Such a precommitment to a causal perspective hinders a proper appreciation of the statistical law of regression.

Every empirical finding is characterized by a nonzero effect size and imperfect measurement reliability. Assuming a retest reliability of $r = .67$, for example, the retest scores x' will be regressive by one third $(1 - r = .33)$ relative to the original scores x. An individual i whose initial z-standardized score is $z(x_i) = 3$, that is, whose score lies three standard deviations above the mean, will probably have a retest score of $z(x_i') = 2$. Likewise, at the study level, an initial mean difference between two study groups of, say, $d' = z_{\text{Experts}} - z_{\text{Laypeople}} = 1.00$ will shrink by the same scaling factor to $d'' = .67$. Although replication studies may sometimes yield stronger results than the original studies because of improvements in the precision of measurement, such an outcome is unlikely. The original findings most likely to stimulate replication studies are those that have large effect sizes. This is so because large effects are most likely to be published, as a premise for replication (Fiedler, 2011). Yet, the effect sizes of the replications tend to be smaller than the original effects, reflecting both the regressive shrinkage of scores at the individual level and the regressive decline of typically inflated (rather than underestimated) initial effects at the study level.

Bidirectional Regression   Why does unreliability not lead as often to increased effect sizes? This question reflects a basic psychological barrier to understanding the regression principle. Even Galton (1886) first misunderstood his data on heredity (Stigler, 1999). Galton found that very tall fathers are taller and that very short fathers are shorter than their sons. This pattern looked as though the height of men becomes more uniform over generations. But Galton also noticed that very tall sons are taller and that very short sons are shorter than their fathers. Now it seemed as though the height of men becomes less uniform. Both trends cannot be true. The logic of regression explains that it is only the variation of the prediction estimates that shrinks, whereas the predictor levels are fixed at their original values. Given two random variables X and Y with equal variance and a less than perfect intercorrelation $(|r_{XY}| < 1)$, the variance of estimates of X shrinks when plotted against fixed levels of Y, but the variance of estimates of Y also shrinks when plotted against fixed levels of X (Furby, 1973).

Now suppose all studies were published and followed up with attempts to replicate. Replications would yield less extreme results when plotted against original results. Yet, the original results would appear less extreme if plotted against replications. The regression law does not imply a real difference between originals and replications. Replications only appear to yield smaller effects because they are typically plotted against (i.e., conditionalized on) the original results. Analogous to the Galton story, one might produce the opposite phenomenon in reverse analyses. Plotting Y against X means to take observed X values for granted, despite the error with which X is measured. Given that $|r_{XY}| < 1$, any value on the X axis belongs to a true value that is less extreme. Consequently, the Y estimates that correspond to fixed levels of X must be less extreme. This does not reflect any essential difference in the variability of X and Y but merely the fact that X is fixed and only Y is allowed to shrink with decreasing r_{XY}.

Everyday Success and Failure   The regression-replication trap has parallels in everyday judgment and decision making. When a political party or candidate wins an election by a landslide, the rational voter expects a more modest outcome the next time around. Landslides are by definition extreme and unusual. Politicians, pundits, and casual observers who are blind to regression will rush to explain both the landslide and the close election following it in causal terms. If they appreciated regression, they would estimate the degree to which election outcomes lack perfect reliability (e.g., by considering the historical record), make a regressive forecast for the next election, and then compare the observed result with the predicted one.

Similar scenarios arise in business, sports, and popular culture. Often, people are hired, promoted, or married at a time when they are at their personal, but unreliable, best. The regression fallacy is to think that this stellar moment reflects a new high plateau ("He/she will never change!") or worse yet, the first step in a journey to ever-improving excellence. Such hopes may be fulfilled in a few cases, but these are hard to identify *before* the fact. The typical scenario is that of regression. The moment of promotion, winning a contest, marriage, and so on, is one in which performance or fortune (i.e., the "evidence") surpasses a high threshold. It is difficult to see that this evidence is but a sample drawn from a latent population. It is the central tendency and the variability of that latent population that characterize the person, not the extraordinary sample retained *because* it passed the threshold.

Insensitivity to regression and the need to explain random variation breeds disappointment, damages careers, and breaks families. Take the plight of well-intentioned, but regression-blind, educators (Stelzl, 1982). Novice teachers often assume that students' academic achievement and social behavior responds to positive reinforcement, and that punishment of failure and misbehavior is ineffectual and undesirable. Failing to take stochastic factors into account, educators who most enthusiastically reward the highest student achievement and the most positive conduct will notice that subsequent performance and conduct are often less outstanding. They may then falsely conclude that praise damages performance. If teachers then resort to punishing poor performance and behavior, they will notice improvements. Over time, regression blindness turns optimistic reinforcers into cynical punishers. This deplorable sequence of events would not occur if teachers could estimate, however crudely, the random element in student behavior, adjust for it, and evaluate the effectiveness of their feedback by comparing student behavior with informed predictions that take regression into account.

How Much Regression? We have emphasized the need to draw rational inferences by comparing observations with predictions informed by the regression logic, not with selective or haphazard past observations. The direction and amount of change that can be expected from regression can be quantified precisely, assuming a standard normal distribution. Let $Y = (X - \mu)$ be the deviation of an observed value X from the population mean μ. The given deviation score of Y will regress to $Y^* = Y \times r$, whereby r is the reliability of measurement. The strength of the regression shift $Y^* - Y$ is $-Y \times (1 - r)$. Regression is an inverse joint function of the extremity of an original, error-prone measurement, multiplied by its unreliability $(1 - r)$. It is negative when original measures are above the mean (i.e., when $Y > 0$) and positive when original measures are below the mean. It increases linearly with both extremity ($|Y|$) and unreliability ($1 - r$).

These implications are relevant for the theoretical analysis of many putative illusions and biases in judgment and decision-making. Even when the parametric regression model is not applicable because the assumption of a metric normal distribution is not met, or because prior knowledge or extraneous influences cause regression to move to some other value than the arithmetic mean, the qualitative and ordinal implications remain: Regression counteracts the apparent trend observed in any (error-prone) deviation measure, and its effect strength increases with extremity and unreliability.

REGRESSION AS A KEY CONCEPT IN PSYCHOLOGICAL EXPLANATIONS

As noted earlier, regression effects are often dismissed as artifacts. Psychologists and other scientists have been slow to reflect on the theoretical potential of regression (cf. Rulon, 1941). One reason for this neglect may lie in implicit philosophical assumptions about what qualifies as an adequate explanation of human judgment and behavior. Most social and personality psychologists seek to explain behavior in terms of internal (intrapsychic) factors such as intentions, needs, or traits, or external factors such as salient stimuli, social influence, or social roles and norms (Ross & Nisbett, 1991). They rarely consider unsystematic error as a source of systematic effects. By contrast, we argue that acceptance of regression as an explanatory construct can enrich psychological theories.

We elaborate this idea in the context of prominent research findings, devoting four subsections to different ways in which unsystematic regression error can generate systematic biases. These four variants of theoretical regression effects, which lie at the heart of different classes of theoretical explanations, are regression in longitudinal assessment, regression in conditional reasoning, differential regression, and regression approaches to subadditivity.

Regression in Longitudinal Assessment

Timing of Interventions   Regression effects pervade longitudinal research in developmental psychology, education, and quality control studies for intervention programs (E. Thorndike, 1924). Intervention studies in business, education, or in the field of public health (e.g., rewards, punishments, therapy, compensatory training, etc.) rarely use designs with random assignment. Their timing depends on abnormal or extreme states or events. The abnormal moments, which elicit interventions (or more generally, actions and reactions), entail regression, and hence any apparent impact of an intervention is ambiguous. The evident success of an intervention may in part or fully be the result of regression.

Eysenck (1965) made this point in his early critique of research on the efficacy of psychotherapy. Even when most patients improve with time, there is no reason for celebration if a similar rate of improvement may be observed as spontaneous remissions in a nonintervention control group. Although psychotherapy research has become more refined since Eysenck's days (Weisz, McCarty, & Valeri, 2006), such control conditions remain rare. Campbell (1996) observed that therapy

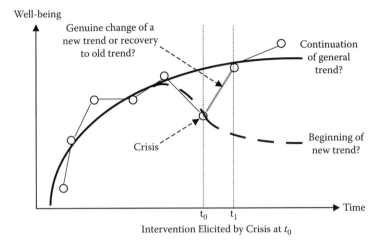

Figure 10.1   Regression provides an alternative account of improvement after an intervention elicited by an unusually low measurement point, or crisis at t_0. The increase between t_0 and t_1 need not reflect the causal impact of the intervention intended to counteract a new downward trend (dashed line). It may simply reflect a normal return to the original trend (solid line), which may be causally independent of the intervention.

is typically introduced or changed at a point of crisis or abnormal peak in the patients' symptoms. If the history of the symptoms prior to intervention is ignored, it is impossible to distinguish the causal impact of the intervention (dashed trend in Figure 10.1) from a regressive return to the old long-term baseline (gray line leading back to the solid curve).

Misattribution and Superstition   Practical intelligence involves the ability to cope with "statistical deceptions." Campbell (1996) considered the case of "Compound Q," which was promoted as a drug to manage AIDS. Although the necessary data were available, researchers did not analyze an extended time series to determine whether the success of the intervention was due to a genuine improvement over the existing trend or merely to a return to the normal trend from an abnormal crisis that motivated the intervention. Campbell cautioned that blindness to regression can be motivated. Agents who are accountable for expensive interventions or new medical developments have little interest in designing studies sensitive enough to test alternative explanations.

Much like scientists' misinterpretations of intervention effects may reflect both the regression trap and vested interests, everyday attribution errors are also subject to both influences. Voters have to judge whether a government's policies have been successful. They must distinguish between illusory failure due to regression (when a government started at a time of abnormal prosperity that would regress statistically to a more modest level) and genuine failure (a reduction in welfare beyond regression). Facing this ambiguity, voters' attributions typically stay consistent with their preferred political standpoint.

People often try to control (and improve) the outcomes in their lives. Some behavior, such as intercessional prayer or taking substances without demonstrated medicinal value, is futile considering the best evidence; yet regression (from a crisis that causes the behavior) makes it look effective, and the person choosing these interventions is vulnerable to an illusion of control (Langer, 1975). The sequence of poor condition, intention to act, taking action, and experiencing improvement, makes it virtually irresistible to see oneself as the author of improvement.

People are not blind to variations in the control they have over their outcomes (Thompson, Armstrong, & Thomas, 1998). With the correlation between true and perceived control less than perfect, regression guarantees that the overestimation of control will be at a maximum when actual control is minimal. The only way to err is to overestimate control. Conversely, if a study was designed in which actual control was perfect, the only way to err would be to underestimate control.

These examples illustrate the manifold ways in which regression effects can account for illusory or superstitious attributions. A final illustration for the counterintuitive nature of regression can be found in the stock market, which is essentially regressive. By analyzing the values of a set of different shares over 15 years, Hubert (1999) showed that investors would have been better off always buying the shares with the lowest annual average profit than buying always the shares with the highest annual profit. Accordingly, successful investment means to anticipate reversals in trends, buying just before an upturn and selling just before a downturn.[1] Because, however, stock prices are not sampled from a population with stable parameters, the estimation of regression to a moving mean becomes an intricate problem.

Moral and Political Reasoning

Blindness to regression lies at the heart of many moral, ethical, and social-political judgments. Consider again a prominent research example. To study the effectiveness of educational or economical programs intended to compensate for existing inequalities in social-economic status or between gender groups, researchers often compare matched groups with "equivalent" test scores, one from an advantaged group and one from a disadvantaged group (McNemar, 1940; R. Thorndike, 1942).

If posttraining performance is lower in the disadvantaged group (e.g., immigrant, minorities, working class people), this is often attributed to the ineffectiveness of the program, or the "genetic" inferiority of the disadvantaged group. Such inferences can be groundless because regression plays a subtle yet powerful role. Note that the two groups are matched only at the sample level. Matching samples from two different populations means that the sample of the advantaged group is likely to underestimate the real performance, whereas the sample drawn from the disadvantaged group is likely to overestimate the real performance. Independent of any causal influence of the training program, a shift toward their respective population means can be expected. This shift needs to be statistically controlled before social interventions can be evaluated. Careful analysis might show that a program has worked, although the apparent sample difference appears to refute this claim.

Regression in Conditional Reasoning

The defining characteristic of regression is the lack of a perfect correlation (Campbell & Kenny, 1999). Temporal instability is but one source of regression effects. In concurrent measurement, the lack of a perfect correlation can signal a lack of reliability, validity, or accuracy. The psychology of judgment and decision making is replete with findings computed as differences between observed and predicted values. These differences are typically chalked up to the "limited capacity" of the human mind to make rational decisions. Upon reflection, however, many of these differences can be understood as a regressive transformation of random variation into systematic discrepancies, or "effects."

Overconfidence   In a typical study, participants receive a list of knowledge questions (e.g., Which river is longer, the Mississippi or the Nile?). For each, they select an answer and indicate their degree of confidence. Judgments are considered well calibrated if the degree of confidence matches the probability of being correct. Overconfidence means that people overestimate the probability of being correct.

Of course, subjective confidence levels vary. Likewise, there is variation in item difficulty. By definition, questions that few (many) people answer correctly are difficult and questions that many people answer correctly are easy. Confidence and accuracy are positively correlated as people have some insight into the quality of their judgments. Yet, when accuracy is plotted against confidence, very high confidence is usually too high, and very low confidence is usually too low (see Figure 10.2). Therefore, subjectively easy items (with high or extremely high confidence) entail overconfidence, whereas subjectively difficult tasks (with low and extremely low confidence) entail underconfidence (Juslin, Winman, & Olsson, 2000).

Studying overconfidence requires a decision as to which criterion will be regressed on what predictor. When regression is done both ways, the same data can show both overconfidence and underconfidence (Dawes & Mulford, 1996; Erev, Wallsten, & Budescu, 1994; Soll, 1996). Consider easy tasks producing high confidence ratings. When the accuracy on these tasks is plotted against confidence, the accuracy corresponding to the highest confidence levels will be less extreme, thus exhibiting overconfidence. When, however, confidence is plotted against accuracy, the confidence for the easiest or most accurate items will be less extreme, thus showing underconfidence. Conversely, the most difficult items with the lowest accuracy will produce overconfidence when confidence is plotted against given accuracy levels. The same items produce underconfidence when the accuracy corresponding to extremely low confidence ratings is actually less extremely low.

Optimistic Bias   Research on self-enhancement, or the so-called illusion of invulnerability, parallels some of the issues illustrated with confidence research (Alicke & Sedikides, 2009). In this paradigm, self-judgments are typically plotted against objective measures, and it is noted that most self-assessments are more favorable than actual performance. Like the hard–easy effect in overconfidence, this effect is most pronounced for low performers. In contrast, high performers underestimate themselves, though less extremely so (Krueger & Mueller, 2002). To

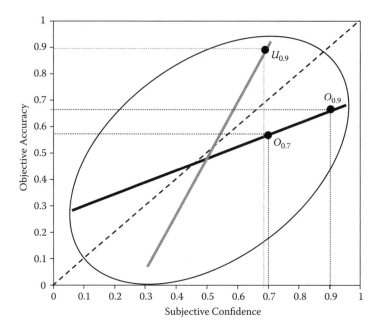

Figure 10.2   The bidirectional nature of regression creates overconfidence and under-confidence in the same data. When objective accuracy is plotted against given values of subjective confidence, overconfidence is apparent in the fact that the objective analogues of high subjective values are clearly lower (see data points $O_{.9}$ and $O_{.7}$). In contrast, undercon-fidence is apparent when subjective confidence estimates are plotted against given objec-tive accuracies. The subjective analogue of high accuracy (see $U_{.9}$) is clearly lower.

account for this regressive pattern, there is no need to attribute different mental capacities or motives to high versus low performers, as Kruger and Dunning (1999) did. The logic of regression alone predicts these opposite judgment biases for high and low performers (Krueger & Wright, 2011). The same logic also predicts that the optimistic bias of low performers can be turned into apparent pessimism if the data are analyzed the other way around. On tasks with extremely low self-attributed percentile values, the actual percentile can be expected to be relatively higher.

A mean-level optimism effect can also be explained with the assumption that judgments under uncertainty do not regress to the midpoint of the response scale but to some optimistic default value above the midpoint of the scale. Although such a response tendency might be called an optimistic bias, it need not be explained in terms of self-serving motives. The same optimism is extended to friends (Epley & Whitchurch, 2008; Krueger, 1998) or other members of the social group (Klar & Giladi, 1997).

Differential Regression as a Source of Biased Comparisons

We have reviewed judgmental biases that reflect a failure to take the conditional nature of regression into account. Depending on whether we observe *Y* conditional on X or X conditional on Y, regression will render Y or X, respectively, less variable and less extreme. According to what might be called *Goldberg's Rule*, "The variance of our predictions should never be larger than that of the criterion we seek to predict. (Never, not just hardly ever)" (Goldberg, 1991, p. 181). Considering the correlation in only one direction may lead to premature conclusions about cognitive or motivational biases.

We now turn to phenomena that arise when two or more sets of judgments are regressive to different degrees. The result is that equivalent targets are judged differently, which is traditionally attributed to perceiver's biases in attention or motivation. Differential regression offers a more parsimonious account. The central idea is that judgments are less extreme for those targets for which the available observations are less reliable. As reliability increases with the size of the sample, one may expect that judgments based on many observations will be more extreme than judgments based on few observations.

Imagine a person playing the role of a classroom teacher (Fiedler, Freytag, & Unkelbach, 2007; Fiedler, Walther, Freytag, & Plessner, 2002). Sixteen simulated boys and girls are presented on the computer screen. Across several sessions, the teacher is giving lessons on different subjects. For each lesson, there is a list of questions on a pull-down menu. On every trial, the teacher selects a question for the class. Some students raise their hands, the teacher calls on one, and the answer is either right or wrong. The individual students differ in their percentage of correct responses (the ability parameter) and their percentage of raising their hand (the motivation parameter). Teachers are asked to assess performance over many trials and to grade all students on both ability and motivation at the end of each lesson.

Figure 10.3 shows the average estimates of student ability as a function of their actual ability parameter (20% versus 50% versus 80%) and successive lessons (from 1st to 4th). Before the first lesson, in the absence of any observations, a reasonable teacher assigns the same intermediate scores to all students. This state of indeterminacy reflects maximal regression, as indicated by the dashed horizontal regression line. After the first session, the learning of student-specific performance remains incomplete, but the slope is already visible. Nevertheless, real parameters of 20% and 80% regress to middling estimates of roughly 46% and 55%, respectively. As the assessment process becomes more complete, the degree of regression declines, reflecting the increasing extraction of judgment-relevant data. Yet, even after many lessons regression is not eliminated. Teachers' judgments never correlate perfectly with student parameters, due to uncontrollable sources of unreliability such as forgetting, attention loss, or fatigue.

Now consider two students that differ in the degree of regression because they are afforded unequal opportunities to learn about their performance. Students with the same high ability parameter (80%) could differ in how often they raise their hand. Assuming unbiased teacher attention, this results in a larger sample of observations or "learning trials" for the more motivated student. However, as the amount of learning determines reliability and regression, this means that high ability will be more apparent for the more motivated student simply because of differential regression. No motivational or cognitive anomalies need to be postulated to predict and explain this basic judgment bias.

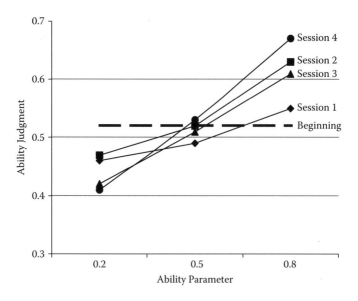

Figure 10.3 Regressive underestimation of high-ability students (0.80) and overestimation of low-ability students (0.20) in simulated classroom studies by Fiedler et al. (2002). The degree of regression decreases with learning experience, from session 1 to session 4.

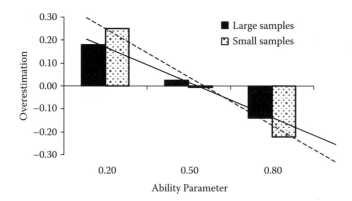

Figure 10.4 Regressive underestimation of high-ability students (0.80) and overestimation of low-ability students (0.20) in simulated classroom studies by Fiedler et al. (2002). Judgments based on small samples are more regressive than judgments based on large samples.

The results plotted in Figure 10.4 show that the same level of student ability led to more extreme judgments when the sample of observations was large rather than small. Small samples created a disadvantage for smart students, whose high ability was underestimated due to enhanced regression, whereas poor students profited from enhanced regression, which prevented teachers from fully recognizing their low ability (Fiedler et al., 2002).

Confirmation Bias and Positive Testing
Differential regression can also explain findings traditionally seen as instances of confirmation bias (Nickerson, 1998; Snyder, 1984). In the simulated-classroom study, teachers were asked to test the hypothesis that boys are superior in math and physics, whereas girls are superior in language. As expected, these instructions triggered a positive-testing strategy (Klayman & Ha, 1987). Focusing on the students representing the focal hypothesis, most teachers gathered more science-related information from boys and more language-related information from girls. As a consequence, judgments of boys and girls were unequally regressive, leading to less positive evaluations of smart girls than equally smart boys in science, and to less positive evaluations of smart boys than equally smart girls in language. These differences in evaluation did not emerge among teachers who gathered samples of the same sizes. In other words, differences in evaluation depended on the regressiveness of available information, not on biased information processing.

Confirmation biases are often attributed to the undesirable effects of stereotypes. Hence, the case for the differential regression hypothesis is particularly strong if its signature pattern of results can be obtained even when it is pitted against the stereotype effect. Indeed, when teachers draw larger samples of girls in science and boys in language, the resulting differences in the evaluation of equally smart boys and girls run counter to the stereotype (Fiedler et al., 2002; Fiedler, Walther, & Nickel, 1999).[2]

Comparing the Self to the Group Average
Differential regression also casts a new light on optimistic biases. Given the general response bias toward high performance estimates and given that people know more about themselves than about others, it follows that judgments of the self are less regressive—and thus more positive—than judgments of others. The regression account correctly predicts a reduced better-than-average effect when the amount of information about others increases (Moore & Small, 2007). By the same logic, a worse-than-average effect can result due to greater self-knowledge, when people compare themselves to the average other with regard to negative attributes (Klar & Giladi, 1997).

Illusory Devaluation of Minorities
The devaluation of minority groups is a robust social-psychological finding that has generated many explanations (Dovidio & Gaertner, 2010). In Hamilton and Gifford's (1976) influential work on illusory correlations, participants receive behavior descriptions associated with members of two groups, denoted A and B. For Group A, the sample of behaviors is twice as large as for Group B. As positive behaviors are twice as frequent as negative behaviors in both groups, the correlation between group and valence is zero. Nevertheless, the prevalent positivity of behavior is more readily apparent for the majority than for the minority, as evident from frequency estimates, group impression ratings, and cued recall of behavior-group associations in countless experiments (Fiedler, 2000; Mullen & Johnson, 1990).

Conventional explanations of illusory correlations focus on cognitive or motivational biases, such as selective memory for the most infrequent combination (i.e., negative behavior by the minority), or a motive to give meaning and identity to groups (McGarty, Haslam, Turner, & Oakes, 1993). However, differential regression is sufficient to produce the effect (Fiedler, 1991). Given more learning trials for the majority than the minority, it is no wonder that a generally high rate of positive behavior is more readily extracted for the former than the latter group (Fiedler, 1996; Klauer & Meiser, 2000).

Enhanced Regression Effects Through Subadditivity

A particularly intriguing class of biases in judgment and decision making arises when superordinate categories are split into subcategories or, conversely, when subcategories merge into superordinate categories. In this context, we encounter subadditivity. The overall subjective quantity $s(A + B)$ that results from merging two subsets or subcategories A and B is smaller than the sum of the subjective component quantities $s(A) + s(B)$. Subadditivity holds for both utilities (Morewedge, Gilbert, Keyzar, Berkovits, & Wilson, 2007) and probabilities (Fiedler & Armbruster, 1994; Tversky & Koehler, 1994). Gaining two times $1000 is worth more, subjectively, than gaining $2000. Tolerating an unpleasant physical examination for 10 minutes is less aversive than tolerating two 5-minute unpleasant examinations on separate days. The estimated risk or likelihood of dying from an accident is smaller than the summed estimate of the likelihood of dying in a traffic accident or a sports accident or a household accident, or a work accident, or a disjunctive list of other accidents.

Subadditivity entails so-called unpacking effects (Rottenstreich & Tversky, 1997; Tversky & Koehler, 1994) or category-split effects (Fiedler, 2002; Fiedler & Armbruster, 1994). The subjective likelihood or utility of a superordinate category (e.g., the number of Japanese cars on U.S. streets) can be increased by unpacking the category into two or more subcategories (e.g., number of Mazda, Toyota, Mitsubishi, Nissan, Honda, or Suzuki cars on U.S. streets). Conversely, packing several subcategories into a superordinate category reduces the overall subjective quantity.

Subadditivity can be derived from the negatively accelerated shape of most psychophysical functions. Large quantities are disproportionally underestimated because the subjective analogues of objective quantities (such as lightness, loudness, or monetary gains) do not increase linearly. The example in Figure 10.5 shows that adding $a + b$ yields a high quantity on the abscissa, the relative underestimation of which is much greater than for the two smaller component quantities together, as evident from the deviation between the subjective function and the dashed linear diagonal.

The Weber–Fechner law captures this psychophysical phenomenon. The difference threshold Δx (i.e., the increment in the stimulus quantity required to notice an increment) increases linearly with the absolute level x of the quantity. With the ratio $\Delta x/x$ constant, an increasingly larger objective input is needed to produce an identical subjective output increment Δx (i.e., a just noticeable difference).

A similar rule can explain why decelerating functions, implying subadditivity, are common in many other areas beyond psychophysics. In prospect theory (Kahneman & Tversky, 1979), the amount of objective gains (losses) needed to add a constant increment in subjective value increases with the absolute level of gains (losses). In

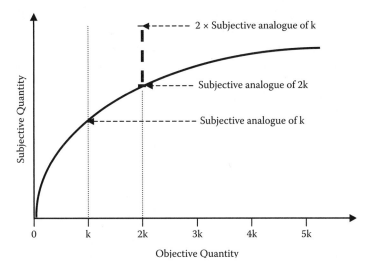

Figure 10.5 Graphical illustration of subadditivity created by negatively accelerated functions: Twice the subjective analogue of k is clearly more than the subjective analogue of 2k.

psychological statistics, too, the increment in sample size required to increase the resulting reliability by a constant factor increases with absolute sample size.[3]

As a rule, the dynamically changing discrepancies between subjective and objective quantities—in psychophysics, utility and subjective probability assessment—entail regression effects, that is, overestimation (underestimation) of small (large) quantities that results from the splitting (merging) of stimulus categories. In a recent study by Fiedler, Unkelbach, and Freytag (2009), participants estimated the number of butterflies of different types they had seen in an extended stimulus series. In one experiment, the objective presentation frequencies for butterfly types A, B, C, and D were 4, 10, 16, and 22, respectively. Frequency estimates were regressive because subjective and objective frequencies were not perfectly correlated. Replicating a standard result in memory for frequencies (cf. Fiedler, 2002; Sedlmeier, 1999), participants overestimated the frequencies of small categories (A and B), and underestimated the frequencies of large categories (C and D). Over- or underestimation was stronger for extreme categories (A and D) than for moderate categories (B and C). When the other determinant of regression, unreliability, was manipulated with a secondary task causing cognitive load, the overall degree of regression increased. This increase was proportionally stronger for extreme than for moderate categories.

Given the general applicability of a regression model to the frequency-judgment task, the question was what happens when some of the stimulus categories are unpacked into smaller subcategories. For example, when type-A butterflies are split into two subcategories, A_1 and A_2, marked by different colors, a small category frequency of 4 was decomposed into two extremely small subcategories with frequencies of 2 each. As the degree of regression increases with extremity, the twofold overestimation of both extremely small subcategories should result in a larger summed estimate $f(A_1) + f(A_2)$ than the pooled estimate of $f(A_1 + A_2)$ in the nonsplit condition. Likewise, the estimated frequency of the large category D (with a frequency of 22), which is usually underestimated due to regression, can be split into two medium subcategories of size 11, which should show little regression (on a reference scale from 2 to 22). As a consequence, they should be no longer underestimated, so that the summed estimates of $f(D_1) + f(D_2)$ should again be clearly higher than the pooled estimate of $f(D_1 + D_2)$ in the nonsplit condition.

In general, the frequency illusions that resulted from the packing and unpacking of stimulus frequencies were well predicted by the general rule of regression. As expected, large quantities (e.g., frequencies) were underestimated and low quantities (frequencies) were overestimated. These discrepancies increased with greater extremity or unreliability of the available information. When the extremity of small frequencies was enhanced or the extremity of large categories was reduced (by splitting a category into smaller subcategories), this increased the subjective frequency of the entire category. The strength of category-split effects increased when cognitive load reduced the reliability of frequency assessment.

Unkelbach and Fiedler (2011) showed that regression-based effects on frequency judgments can carry over to evaluative judgments. The mere-exposure effect is the classic finding that liking for a target or stimulus increases with the frequency with which it has been encountered (Bornstein, 1989; Zajonc, 1968). Replicating this effect, with types of butterflies, Unkelbach and Fiedler found that frequently presented types were rated as more attractive than infrequently presented butterflies. Critically, however, this exposure effect varied with subjective frequencies of presentation, which, in turn, were subject to differential regression. As expected, cognitive load produced greater regression and thus smaller effects of exposure on liking. Moreover, exposure effects became smaller when stimulus categories were split into small or very small subcategories.

CONCLUSION

Despite the reputation of regression as an artifact, a noisy variance component, and a source of uncontrolled error, we have considered regression as a fascinating and enlightening property of the empirical world. Although stochastic in origin, regression effects are bound by well-understood rules that can turn unsystematic error into systematic bias. Analyzing and understanding these lawful manifestations of regression leads to alternative explanations for a host of prominent phenomena in judgment and decision making. Once we theorize in terms of regression as a model with two clearly specified determinants, extremity and unreliability, we encounter novel predictions that cannot be derived from any other theoretical approach.

We have illustrated our core message with reference to four classes of judgment biases, reflecting four different ways in which regression turns into systematic variance. The first class of phenomena includes the most prominent examples of the "regression trap" in the methodological literature. These examples typically point to illusions in the researcher's mind and they refer to misinterpretations of changes in longitudinal designs. When interventions are not initiated in a randomly determined moment but in a crisis or in an extraordinary moment, then any subsequent improvement or return to that baseline does not justify the attribution of a separate cause (e.g., the intervention). Such changes across repeated measures may merely reflect the operation of regression to a general trend or overall mean.

The remaining three classes of phenomena are not included in classical treatises of regression artifacts. They rather reflect the systematic application of regression conceived as a theoretical model of judgment biases in several prominent paradigms. Thus, the second class originates in a critical reanalysis of the data from conditional inference studies. Conditional inferences of one variable from given levels of another variable can be misleading because regression is bidirectional. Accuracy is a regressive function of confidence but confidence is also a regressive function of accuracy. The same judgments can be overconfident and underconfident, depending on whether accuracy is conditionalized on confidence, or confidence on accuracy.

The third scenario is differential regression. Judgments and evaluations of two equivalent targets (e.g., two equally smart students; equally positive groups) will differ when the targets cannot be assessed with the same reliability, due to unequal sample size, motivation, or distance of observations. Fourth, when large target categories are decomposed into smaller subcategories or, conversely, when small categories are merged into larger superordinate categories, the summation of several regression effects can produce strong and systematic biases. Subadditivity arises from the general rule that large quantities tend to be underestimated whereas small quantities tend to be overestimated.

Regression effects can account for many well-known judgmental biases that have been traditionally explained in terms of extraneous causes. The preferred causal explanations for such biases involve intrapsychic constructs, such as stereotypes, wishful thinking, limited memory capacity, or heuristic as opposed to deliberative reasoning. Even though these factors may contribute to some of the biases some of the time, regression alone is a sufficient condition for all these phenomena to occur. For the claim that cognitive or motivational factors produce bias to be compelling, it must be demonstrated that the bias goes beyond what regression can explain. As such a research methodology has rarely been used, the canonical findings conflate to an unknown degree the impact of regression and other causal influences.

Why is there such resistance to regression as an explanatory construct? We suspect that probabilistic thinking in general is counterintuitive and that this remains true for trained scientists (Goldberg, 1991; Rulon, 1941). Formal models of probability did not appear until late in the Renaissance (Gigerenzer, Swijtink, Porter, Daston, Beatty, & Krüger, 1989). Regression is counterintuitive because it is anticyclical; it points in the direction opposite to what appear to be current trends.

In addition to these psychological barriers, theorists and researchers have incentives to explain behavior in causal terms. In experimental science, researchers take it as their mission to isolate unique causal relationships. The ability to detect causal relations is the stated distinction of the experimental method. To explain systematic biases (or other behavioral effects) with variation that is at its root random must seem like a failure to the experimentalist. Hence, we may read and understand the regression critique of overconfidence, and yet continue to believe that overconfidence comes from the enhancement of the ego. We may comprehend the lesson that the stock market behaves regressively, while continuing to invest in stocks that were recent winners. No one has refuted the claim—truism even— that the devaluation of minorities in the illusory-correlation paradigm can reflect regression alone, but textbooks continue to broadcast the view that a memory bias toward rare (i.e., negative) behavior in rare people (i.e., minorities) is the necessary and sufficient source of this effect.

We believe that it is necessary to overcome the resistance to abstract and counterintuitive constructs in theoretical reasoning. Abstract theoretical concepts like regression can expand knowledge and stimulate bold new hypotheses. These concepts can also be translated into vivid and comprehensible theoretical metaphors. One such metaphor portrays regression as a sort of informational erosion. To the extent that the geological ground is weak and "unreliable," and to the extent that the geological surface varies in extremity of altitude, erosion will be manifested in shrinking mountain tops and rising valley floors.

Another physical metaphor, related to the concept of potential energy, construes the multivariate empirical world as a bundle of intertwined rubber strings. Depending on the direction and strength of all kinds of varying extraneous forces that impinge on the world, the individual rubber strings (i.e., variables) are stretched to varying degrees (i.e., contaminated with error variance). As a consequence, the true length of the rubber strings will be overestimated to the extent that they are exaggerated at the time of measurement. The same rubber strings can be expected to shrink on the next occasion, when external forces are eliminated or operating in different directions.

Whatever metaphor of the regression law turns out to be most intelligible and appropriate as an explanatory construct, we believe it will eventually further our theoretical and empirical knowledge. It will not only explain familiar phenomena in human judgment but also help discover new phenomena that can be derived from mental simulations or computer simulations of the regression model proper. Last but not least, systematic analyses of the conditions under which regression is minimized can assist researchers in devising efficient debiasing strategies and remedies to irrational illusions in judgment and decision making.

AUTHOR NOTE

Correspondence regarding this chapter should be addressed to Klaus Fiedler at: kf@ psychologie.uni-heidelberg.de. The research underlying the present paper was supported by a Koselleck grant of the Deutsche Forschungsgemeinschaft awarded to Klaus Fiedler.

NOTES

1. Even when the standard regression model assuming a stable mean is not met in the stock market example, regression often accounts for the lion's share of outcome variance (Hubert, 1999).
2. Following a suggestion by Constantine Sedikides, these authors introduced the term *autoverification effect*.

3. The formula provided by Spearman (1910) and Brown (1910), $R = nr / (1 - r + nr)$ shows the increase in the overall reliability of a test, R, as a function of n, the number of items or responses, and the average reliability of a single item r. This function is negatively accelerated. To achieve a constant increment in reliability, the increment in sample size has to be larger for large than for small n. This is so because increasing n by a factor $k > 1$ increases the entire numerator but only one summand in the denominator by k.

REFERENCES

Alicke, M. D., & Sedikides, C. (2009). Self-enhancement and self-protection: What they are and what they do. *European Review of Social Psychology, 20*, 1–48.

Bornstein, R. F. (1989). Exposure and affect: Overview and meta-analysis of research, 1967–1987. *Psychological Bulletin, 106*, 265–289.

Brown, W. (1910). Some experimental results in the correlation of mental abilities. *British Journal of Psychology, 3*, 276–322.

Campbell, D. T. (1996). Regression artifacts in time-series and longitudinal data. *Evaluation and Program Planning, 19*, 377–389.

Campbell, D. T., & Kenny, D. A. (1999). *A primer on regression artifacts*. London: Guilford Press.

Dawes, R. M., & Mulford, M. (1996). The false consensus effect and overconfidence: Flaws in judgment or flaws in how we study judgment? *Organizational Behavior and Human Decision Processes, 65*, 201–211.

Dovidio, J. F., & Gaertner, S. L. (2010). Intergroup bias. In S. T. Fiske, D. T. Gilbert, & G. Lindzey (Eds.), *Handbook of social psychology* (5th ed., Vol. 2, pp. 1084–1121). Hoboken, NJ: Wiley.

Epley, N., & Whitchurch, E. (2008). Mirror, mirror on the wall: Enhancement in self-recognition. *Personality and Social Psychology Bulletin, 34*, 1159–1170.

Erev, I., Wallsten, T. S., & Budescu, D. V. (1994). Simultaneous over- and underconfidence: The role of error in judgment processes. *Psychological Review, 101*, 519–527.

Eysenck, H. J. (1965). *Fact and fiction in psychology*. Baltimore, MD: Pelican.

Fiedler, K. (1991). The tricky nature of skewed frequency tables: An information loss account of distinctiveness-based illusory correlations. *Journal of Personality and Social Psychology, 60*, 24–36.

Fiedler, K. (1996). Explaining and simulating judgment biases as an aggregation phenomenon in probabilistic, multiple-cue environments. *Psychological Review, 103*, 193–214.

Fiedler, K. (2000). Illusory correlations: A simple associative algorithm provides a convergent account of seemingly divergent paradigms. *Review of General Psychology, 4*, 25–58.

Fiedler, K. (2002) Frequency judgment and retrieval structures: Splitting, zooming, and merging the units of the empirical world. In P. Sedlmeier &. T. Betsch (Eds.), *Frequency processing and cognition* (pp. 67–87). Oxford, UK: Oxford University Press.

Fiedler, K. (2011). Voodoo correlations are everywhere—Not only in neuroscience. *Perspectives on Psychological Science, 6*(2), 163–171.

Fiedler, K., & Armbruster, T. (1994). Two halfs may be more than one whole: Category-split effects on frequency illusions. *Journal of Personality and Social Psychology, 66*, 633–645.

Fiedler, K., Freytag, P., & Unkelbach, C. (2007). Pseudocontingencies in a simulated classroom. *Journal of Personality and Social Psychology, 92*, 665–667.

Fiedler, K., Unkelbach, C., & Freytag, P. (2009). On splitting and merging categories: A regression account of subadditivity. *Memory & Cognition, 37*, 383–393.

Fiedler, K., Walther, E., Freytag, P., & Plessner, H. (2002). Judgment biases in a simu-lated classroom—A cognitive–environmental approach. *Organizational Behavior and Human Decision Processes, 88*, 527–561.

Fiedler, K., Walther, E., & Nickel, S. (1999). The autoverification of social hypoth-esis: Stereotyping and the power of sample size. *Journal of Personality and Social Psychology, 77*, 5–18.

Furby, L. (1973). Interpreting regression toward the mean in developmental research. *Developmental Psychology, 8*, 172–179.

Galton, F. (1886). Regression toward mediocrity in hereditary stature. *Journal of the Anthropological Institute of Great Britain and Ireland, 15*, 246–263.

Gigerenzer, G., Swijtink, Z., Porter, T., Daston, L., Beatty, J., & Krüger, L. (1989). *The empire of chance: How probability changed science and everyday life*. New York: Cambridge University Press.

Goldberg, L. R. (1991). Human mind versus regression equation: Five contrasts. In D. Cicchetti & W. M. Grove (Eds.), *Thinking clearly about psychology: Essays in honor of Paul E. Meehl* (Vol. 1, pp. 173–184). Minneapolis: University of Minnesota Press.

Hamilton, D. L., & Gifford, R. K. (1976). Illusory correlation in interpersonal perception: A cognitive basis of stereotypic judgments. *Journal of Experimental Social Psychology, 12*, 392-407.

Hubert, M. (1999). The misuse of past-performance data. In L. E. Likson & R. A. Geist (Eds.), *The psychology of investing* (pp. 147–157). New York, NY: Wiley.

Jennions, M. D., & Møller, A. P. (2002). Relationships fade with time: A meta-analysis of temporal trends in publication in ecology and evolution. *Proceedings of the Royal Society London B, 269*, 43–48.

Juslin, P., Winman, A., & Olsson, H. (2000). Naive empiricism and dogmatism in confidence research: A critical examination of the hard–easy effect. *Psychological Review, 107*, 384–396.

Kahneman, D., & Tversky, A. (1979). Prospect theory: An analysis of decision under risk. *Econometrica, 47*(2), 263–291.

Klar, Y., & Giladi, E. (1997). No one in my group can be below the group's average: A robust positivity bias in favor of anonymous peers. *Journal of Personality and Social Psychology, 73*, 885–901.

Klauer, K., & Meiser, T. (2000). A source-monitoring analysis of illusory correlations. *Personality and Social Psychology Bulletin, 26*, 1074–1093.

Klayman, J., & Ha, Y. (1987). Confirmation, disconfirmation, and information in hypothesis testing. *Psychological Review, 94*, 211–228.

Krueger, J. (1998). Enhancement bias in the description of self and others. *Personality and Social Psychology Bulletin, 24*, 505–516.

Krueger, J., & Mueller, R. (2002). Unskilled, unaware, or both? The better-than-average heuristic and statistical regression predict errors in estimates of own performance. *Journal of Personality and Social Psychology, 82*, 180–188.

Krueger, J. I., & Wright, J. C. (2011). Measurement of self-enhancement (and self-pro-tection). In M. D. Alicke & C. Sedikides (Eds.), *Handbook of self-enhancement and self-protection* (pp. 472–494). New York: Guilford.

Kruger, J., & Dunning, D. (1999). Unskilled and unaware of it: How difficulties in recogniz-ing one's own incompetence lead to inflated self-assessments. *Journal of Personality and Social Psychology, 77*, 1121–1134.

Langer, E. (1975). The illusion of control. *Journal of Personality and Social Psychology, 32*, 311–328.

McGarty, C., Haslam, S. A., Turner, J. C., & Oakes, P. J. (1993). Illusory correlation as accentuation of actual intercategory difference: Evidence for the effect with minimal stimulus information. *European Journal of Social Psychology, 23*, 391–410.

McNemar, Q. (1940). A critical examination of the University of Iowa studies of mental influences upon the IQ. *Psychological Bulletin, 37*, 63–92.

Moore, D. A., & Small, D. A. (2007). Error and bias in comparative judgment: On being both better and worse than we think we are. *Journal of Personality of Social Psychology, 92*, 972–989.

Morewedge, C. K., Gilbert, D. T., Keyzar, B., Berkovits, M. J., & Wilson, T. D. (2007). Mispredicting the hedonic benefits of segregated gains. *Journal of Experimental Psychology: General, 136*, 700–709.

Mullen, B., & Johnson, C. (1990). Distinctiveness-based illusory correlations and stereotyping: A meta-analytic integration. *British Journal of Social Psychology, 29*, 11–28.

Nickerson, R. S. (1998). Confirmation bias: A ubiquitous phenomenon in many guises. *Review of General Psychology, 2*, 175–220.

Ross, L., & Nisbett, R. E. (1991). *The person and the situation*. New York: McGraw-Hill.

Rottenstreich, Y., & Tversky, A. (1997). Unpacking, repacking, and anchoring: Advances in support theory. *Psychological Review, 104*, 406–415.

Rulon, P. J. (1941). Problems of regression. *Harvard Educational Review, 11*, 213–223.

Sedlmeier, P. (1999). *Improving statistical reasoning: Theoretical models and practical implications*. Mahwah, NJ: Lawrence Erlbaum Associates.

Snyder, M. (1984). When belief creates reality. In L. Berkowitz (Ed.), *Advances in experimental social psychology* (Vol. 18, pp. 247–305). New York: Academic Press.

Soll, J. B. (1996). Determinants of overconfidence and miscalibration: The roles of random error and ecological structure. *Organizational Behavior and Human Decision Processes, 65*(2), 117–137. doi:10.1006/obhd.1996.0011.

Spearman, C. C. (1910). Correlation calculated from faulty data. *British Journal of Psychology, 3*, 271–295.

Stelzl, I. (1982). *Fehler und Fallen der Statistik [Errors and traps of statistics]*. Bern, Switzerland: Huber.

Stigler, S. (1999). *Statistics on the table: The history of statistical concepts and methods*. Cambridge, MA: Harvard University Press.

Thompson, S., Armstrong, W., & Thomas, C. (1998). Illusions of control, underestimations, and accuracy: A control heuristic explanation. *Psychological Bulletin, 123*, 143–161.

Thorndike, E. L. (1924). The influence of chance imperfections on measures upon the relationship of initial score to gain or loss. *Journal of Experimental Psychology, 7*, 225–232.

Thorndike, R. L. (1942). Regression fallacies in the matched groups experiment. *Psychometrika, 7*, 85–102.

Tversky, A., & Koehler, D. J. (1994). Support theory: A nonextensional representation of subjective probability. *Psychological Review, 101*, 547–567.

Unkelbach, C., & Fiedler, K. (2011). *Regression-based frequency illusions and the mere exposure effect*. Manuscript submitted for publication.

Weisz, J. R., McCarty, C. A., & Valeri, S. M. (2006). Effects of psychotherapy on depression in children and adolescents: A meta-analysis. *Psychological Bulletin, 132*, 132–149.

Zajonc, R. B. (1968). Attitudinal effects of mere exposure [Monograph supplement]. *Journal of Personality and Social Psychology, 9*(2, Pt. 2), 1–27.

Section IV

Applications

11

Simple Heuristics for Mate Choice Decisions

PETER M. TODD, SKYLER S. PLACE, and ROBERT I. BOWERS

*M*ate choices are among the most important social decisions we can make. Not only are we making decisions about other people, but our decisions are also informed and influenced by those particular individuals, and by still others that they and we interact with—our mate choices depend on our own experiences with others, and on the experiences that others have had and we can learn from. Thus, our mate choice decisions are about social options, and are based on both individually and socially acquired information.

With all of that information available, both from the chooser's own investigations of potential mates and the appraisals and opinions of others, it may seem as though we need complex algorithms to process it all and make optimal, rational decisions (Krueger, this volume, Chapter 4). But humans typically do not need to gather and use very much information to make good choices. By and large, we can make choices based on the limited data we have by using rather simple decision mechanisms, or heuristics—rules of thumb that allow us to make good decisions without much information or processing. Such heuristics are widely used in all manner of domains of human endeavor, whether social (Hertwig, Hoffrage, & the ABC Research Group, in press; see also Hoffrage & Hertwig, this volume, Chapter 8) or individual (Gigerenzer, Todd, & the ABC Research Group, 1999).

Heuristics play a part throughout our extended search for romantic partners, affecting two critical stages of decision making that we have to interleave. First, when we encounter a new potential mate, we need to assess that individual, typically by learning some things about him or her and then using that information to make an overall judgment of how attractive this individual is to us. Second, we must decide whether this person is attractive *enough* so that we will stop our search and pursue a relationship (taking into account that the other person must also choose us in return)—if not, we continue exploring the mating pool, returning to the first stage when we meet another new potential mate. In making both of these decisions, we can use information that we have gathered ourselves or that we obtain from others. We can limit the information we need to use by employing appropriate heuristics for both individual assessment and sequential search. In this chapter, we explore the types and sources of information used in these stages of mate choice, and the heuristic mechanisms that convert it into adaptive decisions.

In the next section, we begin with a brief overview of the framework of bounded and ecological rationality within which heuristic decision making can be studied. Then we describe the ways in which people can use individually gathered information in making their mate choice decisions, both in the assessment of potential mates and in the search through a sequence of possible mates. Finally, we look at how people can use information from others to guide their mate choices, in terms of what to look for when assessing mates, and how to decide if one's search should stop with the current prospect.

MAKING DECISIONS WITH SIMPLE HEURISTICS

Given the complexity of our social environment and the decisions we must make within it, how can good decisions be made by real minds operating in this uncertain social world? The same question applies to decision making in nonsocial domains, though the complexity is compounded when other individuals are thrown into the mix. The traditional rational approaches to such complex problems would be to deploy complex decision mechanisms (e.g., predicate logic, Bayesian statistics, and so forth), gathering all the available information and processing it fully to reach the optimal conclusions (cf. Hastie & Dawes, 2010). However, humans (and other animals) must often make decisions within narrow psychological and ecological bounds that prevent the use of complex methods. These bounds include the limited time available to make a decision before an opportunity passes (especially in competitive social settings, such as seeking a mate when others are competing within the same limited mating pool; see Todd, 2007), the limited and uncertain information accessible within that time, and the limited ability to process that information, owing to neural constraints of processing power and memory.

To work within these bounds and still behave adaptively, people can rely on "fast and frugal" heuristics (Gigerenzer & Goldstein, 1996; Gigerenzer et al., 1999)—decision rules that use a small amount of time, information, and processing to come up with what are usually good choices, when they are employed in the proper environments. This use in appropriate environments is central to the heuristics' successful application, because it allows them to exploit the fact that information in the world is typically structured in useful ways. For example, if one asks about the socially distributed knowledge of what authors, or places, or products are widely recognized in a given society, one finds systematic patterns relating recognition to the publication rate, or population size, or prevalence of those things, rather than a random or uniform distribution of what is recognized. Higher values on the latter dimensions lead to greater recognition (Goldstein & Gigerenzer, 2002; Pachur, Todd, Gigerenzer, Schooler, & Goldstein, in press). An individual decision maker can capitalize on this structure, which he or she picks up through social interactions (learning about, and hence recognizing, what others mention), by using simple heuristics that employ recognition as a cue in making choices, for instance, preferring what they recognize when deciding which article to cite or which brand of car to buy. By counting on certain information structures to be present in the environment, decision heuristics can be correspondingly simpler, effectively letting the world do some of the work for them.

Using simple heuristics in environments to which they fit can enable decision makers to achieve what Herbert Simon (1990) called *bounded rationality*. In contrast to the largely unachievable dream of unbounded rationality, which assumes optimal processing of all available information without concern for computational or informational costs, Simon saw humans as exhibiting a bounded form of rationality emerging from the interaction of two forces: the cognitive capabilities of the person and the structure of the task environment. These two components complement each other like the two blades of a pair of scissors. For behavior to be adaptive, or boundedly rational, mind and environment must be closely matched. This perspective aligns with that of evolutionary psychology, which assumes that evolution has favored a close fit between mind and environment by honing the former to match the latter (see DeScioli & Kurzban, this volume, Chapter 12). Yet, minds can also shape their own environments, and this is particularly true in social domains. In other words, the adaptive forces flow in both directions between organisms and their world.

The research program of *ecological rationality* aims to identify the particular decision mechanisms that can produce bounded rationality in the presence of particular structures of information in the environment (Gigerenzer et al., 1999; Todd & Gigerenzer, 2007; Todd, Gigerenzer, & the ABC Research Group, in press). Ecological rationality emphasizes the importance of considering both environmental information structure and psychological information-processing mechanisms, and how the former enables and constrains the latter to yield adaptive decisions. The strategy for studying the ecological rationality of particular decision mechanisms proceeds through a sequence of steps including analysis of the environment structure, simulation testing of proposed heuristic mechanisms in constructed test environments, analysis of the information structures in which the heuristics will and will not work well, and empirical investigation of when people actually use these heuristics via lab experiments and field studies.

The simple heuristics in the mind's *adaptive toolbox* (Gigerenzer & Todd, 1999) are composed of even simpler building blocks that guide the search for information or options, stop that search in a frugal manner, and then decide on the basis of the search's results. These heuristics are all proposed and tested in terms of precise cognitive mechanisms that specify exactly what information is used and how it is processed algorithmically, step by step, to produce a decision or judgment. As a consequence, they yield more types of predictions about the course of behavior (e.g., reaction times and cue-search orders in addition to choices made) and are consequently more susceptible to empirical rejection than are broad categories like "social influence."

One important class of heuristics comprises those heuristics that make decisions among a set of currently available options or alternatives by limiting the amount of information they seek about each. The *recognition heuristic* (Goldstein & Gigerenzer, 2002), for example, favors recognized options over unfamiliar ones. Another example is the *take-the-best heuristic* (Gigerenzer & Goldstein, 1999), which chooses between options by searching through relevant cues about them in order of their validity (accuracy), stops as soon as it encounters the first cue that discriminates between the options, and selects the option with the highest value on that cue. A second important type of heuristic searches for options themselves, rather than information about currently available options, in a fast and frugal way. For example, a *satisficing* heuristic (Simon, 1990) uses a preset aspiration level—the minimum value that the searcher will settle for—to search through a sequence of options (e.g., apartments to rent, visited one after another) until the first is found that exceeds that aspiration level. We will discuss examples of both types of heuristics applied to mate choice in the following sections.

USING ONE'S OWN EXPERIENCES TO CHOOSE MATES

Assessing Potential Mates

When a potential mate is encountered, the first stage of choice begins with an assessment of whether that person could be a suitable partner. This stage involves the observation and processing of available cues about that person. There are many cues that are associated with mate quality in humans, including height, weight, facial attractiveness and averageness, skin texture and tone, jaw size, waist-to-hip ratio, musculature, voice, movement, scent, cultural decoration, intelligence, sense of humor, warmth and kindness, health, social status, fidelity, interest in having a family, general mood, and so on (Grammer, Fink, Møller, & Thornhill, 2003; Miller & Todd, 1998). (Here we focus on these cues being assessed by the mate seeker personally; later we consider using the assessments made by others.) The traditional rational approach to processing these cues into an overall judgment of mate quality would be to gather all the information available, and then use it all—possibly weighting some of the cues more strongly than others—to make a comparison between the potential mate and some standard. The standard could take a number of forms, including a prototypical attractive individual with the prototype inherited or learned from one's culture or other experience, another potential mate who might be currently available (for instance, when choosing which of two possible romantic partners to pursue), or even be the mate-seeker himself or herself. In the last case, the mate-seeker could weigh and compare the cues so that similarity with the potential mate is highly valued (likes attract), or so that different cues trade off between the seeker and potential mate (opposites attract or complements attract). Men, for example, tend to trade off wealth and status for youth and attractiveness in women (Todd, Penke, Fasolo, & Lenton, 2007).

Fully rational decision models have serious drawbacks that make them at least partly unrealistic for real mate choice. First, they assume people take the time and make the effort to learn all these attributes about the person they are interested in, when clearly many mate choice decisions (particularly those in the negative direction, rejecting a potential mate) can be made almost instantaneously. Second, rational models assume that all the necessary cues will be available simultaneously but different sexual cues require different lengths of time to assess: physical beauty and other cues at the beginning of the list given earlier can be perceived immediately, whereas recognizing infidelity or stability of mood could take weeks to years. Third, these models typically assume a linear combination of the cues involved, although there are recognized nonlinearities in how cues in mate choice interact (Miller & Todd, 1998). Linear models also assume that any given cue can be traded off against any other, such that beauty for instance could compensate for infidelity, which often will not be the case.

Contrary to the assumptions of rational models, people often apply simple mate choice heuristics that do not require consideration of all the available information, nor linearly combine what cues they do use. For instance, a strategy like take-the-best may be used to compare the attractiveness of pairs of potential mates, by starting with the mate seeker's most important cue and determining whether the two options differ on that cue; if so, stop cue search and accept (or pursue) the person who is more attractive; if not, go on to the next most important cue and repeat the process (Czerlinski, Gigerenzer, & Goldstein, 1999). The fact that many cues of mate quality are significantly correlated (Grammer et al., 2003) means that this heuristic approach will often lead to the same choices, no matter which particular cues are used. Another strategy, avoid-the-worst (Grammer, Fink, Juette, Ronzal, & Thornhill, 2001), also makes comparisons between potential mates on the basis of a single cue but starts with the least attractive cues. This heuristic implies a more risk-averse strategy of avoiding undesirable mates. With greater time pressure to make decisions quickly, such as when faced with an abundance of possible options at a party or at a speed-dating event, the amount of information used in mate choice decreases even more (Lenton & Francesconi, 2010).

When deciding about a single potential mate rather than comparing multiple possibilities, the fact that mate quality cues have different assessment times points to another heuristic choice mechanism. Mate seekers can filter prospects through a sequence of aspiration levels spread out over time. For instance, they can first use physical appearance to decide with whom to talk, then use conversation to decide with whom to form a short-term relationship, and finally use interest in having a family to decide with whom to have children. In this sequential aspiration model (Miller & Todd, 1998), mate choice consists of a series of hurdles that the potential partner must exceed. The aspiration levels themselves for the different cues may be set at different values depending on the type of relationship sought (Kenrick, Sadalla, Groth, & Trost, 1990).

Deciding When to Stop a Mate Search

The previous section described how good choices can be made among potential mates by using decision heuristics that search for and use little information about each alternative. But what about the second stage of mate choice, where the alternatives themselves must be sought—in that case will more search, finding more alternatives to choose from, be better than less search? The rational approach prescribed by economists says to do exactly that, looking for more alternatives until the cost of further search outweighs any potential benefits (Stigler, 1961) and then taking the best alternative seen so far. The mate choice situation typically does not allow such an approach. The costs of searching for further possible mates are largely unknown; it is typically not even known how long it will be until the next candidate comes along. Likewise, it is unknown what potential benefits future options might bring. Critically, and in contrast to the assumptions of traditional rational models, there often is no possibility of returning to an option once it has been rejected. Despite these serious ecological constraints, there are simple heuristics that can handle such sequential decision tasks rather well.

Sequential search is ubiquitous and it pervades both social and nonsocial domains whenever desirable resources are distributed in time or space and cannot be considered (or at least not encountered) simultaneously. Searching for mates or friends, houses or habitats, jobs, parking spaces, shopping bargains, or restaurants to eat at all involve sequential decisions of this sort. Some of these searches are social in that what is being searched for is another person, who may or may not want to be chosen (e.g., reluctant potential partners); some are social in that multiple people may be competing with one another in the same search (e.g., for a luxury apartment or a tenure-track position). These different social effects can lead to different pressures on the decision making to be done (Todd, 2007). Yet, often social and nonsocial searches are analyzed in similar ways (for example, by using the logic of optimal patch-leaving decisions; Charnov, 1976). At the highest level, the challenge in all of these cases is that whatever option is currently available—for instance, the potential mate who is currently in the social orbit—a better option could become available in the future. How then can one decide when to stop searching and pursue the current (or some previous) option?

Mate search belongs to a particularly challenging class of search domains that adds additional complications to the challenge of when to stop. In situations where there is competition for specific alternatives, as when seeking a mate, buying unique items such as antiques or houses, or looking for a job or job candidate, once the searcher has passed by an alternative and decided not to choose it, there may be no chance to change one's mind and return to that alternative later, because someone else will have married the person previously spurned or bought the house previously rejected. (Technically, these search settings have little or no possibility of *recall* of previous options.) This, coupled with the aforementioned lack of knowledge about the range of possible alternatives ahead, means the searcher is effectively stuck at the present moment in time, not knowing what will come in the future, and unable to return to what has been passed by in the past.

In a search situation like this, where the distribution of available alternatives is unknown, there is no recall and no switching between alternatives (only one final choice can be made), then searching with an aspiration level can be appropriate—what Simon (1956, 1990) called satisficing heuristics. This method divides the search into two phases: In the first phase, alternatives are looked at without selecting any of them, so that the searcher can gather information about the available options. This information is used to set an aspiration level at the minimum value that the searcher will try to get in further search. The second phase consists of looking at additional alternatives, until one is found that exceeds the aspiration level set in Phase 1. Search is stopped at that point and that alternative is chosen.

The question then becomes how to set the appropriate aspiration level. This is further complicated by the fact that, most of the time, mate search (and other related kinds of search) are two sided, which means the searchers are being searched by others at the same time, and choice must therefore be mutual. Two people aiming to marry must both decide to tie the knot together, and job applicants must select their employer and be selected in return. Although one-sided search (as exemplified by the dowry problem; Ferguson, 1989; Todd & Miller, 1999) can be solved by just learning about the range of potential mates and picking the best one, this added challenge of mutual search can be solved by the searchers learning about *themselves*—their own relative position within their pool of fellow mate seekers. They can then use this self-knowledge to determine how high they should aim their search aspirations rather than merely setting an aspiration level based on the values of a small sample of available options as in one-sided search (see Kalick & Hamilton, 1986, for early mate search models with and without self-knowledge, showing that search can be sped up with such knowledge).

Again, there are standard economic approaches to this "two-sided matching problem" that make unrealistic assumptions about the capabilities of an individual searcher, such as full knowledge of all the available mates and of one's preferences over them (Roth & Sotomayor, 1990). For real people using bounded rationality, however, heuristics can be used to make good choices. To first find out what kind of heuristics may fare well in this environment in principle, we can test some possibilities via computer modeling. Todd and Miller (1999) set up a simulation similar to a classroom demonstration called the Pairing Game (Ellis & Kelley, 1999) in which two sets of individuals with numbers on their foreheads must wordlessly find a good and willing partner—bearing as high a number as possible—from the other set. In the model, 100 "male" and 100 "female" individuals were created, each with some attractiveness value drawn from a uniform distribution from 0 to 100. As in the Pairing Game and in real life, individuals did not innately know their own attractiveness value, but they could "see" the values of all potential mates they encountered. Individuals met in male–female pairs, assessed each other, and decided whether or not to make a proposal to each other.

This meeting and assessing process happened in two phases. In the first, the "adolescent" phase, proposals and rejections did not result in actual pairing, but could be used to set or adjust an aspiration level that determined to whom later proposal offers were made. In the following "adult" phase, the aspiration level set during the adolescent phase was fixed and used to make decisions during the rest of the search. These proposal and rejection decisions were now "real" in that mutual proposals resulted in a pair being made and that couple leaving the simulation. (In reality, there need be no clear demarcation between these two phases, and learning and choice can go on simultaneously at some point.) It is this necessity for mutual agreement that makes this scenario different from the one-sided search case described earlier, and adds an even greater challenge to this type of social decision making. Here, the decisions of potential mates play a critical role in determining each searcher's own mating fate, and the decision strategies should take this into account.

In the mutual search setting, a strategy fares poorly if it ignores the social information available about oneself from the potential mates one encounters—that is, their offers and rejections—and instead just looks for high-quality mates above the learned threshold. What happens when this "ignorant" strategy, which was appropriate for one-sided search, is used in the mutual search case is that most everyone quickly ends up with very high aspiration levels, and so only those with very high mate values will find willing mates (Todd & Miller, 1999). This problem is lessened if a linear function relating attractiveness to likelihood of courtship is used rather than a threshold heuristic (for example, Kalick & Hamilton, 1986), but then the mutual search process can take an unrealistically long time as individuals still refuse to adjust their threshold in the face of lack of success on the mating market. Ignoring the decisions made by others in the social environment, and trying to get the best mate possible without regard for one's own attractiveness on the market, results in unrealistic outcomes for many searchers in these models.

In contrast, if individuals somehow knew their own mate value and used it as their aspiration level, then most of the population could quickly find a well-matched partner (for example, the second model in Kalick & Hamilton, 1986). But individuals do not have built-in knowledge of their relative ranking in the current mate market. If they wanted to use it in their decisions, they would have to infer it or learn it. A reasonable approach to this problem could be to use the assessments that others make of oneself as a cue about one's own mate value, which the others *can* see. One could raise one's self-appraisal, and hence one's aspiration level, during the adolescent phase every time an unexpected offer is received and lower it after every unexpected rejection. This process fits with intuitions about how romantic successes and failures can induce self-esteem to go up and down, which in turn can affect how high or low people aim in their next romantic endeavors (Kavanagh, Robins, & Ellis, 2010).

With this simple heuristic, taking into account all of the decisions made by others, many more pairs are formed, at least if the adolescence period is not too long, and the individuals in "married" pairs are well matched to each other. In other simulations, modifications of this type of aspiration-adjusting mutual search rule have come even closer to matching some of the coarse statistics of human mating behavior (Simão & Todd, 2003). A variety of indirect evidence about real human mate choice is at least consistent with these aspiration-adjustment mechanisms. For instance, individual self-esteem goes up and down with dating success or failure, which could be the basis of an aspiration level for further search (Kavanagh et al., 2010; Kenrick, Groth, Trost, & Sadalla, 1993; Kirkpatrick & Ellis, 2001). Additional search may be curtailed by an emotional mechanism—falling in love—that could act to adjust one's goals in choosing a mate so that only the current partner meets those aspirations (Miller & Todd, 1998). Furthermore, at the population level, demographers have long puzzled over a common skewed-bell-shape pattern in the distribution of ages at which people first get married (Coale, 1971), which rises rapidly in the late teens and then falls in the 30s and trails off into the 50s and 60s with still a few first marriages occurring; this same pattern is reproduced in the simulations of marrying mate-searching agents in terms of the time it takes for pairs to be formed (Todd, Billari, & Simão, 2005). But we need to find more direct and fine-grained methods for testing whether individual people actually use something like this type of heuristic as they search through a sequence of mates.

Because the adolescent and adult periods of mate search in real life take so long, it would be preferable to find a way to watch people's sequential mate search processes distilled down into an easily observable sped-up version of reality. Just such an opportunity is afforded by the phenomenon of speed dating: a commercially sponsored occasion of rapid-fire sequential mate choice. At speed-dating events, several men and women seeking dates meet and assess each other in a sequence of short, individual dates over the course of an evening, talking to each potential partner for about five minutes and then deciding whether they would like to meet that person again for an extended date.

Researchers have begun to use speed dating as a source of data about the mate choices that people make (Finkel & Eastwick, 2008; Kurzban & Weeden, 2005; Lenton & Francesconi, 2010; Todd et al., 2007). By gathering data about the mate quality cues and preferences that speed daters had, as well as the offers and rejections that they made and received as they met a sequence of potential mates, Beckage, Todd, Penke, and Asendorpf (2009) were able to determine how well different search heuristics accounted for the pattern of offers that each individual made. They found that the aspiration-adjusting rules that took into account the feedback from other speed daters predicted more of the offers than either an "ignorant" one-sided search rule or a fixed aspiration level, further supporting the use of this type of simple search heuristic. This finding held for both men and women, who would be predicted to use the same sort of heuristic since they face the same information-processing challenges in this mutual long-term mate choice setting; however, they are likely to have different baseline threshold levels, reflecting differential choosiness between the sexes (cf. Todd et al., 2007).

USING OTHERS' EXPERIENCES TO MAKE MATE CHOICES

Both the assessment and search processes described in the previous section rely on information gathered by the individual seeking a mate. Some of this information is about the potential mates, acquired as cues observed during the assessment stage; some is about the mate seeker himself or herself, acquired as feedback (interest or rejections) during the sequential search stage. Together these processes implement two broad approaches to mate choice: First, select someone you like (irrespective of whether the person likes you) by evaluating highly those potential mates with good quality cues and ignoring the feedback about yourself that you get from them and others during search. Second, select someone who likes you by using past experience on the mating market to assess your own relative attractiveness and then pursuing those potential mates who have cues indicating they are of a similar level of attractiveness. In both approaches, choices depend only on the mate seeker's own experiences.

This unilateral strategy ignores a lot of potentially useful information acquired through the experiences of others in the surrounding social environment—namely, what and whom others find attractive. By capitalizing on such socially obtained information, a different approach to mate choice becomes possible: Select someone that *others* like. This, like the individual-experience approach, is also implementable by means of simple heuristics, in particular various forms of mate choice copying, using social imitation. These heuristics selectively employ information gathered by others to reduce the amount of information that the mate seeker must individually acquire. In particular, a mate seeker can learn about and adopt others' preferences for a particular individual, short-cutting the second mate choice decision stage (search); this strategy is known as individual-based mate choice copying. Alternatively, a mate seeker can learn about and take on others' preferences for particular traits, altering the first mate choice decision stage (assessment); this is trait-based mate choice copying. We consider each of these copying heuristics in turn.

Copying the Mate Choices of Others

The simplest way of using the experience of others to guide one's own mate choices is to copy the choices they have made. If someone else finds that potential mate worth pursuing, they do so, too. This form of social imitation has the benefit of removing the need to directly observe cues about a potential mate. It provides additional or more accurate information about those cues if the copied person has spent more time assessing them or is a more expert judge (Dugatkin, 2000; Little, Burriss, Jones, DeBruine, & Caldwell, 2008). As a consequence, this strategy can allow the mate seeker to skip over much or all of the first assessment stage of mate choice and even to stop the second search stage at the current potential mate without bothering to look further. Individual-based mate copying may also have costs, however, such as entering into competition with the other(s) that one is copying. Clearly, selecting someone who attracts many others means competition. The risk may be worth taking, however, if the highest quality individuals in the local environment are also the ones most likely to garner the positive interest of others.

Mate choice copying in humans has been explored by looking at how attracted participants are to potential dates based on the current available social information. When asked about the attractiveness of potential dates who are labeled as single compared with those labeled as in a relationship, participants prefer the latter, indicating mate choice copying. They prefer someone that another person has also preferred and chosen to date (Eva & Wood, 2006; Waynforth, 2007). Researchers have also looked at changes in attractiveness judgments given more realistic opportunities to observe a potential date. A picture of the potential date is shown by itself and participants rate how interested they are in dating that person. Then, the participants watch video clips of that same person on a speed date and predict the outcome. If after watching the interaction, the participants judged the same-sex dater to have been interested in the opposite-sex dater, they are more likely to be interested in the potential date themselves (again signifying mate copying) than if they thought the couple were not interested in each other (Place, Todd, Penke, &

Asendorpf, 2010). These laboratory experiments are controlled ways to learn about the social heuristics that individuals might be using in the real world.

However, it may not be adaptive to be influenced by the preferences of *everyone* (Waynforth, 2007). If someone very unattractive or very different from ourselves is interested in a potential date, that piece of information may not be particularly useful. The qualities of the person expressing interest in a suitor can be as important as the presence of interest itself (as seen in other species; for example, Vakirtzis & Roberts, 2009; Witte & Godin, 2010). For a mate choice copying heuristic to be adaptive, it has to be applied only when using this social information is a good shortcut. Recent findings have shown exactly this (Place et al., 2010): individuals pay much more attention to the dating decisions of attractive same-sex peers and also take into account how attractive those peers are relative to themselves. Attractive individuals are influenced by the choices of only the most attractive peers, whereas those who think they are average copy the choices of average or more attractive competitors.

An important component of mate copying, being able to utilize social information from the local environment about others' mate choices, is the ability to decipher the romantic interest between others. You need to know who likes whom to be able to copy their decisions, and you do not want to mistakenly go after someone whom nobody likes. Humans can read the romantic intentions of others fairly accurately and very rapidly, using rather limited information (Place, Todd, Penke, & Asendorpf, 2009). You do not need to know what people are saying or whether they share common interests or political or religious beliefs; the nonverbal signals that individuals produce during conversation are often far more telling than *what* they are saying. In fact, how *much* individuals are moving appears to be a tell-tale sign of their romantic interest (Grammer, Honda, Juette, & Schmitt, 1999). It does not seem to matter if the motion is hair-flipping, crossing and uncrossing legs, or gesticulating with arms and hands—greater amounts of motion are associated with greater likelihood of being interested in one's partner. Humans have the ability to assess this global aspect of motion and can tune into such nonverbal signals (Place, 2010). The human individual-based mate choice copying heuristic thus makes use of another heuristic that is sensitive to whole-body motion to decipher romantic interest. The ability to rapidly decode social information enables people to use this information in their mate choice decisions, piggybacking on the time and effort others have already invested in getting to know the potential suitors around them.

Copying the Preferred Traits of Others

In addition to learning about individuals one at a time, social information can also be applied to learning about qualities of successful individuals. If Mary Ellen likes John, what does this tell an observer about Stuart, who has perceptible qualities in common with John? If what is copied is not the specific choice, but preferences for perceptible traits of mates, candidates like Stuart benefit from the mating successes of similar others. Where this happens, mate choice preferences for traits can spread socially throughout a population, which may have consequences for how social learning impacts mate choice, what function it fulfills, and the costs it imparts.

Does mate choice copying generalize to those with shared perceptible traits? Positive evidence has been found in several species of animals. Coturnix quail hens shown artificially decorated males mating thereafter came to show preferences for other males with similarly marked plumage (White & Galef, 2000). Similarly, while female guppies initially prefer males with more orange coloring over less, they reverse this preference after observing model females affiliating with the duller of two males (Godin, Herdman, & Dugatkin, 2005). Notably, this change in preference is not specific to the male observed but generalizes to affect preferences for other, new males with the manipulated trait. These and similar results with finches and fruit flies indicate the presence of trait-based copying among these species.

To study this question in humans, a modification to the procedure described in the previous section can be used. After showing participants social information about a target speed dater in the form of apparent interest from another speed dater (as in Place et al., 2010), they are asked to rate photos of that first target person and others. Individual-based mate choice copying is present if the target dater increases more in attractiveness after being shown receiving social interest than receiving no social interest. To answer whether this effect generalizes to similar others, participants are also asked to rate faces that have been manipulated to be similar to the dater receiving apparent mating interest. There are different ways in which people may be perceptually similar. People may resemble each other facially, or in the way they dress or wear their hair. This difference is important, as facial traits are strongly heritable, whereas how people choose to present themselves, how they keep their hair and the clothes they wear, are characteristics primarily obtained through cultural membership. Strikingly, only preferences for the latter, culturally acquired, sort of trait appear to be learned about via generalized trait-based copying; preferences for facial traits do not appear to be passed on socially in this way (Bowers, Place, Todd, Penke, & Asendorpf, 2010). This is good use of information if the mate choices of others are indicative of behavioral or personality characteristics that are not well predicted by facial traits.

Both of these uses of social information may be valuable to a mate seeker. However, they differ in an important respect regarding function, to which the mate seeker's level of experience becomes relevant. In contrast to experienced mate seekers, novices still have much to learn about general qualities of a good mate. Moreover, if the traits of chosen mates are noisy indicators of quality, relying exclusively on such information to learn about whom to mate with may lead to poorer choices. As the mate seeker gains experience in assessing mates independently and accurately, the initially modest benefit of attending to such information could further diminish. Thus, continuing to use this information could interfere with independent mate assessments and lower the accuracy of choice.

In short, copying preferences for traits may best serve the least experienced mate seekers. In contrast, information regarding otherwise hard-to-know qualities of specific individual candidates is relevant to even the most experienced mate seeker. If social information use has undergone selective shaping under such conditions, trait-based copying but not individual-based copying should vary with age. Indeed, this is the empirically observed pattern among women. In a study, 18- and 19-year-old female participants, but not older, appeared to generalize preference for the traits of successful male daters (Bowers et al., 2010). Males of a similar age (18–23 years) did not show this pattern, leaving the possibility that the age-dependence effect may develop later for them.

In summary, the evidence suggests that humans, as some other species, not only use socially gathered mate choice information to adjust their preferences for specific individuals but also use this information to alter how they assess other potential mates, generalizing their adjusted preferences to similar others. Among humans, this generalization of copied preferences appears to be cue specific and age specific in ways that match the functions fulfilled. Copying of others' choices may lead to the social transmission of preferred traits of style throughout a population, specifically among very young adults.

CONCLUSION

Mate choice is a rich social decision domain. There is a lot of information available about the mates themselves, and about others' opinions of those individuals, all of which can be used to inform one's choices. Does this mean that a complex cognitive mechanism is needed to process all of that information into the best choice? We have argued here that the mind need not resort to unattainable extremes of information processing postulated by traditional rationality; rather, it can draw on a collection of simple heuristics to solve the particular problems of mate choice. Similar heuristic shortcuts, for assessing individuals, deciding when an individual is good enough as a partner, and copying the preferences of others to guide that assessing and deciding, may be used in other social domains where interaction partners are sought, including friendship, trade, and cooperation. Research on social decision making should proceed in these directions by assessing the often simple mechanisms in the mind; the rich and reliable structure in the social environment; and the way the two fit together to achieve ecological, and social, rationality.

REFERENCES

Beckage, N., Todd, P. M., Penke, L., & Asendorpf, J. B. (2009). Testing sequential patterns in human mate choice using speed dating. In N. Taatgen and H. van Rijn (Eds.), *Proceedings of the 2009 Cognitive Science Conference* (pp. 2365–2370). Cognitive Science Society. Online at: http://csjarchive.cogsci.rpi.edu/proceedings/2009/index.html.

Bowers, R. I., Place, S. S., Todd, P. M., Penke, L., & Asendorpf, J. B. (2010). *Generalization of mate choice copying in humans.* Manuscript in preparation.

Charnov, E. L. (1976). Optimal foraging, the marginal value theorem. *Theoretical Population Biology, 9,* 129–136.

Coale, A.J. (1971). Age patterns of marriage. *Population Studies, 25,* 193–214.

Czerlinski, J., Gigerenzer, G., & Goldstein, D.G. (1999). How good are simple heuristics? In G. Gigerenzer, P. M. Todd, & the ABC Research Group, *Simple heuristics that make us smart* (pp. 97–118). New York: Oxford University Press.

Dugatkin, L. A. (2000). *The imitation factor: Evolution beyond the gene.* New York: Free Press.

Ellis, B. J., & Kelley, H. H. (1999). The pairing game: A classroom demonstration of the matching phenomenon. *Teaching of Psychology, 26,* 118–121.

Eva, K. W., & Wood, T. J. (2006). Are all the taken men good? An indirect examination of mate-choice copying in humans. *Canadian Medical Association Journal, 175*(12), 1573–1574.

Ferguson, T. S. (1989). Who solved the secretary problem? *Statistical Science, 4,* 282–296.

Finkel, E. J., & Eastwick, P. W. (2008). Speed-dating. *Current Directions in Psychological Science, 17,* 193–197.

Gigerenzer, G., & Goldstein, D.G. (1996). Reasoning the fast and frugal way: Models of bounded rationality. *Psychological Review, 103,* 650–669.

Gigerenzer, G., & Goldstein, D.G. (1999). Betting on one good reason: The take the best heuristic. In G. Gigerenzer, P. M. Todd, & the ABC Research Group, *Simple heuristics that make us smart* (pp. 75–95). New York: Oxford University Press.

Gigerenzer, G., & Todd, P. M. (1999). Fast and frugal heuristics: The adaptive toolbox. In G. Gigerenzer, P. M. Todd, & the ABC Research Group, *Simple heuristics that make us smart* (pp. 3–34). New York: Oxford University Press.

Godin, J.-G. J., Herdman, E. J. E., & Dugatkin, L. A. (2005). Social influences on female mate choice in the guppy, *Poecilia reticulata*: Generalized and repeatable trait-copying behaviour. *Animal Behaviour, 69*(4), 999–1005.

Goldstein, D. G., & Gigerenzer, G. (2002). Models of ecological rationality: The recognition heuristic. *Psychological Review, 109,* 75–90.

Grammer, K., Fink, B., Juette, A., Ronzal, G., & Thornhill, R. (2001). Female faces and bodies: N-dimensional feature space and attractiveness. In G. Rhodes & L. Zebrobwitz (Eds.), *Advances in visual cognition: Vol. I. Facial attractiveness* (pp. 91–125). Westport, CT: Ablex.

Grammer, K., Fink, B., Møller, A.P., & Thornhill, R. (2003). Darwinian aesthetics: Sexual selection and the biology of beauty. *Biological Reviews, 78*(3), 385–407.

Grammer, K., Honda, M., Juette, A., & Schmitt, A. (1999). Fuzziness of nonverbal courtship communication unblurred by motion energy detection. *Journal of Personality and Social Psychology, 77*(3), 487–508.

Hastie, R., & Dawes, R.M. (2010). *Rational choice in an uncertain world: The psychology of judgment and decision making* (2nd ed.). Thousand Oaks, CA: Sage.

Hertwig, R., Hoffrage, U., & the ABC Research Group (in press). *Simple heuristics in a social world.* New York: Oxford University Press.

Kalick, S. M., & Hamilton, T. E. (1986). The matching hypothesis reexamined. *Journal of Personality and Social Psychology, 51,* 673–682.

Kavanagh, P. S., Robins, S., & Ellis, B. J. (2010). The mating sociometer: A regulatory mechanism for mating aspirations. *Journal of Personality and Social Psychology, 99*(1), 120–132.

Kenrick, D. T., Groth, G. E., Trost, M. R., & Sadalla, E. K. (1993). Integrating evolutionary and social exchange perspectives on relationships: Effects of gender, self-appraisal, and involvement level on mate selection criteria. *Journal of Personality and Social Psychology, 64,* 951–969.

Kenrick, D. T., Sadalla, E. K., Groth, G., & Trost, M. R. (1990). Evolution, traits, and the stages of human courtship: Qualifying the parental investment model. *Journal of Personality, 58,* 97–116.

Kirkpatrick, L. A., & Ellis, B. J. (2001). An evolutionary-psychological approach to self-esteem: Multiple domains and multiple functions. In G. Fletcher & M. Clark (Eds.), *The Blackwell handbook of social psychology—Vol. 2: Interpersonal processes* (pp. 411–436). Oxford, UK: Blackwell.

Kurzban, R., & Weeden, J. (2005). HurryDate: Mate preferences in action. *Evolution and Human Behavior, 26*(3), 227–244.

Lenton, A. P., & Francesconi, M. (2010). How humans cognitively manage an abundance of mate options. *Psychological Science, 21,* 528–533.

Little, A., Burriss, R. P., Jones, B. C., DeBruine, L. M., & Caldwell, C. A. (2008). Social influence in human face preference: Men and women are influenced more for long-term than short-term attractiveness decisions. *Evolution and Human Behavior, 29*(2), 140–146.

Miller, G. F., & Todd, P. M. (1998). Mate choice turns cognitive. *Trends in Cognitive Sciences, 2,* 190–198.

Pachur, T., Todd, P. M., Gigerenzer, G., Schooler, L. J., & Goldstein, D. G. (in press). When is the recognition heuristic an adaptive tool? In P.M. Todd, G. Gigerenzer, & the ABC Research Group, *Ecological rationality: Intelligence in the world.* New York: Oxford University Press.

Place, S. S. (2010). *Non-independent mate choice in humans: Deciphering and utilizing information in a social environment.* Unpublished dissertation, Indiana University, Bloomington.

Place, S. S., Todd, P. M., Penke, L., & Asendorpf, J. B. (2009). The ability to judge the romantic interest of others. *Psychological Science, 20*(1), 22–26.

Place, S. S., Todd, P. M., Penke, L., & Asendorpf, J. B. (2010). Humans show mate copying after observing real mate choices. *Evolution and Human Behavior, 31*(5), 320–325.

Roth, A. E., & Sotomayor, M A. O. (1990) *Two-sided matching: A study in game-theoretic modeling and analysis.* Cambridge, UK: Cambridge University Press.

Simão, J., & Todd, P. M. (2003). Emergent patterns of mate choice in human populations. *Artificial Life, 9,* 403–417.

Simon, H. A. (1956). Rational choice and the structure of environments. *Psychological Review, 63,* 129–138.

Simon, H. A. (1990). Invariants of human behavior. *Annual Review of Psychology, 41,* 1–19.

Stigler, G. J. (1961). The economics of information. *Journal of Political Economy, 69,* 213–225.

Todd, P. M. (2007). Coevolved cognitive mechanisms in mate search: Making decisions in a decision-shaped world. In J. P. Forgas, M. G. Haselton, & W. von Hippel (Eds.), *Evolution and the social mind: Evolutionary psychology and social cognition* (Sydney Symposium of Social Psychology series) (pp. 145–159). New York: Psychology Press.

Todd, P. M., Billari, F. C., & Simão, J. (2005). Aggregate age-at-marriage patterns from individual mate-search heuristics. *Demography, 42*(3), 559–574.

Todd, P. M., & Gigerenzer, G. (2007). Environments that make us smart: Ecological rationality. *Current Directions in Psychological Science, 16*(3), 167–171.

Todd, P.M., Gigerenzer, G., & the ABC Research Group (in press). *Ecological rationality: Intelligence in the world.* New York: Oxford University Press.

Todd, P. M., & Miller, G. F. (1999). From pride and prejudice to persuasion: Satisficing in mate search. In G. Gigerenzer, P. M. Todd, & the ABC Research Group, *Simple heuristics that make us smart* (pp. 287–308). New York: Oxford University Press.

Todd, P. M., Penke, L., Fasolo, B., & Lenton, A. P. (2007). Different cognitive processes underlie human mate choices and mate preferences. *Proceedings of the National Academy of Sciences USA, 104*(38), 15011–15016.

Vakirtzis, A., & Roberts, S. (2009). Mate choice copying and mate quality bias: Different processes, different species. *Behavioral Ecology, 20*(4), 908–911.

Waynforth, D. (2007). Mate choice copying in humans. *Human Nature, 18*(3), 264–271.

White, D. J., & Galef, B. G., Jr. (2000). "Culture" in quail: Social influences on mate choices of female *Coturnix japonica. Animal Behaviour, 59,* 975–979.

Witte, K., & Godin, J.-G. J. (2010). Mate choice copying and mate quality bias: are they different processes? *Behavioral Ecology, 21*(1), 193–194.

12

The Company You Keep
Friendship Decisions From a Functional Perspective

PETER DeSCIOLI and ROBERT KURZBAN

INTRODUCTION

*M*any researchers in social psychology and judgment and decision making focus on identifying mental mistakes and troubleshooting people's decisions. The focus on biases and errors leads researchers to underestimate the intelligence of evolved computational systems. Here we examine this issue in the context of human friendship decisions. Social psychologists have long claimed that people's friendship choices are surprisingly unintelligent, based on strategically irrelevant factors such as proximity, familiarity, similarity, or very simple reinforcement learning. However, this view is becoming increasingly untenable as research on many nonhuman species uncovers sophisticated computational control systems that intelligently regulate behavior in cooperative relationships. We argue, in sharp contrast, that human friendship is caused by complex computational machinery that performs a strategic alliance-building function.

Intricately Complex Computational Systems That Make Us Smart

Natural computational systems are strikingly intelligent. The minds of bumblebees, fiddler crabs, blue jays, and humans are highly complex computational control systems that far outperform even the most advanced artificial intelligence systems made by human engineers. Human scientists can barely fathom what it takes to build a fully functional autonomous robot that can successfully navigate landscapes, capture prey, avoid predators, fight rivals, court mates, and perform other feats routinely accomplished by animal minds.

Nevertheless, scholars have long disparaged the human mind as stupid, biased, and irrational. Francis Bacon (1620) famously decried the "idols of the mind" and complained that "the human understanding is like a false mirror" that "distorts and discolors the nature of things." For instance, Bacon observed that "the human understanding when it has once adopted an opinion … draws all things else to support and agree with it," what psychologists now call "confirmation bias" (Nickerson, 1998). Bacon also noticed that "human understanding is moved by those things most which strike and enter the mind simultaneously and suddenly, and so fill the imagination," what psychologists now call "availability bias" (Tversky & Kahneman, 1973) or related "anchoring" effects (Hastie & Dawes, 2010, pp. 71–72). Bacon's insights had applications in the development of the scientific method, which aimed to produce knowledge by circumventing human cognitive weaknesses. Similarly, many modern researchers in social psychology and judgment and decision making seek to identify cognitive errors (for example, Ariely, 2008) and with important applications, such as reducing prejudice (Aronson & Patnoe, 1997) or facilitating negotiations (Bazerman, Curhan, Moore, & Valley, 2000).

So, is the human mind smart or stupid? Psychologists have learned a lot about animal minds since Bacon's *Novum Organum*. The cognitive revolution and advances in computer science have led to the computational theory of mind: Minds are information-processing programs that are run on the hardware of the brain (Pinker, 1997). As such, minds can be described in terms of the underlying machine code—their neural implementation—or, more practically, at higher levels of abstraction in terms of the pseudocode that describes the operations performed by the system. As this theory developed, artificial intelligence researchers started trying to match the performance of animal minds on tasks such as vision and locomotion, and only then did they begin to realize the intricate functional complexity of natural computational systems (Minsky, 1985; Pinker, 1997).

Modern computer systems such as "smart" phones or autonomous robots are packed with elaborate computer programs, each consisting of labyrinthine control structures represented by up to millions of lines of code. Yet these artificial intelligence systems cannot perform many of the simplest tasks that animal minds routinely accomplish. How many programs and how many lines of code would be required to successfully operate the body of a housefly, much less a human? These observations suggest that human operating systems and their specialized applications are orders of magnitude more sophisticated and complex than what has so far been produced by the coordinated efforts of thousands of professional computer engineers. In short, the human mind is smart, dazzlingly so.

People make mistakes, of course, and there is a place for Baconian criticism and its applications in troubleshooting human decisions. After all, like any good program, animal minds have error-checking subroutines, and Bacon's insights and their lasting appeal probably stem from human error-checking abilities. Baconian scholars do not stand outside of the minds they critique, and thus their error-checking successes must be properly credited to the competencies of their "irrational" minds.

However, to take "irrationality" as the basic character of the human mind is misguided. The fundamental question for psychology is "How can intelligence emerge from nonintelligence?" (Minsky, 1985, p. 17). Unlike inanimate rocks, planets, and stars, animals are physical systems that navigate landscapes, communicate with others, and replicate their complex structures in offspring. No amount of "irrationality" or "bias" can explain the difference between an intelligent living grasshopper and an unintelligent dead grasshopper (though both are composed of the same unintelligent parts). Instead, this difference can be explained by the *functions* performed by (intact) grasshopper minds.

The focus on cognitive shortcomings causes researchers to lose sight of the big picture: *explaining* decision-making systems, not just *troubleshooting* them. This mistake can be called the "bias bias" or the "troubleshooting bias" (see also Krueger & Funder, 2004). The bias bias causes researchers to greatly underestimate the complexity and performance of human cognitive systems including our focus here, human friendship systems.

Why Do Animals Seem So Smart and People Seem So Stupid?

In the deer mouse *P. maniculatus*, females mate with multiple males and their sperm compete for fertilization inside the female's reproductive tract. To increase their swimming speed, sperm form cooperative groups of 2 to 40 individuals. The sperm "choose" their partners carefully: They sense others' genetic relatedness and select partners based on this variable, thereby gaining an evolutionary advantage (Fisher & Hoekstra, 2010). How smart!

Social psychologists like to say that humans are not very choosy about their friends. They claim that despite the feeling that friends are special, in reality we make friends with whoever just happens to be around. A leading social psychology textbook claims that "the single best predictor of whether two people will get together is physical proximity" (Brehm, Kassin, & Fein, 2002). If social psychologists are correct, then brainless mouse sperm show more intelligence than humans, choosing partners based on a relevant property rather than simple proximity.

Some of our primate relatives are particularly strategic in their social relationships. Indeed, researchers often describe primate social behavior as "Machiavellian" (Byrne & Whiten, 1988; Whiten & Byrne, 1997), drawing a comparison with the famous political strategist Niccolò Machiavelli. For example, monkeys choose friends carefully, preferring high-ranking individuals; they compete for the best partners but are sometimes willing to settle for less desirable friends; and they jealously prevent the formation of rival relationships (Harcourt, 1992; Schino, 2001; Seyfarth, 1977). These abilities are vitally important because, as Seyfarth and Cheney (2002) noted, primates "live in large groups where an individual's survival and reproductive success depends on its ability to manipulate others within a complex web of kinship and dominance relations" (p. 4141). Strategic behavior is not limited to primates. Research on dolphins, for instance, shows that "patterns of alliance affiliation among males may be more complex than are currently known for any non-human, with individuals participating in 2–3 levels of shifting alliances" (Connor, 2007, p. 587).

In contrast, many researchers describe humans as strategically inept in relationships. Friend choices are claimed to be shaped by factors as arbitrary as whether individuals live next door or two doors down (Festinger, Schachter, & Back, 1950). Other researchers have claimed that mere familiarity (Zajonc, 1968) and similarity (McPherson, Smith-Lovin, & Cook, 2001) shape human friendships. Exchange theorists (Homans, 1958) argue that friendships are based on Skinnerian reinforcement generated by the prior stream of benefits emitted by the friend. These theories paint an unflattering picture of our species' strategic sophistication. The gap between the literatures on animals and people creates a puzzle: Why do animals seem so smart and people seem so stupid?

The discrepancy might be resolved, in part, by looking closer at the questions pursued in animal and human investigations. Human research has focused on the question: What determines whether someone *becomes a friend versus remains a stranger*? Animal research has asked: What determines whether an individual becomes a *friend versus an adversary*? These are obviously very different questions. For instance, hyenas recognize all clan members individually (up to 90) and friendships are invariably formed within the clan (Holekamp, Sakai, & Lundrigan, 2007). Hyenas do not form friendships with strangers, so there is no answer to the "friend versus stranger" question. Instead, hyena cognitive systems sort through known individuals to identify promising friend prospects, and the details of these systems provide answers to the "friend versus adversary" question. The same is true of nonhuman primates, many premodern human societies, and, presumably, our hominid ancestors. Friendships with strangers might not have occurred sufficiently frequently in the ancestral world to select for specialized adaptations (Seabright, 2004). In contrast, within-group friendship formation was a recurrent adaptive problem that could plausibly have shaped cognitive mechanisms for sorting the social world into friends and foes.

Shifting focus to what determines friend versus adversary, many of the discrepant human findings dissipate. For instance, although proximity does create friends (versus strangers), it is even more likely to create enemies (Ebbesen, Kjos, & Konecni, 1976). Similarly, more than liking, familiarity breeds contempt (Norton, Frost, & Ariely, 2007). Thus, humans might not be less discriminating than monkeys or hyenas once the proper comparisons are made. If human friendship is strategic, its sophistication will not be found in how strangers become friends but in how people sort known individuals into best friends, lesser friends, and enemies.

THE STRATEGIC FUNCTION OF HUMAN FRIENDSHIP

Friendship is a human universal. People everywhere invest in nonkin, nonsexual relationships, despite costs to self, family, mates, and groups. The significance of friendship is underscored in cultures that enact friendship unions in formal ceremonies, such as "blood covenants" found widely across continents and historical periods (Černy, 1955; Evans-Pritchard, 1933; Trumbull, 1893). The social importance of friendship rites is comparable to marriage ceremonies, and they are sometimes more binding than marriage (Kiefer, 1968; Roscoe, 1923). The universality of friendship provides a clue that this behavior is caused by specialized species-typical cognitive mechanisms, and hence, that the function of these mechanisms can be productively investigated.

Potential functions of friendship are sometimes put on display in friendship rituals found in different cultures. For example, the Azande of north central Africa held friendship ceremonies in which each of the two friends consumed the other's blood and then made a ritual address enumerating friendship obligations (Evans-Pritchard, 1933). The address included clauses requiring the friend to provide aid in conflicts (even if this undermined the local authorities), protect the partner's children, share material resources, avoid adultery against the partner, and provide their daughters for marriage. The friendship rites of the Azande and other cultures can be used as one source for hypotheses about the function of friendship. Indeed, many of the functions identified in these rituals reflect common biological functions for social relationships that are also found in nonhuman species, including agonistic support, alloparenting, and food sharing.

Is Friendship Exchange?

Although there are a number of competing theories of friendship (e.g., propinquity theory), for brevity, here we focus on reciprocal altruism (Trivers, 1971), the biological framework most frequently invoked to explain friendship. On this account, human friends function as exchange partners, from whom gains in trade can be profitably extracted, provided that cheaters can be detected and avoided. Consistent with this idea, friendship rites are sometimes used to cement trade relations (Herlehy, 1984). However, while reciprocity likely explains much of human sociality (Axelrod, 1984), the application to close long-term friendships has several problems (Silk, 2003).

First, people adamantly deny that friendships are exchange relationships, regarding this very idea as taboo (Fiske & Tetlock, 1997). Instead, friendship is viewed as a communal relationship in which benefits given and received are not carefully monitored (Clark, 1984; Clark & Mills, 1979). Whether or not this folk intuition is correct, reciprocal altruism does not explain why human minds draw the exchange–communal distinction.

Second, reciprocal altruism does not explain the fact that friends help each other in catastrophes when the expected benefits from future repayment are outweighed by the costs of helping (Tooby & Cosmides, 1996). A sudden catastrophe can render an individual unable to reciprocate, and therefore, if reciprocity is the correct explanation, debilitated individuals should be abandoned by their friends. In fact, people often help friends through sickness and injury—even when repayment is unlikely—serving an insurance function that might be explicable in terms of commitment mechanisms (Tooby & Cosmides, 1996).

Third, social exchange does not explain the dark side of friendship: relational aggression such as extortion, jealousy, and exclusivity (for review, see Archer & Coyne, 2005). The earliest friendships are exclusive: preschoolers reject outsiders trying to join their play group about half of the time (reviewed in Shantz, 1987, p. 293). Many children hold friendships hostage to extort favors, for example, "I'm not your friend unless you …" (Crick & Grotpeter, 1995); they jealously prevent friends from forming close relationships with others (Parker, Low, Walker, & Gamm, 2005); they spread malicious rumors to damage others' friendships

(Owens, Shute, & Slee, 2000a, 2000b); and all of these behaviors persist despite considerable efforts to stop them (for example: www.opheliaproject.org). Relational aggression continues into adulthood (for example, in the workplace, Kaukiainen et al., 2001, and in international relations, Snyder, 1997). These phenomena are left unexplained by reciprocal altruism, which is mute on interactions beyond exchange dyads, such as sabotage of rival friendships.

THE ALLIANCE HYPOTHESIS FOR HUMAN FRIENDSHIP

Another idea is that friendships function as alliances (DeScioli, 2008; DeScioli & Kurzban, 2009). In order to evaluate this idea, we discuss how alliances work, cognitive programs for managing alliances, and evidence relevant to the alliance hypothesis.

How Alliances Work

Organisms, humans included, frequently have conflicts of interest. Sometimes these conflicts are zero-sum games in which benefits to one party are costs to the other. More often, however, disputes are non-zero-sum and mixed motive games in which agents have conflicting interests over the outcomes, but they also share a common interest in reducing the costs of fighting (for example, Hawk-Dove, Chicken, or War of Attrition games; Maynard Smith, 1982; Schelling, 1960). These conflicts have led to the evolution of both adaptations for damaging opponents and adaptations for reducing fighting costs such as signaling mechanisms (for example, caterpillars; Scott et al., 2010). Via these adaptations, different balances of opposed and shared interest lead to variation in overt hostility ranging from the bloody brawls between male elephant seals (Haley, 1994) to more subtle disagreements between mother and fetus (Haig, 1993).

A long history of conflict has armed organisms with a vast arsenal of weaponry including chemical toxins, stinging barbs, razor-sharp claws, venomous fangs, and massive antlers. The arsenal also includes intelligent computational control systems that guide the deployment of weaponry in hostile encounters. Furthermore, some organisms are able to mobilize other organisms' weaponry in disputes by interfacing with those organisms' control systems, that is, they are able to recruit allies. The capacity to recruit allies adds layers of complexity to conflicts because the outcomes depend not only on individuals' fighting abilities but also the abilities of intervening allies (Harcourt, 1992).

Alliance relationships are fundamentally different from exchange relationships. In exchange relationships, the gains an individual enjoys occur by virtue of mutually profitable transactions with others. While mutual gains in wealth can generate any number of externalities to third parties, externalities are not a necessary feature of mutually profitable exchanges.

More concretely, two people on a desert island can engage in exchange, making both participants better off while making no one worse off (i.e., creating "Pareto improvements"; Frank, 2001). Alliances are fundamentally different. When two agents form an alliance, this necessarily harms third parties: Two people on a desert island cannot form an alliance because there are no others to ally against.

The simplest form of an alliance problem is described by the Simple Majority Game (von Neumann & Morgenstern, 1944). In this game, there are three players. Each player has only one decision to make, choosing one of the other two players. If two players choose each other, an "alliance" is formed, and they get a positive payoff of one-half; the third player gets –1. (If a "cycle" occurs, with each choosing a different person, they all get zero.) In other words, any two players can team up and take 1 point from the third player and then divide the spoils, each getting ½ point.

Notice that Pareto improvements are not possible in this game. More complex alliance problems can be described by adding more players, more strategies, non-zero-sum payoffs, uncertainty, asymmetries, and so forth, but a basic constant property of these games is that helping one individual, by allying with them, necessarily makes others worse off.

In games with this type of structure, from the perspective of third parties, the relationship between two players, unlike exchange, imposes costs on the excluded individual(s). Liska (1962), in his classic treatment of alliances, captured this idea in his claim that "alliances are against, and only derivatively for, someone or something" (p. 12). Alliances are threatening to others in a way that bilateral exchange relationships are not.

This feature of alliances is apparent in international relations. One famous and clear case is the Molotov–Ribbentrop Pact in August 1939. This agreement of nonaggression between Germany and the Soviet Union was perceived as a major threat by Allied nations, much greater than the earlier commercial agreements between the two nations. The pact made the subsequent invasion of Poland much less risky for Germany because Germany no longer needed to worry about the Eastern Front. Similarly, in 1917 the United States felt threatened when Germany proposed an alliance with Mexico in the famous Zimmermann Telegram, and shortly after the telegram was made public, the United States declared war against Germany. Politically, alliances are genuinely threatening to third parties.

A key problem in alliance contexts is avoiding being on the losing side of conflicts. Frequently, the side that wins is the one with the larger number of individuals, particularly because of the tactical advantages associated with numerical superiority (Adams & Mesterton-Gibbons, 2003). To avoid being in the minority, disputants need to recruit allies to try to gain numerical superiority. Third parties, on the other hand, need to choose sides carefully by considering which side will attract more allies and ultimately prevail.

These considerations lead to a key strategy for choosing sides: *bandwagoning* (Snyder, 1997). To pursue a bandwagon strategy, individuals assess who is most likely to win the incipient conflict and support that disputant. This strategy helps individuals avoid being on the losing side of disputes. In international relations, bandwagoning can be seen in late entrants to conflicts that are nearly decided, with previously neutral nations opportunistically entering on the side that is winning. Bandwagoning tends to produce positive feedback loops, with the side that is winning gaining additional allies, making victory even more likely.

A second way to choose sides in disputes is to support the individual who is more likely to side with oneself in future conflicts—*alliance building*. Siding with these loyal individuals furthers one's long-term interests by supporting those who are likely to be one's own future supporters. When individuals use this strategy, close allies become valuable and, as a consequence, a feedback loop is generated. If you know that I will aid you in your future conflicts, then I am a very valuable ally, and you benefit by keeping me safe and free from harm. I, in turn, now value you even more, given that you are motivated to maintain my health and safety. This dynamic can be described as an "integrative spiral" (Snyder, 1984) or as alliance building.

Individuals frequently have relationships with both sides in a conflict, particularly because human social networks are locally dense (Feld, 1981). In this case, individuals will have to be able to prioritize one ally over another. That is, they need to be able to determine for all possible pairwise conflicts which side they will favor. One way to do this is to maintain a ranking of allies that prioritizes one's alliances.

If individuals maintain a friend ranking, then the set of all group members' rankings of all other group members defines a "loyalty landscape." The loyalty landscape largely determines individuals' fighting power because it specifies the distribution of support for all possible conflicts. Therefore, like in dyadic conflict (Parker, 1974), individuals stand to gain by assessing, probing, displaying, concealing, and manipulating information about the loyalty landscape.

Mechanisms for Building Alliances

Decision-making systems for managing alliances should implement good strategies. Alliances pose special problems such as choosing sides in disputes, avoiding being on the losing side, and protecting one's reliable supporters. To effectively solve these problems, individuals need cognitive systems that monitor, seek, and encode the relevant information, usefully process the information, and produce behavioral output that is strategically intelligent and advantageous.

To pursue a bandwagon strategy, individuals need systems to predict which side in a conflict will win. A variety of cues could be used. Individuals could assess size, strength, agility, and other physical attributes. They could also track histories of conflict outcomes, monitor others' fighting records, and make transitive inferences based on previous fight outcomes. They might also need to parse and represent local status hierarchies. In hyenas, for instance, individuals maintain representations of the relative status of the different members of the social group. They use this information to choose sides in conflicts, always siding with the higher status individual (Engh, Siebert, Greenberg, & Holekamp, 2005). Similar evidence shows a bandwagon strategy, based on status, in baboons (Cheney, 1977) and rhesus macaques (Chapais, 1983).

Pursuing an alliance-building strategy is even more computationally demanding. This strategy involves siding with the individual who is most likely to side with oneself in future conflicts. If Ego is choosing sides in a fight between Alpha and Bravo, then in order to choose based on which of the two will be more likely to support Ego in the future, Ego must know how Alpha and Bravo each rank their allies. Then, Ego should choose the individual who ranks Ego higher. For example, if Alpha ranks Ego as their third best ally, then Alpha will often support Ego but not against Alpha's first and second rank ally. Hence, if Bravo ranks Ego first or second, then Ego should side with Bravo because Bravo's support is more reliable.

Importantly, individuals cannot afford to wait until a fight breaks out to try to gather and process this information. To make intelligent alliance tradeoffs, individuals need to assess and probe alliance information well in advance of quickly escalating disputes. And they need to process this information and produce a representation of their relative loyalties to others, that is, a ranking of friends. Friend ranking requires collapsing across friends' many qualities to rank partners along a single dimension of one's loyalty.

Further, in order to rank friends advantageously, Ego needs to know how their friends rank Ego. This requires maintaining representations of *others' representations*, a data structure that captures other individuals' loyalties to oneself and others. This information can be used to represent the "loyalty landscape," the set of all group members' rankings of all other group members.

The computational requirements for choosing sides among allies are different from those that are required for exchange partners. The value of exchange partners derives from the possibility of reaping gains in trade, and therefore requires the ability to track information that is relevant to these gains. For instance, given the key adaptive problem of preventing being cheated in exchanges (Cosmides & Tooby, 1992), information about cheating behavior should be recorded. Also relevant to these relationships is the probability of continued interaction, since the shadow of the future is important for iterated reciprocity. In contrast, managing alliances requires computations for choosing sides in disputes such as a ranking of others. Moreover, people need to monitor their own position in others' rankings, tracking friends' friends, and if necessary to take steps toward disrupting rival relationships.

Evidence From Relational Aggression

If the alliance hypothesis is correct, then humans should be capable of monitoring and manipulating alliances to their own strategic advantage. That is, they should be capable of representing and interacting with the loyalty landscapes in which they live. One straightforward way to manipulate the loyalty landscape is to damage relationships in the local social network. By severing bonds between people in their network, individuals can change the loyalty landscape and potentially improve their strategic position, that is, their ability to recruit alliance support relative to others. We will discuss three basic socially destructive maneuvers: (1) damaging or threatening damage to one's own friendships, (2) damaging friends' other friendships, and (3) damaging friendships between one's rivals. We argue that humans show all three of these strategic maneuvers and that this evidence supports the idea that friendship is caused by cognitive mechanisms specialized for handling alliance problems.

Humans use a variety of strategies aimed at damaging relationships among people in their social networks (Archer & Coyne, 2005). However, the "relational aggression" literature has largely taken a troubleshooting perspective toward this phenomenon, missing the strategic implications. Relational aggression, like physical aggression, leads to harmful outcomes for the victims of aggression, and research in this area has focused on its social harms, often regarding aggression as pathological. However, considering behavior in the context of strategy rather than pathology can be illuminating.

One of the most basic forms of relational aggression is damaging or threatening damage to one's own friendships (reviewed by Archer & Coyne, 2005). Preschool children become angry with others and respond by covering their ears and giving the silent treatment. They also extort others by saying that they will end the friendship unless the other person does what they want. This strategy continues into adulthood in both personal friendships (Bernstein, 2010, "How to break up with a friend") and workplace relationships (Kaukiainen et al., 2001). It also appears in international politics. A newspaper reported that "China called German Chancellor Angela Merkel's meeting with the Dalai Lama a serious mistake and warned Berlin that the meeting had damaged bilateral ties"—the adult equivalent of "I won't be your friend anymore."

Some people might view Chinese leaders and other adults as childish for using these tactics, but we can alternatively view children as precocious political strategists. When a preschool child threatens "I'm not your friend anymore unless ...," what does this imply about their cognitive abilities for representing the social world? They need to represent themselves as having a distinct form of relationship, a friendship, with the listener. They need to represent the counterfactual that they do not have a friendship with the listener. They need to make inferences based on this counterfactual about its consequences both for the self and for the listener and compare these consequences with the current state of affairs. They need to represent that the listener can represent actual and counterfactual states of relationships, and that the listener prefers a state of friendship over an alternative state. They need to represent that listeners will actively take steps to avoid a change in state to their friendship, and specifically that the steps they will take will be those specified in the threat. They should also estimate the probability that the threat will be successful, given the costs and benefits to the listener, and the expected benefits of success compared to the costs of failure.

This task description is just a brief high-level sketch of what would be needed to effectively deploy threats to damage one's relationships. If it is true that children effortlessly perform these threats, then how can we explain these abilities? Obviously, parents do not teach children how to exploit their peers with threats. If anything, the opposite is true: Parents suppress their children's developing Machiavellian aims because these aggressive maneuvers, however intelligent, are not very nice. Instead, these abilities might reflect reliably developing cognitive machinery specialized for managing friendships.

A second important form of relational aggression is damaging friends' other friendships. People often feel jealousy about their friends' friends, a negative experience associated with behaviors aimed at disrupting the rival relationship. Children bring a broad range of tactics to bear on the problem of rival relationships, including gossip, ridicule, name calling, rumors, and breaking confidences (Archer & Coyne, 2005; Hess & Hagen, 2002; Parker et al., 2005). And these strategies continue into adulthood in personal relationships (Forrest, Eatough, &

Shevlin, 2005) and in the workplace (Kaukiainen et al., 2001). The alliance model can explain jealousy because one's friends' alternative friendships represent potential threats. When others are placed above oneself in friends' friendship queues, one has endured the cost of losing support in potential conflicts with this interloping individual.

Friendship jealousy implies sophisticated cognitive abilities. Most obviously, it would not be possible for people to experience friendship jealousy if they were unable to track third-party relationships, that is, their friends' friendships. In the nonhuman animal literature, this cognitive ability is regarded as highly sophisticated and has been observed in only a small number of species (Connor, 2007; Engh et al., 2005; Harcourt, 1992). This only scratches the surface of the cognitive abilities required to engage in the long-term multistage campaigns that people wage to protect their close friendships from interlopers.

A third form of relational aggression is damaging friendships among one's rivals. In this case, neither of the individuals is a close friend with Ego, but Ego can improve their strategic position by weakening alliances between potential rivals. This tactic is frequently used in international relations, such as in Germany's propaganda efforts to drive wedges between England and France, or between America and the European allies in the Second World War. In nonhuman primates, studies have found that high status individuals frequently prevent lower status individuals from grooming each other in order to impede rival alliances (Harcourt, 1992). Research on schoolchildren shows that they engage in malevolent gossip and spread false rumors aimed at damaging others' friendships (Owens et al., 2000a, 2000b). Interestingly, when participants were asked why they engaged in damaging and false gossip, they could offer little insight beyond that it "created excitement." This vacuous self-report (Why is malicious gossip experienced as exciting?) suggests that any underlying strategies are consciously inaccessible.

A number of organizations have made efforts to reduce relational aggression (for example: www.opheliaproject.org). Recent high-profile cases of school violence and suicide have been attributed to the effects of social bullying, exclusion, harassment, gossip, and other forms of social aggression. However, this strategic behavior is resistant to instruction aimed at suppressing it. People are natural political strategists and they will use the tactics available to them to gain advantages. Relational aggression surely can (and should) be reduced, but it might be difficult to directly suppress. An alternative approach is to focus on the relevant social environments and the costs and benefits at stake in disputes. It might be possible to reduce the frequency and stakes of disputes, and hence to reduce the advantages associated with political maneuvering, thus indirectly curbing relational aggression.

In sum, the alliance model readily explains why close friendships have substantial amounts of conflict (Bushman & Holt-Lunstad, 2009). A study of teenage girls, for example, found that "fights over friends were part of the day-to-day life of the girls," and the school principal reported that these fights were "based upon changing allegiances between the kids, the stealing of friends" (Owens et al., 2000b, p. 37). In everyday life, people frequently denigrate relational aggression as childish, petty, or pathological. These disparaging judgments serve our interests because each of us stands to gain by reproaching and suppressing the

Machiavellian strivings of others (while hypocritically engaging in the same tactics ourselves; Kurzban, 2010). If, however, we hold aside the usual social politics and view relational aggression from an engineering perspective, then it appears as a marvel of functional design in which cognitive mechanisms strategically manipulate a complex landscape of alliances. The day that an artificial intelligence system can keep up with schoolchildren's gossip is far off indeed.

Testing the Alliance Model: Predictors of Friend Rank

The alliance model of friendship identifies the relative position that one occupies in others' queue of friends as the key variable that determines the value of each friend as an ally to oneself. In the limit, being someone else's best friend, at the top of the queue, is the most valuable form of friendship.

This idea can be contrasted with the properties that people look for in friends on alternative models. For example, on homophily or assortment models, one is attracted to those who share similar properties. Exchange models, of course, point to the value of others in terms of their willingness to exchange, their capacity to exchange, and their trustworthiness. Other models hint that friends might be chosen on the basis of popularity (Levine & Kurzban, 2006) or culturally valued abilities (Henrich & Gil-White, 2001). Models based on familiarity or proximity make similarly straightforward predictions about what variables will correlate with closeness.

These different models make different predictions. The alliance model would be undermined if people named as close friends individuals who (they perceive to) rank many other people above them in their friendship queues. Similarly, the alliance model predicts that people will fill their precious best friend slot with someone who values Ego above all (or most) others. Last, if people choose their best friends based on properties (e.g., attractiveness, intelligence, and so forth) rather than where one ranks in the friendship queue, then the alliance model is undermined. Symmetrically, homophily, popularity, and exchange models predict that best friends will be chosen on the basis of these features. For instance, if friendship is for exchange, then the underlying mechanisms should be designed to prefer those individuals who are promising exchange partners; relative rank should not matter.

We conducted investigations to test these predictions of the respective models (DeScioli & Kurzban, 2009). We used three samples: a sample of undergraduates, a sample of people in a park in Philadelphia, and an Internet sample from Amazon's "crowdsourcing" Web site, Mechanical Turk. In each sample, we asked subjects to consider their top ten friends, from best friend to tenth closest friend, and answer some questions about the properties of each of these friends, including variables central to each of the models mentioned earlier.

This procedure puts these models at risk because each model makes clear predictions about what measurements ought to relate to friendship rank. For the present purpose, our main interest is the key alliance measure: We asked people where they thought they were ranked in each of their top ten friends' queues of closest friends. For each of their friends, participants indicated how their friend would rank them among other friends, that is, their perceived rank. If this rank does not predict one's own ranking of closeness, then doubt would be cast on the alliance model. For each friend, participants also rated similarity, benefits derived from the relationship, secret sharing, caring, intelligence, attractiveness, popularity, friendship duration, frequency of contact, sex, and age.

Among all of the variables that we measured, perceived rank was the best predictor of how subjects ranked their own friends. Across the three samples, the average raw correlation of perceived rank with the participant's ranking was .71, .50, and .68, respectively. These were the highest correlations for any of the 12 variables we measured. We used logistic regression to look at the effects of each variable controlling for the other 11 variables. We observed consistent effects for perceived rank, benefits, similarity, and secret sharing. In all three samples, however, perceived rank emerged as the strongest predictor of participants' rankings of friends. This evidence shows that, consistent with an alliance-building function, participants' perceptions of how others rank them were systematically related to their representations of relative closeness to their friends.

CONCLUSION

Friendship is a crucial part of human sociality, but its biological function remains poorly understood (Silk, 2003). Progress has been impeded by two problems that plague the social sciences. First, friendship is treated as functionless, rather than as the product of evolved functional mechanisms. Second, friendship decisions have been viewed as unsophisticated, based on simple rules such as attraction to proximate individuals, which stands in stark contrast to the complexity of other species' mechanisms for social life.

Instead, we suggest that the human mind has an extraordinarily intelligent cognitive machine that operates as a political strategist guiding our friendship decisions—a computational system that is far more strategically sophisticated than the most advanced professionals in political strategy. Just as the human mind is better at solving problems in computer vision than professional computer engineers, so too is the mind better at solving problems in political strategy than professional political strategists.

If friend cognition is as intelligent as we suggest, then understanding friendship will be difficult. There might be some aspects of friendship that cannot be understood until our theoretical knowledge of strategy becomes further developed. For biomechanics, Steven Vogel (1998) pointed out that "The biomechanic usually recognizes nature's use of some neat device only when the engineer has already provided us with a model" (p. 18). Similarly, we might need better theories of alliance strategy in order to understand friendship decisions.

Friendship systems solve an adaptive problem. We think that the problem has to do with strategic dynamics, specifically how to muster support when conflicts arise and how to avoid being on the losing side in fights. We think the current evidence cuts against the theory that friendship is for economic exchange. Whatever the function of friendship systems, they should be approached without the limiting lens of the "bias bias," the tendency to characterize human cognitive systems as error prone rather than computationally sophisticated. They are the product of the same evolutionary process that generated incredible feats of engineering ranging from a hummingbird's ability to hover to a lizard's ability to walk on water to our immune system's ability to neutralize pathogens.

It is a mistake to assume that the systems designed to navigate the social world will be a great deal less sophisticated. We look forward to future research that takes human friend-making decision systems to be at least as complex as other evolved systems.

REFERENCES

Adams, J., & Mesterton-Gibbons, M. (2003). Lanchester's attrition models and fights among social animals. *Behavioral Ecology, 14*, 719–723.

Archer, J., & Coyne, S. M. (2005). An integrated review of indirect, relational, and social aggression. *Personality and Social Psychology Review, 9*, 212–230.

Ariely, D. (2008). *Predictably irrational: The hidden forces that shape our decisions.* New York: Harper Collins.

Aronson, E., & Patnoe, S. (1997). *The jigsaw classroom: Building cooperation in the classroom* (2nd ed.). New York: Addison Wesley Longman.

Axelrod, R. (1984). *The evolution of cooperation.* New York, NY: Basic Books.

Bacon, F. (1620). *Novum organon.* Retrieved from the Constitution Society, http://www.constitution.org/bacon/nov_org.htm.

Bazerman, M. H., Curhan, J. R., Moore, D. A., & Valley, K. L. (2000). Negotiation. *Annual Review of Psychology, 51*, 279-314.

Bernstein, E. (2010, March 23). How to break up with a friend. *Wall Street Journal*, p. D1.

Brehm, S. S., Kassin, S. M., & Fein, S. (2002). *Social psychology.* New York: Houghton Mifflin.

Bushman, B. B., & Holt-Lunstad, J. (2009). Understanding social relationship maintenance among friends: Why we don't end those frustrating friendships. *Journal of Social and Clinical Psychology, 28*, 749–778.

Byrne, R. W., & Whiten, A. (Eds.). (1988). *Machiavellian intelligence: Social expertise and the evolution of intellect in monkeys, apes, and humans.* Oxford, UK: Clarendon Press.

Černy, J. (1955). Reference to blood brotherhood among Semites in an Egyptian text of the Ramesside Period. *Journal of Near Eastern Studies, 14*, 161–163.

Chapais, B. (1983). Reproductive activity in relation to male dominance and the likelihood of ovulation in Rhesus Monkeys. *Behavioral Ecology and Sociobiology, 12*, 215–228.

Cheney, D. L. (1977). The acquisition of rank and the development of reciprocal alliances among free-ranging immature baboons. *Behavioral Ecology and Sociobiology, 2*, 303–318.

Clark, M. S. (1984). Record keeping in two types of relationships. *Journal of Personality and Social Psychology, 47*, 549–557.

Clark, M. S., & Mills, J. (1979). Interpersonal attraction in exchange and communal relationships. *Journal of Personality and Social Psychology, 37*, 12–24.

Connor, R. C. (2007). Dolphin social intelligence: Complex alliance relationships in bottlenose dolphins and a consideration of selective environments for extreme brain size evolution in mammals. *Philosophical Transactions of the Royal Society B, 362*, 587–602.

Cosmides, L., & Tooby, J. (1992). Cognitive adaptations for social exchange. In J. Barkow, L. Cosmides, & J. Tooby (Eds.), *The adapted mind* (pp. 163–228). New York: Oxford University Press.

Crick, N. R., & Grotpeter, J. K. (1995). Relational aggression, gender, and social-psychological adjustment. *Child Development, 66*, 710–722.

DeScioli, P. (2008). *Investigations into the problems of moral cognition.* Unpublished doctoral dissertation, University of Pennsylvania, Philadelphia.

DeScioli, P., & Kurzban, R. (2009). The alliance hypothesis for human friendship. *Public Library of Science ONE, 4*(6), e5802.

Ebbesen, E. B., Kjos, G. L., & Konecni, V. J. (1976). Spatial ecology: Its effects on the choice of friends and enemies. *Journal of Experimental Social Psychology, 12*, 505–518.

Engh, A. L., Siebert, E. R., Greenberg, D. A., & Holekamp, K. E. (2005). Patterns of alliance formation and postconflict aggression indicate spotted hyaenas recognize third-party relationships. *Animal Behavior 69*, 209–217.

Evans-Pritchard, E. E. (1933). Zande blood-brotherhood. *Africa: Journal of the International African Institute, 6*, 369–401.

Feld, S. L. (1981). The focused organization of social ties. *The American Journal of Sociology, 86*, 1015–1035.

Festinger, L., Schachter, S., & Back, K. (1950). *Social pressures in informal groups: A study of a housing project.* New York: Harper.

Fisher, S. H., & Hoekstra, H. E. (2010). Competition drives cooperation among closely related sperm of deer mice. *Nature, 463*, 801–803.

Fiske, A. P., & Tetlock, P. E. (1997). Taboo trade-offs: Reactions to transactions that transgress the spheres of justice. *Political Psychology, 18*, 255–297.

Forrest, S., Eatough, V., & Shevlin, M. (2005). Measuring adult indirect aggression: The development and psychometic assessment of the indirect aggression scales. *Aggressive Behaviour, 31*, 84–97.

Frank, R. H., (2001). The economist as public intellectual: A case for selling Pareto improvements. *Eastern Economic Journal, 27*, 221–225.

Haig, D. (1993). Genetic conflicts in human pregnancy. *The Quarterly Review of Biology, 68*, 495–532.

Haley, M. P. (1994). Resource-holding power asymmetries, the prior residence effect, and reproductive payoffs in male northern elephant seal fights. *Behavioral Ecology and Sociobiology, 34*, 427–434.

Harcourt, A. H. (1992). Cooperation in conflicts: Commonalities between humans and other animals. *Politics and the Life Sciences, 11*, 251–259.

Hastie, R. K., & Dawes, R. M. (2010). *Rational choice in an uncertain world: The psychology of judgment and decision making.* Thousand Oaks, CA: Sage.

Henrich, J., & Gil-White, F. J. (2001). The evolution of prestige: Freely conferred status as a mechanism for enhancing the benefits of cultural transmission. *Evolution and Human Behavior, 22*, 165–196.

Herlehy, T. J. (1984). Ties that bind: Palm wine and blood-brotherhood at the Kenya coast during the 19th century. *The International Journal of African Historical Studies, 17*, 285–308.

Hess, N.C., & Hagen, E. H. (2002). *Informational warfare.* Unpublished manuscript.

Holekamp, K. E., Sakai, S. T., & Lundrigan, B. L. (2007). Social intelligence in the spotted hyena (Crocuta crocuta). *Philosophical Transactions of the Royal Society B, 29*, 523–538.

Homans, C. G. (1958). Social behavior as exchange. *The American Journal of Sociology, 63*, 597–606.

Kaukiainen, A., Salmivalli, C., Bjorkqvist, K., Osterman, K., Lahtinen, A., Kostamo, A., & Lagerspetz, K. (2001). Overt and covert aggression in work setting in relation to the subjective well-being of employees. *Aggressive Behavior, 27*, 360–371.

Kiefer, T. M. (1968). Institutionalized friendship and warfare among the Tausug of Jolo. *Ethnology, 7*, 225–244.

Krueger, J. I., & Funder, D. C. (2004). Towards a balanced social psychology: Causes, consequences and cures for the problem-seeking approach to social behavior and cognition. *Behavioral and Brain Sciences, 27*, 313–327.

Kurzban, R. (2010). *Why everyone (else) is a hypocrite: Evolution and the modular mind.* Princeton, NJ: Princeton University Press.

Levine, S. S., & Kurzban, R. (2006). Explaining clustering in social networks: Towards an evolutionary theory of cascading benefits. *Managerial and Decision Economics, 27*, 173–187.

Liska, G. (1962). *Nations in alliance: The limits of interdependence.* Baltimore, MD: Johns Hopkins Press.

Maynard Smith, J. (1982). *Evolution and the theory of games.* Cambridge, UK: Cambridge University Press.

McPherson, M., Smith-Lovin, L., & Cook, J. M. (2001). Birds of a feather: Homophily in social networks. *Annual Review of Sociology, 27*, 415–444.

Minsky, M. L. (1985). *The society of mind.* New York: Simon & Schuster.

Nickerson, R. S. (1998). Confirmation bias: A ubiquitous phenomenon in many guises. *Review of General Psychology, 2,* 175–220.

Norton, M. I., Frost, J. H., & Ariely, D. (2007). Less is more: The lure of ambiguity, or why familiarity breeds contempt. *Journal of Personality and Social Psychology, 92*, 97–105.

Owens, L., Shute, R., & Slee, P. (2000a). "Guess what I just heard!": Indirect aggression among teenage girls in Australia. *Aggressive Behavior, 26*, 67–83.

Owens, L., Shute, R., & Slee, P. (2000b). "I'm in and you're out …": Explanations for teenage girls' indirect aggression. *Psychology Evolution & Gender, 2*, 19–46.

Parker, G. A. (1974). Assessment strategy and the evolution of fighting behaviour. *Journal of Theoretical Biology, 47*, 223–243.

Parker, J. G., Low, C. M., Walker, A. R., & Gamm, B. K. (2005). Friendship jealousy in young adolescents: Individual differences and links to sex, self-esteem, aggression, and social adjustment. *Developmental Psychology, 41*, 235–250.

Pinker S. (1997). *How the mind works.* New York: W. W. Norton.

Roscoe, J. (1923). Uganda and some of its problems: Part I. *Journal of the Royal African Society, 22*, 96–108.

Schelling, T. C. (1960). *The strategy of conflict.* Cambridge, MA: Harvard University Press.

Schino, G. (2001). Grooming, competition and social rank among female primates: A metaanalysis. *Animal Behaviour, 62*, 265–271.

Scott, J. L., Kawahara, A. Y., Skevington, J. H., Yen, S., Sami, A., Smith, M. L., & Yack, J. E. (2010). The evolutionary origins of ritualized acoustic signals in caterpillars. *Nature Communications, 1*, 1–9.

Seabright, P. (2004). *The company of strangers: A natural history of economic life.* Princeton, NJ: Princeton University Press.

Seyfarth, R. M. (1977). A model of social grooming among adult female monkeys. *Journal of Theoretical Biology, 65*, 671–698.

Seyfarth, R. M., & Cheney, D. L. (2002). What are big brains for? *Proceedings of the National Academy of Sciences, USA, 99*, 4141–4142.

Shantz, C. U. (1987). Conflicts between children. *Child Development, 58*, 283–305.

Silk, J. (2003). Cooperation without counting: The puzzle of friendship. In P. Hammerstein (Ed.), *Genetic and cultural evolution of cooperation* (pp. 37–54). Boston: MIT Press.

Snyder, G. H. (1984). The security dilemma in alliance politics. *World Politics, 36*, 461–495.

Snyder, G. H. (1997). *Alliance politics.* Ithaca, NY: Cornell University Press.

Tooby, J., & Cosmides, L. (1996). Friendship and the banker's paradox: Other pathways to the evolution of adaptations for altruism. *Proceedings of the British Academy, 88,* 119–143.

Trivers, R. L. (1971). The evolution of reciprocal altruism. *Quarterly Review of Biology, 46,* 35–57.

Trumbull, H. C. (1893). *The blood covenant: A primitive rite and its bearings on scripture.* Philadelphia: J. D. Wattles.

Tversky, A., & Kahneman, D. (1973). Availability: A heuristic for judging frequency and probability. *Cognitive Psychology, 5,* 207–232.

Vogel, S. (1998). *Cats' paws and catapults: Mechanical worlds of nature and people.* New York: W. W. Norton.

von Neumann, J., & Morgenstern, O. (1944). *The theory of games and information.* Princeton, NJ: Princeton University Press.

Whiten, A., & Byrne, R. W. (Eds.). (1997). *Machiavellian intelligence II: Extensions and evaluations.* Cambridge, UK: Cambridge University Press.

Zajonc, R. B. (1968). Attitudinal effects of mere exposure. *Journal of Personality and Social Psychology Monograph, 9*(2, Pt. 2), 1–27.

13

The Social Psychology of the Wisdom of Crowds

RICHARD P. LARRICK,
ALBERT E. MANNES, and JACK B. SOLL

*P*icture yourself taking part in a classroom psychology experiment on perception. You and nine other subjects are being asked to judge the lengths of lines in a vision test. The experimenter holds up a large card that contains three lines of different lengths, marked A, B, and C, and a target line. The subjects are asked: Which of A, B, or C is the same length as the target? For each card, all subjects take turns reporting which line matches the target. The first few sets of cards are unremarkable. Everyone states what is clear to the eye. On the fifth trial, the obvious answer to you is B, but the first person says C (you find this mildly amusing). However, the second person also says C. The third says C, and then the fourth. Everyone says C. When it is your turn to answer, what do you say? Before hearing the response of others, you thought the answer was obviously B. But the unanimous opinion of others is C.

All students of social psychology recognize the famous Asch (1955) experiment, and most remember that three of four subjects at some point conform to a group answer that defies their own perceptions. Deutsch and Gerard (1955) introduced the term *normative social influence* to characterize the tendency for people to give public responses that allow them to fit in with others even when they privately disagree. However, Asch's classic study has come to symbolize more. In its own time—an era of totalitarian governments that repressed individualism and McCarthyite pressures in the United States that did likewise—Asch's study reinforced a suspicion of groups and a celebration of the lone, independent individual.

Early conformity research was criticized for leaving the widely held but misleading impression that people yield too much to the judgments of others, thereby harming themselves. Some authors (Allen, 1965; Campbell, 1961) suggested that this pessimistic conclusion is misleading because it was foreordained by the

227

experimental design. In the Asch study, the other nine group members were only pretending to be subjects and had been planted to give consistently false answers before the true subject responded. Allen observed, "[M]ost psychological experiments in this area have been designed in such a manner that conformity was by necessity maladaptive: factually incorrect, detrimental to the group and the individual, or simply dishonest" (1965, p. 136).

In response, some authors stressed the adaptive value of conformity. Under uncertainty, people look to others for information (Deutsch & Gerard, 1955; Festinger, 1954), and groups are usually a valid source of information (Campbell, 1961). Allen observed that "a person may go along with beliefs expressed by most of the other people around him because he realizes that opinions shared by many are often more likely to be correct than the opinions held by a single individual. ... In some situations conformity is constructive and appropriate; in other situations it is not" (1965, pp. 136–137). (See Kameda & Tindale, 2006, and Krueger & Massey, 2009, for recent analyses of the adaptiveness of conformity.)

This chapter builds on the questions raised by classic social psychology experiments on conformity to examine the wisdom of relying on crowds. We review two general sets of questions. The normative questions ask what is rational or optimal: How accurate are the judgments of collectives? When individuals disagree with the judgments of others, should they change their judgment or hold firm to their initial opinion (Bell, Raiffa, & Tversky, 1988)? The descriptive questions ask what people actually do when they have access to the judgments of others: Do individuals understand why they should listen to others? Do they effectively decide when to listen to others (Bell, Raiffa, & Tversky, 1988)?

To address these questions, we build on a research tradition that differs markedly from the Asch tradition. The Asch situation was by nature misleading. In more mathematical terms, the answers from the false group members were unrepresentative of true answers. Brunswik (1955) famously argued that decision makers need to be presented with representative stimuli to assess how well they use information (Dami, Hertwig, & Hoffrage, 2004). To understand whether groups yield accurate answers and whether subjects are able to benefit from group accuracy, one needs to study processes in which representative judgments are elicited and shared with decision makers.

The remainder of the chapter is divided into two main sections. First, we describe recent research on the wisdom of crowds. This innovative literature combines decades of research in different fields showing the benefits of combining information across people. We analyze the conditions that make crowds effective to answer the normative questions of how and when crowds are wise. We then examine the descriptive question of how people use the judgments of others. We review a growing body of research showing that people are egocentric in their use of judgments: They rely too much on their own judgments and miss the opportunity to learn from others.

THE WISDOM OF CROWDS

Some of the earliest studies in social psychology examined whether groups were fundamentally different from individuals. In the 1920s, researchers examined whether groups were smarter than individuals (see Larrick & Soll, 2006, for a historical review). In one early study students estimated the temperature in a classroom. When the estimates were averaged, the result was more accurate than the estimate of a typical group member. It should be noted that individual members of this "group" never interacted with one another. Where did the benefits come from? Early authors were surprised by this result and attributed it to some mysterious group property. As one writer put it, "In every coming together of minds … [t]here is the Creative Plus, which no one mind by itself could achieve" (Overstreet, 1925, as cited in Watson, 1928). In time, researchers recognized that the power of groups came from something much simpler but still elegant: Combining judgments takes individual imperfection and smoothes the rough edges to isolate the collective's view of the truth. Or, to put it more mathematically and mundanely, averaging cancels error.

Subsequent research in the forecasting literature demonstrated that simple combination methods that weight people equally, such as averaging judgments, often perform as well as more sophisticated statistical methods of combination (Armstrong, 2001; Clemen, 1989). The power and simplicity of averaging was summed up in the title of James Surowiecki's 2004 best-selling book, *The Wisdom of Crowds*.

Consider a brief example that illustrates the power of averaging. Imagine two professors estimating the number of students who are likely to apply to a program in neuroscience. Their goal is to get as close to the truth as possible. Being too high or too low is equally bad (e.g., being 5 high or 5 low will be treated as a miss of 5). Professor L estimates 40. Professor H estimates 60. Their average guess is 50. If the truth turns out to be 47, the judges have missed by 7 and 13, respectively, and their average miss is 10. But the average of the judges' guesses, 50, missed the true value of 47 by only 3—a substantially smaller error than the average miss of 10. Why does this happen? The judgments of 40 and 60 "bracket" the truth: The high error and low error offset each other. It is bracketing that gives averaging its power (Larrick & Soll, 2006; Soll & Larrick, 2009).

Now suppose that the truth is 37. Both professors have overestimated (by 3 and 23, respectively), and the average performance of the professors has missed by (3 + 23)/2 = 13. The average guess of 50 also misses by 13. In cases like this—where both judges fall on the same side of the truth—averaging "locks in" the average individual error. This is the worst case scenario for averaging. With bracketing, averaging will be more accurate than the average individual error.

Of course, Professor L is more accurate than Professor H in both examples. Picking Professor L's lone judgment would have done well in the second scenario although fallen short of the average in the first scenario. It is tempting to declare Professor L smarter than the average. Research on groups frequently compares group performance to the performance of the "best member." It is important to point out, however, that in judgments under uncertainty the best member standard can be misleading when defined post hoc. Even when there is skill in judgment, there is luck as well, and it takes a large sample to know whether one judge is truly more accurate than another. The critical questions are whether (a) one judge is *reliably* better than another judge by *a substantial margin* over time and

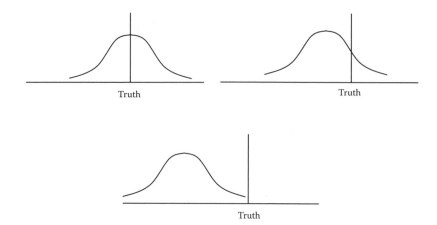

Figure 13.1   Three distributions of individual judgments in which judgments are evenly distributed around the truth (top left panel), bracket the truth (top right panel), or are biased below the truth (bottom panel).

(b) whether the difference in ability is *detectable* from available cues in advance. In this example, could one know anything in advance about Professors L and H (or their answers) that would lead one to heavily favor the judgment of one over the other before knowing the outcome? Averaging is powerful, because, thanks to bracketing, it must perform better than the average judge and can often perform much better. This performance makes it superior to choosing individual judges when judges are roughly similar in ability or when it is hard to distinguish their ability in advance.

The idea of bracketing generalizes to larger crowds.[1] To illustrate, the *Wall Street Journal* surveys a panel of about 50 economists every six months to make macroeconomic forecasts about inflation, unemployment, and so forth. The resulting diagram of forecasts often looks like a reasonable approximation of a normal distribution (see three hypothetical examples in Figure 13.1). When the truth is added to the plot six months later, it is often the case that the crowd of economists is roughly centered on the truth (top left panel). Even when the distribution is not centered on the truth, it often brackets the truth (top right panel). Given some degree of bracketing, the average of the crowd is by mathematical necessity more accurate than the average individual.[2] When there is no bracketing—that is, the whole crowd is biased strictly above or below the truth as in the bottom panel—the average of the crowd is still as accurate as the average individual. Averaging the answers of a crowd, therefore, ensures a level of accuracy no worse than the average member of the crowd and, in some cases, a level better than nearly all members.

Conditions for Crowds to Be Wise

Crowds, of course, are not always wiser than individuals. The degree to which crowds are more accurate than individuals is a function of two factors: expertise and diversity. First, the crowd needs to consist of individuals with some knowledge or expertise about the issue in question. This could be based on past education or past experience. In quantitative judgments, expertise allows individuals to use imperfect evidence to make predictions that will fall close to the truth over many judgments.

Second, the crowd needs to hold diverse perspectives on the judgment in question. As a result of holding diverse perspectives, different individuals will bring different areas of expertise to bear on a judgment and therefore make different mistakes. For example, imagine two professors predicting the academic ability of graduate school applicants. One professor tends to focus on past research experience; the other focuses on grades. Both cues are valid—both cues are predictive of future performance. Moreover, the cues are not perfectly correlated, so over many cases, they often lead to conflicting conclusions. Thus, when one professor is optimistic about a student who has a good deal of research experience and the second professor is pessimistic because the student has low grades, their average assessment is more complete and likely to be more accurate than their individual assessments. Relying on a subset of cues introduces errors that can be offset by including the additional valid cues used by other judges.

To appreciate the effect of diversity on judgment, consider its absence. Imagine a marketing team evaluating the revenue potential of new possible products. If all of the marketers have worked in the same company on the same past products at the same period of time, they have developed a shared set of experiences that guide their judgment about which new products are best. As a result, they are likely to hold shared opinions such as "customizability is more attractive to people under 40 than to people over 40." The consequence is that they share the same expertise—and the same blind spots. Forecasting researchers term this pattern "positively correlated forecast errors" and show mathematically that it reduces the value of aggregating judgments across people because similar errors cannot cancel each other. Sociologists who study social networks refer to shared patterns of knowledge as *redundant* (Burt, 1992, 2004). The word redundant evokes the right image: In the extreme, the knowledge of one person is a pretty good substitute for another person's. From a wisdom-of-crowds perspective, it is as if you do not have a crowd; your crowd is effectively one.

There are two ways to foster diversity. Differences in perspective are created through who is in the group (composition) and how they share information (process).

Composition

Research in the forecasting literature (Clemen & Winkler, 1986) has demonstrated the value of combining forecasts from different econometric models based on different economic schools of thought. The organizational literature has emphasized cross-functional teams as the best source for new ideas (Cronin & Weingart, 2007). A company does not want a new product designed by marketers alone—marketers will give it a fantastic look with many features but may pay less attention to the cost of production. The company needs expertise in other areas (finance, engineering, etc.) to ensure that the product meets a more optimal set of objectives.

Network sociologists propose enhancing diversity by finding gaps in the social network (Burt, 1992). The premise is that in tightly knit groups, people talk a great deal, and come to know and value the same things. They become redundant. From a group's vantage point, new ideas and new perspectives lie outside their own boundaries—even in other closely knit groups. The beauty of separation is that separated groups are likely to have evolved different views that are redundant *within* a group but nonredundant *between* them (Burt, 2004).

Creating diversity through composition can be challenging. One obstacle is that in-groups that share a similar perspective often look down on out-groups (DiDonato, Ullrich, & Krueger, 2011). Members of the marketing group suspect that members of the finance group are just bean counters who will stifle creativity. A second obstacle is that real differences in language and thinking impede collaboration between groups (Cronin & Weingart, 2007). These obstacles tend to lead people to associate with similar others. Sociologists term this tendency *homophily*; informally, it is the tendency for birds of a feather flocking together. Thus, when people assemble teams, they often select members based on common experience, common training, and common attitudes. This facilitates harmony but limits diversity.

Process   The second source of diversity is the process a group or collective uses to elicit judgments. A good group process ensures that individuals think independently before sharing their judgments. Why is independence important? Imagine being in an experiment in which you are asked to estimate the years in which important events happened. Imagine also that before you see a question, you see the real answer from another subject. For example, you see 1300 followed by the question "In what year was the Magna Carta written?" To what extent is your answer influenced by first seeing the answer of another subject? Koehler and Beauregard (2006) found that when answers were given without seeing other answers—that is, when answers were independent—they were typically 50 years apart (median value). When answers were given after seeing someone else's answer, however, they differed by only 10 years from the answer that was seen. Cognitive psychologists have called this general phenomenon *anchoring* (Tversky & Kahneman, 1974). Anchoring occurs because people start with a number, such as the year 1300, and unconsciously recruit evidence consistent with it (Chapman & Johnson, 1999; Mussweiler & Strack, 1999) and then fail to adjust sufficiently from it (Epley & Gilovich, 2001).

Whether a deliberate strategy or an unconscious anchoring process, people rely on others to form their judgments. Deutsch and Gerard (1955) called this tendency *informational influence* and contrasted it with the *normative influence* illustrated in the Asch study. Recall that participants in the Asch experiment would often publicly report an answer with which they disagreed privately. Informational influence, on the other hand, occurs when people use the judgments of others to reduce their own uncertainty. It results in a new opinion—public and private—that incorporates the beliefs of others.

Because of anchoring and informational influence, single judgments in a group can propagate through the judgments of others if the others have not first formed an opinion. For example, having one person start a discussion with an opinion ("we should increase inventory by 20%") tends to lead others to think in small variations of that opinion. The result is that both the initial accuracy and the initial error in the first judgment are spread to those who hear it (economists have studied this phenomenon under the name *information cascades*; see Krueger & Massey, 2009, for a review). Anchoring and informational influence produce *positively correlated error* and *redundancy*, which amount to reducing the effective sample size.

Better group processes ensure that members think independently to form their judgments before sharing them. Research on brainstorming has found that working independently leads to a bigger and better pool of ideas than working face to face (Girota, Terwiesch, & Ulrich, 2010; Paulus & Yang, 2000). This effect occurs, in part, because independent ideas are generated in parallel, whereas face-to-face conversations require taking turns. But some of the effect is due to groups developing a common way of thinking about a question due to anchoring and informational influence. The danger of anchoring during group discussion has led one forecasting expert (Armstrong, 2006) to propose that many decisions would be better made if groups shared information without ever meeting.

Crowds Versus Individual Experts

To say that a crowd is wise invites the question, "Compared to what?" The implicit comparison in these examples has been to the average individual in the crowd. Indeed, for quantitative judgments, the average of the crowd can never be worse than the average individual in the crowd. With a high rate of bracketing, averaging will be far superior to the average individual. However, the average individual is not the only standard by which to judge a crowd. One can also ask how well averaging performs compared with the best member of the crowd (Luan, Katsikopoulos, & Reimer, in press). For this comparison to be informative, it is important to predict beforehand who the best judge will be. As noted earlier, it is always possible to determine the best performer after the fact.

There can be significant barriers to accurate identification of expertise. If there is no reliable track record of performance, one needs to rely on other cues. In a group discussion, members often rely on confidence and verbosity as cues to expertise (Littlepage, Robison, & Reddington, 1997). Unfortunately, cues like confidence often correlate weakly with actual accuracy (Burson, Larrick, & Klayman, 2007). Consequently, group members often inaccurately rank order the expertise of the members of their group (for example, Miner, 1984).

Even if one has access to past performance, the sample may not be large enough to allow a valid inference of stable ability. If you track the best performers in *The Wall Street Journal* data from one period to the next, they are no more accurate than the average judge in later periods (Mannes, Soll, & Larrick, 2011). Why? Performance is a function of both skill and luck. More formally, apparent experts in one period of time regress to the mean of performance in the next period (for a discussion of regression to the mean, see Chapter 10 by Fiedler and Krueger in this volume).[3] As a result, one is better off using the average of the whole sample of economists in the current period than to bet on the winner from the last survey.

Whether one should pick a single expert or rely on a crowd depends not just on access to valid evidence about the ability of judges, but also the presence of a large difference between the best judge and other judges. The benefits of diversity are so strong that one can combine the judgments from individuals who differ a great deal in their individual accuracy and still gain from averaging. In a two judge case, one judge can be 50% more accurate than another judge and averaging will still outperform the better judge with realistic rates of bracketing (Soll & Larrick, 2009). For example, if over many prediction periods one economist tends to miss true GNP (gross national product) increases by $50 billion on average and a second economist tends to miss by $75 billion, there is still a benefit to combining their judgments. It takes a large difference in ability to justify choosing one judge instead of averaging.

In sum, there are many advantages to averaging a crowd over choosing single experts. First, when judges are similar in ability, it allows their errors to cancel. Second, when judges differ in ability but differences are hard to detect, an averaging strategy is sure to give at least some weight to the best performers; by contrast, trying to pick a single expert based on available cues could put all the weight on a less accurate judge. Finally, an averaging strategy can be implemented even in the absence of evidence about relative expertise.

Types of Crowd Judgments

Most of the examples offered so far have focused on quantitative judgments under uncertainty. But the benefits of crowds can apply to many tasks. When choosing among options, majority rule performs well compared to more complex approaches (Hastie & Kameda, 2005; Sorkin, Luan, & Itzkowitz, 2004). In the popular game show *Who Wants to be a Millionaire?* the studio audience answered the trivia questions correctly 91% of the time (Surowiecki, 2004). More qualitative tasks also benefit from crowds. Research on creativity has shown that once a person has pursued one approach to solving a problem, it is hard for the person to generate other approaches. Brainstorming overcomes this problem by tapping the diverse perspectives of a group to generate a larger and more complete pool of ideas (Girotra et al., 2010; Paulus & Yang, 2000). Bond, Carlson, and Keeney (2008) asked business students to generate objectives for their summer job (e.g., pay level, location, growth opportunities, relevance to future career plans, and so forth). They found that students listed about seven objectives on average. However, when students were then presented with both their own objectives along with a list of objectives generated by others, they tended to find another seven objectives that were as important as the ones they had generated on their own. Groups are smarter than individuals in creating a wider range of creative ideas, objectives, and alternatives.

Technology has made it easier to draw on the wisdom of crowds. Some tools are as simple as aggregating average ratings on consumer Web sites. Others are more complex, such as prediction markets, in which people wager real or pretend money to bet on future events, such as sports. (A famous but short-lived Department of Defense market had people betting for and against the timing of future terrorist attacks; betting "for" an attack was perceived as distasteful.) Similarly, corporations have used internal "idea jams" to tap employee perspectives on innovation opportunities and have used external "crowd sourcing" to reach a broad pool of diverse entrepreneurs to address unsolved technological problems they currently face.

The Individual as a Crowd

Research on the wisdom of crowds supports the old saying that two heads are better than one. It is interesting that the insights from this literature have also been used to show that one head can be nearly as good as two (Herzog & Hertwig, 2009; Vul & Pashler, 2008), as long as a judge follows the principles of relevant knowledge and diverse perspectives. The key insight is that people typically rely on only a sample of the evidence available to them at any given time. But what if people had a reset button, so that they could retrieve facts from memory anew or handle the same facts in a new way?

One way to free people from their original answers is to delay a second answer (Vul & Pashler, 2008) so that people forget their initial perspectives and think about the problem differently the second time around. Another way to free people is to have them try to construct a fresh perspective. To demonstrate this possibility, Herzog and Hertwig (2009) had participants make estimates about quantitative values they did not know with certainty (specifically, dates in history). All participants gave two answers to the same question, and the authors constructed an average of the first and second judgments for each individual. In one condition, participants simply gave a second estimate following their first estimate. This condition did little to increase diversity—people simply anchored on their initial opinions—and there was no benefit from averaging. In a second condition, participants were told to assume that their first answer was incorrect, think of some reasons it might be wrong, and then "based on this new perspective, make a second, alternative estimate" (p. 234). This process of *second guessing* increased bracketing; as expected, the average of the first and second judgments was significantly more accurate than the first estimate. A lesson of Herzog and Hertwig's study is that we each carry around our own crowd, but we gain the wisdom only if we ask different members of the crowd.

HOW WELL DO PEOPLE USE CROWDS?

Strategies for Combining Judgments

Given that crowds are often wise, an important question for social psychology is whether people understand the value of combining knowledge across people. How well do people use judgments of others? This has become a growing area of research in recent years. Most research has focused on a very simple version of a crowd: two-person collectives involving the self (Sniezek & Buckley, 1995; Yaniv & Kleinberger, 2000). In these studies, people make estimates and then learn actual, representative estimates of others. The source of estimates is often called an *advisor* and the literature as a whole has come to be known as "advice taking." The advice-taking literature has used a wide range of quantitative stimuli, including estimating ages or weights of people from photographs, years in which historical events occurred, temperatures of cities, and so on. Studies that have focused on accuracy then compare initial and revised estimates to the truth and typically pay subjects for the closeness of their judgment. A smaller amount of research has looked at how people use the estimates of larger collectives of which they might or might not be members. We consider these two areas of research separately.

Using Advice From One Other Person   One of the most robust findings in the advice-taking literature is that people underweight advice from another and overweight their own opinions (see Bonaccio & Dalal, 2006, for a review). A common result is that, on average, people tend to adjust their estimates 20% to 30% of the way toward advice (Harvey & Fischer, 1997; Soll & Larrick, 2009; Yaniv, 2004), a phenomenon that Yaniv and Kleinberger (2000) labeled *egocentric discounting*. For example, imagine estimating the age of someone from a photograph. You might make an initial estimate of 42 years old, see an advisor's estimate of 50, and adjust your answer to 44. The initial estimate and advice in this example are 8 years apart. The revised answer of 44 reflects a movement of 2/8, which translates to putting 25% weight on advice (WOA) and keeping 75% weight on your initial answer.

Subsequent research has found that 20% to 30% weight on advice is not descriptive of how people actually revise their judgments. The common pattern of 20% to 30% weight on advice is an average result of more extreme underlying behavior. Soll and Larrick (2009) showed that people often either choose one of the two answers (typically their own) or use an equal-weighted average. In their studies, the 30% mean weight on advice reflected a pattern of frequently ignoring advice entirely (0% WOA), sometimes averaging their initial estimates with advice (50% WOA), and occasionally ignoring their own initial estimates and fully accepting advice (100% WOA). The most common response in these studies was 0% weight on advice. Such an extreme strategy takes no advantage of the error-canceling benefits of a two-person crowd and significantly hurts final accuracy. Subjects would have formed more accurate final estimates if they had given *equal* weight to their own estimates and advice (Soll & Larrick, 2009).[4]

Why do people put so much weight on their own estimates? Several explanations have been offered. First, many people have an incorrect theory of combining judgments (Larrick & Soll, 2006), believing that averaging leads to mediocrity. Specifically, they incorrectly believe that the average judgment in a crowd is no more accurate than the average judge. Holding this incorrect belief is significantly related to ignoring advice (Larrick & Soll, 2006).

Other explanations for ignoring advice have focused on more psychological assumptions. Harvey and Harries (2004) proposed that people believe that the advisor is substantially less accurate than oneself. Yaniv and his colleagues (Yaniv, 2004; Yaniv & Kleinberger, 2000) proposed that people weight their own answers more highly because they know the reasons for their own judgments but not those behind the judgments of others. Soll and Mannes (2011) tested both explanations by directly measuring subjects' perceptions of their accuracy relative to their advisor and by systematically providing or withholding cues at the time of revision (where seeing cues can remind subjects of their reasons for their initial answer).

They found some evidence for inflated perceptions of the self, but not enough to explain the frequent use of 0% WOA. Moreover, they found no effect of having access to reasons on WOA. They proposed that the tendency to hold on to one's judgment may be less cognitive and more motivational: One's judgments are part of oneself and, like possessions, letting go of them is painful. Moreover, there may be an asymmetry in the regret of changing one's mind. Actively giving up an initially accurate answer for a worse one may lead to more regret than passively holding on to an inaccurate answer and foregoing improvement (see Chapter 15 by Baron in this volume).

The advice-taking literature has found that a number of factors affect the weight placed on advice. Some factors are rational: Subjects weight advice more heavily when advisors are more experienced or knowledgeable (Harvey & Fischer, 1997; Soll & Larrick, 2009), when advisors express greater confidence in the quality of their advice (Sniezek & Buckley, 1995; Sniezek & Van Swol, 2001; Soll & Larrick, 2009), and when the subject finds the task difficult (Gino & Moore, 2007). As long as people use these advisor characteristics according to their validity, shifting weight to more expert advisors is an effective response to these cues. Other factors are more psychological: Decision makers weight advice less heavily when they feel powerful (See, Morrison, Rothman, & Soll, 2011) and when they experience emotions that increase feelings of certainty, such as anger (Gino & Schweitzer, 2008). This research identifies a practical set of factors that reduces the use of advice and can help practitioners in different fields, such as business and medicine, recognize when egocentric discounting will be at its greatest.

Combining Judgments From a Collective

A smaller stream of research has focused on how people combine the opinions of multiple others. Most studies in this area have looked at how people combine judgments across a panel of experts. In these studies, subjects have not made their own initial judgment but are neutral arbiters deciding how to balance the judgments of others (Budescu, 2006; Harvey, Harries, & Fischer, 2000; Yaniv, 1997). Budescu and colleagues (Budescu, 2006; Budescu, Rantilla, Yu, & Karelitz, 2003) have found that people tend to weight expert judgments in proportion to the expertise of different judges.

Two studies in this area have looked at advice taking from a group. As in the two-person advice research, these studies involve having people make an initial judgment and then revise it after seeing the estimates of a group (Mannes, 2009; Yaniv & Milyavsky, 2007). Yaniv and Milyavsky (2007) found that people cherry-pick the advice from a larger crowd, focusing on the judgments most consistent with their own. Subjects effectively use their first guess as a standard of accuracy and dismiss discrepant advice. From a wisdom-of-crowds perspective, this is dangerous: It ignores the benefits of incorporating diverse perspectives to cancel error. Mannes (2009) explored the extent to which people listen to the average judgment from crowds of different sizes. Normatively, subjects would be wise to put less weight on themselves and more weight on the crowd as the crowd grows in size (reflecting a basic principle in statistics known as the *law of large numbers*). In addition, if all judges are expected to be equally accurate in advance, subjects would be wise to put the same weight on themselves as they do on each member of the crowd (i.e., a $1/n$ weight on their own judgment and a $(n − 1)/n$ weight on the crowd's advice). Mannes found that people put more weight on larger crowds, as they should from a normative perspective, but not enough weight. They put only 60% weight on advice from a nine-person crowd where equal weighting would require more than 90% weight. The consequence of egocentric weighting is that subjects paid a significant price in the accuracy of their final judgments.

Future Directions for the Psychology of the Wisdom of Crowds

The main conclusion from existing research is that people use crowds too little: They put too much weight on their own judgment and thereby miss out on the benefit of diverse perspectives for reducing error. This is a young and growing area of research. What are some of the unanswered questions? Perhaps a key issue that arises in the existing work is that advice is quantitative, impersonal, and unsolicited—it consists of seeing numerical estimates made by others (including group averages) and making conscious decisions about how best to combine them with one's own independent estimates. The use of crowd judgments should be explored in other ways.

First, advice *seeking* could be an important variable to study. How often do people seek advice? Perhaps the easiest way to reduce error in judgment is to seek other's opinions, and the failure to do so has the same negative consequences as ignoring advice. We suspect people seek advice less often than they should. How does seeking advice affect its use? The act of seeking advice is likely to increase the extent to which advice is used (Gino, 2008) and thereby improve judgment. It is also possible that seeking advice will lead people to pick a single expert and put too much faith in that single piece of advice.

Second, other advice-taking contexts may change openness to advice, such as face-to-face interactions or interactions with richer information sharing. Richer information sharing may lead to deeper information processing. Face-to-face interactions may evoke processes such as empathy and mimicry that produce greater yielding to others.

Third, the benefits of independence should be carefully examined. Earlier we argued that independence increases diversity of perspective and thereby makes a crowd more accurate. Asch captured this idea when writing that "consensus, to be productive, requires that each individual contribute independently out of his experience and insight" (1955, p. 34). In this view, individual judgments are "inputs" to a combination process and they are more valuable if they are independent. However, individual judgments can also be "outputs" from exposure to the judgments of collectives. Egocentric discounting of advice is an example of an inferior output. In output situations there may be a benefit if the individual does *not* have an independent opinion: Anchoring on a crowd may actually yield more accurate judgments because it ensures that individual judges are using a larger sample—even if unwittingly.

Consider a study that predates Asch. Jenness (1932) asked students to estimate the number of beans in a jar. They made their estimates in a prescribed sequence: first individually, then by consensus in a three-person group, and then individually again. The initial individual guesses missed the true value (811) by 305 on average. The group consensus answers missed the value by just 91, producing a substantial improvement over their initial individual guesses. Strikingly, however, their final individual guesses missed by 122 on average—worse than the group answers. What went wrong? By reasserting their independence and deviating from the group answer, the subjects in Jenness's study were less accurate than if they had simply placed their faith in the crowd.

Thus, we can think of crowd processes as having two stages. Independence is important at Stage 1, the input stage, because the effective sample size is increased when different judges make different errors. However, independence may be unimportant or even detrimental at Stage 2, the output stage, when a decision maker uses others' judgments to form a final opinion that he or she is going to act on. Campbell adopted the Stage 2 perspective when he argued that, "[I]n Asch's famous situation, the single true subject might rationally decide that, since everybody's eyes are imperfect, and since it would be so extremely infrequent that so many Swarthmore students would deliberately lie in a situation like this, it is more probable that his own eyes are wrong than that all of the others are wrong. He might, therefore, rationally decide that, if asked to bet, he would bet with the majority" (1961, p. 123). In contrast to the view inherited from the Asch tradition, social influence may actually be beneficial. Normative and informational influence may serve as a *cognitive repair* (Heath, Larrick, & Klayman, 1998) that mitigates depending too much on one's own judgments. Influence ensures that people incorporate the wisdom of the crowd in their own judgments.

NOTES

1. One can conceive of bracketing in a group as the rate at which randomly selected pairs bracket the truth or as a ratio of the proportion of the crowd falling on each side of the truth. For example, if 60% of the crowd is high and 40% low, the pairwise bracketing rate is $1 - [(.6 \times .6) + (.4 \times .4)] = .48$, and there is a 1.5 (.6/.4) ratio.
2. This mathematical necessity can be proven by applying Jensen's inequality. Let Judge i's estimate on quantity j be represented as $X_{ij} = T_j + D_{ij}$, where T_j is the correct answer and D_{ij} is the deviation, $i = 1, 2, ..., n$, and $j = 1, 2, ..., m$. Let $w_1, w_2, ..., w_n$ be the weights assigned to n judgments, where $W_i = 1$. Accuracy on a given estimate is a function of the deviation, $f(D)$. Typically, $f(D)$ is increasing in $|D|$, so higher scores reflect lower accuracy. For a quantity j, the deviation for a weighted average is the weighted average of the deviations of the individual estimates:

$$f(w_1 x_{1j} + w_2 x_{2j} + ... + w_n x_{nj} - T_j) = f\left(\sum_{i=1}^{n} w_i D_{ij}\right).$$

The right-hand side of the preceding equation gives the accuracy of a weighted average. If f is a convex function, then Jensen's inequality states that

$$\sum_{i=1}^{n} w_i f(D_{ij}) \geq f\left(\sum_{i=1}^{n} w_i D_{ij}\right).$$

In this chapter, we focus on absolute error as our accuracy standard because it is neutral in punishing larger versus small errors. Past forecast research has focused on squared error as the loss function, which implies that larger errors are worse than smaller ones. When squared error is used as the loss function, averaging is more accurate than the average judge even when there is no bracketing.

Aggregation also improves judgment using other criteria for accuracy, such as correlations with the truth.

3. Denrell and Fang (2010) showed that when a *Wall Street Journal* economist "wins" one period with more extreme judgments—that is, judgments that are outliers compared to the rest of the group—they are actually less accurate than the average judge in subsequent periods.

4. In these studies, subjects made judgments independently (yielding bracketing rates of 30% to 40%), were randomly assigned advisors from their own subject population (yielding small average differences in expertise between judges), and given cues to expertise such as self-expressed confidence or a small sample of past performance (which are weak cues). All of these features, which favor averaging, were known by subjects.

REFERENCES

Allen, V. L. (1965). Situational factors in conformity. *Advances in Experimental Social Psychology, 2*, 133–175.

Armstrong, J. S. (2001). *Principles of forecasting: A handbook for researchers and practitioners*. Boston: Kluwer Academic.

Armstrong, J. S. (2006). Should the forecasting process eliminate face-to-face meetings? *Foresight: The International Journal of Applied Forecasting, 5*, 3–8.

Asch, S. E. (1955). Opinions and social pressure. *Scientific American, 193*, 31–35.

Bell, D., Raiffa, H., & Tversky, A. (1988). *Decision making: Descriptive, normative, and prescriptive interactions*. Cambridge, UK: Cambridge University Press.

Bonaccio, S., & Dalal, R. S. (2006). Advice taking and decision-making: An integrative literature review, and implications for the organizational sciences. *Organizational Behavior and Human Decision Processes, 101*, 127–151.

Bond, S. D., Carlson, K. A., & Keeney, R. L. (2008). Generating objectives: Can decision makers articulate what they want? *Management Science, 54*, 56–70.

Brunswik, E. (1955): Representative design and probabilistic theory in a functional psychology. *Psychological Review, 62*, 193–217.

Budescu, D. V. (2006). Confidence in aggregation of opinions from multiple sources. In K. Fiedler & P. Juslin (Eds.), *Information sampling and adaptive cognition* (pp. 327–352). Cambridge, UK: Cambridge University Press.

Budescu, D. V., Rantilla, A. K., Yu, H.-T., & Karelitz, T. M. (2003). The effects of asymmetry among advisors on the aggregation of their opinions. *Organizational Behavior and Human Decision Processes, 90*, 178–194.

Burson, K. A., Larrick, R. P., & Klayman, J. (2006). Skilled or unskilled, but still unaware of it: how perceptions of difficulty drive miscalibration in relative comparisons. *Journal of Personality and Social Psychology, 90*, 60–77.

Burt, R. S. (1992). *Structural holes*. Cambridge, MA: Harvard University Press.

Burt, R. S. (2004). Structural holes and good ideas. *American Journal of Sociology, 110*, 349–399.

Campbell, D. T. (1961). Conformity in psychology's theories of acquired behavioral dispositions. In I. A. Berg & B. M. Bass (Eds.), *Conformity and deviation* (pp. 101–142). New York: Harper & Brothers.

Chapman, G. B., & Johnson, E. J. (1999). Anchoring, activation and the construction of values. *Organizational Behavior and Human Decision Processes, 79*, 115–153.

Clemen, R. T. (1989). Combining forecasts: A review and annotated bibliography. *International Journal of Forecasting, 5,* 559–609.

Clemen, R. T., & Winkler, R. L. (1986). Combining economic forecasts. *Journal of Business and Economic Statistics, 4,* 39–46.

Cronin, M. A., & Weingart, L. R. (2007). Representational gaps, information processing, and conflict in functionally diverse teams. *Academy of Management Review, 32,* 761–773.

Dami, M. K., Hertwig, R., & Hoffrage, U. (2004). The role of representative design in an ecological approach to cognition. *Psychological Bulletin, 130,* 959–988.

Denrell, J., & Fang, C. (2010). Predicting the next big thing: Success as a signal of poor judgment. *Management Science, 56,* 1653–1667.

Deutsch, M., & Gerard, H. B. (1955). A study of normative and informational social influences upon individual judgment. *Journal of Abnormal and Social Psychology, 51,* 629–636.

DiDonato, T. E., Ullrich, J., & Krueger, J. I. (2011). Social perception as induction and inference: An integrative model of intergroup differentiation, ingroup favoritism, and differential accuracy. *Journal of Personality and Social Psychology, 100,* 66–83.

Epley, N., & Gilovich, T. (2001). Putting adjustment back in the anchoring and adjustment heuristic: Differential processing of self-generated and experimenter-provided anchors. *Psychological Science, 12,* 391–396.

Festinger, L. (1954). A theory of social comparison processes. *Human Relations, 7,* 117–140.

Gino, F. (2008). Do we listen to advice just because we paid for it? The impact of cost of advice on its use. *Organizational Behavior and Human Decision Processes, 107,* 234–245.

Gino, F., & Moore, D. A. (2007). Effects of task difficulty on use of advice. *Journal of Behavioral Decision Making, 20,* 21–35.

Gino, F., & Schweitzer, M. (2008). Blinded by anger or feeling the love: How emotions influence advice taking. *Journal of Applied Psychology, 93,* 1165–1173.

Girotra, K., Terwiesch, C., & Ulrich, K. T. (2010). Idea generation and the quality of the best idea. *Management Science, 56,* 591–605.

Harvey, N., & Fischer, I. (1997). Taking advice: Accepting help, improving judgment, and sharing responsibility. *Organizational Behavior and Human Decision Processes, 70,* 117–133.

Harvey, N., & Harries, C. (2004). Effects of judges' forecasting on their later combination of forecasts for the same outcomes. *International Journal of Forecasting, 20,* 391–409.

Harvey, N., Harries, C., & Fischer, I. (2000). Using advice and assessing its quality. *Organizational Behavior and Human Decision Processes, 81,* 252–273.

Hastie, R., & Kameda, T. (2005). The robust beauty of majority rules in group decisions. *Psychological Review, 112,* 494–508.

Heath, C., Larrick, R. P., & Klayman, J. (1998). Cognitive repairs: How organizations compensate for the shortcomings of individual learners. *Research in Organizational Behavior, 20,* 1–37.

Herzog, S. M., & Hertwig, R. (2009). The wisdom of many in one mind: Improving individual judgments with dialectical bootstrapping. *Psychological Science, 20,* 231–237.

Jenness, A. (1932). The role of discussion in changing opinion regarding a matter of fact. *Journal of Abnormal and Social Psychology, 27,* 279–296.

Kameda, T., & Tindale, R. S. (2006). Groups as adaptive devices: Human docility and group aggregation mechanisms in evolutionary context. In M. Schaller, J. Simpson, & D. Kenrick (Eds.), *Evolution and social psychology* (pp. 317–341). New York: Psychology Press.

Koehler, D. J., & Beauregard, T. A. (2006). Illusion of confirmation from exposure to another's hypothesis. *Journal of Behavioral Decision Making, 19,* 61–78.

Krueger, J. I., & Massey, A. L. (2009). A rational reconstruction of misbehavior. *Social Cognition, 27,* 785–810.

Larrick, R. P., & Soll, J. B. (2006). Intuitions about combining opinions: Misappreciation of the averaging principle. *Management Science, 52,* 111–127.

Littlepage, G. E., Robison, W., & Reddington, K. (1997). Effects of task experience and group experience on group performance, member ability, and recognition of expertise. *Organizational Behavior and Human Decision Processes, 69,* 133–147.

Luan, S., Katsikopolous, K. V., & Reimer, T. (in press). The "less-is-more" effect in group decision making. In R. Hertwig, U. Hoffrage, & the ABC Research Group. *Simple heuristics in a social world.* New York: Oxford University Press.

Mannes, A. E. (2009). Are we wise about the wisdom of crowds? The use of group judgments in belief revision. *Management Science, 55,* 1267–1279.

Mannes, A. E., Soll, J. B., & Larrick, R. P. (2011). *The wisdom of small crowds.* Unpublished manuscript.

Miner, F. C. (1984). Group versus individual decision making: An investigation of performance measures, decision strategies, and process losses/gains. *Organizational Behavior and Human Performance, 33,* 112–124.

Mussweiler, T., & Strack, F. (1999). Hypothesis-consistent testing and semantic priming in the anchoring paradigm: A selective accessibility model. *Journal of Experimental Social Psychology, 35,* 136–164.

Paulus, P. B., & Yang, H. C. (2000). Idea generation in groups: A basis for creativity in organizations. *Organizational Behavior and Human Decision Processes, 82,* 76–87.

See, K. E., Morrison, E. W., Rothman, N. B., & Soll, J. B. (2011). *Powerful and unpersuaded: The implications of power for confidence, advice-taking, and accuracy.* In press.

Sniezek, J. A., & Buckley, T. (1995). Cueing and cognitive conflict in Judge-Adviser decision making. *Organizational Behavior and Human Decision Processes, 62,* 159–174.

Sniezek, J. A., & Van Swol, L. M. (2001). Trust, confidence, and expertise in a judge-advisor system. *Organizational Behavior and Human Decision Processes, 84,* 288–307.

Soll, J. B., & Larrick, R. P. (2009). Strategies for revising judgment: How (and how well) people use others' opinions. *Journal of Experimental Psychology: Learning, Memory and Cognition, 35,* 780–805.

Soll, J. B., & Mannes, A. E. (2011). Judgmental aggregation strategies depend on whether the self is involved. *International Journal of Forecasting, 27,* 81–102.

Sorkin, R. D., Luan, S., & Itzkowitz, J. (2004). Group decision and deliberation: A distributed detection process. In D. Koehler & N. Harvey (Eds.), *Handbook of judgment and decision making* (pp. 464–484). New York: Oxford University Press.

Surowiecki, J. (2004). *The wisdom of crowds: Why the many are smarter than the few and how collective wisdom shapes business, economies, societies, and nations.* London: Little, Brown.

Tversky, A., & Kahneman, D. (1974). Judgment under uncertainty: Heuristics and biases. *Science, 185,* 1124–1131.

Vul, E., & Pashler, H. (2008). Measuring the crowd within: Probabilistic representations within individuals. *Psychological Science, 19,* 645–647.

Watson, G. B. (1928). Do groups think more efficiently than individuals? *Journal of Abnormal and Social Psychology, 23,* 328–336.

Yaniv, I. (1997). Weighting and trimming: heuristics for aggregating judgments under uncertainty. *Organizational Behavior and Human Decision Processes, 69,* 237–249.

Yaniv, I. (2004). Receiving other people's advice: Influence and benefit. *Organizational Behavior and Human Decision Processes, 93,* 1–13.

Yaniv, I., & Kleinberger, E. (2000). Advice taking in decision making: Egocentric discounting and reputation formation. *Organizational Behavior and Human Decision Processes, 83,* 260–281.

Yaniv, I., & Milyavsky, M. (2007). Using advice from multiple sources to revise and improve judgments. *Organizational Behavior and Human Decision Processes, 103,* 104–120.

14

Cognitive, Affective, and Special-Interest Barriers to Wise Policy Making

LISA L. SHU, CHIA-JUNG TSAY, and MAX H. BAZERMAN

Why do legislators allow inefficient policies to persist rather than passing legislation that could improve society overall? This question has primarily been addressed by political scientists, but psychologists can contribute ways to overcome the problem. We review how psychological aspects of decision making result in policies that fail to achieve their intended effect of the greatest utilitarian good. We cover a multitude of barriers to the creation of better policies, ranging from ordinary cognitive and affective biases that affect both individuals and organizations to the special-interest groups that capitalize on these biases. We also recommend techniques to help legislators overcome these barriers and pass legislation that benefits society at large.

Many ineffective government policies stem from the failure to identify and make optimal trade-offs by accepting small losses in exchange for larger gains. One positive change would be the type of policy change that economists call *Pareto improvements*. A Pareto improvement is a policy shift that helps some people and harms no one. However, true Pareto improvements at the societal level are rare; most changes require sacrifices from some. Thus, a more realistic goal for policy makers is *near-Pareto improvements*—those that greatly benefit some while imposing comparatively trivial losses upon others. Stiglitz (1998) argues that "if everyone except a narrowly defined special-interest group could be shown to benefit, surely the change should be made" (p. 4). This is especially true if the special-interest group that stands to lose from a policy change has already manipulated the political system to its advantage.

COGNITIVE BARRIERS IN POLICY MAKING

Why do policy makers often fail to achieve optimal trade-offs through near-Pareto improvements? Research in political science and social psychology has revealed links between cognition and decision making that shed light on this question. Countering the myth of policy makers as rational actors equipped with complete, accurate information about alternatives and consequences, research reveals that when considering issues of high complexity, decision makers are typically constrained by time, imperfect knowledge, and overreliance on general rules of thumb.

As we describe in this section, common cognitive biases can have a strong impact on agenda setting and policy formulation (Rosati, 2000), through effects such as loss aversion (Kahneman & Tversky, 1979) and the heightened salience of short-term considerations (Loewenstein & Thaler, 1989).

Loss Aversion

Loss aversion refers to the common tendency to overweight considerations of losses relative to gains (Kahneman & Tversky, 1979; Tversky & Kahneman, 1991). People generally expect the pain of losing to be larger than the pleasure of an equivalent-sized gain—a major barrier to the passage of legislation that contains such trade-offs.

Bazerman, Baron, and Shonk (2001) posed the following question:

A. If you die in an accident, your heart and other organs will be used to save other lives. In addition, if you ever need an organ transplant, there will be a 90% chance that you will get the heart.

B. If you die in an accident, you will be buried with your heart and other organs in your body. In addition, if you ever need an organ transplant, there will be a 45% chance that you will get the heart.

Which choice is more appealing to you? If you are like most people, Option A seems like the clear winner. Yet over 40,000 Americans are currently waiting for an organ transplant, and at least one-third of them probably will die waiting. Meanwhile, only 40% to 50% of the yearly 11,000 eligible donors actually donate their organs.

Policy discussions regarding organ donation have tended to focus on how to divide a small pie, that is, whether states or federal decision makers should determine who gets the limited number of organs. Overlooked in this debate is the question of how to expand the number of available organs.

A simple policy change could double the number of available organs. Consider that in the United States, citizens provide their explicit consent for organ donation after death. This system favors donors over recipients, despite the fact that recipients have much more to gain than donors have to lose. Meanwhile, many European countries have alleviated their organ shortages through a simple policy change (Johnson & Goldstein, 2003). Instead of instituting "required request," they have a system of "presumed consent": unless a citizen explicitly objects, he or she is assumed to be a potential donor. Because defaults strongly affect choice, this change has saved thousands of lives (Thaler & Sunstein, 2008). Donations soared by 140% in Belgium after a presumed consent law was introduced. Meanwhile, the United States continues to pass up thousands of potential organ donations each year.

Current U.S. law makes organ donation an action and the withholding of donation an omission of action. People view harms arising from omissions as less blameworthy than those from actions (Baron, 1990). Yet, Ritov and Baron (1990) show that the distinction between acts and omissions is arbitrary, created entirely by the default in the organ donation law.

Presumed consent changes the default. In return for the small risk that an individual's true preference will be ignored—because of pressure to consent, for example—many lives are saved. Interestingly, even though the omissions of non-donors inflict a death sentence on others, most do not regard their omission as immoral. In contrast, when consent is presumed, potential donors are forced to confront refusal as a harmful act. Tversky and Kahneman noted that "the adoption of a decision frame is an ethically significant act" (1981, p. 458). In the life-and-death cases of organ donation, defaults matter.

The omission bias thrives on the human tendency to maintain the status quo (Samuelson & Zeckhauser, 1988). Changes to government policy require action. As system justification theory suggests, existing social structures and policies may be perceived as just and legitimate (Jost & Banaji, 1994). Furthermore, just as we tend to focus on losses rather than gains when contemplating a change, we are also more likely to be concerned with the risk of change than the risk of failing to change. This status quo bias can lead to a dysfunctional desire to maintain a broken system (Bazerman, Baron, & Shonk, 2001).

The endowment effect, an important instance of the status quo bias, describes the gap between seller and buyer preferences—namely, sellers are more reluctant to give up a possession than buyers are eager to acquire it. In a famous set of experiments, Kahneman, Knetsch, and Thaler (1990) randomly gave mugs or pens to some participants, who were assigned to sell the objects. Other participants were assigned the role of buyer. Participants showed a staggering inability to agree on price. In one experiment, the average seller's price of $5.75 for a mug was more than twice the average buyer's price of $2.25 for the same mug. As a consequence, very few trades were made. In both laboratory and field experiments, people arbitrarily assigned to be buyers and sellers are unwilling to agree on a trading price (Cummings, Brookshire, & Schulze, 1986).

Most legislation assumes that resources will be allocated efficiently and optimally regardless of initial ownership (Coase, 1960). Yet, undermining the rationale behind government auctions of everything from radio spectrum to mobile phone licensing, the endowment effect suggests that the volume of trade will be low (due to buyer unwillingness to pay and seller unwillingness to accept). This phenomenon limits market efficiency and has important consequences for policies concerning the protection and allocation of public goods such as clean water and air. As an example, one of the largest environmental initiatives to date, cap-and-trade, is a market-driven solution to forestall climate change. The plan sets a ceiling on total pollutant emissions and allows corporations to trade emission permits to comply with the law. Cap-and-trade assumes that creating a market for emission permits allows trading to determine an efficient way to allocate the right to pollute. However, if buyers and sellers have trouble agreeing on price because of the endowment effect, then the total volume of trade will be limited, making it difficult to set fair prices.

Policy bundling is one strategy to overcome the loss aversion underlying the endowment effect (Milkman, Mazza, Shu, Tsay, & Bazerman, 2009). In one study, a bill that would impose costs in Domain A (e.g., job losses in Town X) and benefits in Domain B (e.g., acres of forest preserved in Town X) was combined with a matched bill that had the inverse structure in another town: benefits in Domain A (e.g., job gains in Town Y) and costs in Domain B (e.g., acres of forest lost in Town Y). In the combined bill, the costs and benefits of two separate bills generated net benefits in two domains. Although participants demonstrated loss aversion when evaluating each bill separately (through their unwillingness to support each individual bill), they overcame this aversion when considering the combined bill. This type of policy bundling could potentially allow policy makers to consider the overall advantages of legislation that contain necessary costs.

The Mythical Fixed Pie

Should the United States and Russia both reduce their nuclear arsenals by a third? The U.S. Senate faced this question as it considered the ratification of an agreement the Obama administration had reached with the Russian government. Some conservatives opposed the agreement, swayed more by thoughts of potential losses of U.S. strength than by thoughts of potential gains (reduction of the Russia arsenal).

Decades ago, former United States Congressman Floyd Spence (R-South Carolina) assessed a proposed agreement over nuclear warheads between the United States and the Soviet Union as follows: "I have had a philosophy for some time in regard to SALT [the proposed agreement], and it goes like this: the Russians will not accept a SALT treaty that is not in their best interest, and it seems to me that if it is their best interests, it can't be in our best interest" (cited in Ross & Stillinger, 1991, p. 403). Spence's attitude overlooked the possible benefits of disarmament and consequently may have exposed the world to a higher probability of nuclear annihilation.

Spence's faulty reasoning is consistent with the tendency of many people to oversimplify negotiations by viewing them as *fixed pies*—fights over a limited amount of resources whose size cannot be increased (Neale & Bazerman, 1991). For example, environmental and industry leaders often adopt polarized views in disputes over regulation, land, and conservation. Yet most negotiations involve a number of issues, each with multiple dimensions. When parties have different assessments of the importance of these dimensions, they can make trade-offs to improve the overall quality of the agreement for both parties. Unfortunately, our intuition leads us to focus on losses rather than gains (Malhotra & Bazerman, 2007).

How can legislators overcome the fixed-pie mind-set? One solution is deliberate, complex thinking about problems. Integrative complexity describes the degree to which one considers problems from multiple perspectives (Tetlock, Peterson, & Lerner, 1996). Low levels of integrative complexity—associated with viewing negotiations in black and white—leads policy makers to recognize all the advantages of a favored option and none of its drawbacks, or all the drawbacks of the opposition and none of its strengths. Utilitarian government policies result from integratively complex thinking that avoids the intransigent positions found in most political, economic, or environmental negotiations (Gruenfeld, 1995; Tetlock, Peterson, & Lerner, 1996). Policy makers can increase the complexity of their decision making by identifying the pros and cons of various options and searching for the best overall balance. In 1990, the Environmental Protection Agency (EPA) and Unocal Corporation cleverly did so in the realm of air pollution (Bazerman & Hoffman, 1999). Rather than undertaking costly and inefficient refinery renovations, Unocal launched a program to clear the air more cheaply: they bought pre-1971 high-polluting vehicles from the Los Angeles area for $600 apiece and scrapped them. Unocal determined and documented that it prevented nearly 13 million pounds of air pollution per year from contaminating the L.A. basin. That level of reduction would have cost 10 times as much and taken 10 times as long had it been undertaken at the company's refinery (Stegemeier, 1995).

Discounting the Future

Would you prefer to be paid $10 today or $12 next week? People often say they would prefer to receive $10 today, ignoring the opportunity to earn a 20% premium for a weeklong investment. By overweighting the present benefit and discounting the larger long-term return, people focus too much on short-term considerations and often forgo much higher longer term returns (Loewenstein & Thaler, 1989).

Legislators are notorious for focusing on short-term rather than long-term goals. Near the end of each term, the prospect of reelection exacerbates the tendency to overweight present costs relative to future benefits. From society's perspective, policy makers who overweight present concerns are not merely shortsighted, but also unintentionally immoral, as their present-day decisions will rob future generations of opportunities and resources (Ackerman & Heinzerling, 2004).

Of course, policies require collective action to have their intended effect (Aidt, Dutta, & Loukoianova, 2003). Citizens often forgo much larger benefits that would accrue in the future in favor of benefits available today (Loewenstein & Thaler, 1989). For example, most U.S. citizens would agree that the nation should curtail domestic consumption of nonrenewable energy sources and reduce its contribution to climate change. Yet most also prefer to consume resources today in lieu of conserving for tomorrow, even when they could benefit financially from a change (e.g., installing a smart meter on their home or trading a standard car for a hybrid model).

Such intertemporal choices—those involving trade-offs among costs and benefits that accrue in different periods—are important and ubiquitous (Frederick, Loewenstein, & O'Donoghue, 2002). They represent just one category of intrapersonal conflict between an individual's "multiple selves" (Bazerman, Tenbrunsel, & Wade-Benzoni, 1998). We will return to this phenomenon in our discussion of the tension between reason and emotion.

AFFECTIVE BARRIERS IN POLICY MAKING

Looking beyond decision making as simply a cognitive process, researchers have begun to investigate the emotional influences that can color, inform, and impede wise policy making. Earlier work revealed both cognitive and affective bases of attitudes toward social policies such as abortion, affirmative action, and welfare (Eagly, Mladinic, & Otto, 1994) and suggested the need to further elaborate how affect influences cognitive processes in policy decision making (Geva, Mayhar, & Skorick, 2000). Recent research on affect has revealed the many ways in which emotions significantly impact endorsement and support for policies, as well as the ways in which citizens actively engage with political life. Emotions can serve as a basis of judgment (Schwarz, 2000), as a lens through which we process information (Marcus & MacKuen, 1993), and as informational cues (DeSteno, Petty, Rucker, Wegener, & Braverman, 2004). Neuroscientific research points to the biological roots of emotions, including bodily states and neural systems, in decision making under uncertainty (Naqvi, Shiv, & Bechara, 2006). Thus, it is important to examine the many ways in which emotions impact policy makers.

Although some work suggests that certain social policy decisions tend to be based primarily on cognition (Dovidio, Esses, Beach, & Gaertner, 2002), emotions may play a strong role in other policy preferences (Gordon & Arian, 2001). Exploring the influence of emotional states on citizens' support for social policies, Gault and Sabini (2000) found that differences in both affective states and traits can lead to different policy preferences. Emotion effects can also extend beyond policy endorsement and into the level of engagement with and attention to elections and political life (Marcus & MacKuen, 1993).

Emotions and Attribution

In early emotion research, temporary mood states were found to influence the use of heuristics and stereotyped judgment (Bodenhausen, Kramer, & Suesser, 1994) and the occurrence of the *fundamental attribution error* (the tendency to give too much weight to personality factors rather than situational factors when assessing others' behavior) through the induction of different cognitive processing strategies (Forgas, 1995). Later research showed that certainty-associated emotions (such as happiness, disgust, anger, or contentment) result in more heuristic processing, whereas uncertainty-associated emotions (such as hope, worry, surprise, or fear) result in more systematic processing (Tiedens & Linton, 2001). Mood effects on social judgment are most likely when complex information is open to multiple interpretations and requires constructive, transformative processing (Forgas, 1995).

The joint effects of emotions and attribution have been explored in the realm of international conflict. In examining Israeli Jews' responses to the Arab–Israeli conflict, Bizman and Hoffman (1993) found that participants' perceived locus, controllability, and stability regarding the issue predicted their outcome expectations, emotional responses to ethnic groups, and support for different strategies of conflict resolution. For participants who perceived themselves to have less control over the issue, attributing the conflict to Israel was associated with increased shame and guilt, as well as a preference for negotiation and concession over nonresolution.

Mood Congruence

The close relationship between emotions and cognition is also evident in perception and free association. People pay special attention to mood-congruent information, and better recall and recognize information that is mood congruent (Bower, 1981). For example, inducing unpleasant moods resulted in participants recalling a greater percentage of unpleasant experiences. Inducing anger or happiness also affected cognitive processes such as social perception and snap judgment; angry participants were more likely to find fault with others, whereas happy participants had more charitable interpretations of others.

DeSteno et al. (2004) found that these effects extend into the political world. Specific emotions can inflate expectations of affectively congruent events. For example, when citizens are primed to experience anger while receiving political messages, they tend to expect angering events. These effects can influence the impact of a candidate's message and shift public support toward certain policies. Beyond primed emotions, naturally occurring emotions also affect predictions of probability regarding the media, local issues, and state political and economic issues (Mayer, Gaschke, Braverman, & Evans, 1992). Such emotions, as well as primed affect, can contribute to suboptimal decisions through effects on how events and information are understood.

Framing and Preference Reversals

Emotional responses can mediate the effect of framing on opinions about public policies. In one study, more emotionally engaging frames elicited emotions such as sympathy and pity, which were then associated with increased opposition to mandatory minimum sentencing (Gross, 2008). Such findings suggest that framing may evoke specific emotions that lead to distinct policy preferences (Zebel, Zimmermann, Viki, & Doosje, 2008).

Emotional responses may also help explain preference reversals, and specifically the tendency to prefer one option when alternatives are presented one at a time (*separate evaluation*) but a different option when the same options are simultaneously presented (*joint evaluation*) (Bazerman, Loewenstein, & White, 1992). A more cognitive explanation for preference reversals centers on the relative difficulty of evaluating two options separately versus side by side (Hsee, Loewenstein, Blount, & Bazerman, 1999). The emotional component of such inconsistencies has emerged in preferences on social, public health, and environmental issues (Kahneman & Ritov, 1994). When issues are presented separately, people prefer more "affectively arousing" choices than when issues are presented together. For example, interventions to help "dolphins threatened by pollution" were more important to participants than "skin cancer in farm workers" when these issues were presented one at a time. But when choosing between the two issues simultaneously, participants were more than twice as likely to vote to help the farm workers. The affect heuristic (Slovic, Finucane, Peters, & MacGregor, 2002) explains the tendency to prefer emotionally driven, vivid options under separate evaluation, whereas joint assessment promotes more logical, deliberate processing and thus more rational decision making (Bazerman, Tenbrunsel, & Wade-Benzoni, 1998).

Finally, preference reversals may have more subtle implications for the different decision-making contexts that policy makers versus constituents face. Joint comparison may allow for a more systematic consideration of overall value and relevance, and policy makers typically vote and choose among several alternate policies at a time. By contrast, their constituents learn about a single policy at a time. Policy makers may project their preferences in the joint evaluation mode onto their predictions and choices, potentially overweighting differences that seem distinct but are actually less significant when experienced by their constituents. This inconsistency might be ameliorated if policy makers also simulate the single evaluation experience as they make decisions (Hsee & Zhang, 2004).

The Emotional and Reasoned Selves: Want Versus Should Options

Many policies ask citizens to trade current sacrifices for longer term benefits. For example, people may believe they should support a gas tax to help balance the federal budget, yet at the same time, they do not actually want the tax to be implemented. Examining this tension between reason and emotion, the *multiple-selves theory* (Schelling, 1984) suggests that an internal conflict exists between an emotionally guided "want" self and a deliberate and reflective "should" self. The want self favors decisions that provide immediate gratification, whereas the should self understands the value of alternatives that better serve our long-term interests (Bazerman & Moore, 2008).

Policy proposals fail when voters' "want" desires overwhelm their "should" desires by inflating the importance of the immediate costs associated with policy implementation. Rogers and Bazerman (2008) show that people will be more likely to support environmental policies with immediate costs but long-term benefits when the policies will be implemented after a time delay—even a short one—rather than immediately. This finding indicates that the temporal element of the want–should conflict affects the degree to which citizens and legislators will endorse certain policies. Adding even a slight delay to policy implementation could help people overcome the strong influence of their emotional "want" concerns about immediate costs and focus on longer term "should" concerns that will reap benefits tomorrow.

The vividness of an issue can also trigger emotional reactions that appeal to the want self. People sometimes misallocate scarce resources to address vivid concerns (Bazerman & Moore, 2008) rather than devoting them to problems that would benefit more from funds. In one study, participants' decisions about their recommended course of action regarding nuclear defense and weapons production were associated with the availability of nuclear-related images and emotional responses to nuclear war (Chibnall & Wiener, 1988). In addition, those who most quickly recalled images of nuclear war were more likely than other participants to support continued or increased arms production. This finding is in keeping with the availability heuristic, which indicates that people will estimate a high likelihood of events that they can easily imagine (Tversky & Kahneman, 1974).

Specific Emotions, Risk Perception, and Policy Preferences

Some of the recent research on affect has moved beyond a valence-based view of positive versus negative emotions to explore how specific emotions, such as anger, sadness, and fear, activate distinct cognitive predispositions through which people appraise events (Lerner & Keltner, 2000). This research finds that incidental emotions—those unrelated to the decision at hand—influence the cognitive biases discussed earlier in this chapter, such as the endowment effect, loss aversion, and the status quo bias. For example, Lerner, Small, and Loewenstein (2004) distinguish between the effects of specific negative emotions on the endowment effect. In one experiment, incidental disgust triggered the desire to expel and led to lower selling and choice prices, whereas incidental sadness led to the desire to change one's circumstances and thus to lower selling prices but higher choice prices. Importantly, and perhaps surprisingly, participants were not aware of how these emotions affected their decisions. Incidental emotions may be momentary and mild, but their consequences can be far reaching (Andrade & Ariely, 2009).

This nuanced understanding of specific emotions has implications for policy decisions. For example, perceived threat and anxiety are both common reactions to terrorism, yet they have distinct and even contradictory effects on policy endorsement. In one study, anxiety led to greater risk aversion and reduced support for military action, whereas perceived threat led to increased support for more aggressive antiterrorism policies, including government monitoring of telephones and e-mail messages (Huddy, Feldman, Taber, & Lahev, 2005). In another study, perceived foreign threat heightened participants' sense of national identity, which led them to feel intolerant of international diversity and to endorse policies of assimilation (Davies, Steele, & Markus, 2008).

Threat has also been linked to the information processing of other types of conflict. When participants in one study perceived a high level of threat, they preferred more incendiary policies regarding the Arab–Israeli conflict, suggesting that their choices were dominated by emotion rather than reason (Gordon & Arian, 2001). By contrast, under low levels of threat, cognitive factors are good predictors of support for policies. The more affectively led want self and the more rational and deliberate should self could explain the finding that fear predicts support for punitive crime policies, whereas the preference for preventive policies is mediated by cognitive complexity (Sotirovic, 2001).

In a study of the occupation of Iraq after the 2003 collapse of Saddam Hussein's regime, Iyer, Schmader, and Lickel (2007) found that a nation's foreign policy can elicit specific self-critical emotions, such as shame, in its citizens. These emotions then predicted intentions to support opposition campaigns. Both shame and anger predicted whether American participants preferred for the United States to withdraw troops from Iraq; when anger was directed at the in-group and its representatives, it also predicted the preference to compensate Iraq for the invasion and confront those responsible for it.

Turning to the effects of specific emotions on risk perception, earlier calls for a sociocognitive approach to risk (Vertzberger, 1995) that focuses on decision makers' actual preferences and behaviors as a social construct have been energized by recent research on affect and risk. Emotions affect risk perceptions (Bazerman & Moore, 2008), leading to more optimistic or pessimistic risk assessments and changes in risk-seeking versus risk-averse behaviors. Specifically, anger tends to prompt optimistic risk assessments, and fear leads to more risk-avoidant choices (Lerner, Gonzalez, Small, & Fischhoff, 2003). These effects remain even when the emotions are incidental to the situation (Lerner & Tiedens, 2006). Such emotions can impact not only risk perceptions, but also policy preferences, such that both primed and naturally occurring emotions produce shifts in views toward terrorism policies. In one study, anger, as compared with sadness, increased support for vengeful policies and decreased support for conciliatory policies (Lerner et al., 2003).

THE SOCIAL PSYCHOLOGY OF DISINFORMATION CAMPAIGNS

Most wise legislation has opponents. Despite the fact that tobacco killed about 100 million people in the 20th century and is projected to kill as many as a billion people in the 21st century, there remain some who oppose government regulation of the tobacco industry (see Proctor, 2001, and Bazerman & Tenbrunsel, 2011, for reviews). Similarly, despite the continual pattern of auditor corruption, lack of independence, and massive financial scandals, many argue that auditor dependence on clients is not a problem that needs to be addressed (Antle, 1984). And despite a clear consensus among scientists who are not paid for their opinion that the earth is warming and that humans are exacerbating the problem, the deniers of climate change continue to receive ample media coverage.

Special-interest groups intentionally distort information to influence government policy. Politicians and other professionals face psychological obstacles in confronting and overcoming these corrupting influences, and citizens fail to hold elected officials accountable for them. Most citizens would agree that it is wrong to cheat, steal, and lie. But we have less to say when special-interest groups unethically promote laws and regulatory systems that can be predicted to fail to maximize the interests of our broader society. Nor do most people object when politicians, historians, economists, scientists, doctors, and other professionals contort their supposedly unbiased views in the service of special-interest groups for their own personal gain.

Across industries and time, special-interest groups use a number of common strategies to maintain the status quo that work against society's best interest. As noted previously, when contemplating a potential policy change, citizens and politicians tend to be more concerned about the risk of change than about the risk of failing to change. This tendency contrasts with a more rational analysis that would compare whether the expected gains of a policy exceed expected losses.

But individual-level loss aversion leads us to reject even policies that have smaller losses than gains. Thus, loss aversion at the individual level supports the status quo, corrupt institutional processes, and deficient public policies. In particular, special-interest groups use the following three tactics that capitalize on maintaining the status quo: (1) obfuscation; (2) the claimed need to search for a smoking gun; and (3) shifting views of the argument against change.

Obfuscation

One way that special-interest groups delay governmental response is through obfuscation, or the practice of communicating in a deliberately confusing or ambiguous manner with the intention of misleading the listener. These groups strive to create reasonable doubt about change in the minds of citizens and policy makers in order to promote the status quo. Psychologically, the status quo becomes even more attractive when ambiguity about the costs and benefits of change exists. This ambiguity also allows citizens to hold on to existing beliefs through motivated reasoning, such that they distort information and perspectives in a belief-consistent way—discounting those who do not support their beliefs and quickly accepting those who do (Edwards & Smith, 1996; Lord, Ross, & Lepper, 1979).

Ample evidence suggests that the U.S. tobacco industry knew far more about the hazards of cigarette smoking before the public health community did (Proctor, 2001). To avoid antismoking measures, the tobacco industry intentionally and strategically created confusion about the health effects of smoking since at least early 1950 (Brandt, 2007). The tobacco industry is now following the same strategy in the domain of second-hand smoke. Since 1981, strong evidence has been available that second-hand smoke causes lung cancer, but the tobacco industry has countered by fostering doubt about this scientific research in the public mind.

Similarly, the coal, oil, and automotive industries have obfuscated over the last decade on the role of humans in creating the problem of climate change. Even after clear consensus emerged among impartial scientists (those not paid for their views), the oil and coal industries spent enormous amounts of time and money communicating to the public that some "experts" doubt the existence of climate change—and that even if it did exist, these experts doubt the role of humans in perpetuating it. Similar patterns can be found across industries and among other special-interest groups (Bazerman & Tenbrunsel, 2011).

The Search for a Smoking Gun

In most developed economies, an auditing profession exists to provide outside parties with the assurance that an independent, impartial auditor can vouch for the stated financial condition of publicly traded companies. Which of the following strategies, taken from Bazerman, Moore, Tetlock, and Tanlu (2006), do you think would better ensure the integrity of the auditing profession?

1. In order to maintain auditor independence, auditors are prohibited from establishing durable long-term cooperative partnerships with their clients, from providing nonaudit services to their clients, and from taking jobs with their clients.
2. Begin with a variety of incentives that motivate auditors to want to please their clients. Next, try to identify a complex set of legislative and professional incentives to counteract the corrupting influences created by the desire to please the client.

Bazerman et al. (2006) offered this rhetorical question to highlight the absurdity of current rules regarding auditing. Most agree it makes more sense to begin with a truly independent system than to add patches to an existing, corrupt system—one in which auditors are dependent on their clients for future auditing and consulting business. Auditors rely on their clients to provide data to conduct audits; they knowingly anticipate an error rate of 5% to 10% in client-provided data. Accounting firms' internal models often build in this margin of error by representing valuation in intervals. Auditors' current dependence on appeasing clients in order to gain (or keep) future business puts pressure on auditors to report the maximum valuation in their predetermined range. Such inflation in value is compounded in cases of parent corporations with multiple subsidiaries (some of which are created explicitly to confound a fair assessment of value). Yet in public Securities and Exchange Commission (SEC) hearings in 2000, the auditing industry succeeded in convincing the federal government that no clear evidence exists of audit conflicts of interest. The CEOs of the Big Five accounting firms testified there was no evidence of a single audit being tainted as a result of the auditing–consulting relationship. Without a smoking gun, they argued, no change was necessary. Consequently, only trivial changes were made to the existing system.

Bazerman et al. (2006) argued that in 2000, a smoking gun should not have been necessary to conclude that massive changes were needed to create auditor independence. How could unbiased opinions be expected from firms whose financial survival relies on preserving long-term client relationships? In fact, soon after the SEC hearings, Big Five accounting firm Arthur Andersen collapsed after being implicated in the fall of energy-trading giant Enron, and a wave of other spectacular accounting scandals followed. Even after these disasters, facing significant political pressure, Congress implemented only minor changes to the system, in the form of the Sarbanes–Oxley Act. As this story makes clear, when society waits for a smoking gun, it typically waits too long.

Shifting Views of the Facts

Special-interest groups that oppose wise reforms typically present their own distorted view of the "facts." Often, as knowledge of the issue develops, the special-interest groups' positions become untenable. When maintaining these facts is not possible, these groups simply change their position and deny their past connection to claims they now acknowledge, in the face of overwhelming evidence, to be clearly false. The tobacco industry, for example, long held fast to the view that cigarettes were not only harmless, but that smokers might even achieve some positive health benefits from them. Then, as evidence of the connection between lung cancer and smoking mounted, the industry acknowledged that cigarettes might be one of many possible causes of lung cancer but argued that no specific cancer could be traced to cigarettes and that the causal path was unclear. Soon after seven industry CEOs testified to Congress in 1994 that cigarettes do not cause cancer, all seven CEOs were replaced. Once the tobacco companies admitted that cigarette smoking caused lung cancer, in a breathtaking about-face, they argued that smokers who developed lung cancer should not be allowed to sue the industry for damages, since it was public knowledge that tobacco might be harmful. They made this claim despite the industry's disinformation campaigns across decades and its persistent attempts to turn teenagers into addicts (Brandt, 2007).

Similarly, the U.S. auditing industry transitioned from the claim that its reputation protected it from conflicts of interest to the view that disclosure of conflicts of interest is an effective response. When accounting disasters made it clear that disclosure was not an effective solution to the problem, the auditors changed their views again. This time, they argued that solving the problem of independence would not be worth the cost—ignoring the fact that if audits are not independent, there is no reason for them to be conducted. Here again, the goal of this special-interest group was to maintain the status quo, not to pursue wise policy.

The same behaviors have occurred in the debate over climate change. After decades of obfuscation, the oil industry has made a relatively rapid shift in recent years: from insisting that manmade global warming does not exist, to claiming global warming is not caused by human actions, to arguing that it would not be worth the enormous costs to fix the problem.[1] Essentially, the industry has tried to maintain the most reactionary view that is defensible, shifting its positions only out of necessity.

Across these three strategies, special-interest groups have successfully used our biases against us, capitalizing on the uncertainty and ambiguity that fuel the status quo effect.

CONCLUSION

In this chapter, we have reviewed a multitude of barriers to the creation of wise policies, including those that are innate—both cognitive and affective—as well as those that special-interest groups create. By identifying these systematic and predictable roadblocks, we hope to help citizens and policy makers overcome these barriers, design policies that avoid these pitfalls in our decision-making processes, and ultimately support the passage of wiser legislation.

We believe that psychologists deserve a role in helping to improve government policies, especially in light of the influence that economists currently have in government. It is common for economists to spend time in Washington without damage to their academic career. By contrast, social psychologists rarely spend time in Washington, and if they do, their colleagues may perceive them to be transitioning away from scholarly research. It is not surprising that economics has become the dominant social science in the highest spheres of influence. But we also need a better understanding of the psychology of decision making in government. To make this contribution, psychologists must become willing to move across traditional career boundaries and constraints, to take the risk of cross-disciplinary exchange, and to invest in the public policy-making process.

Additionally, for psychological findings to have an influence on public policy, psychologists must become more comfortable with prescriptive frameworks. Most research psychologists take pride in being descriptive, not prescriptive, with behavioral decision researchers serving as exceptions (Bazerman & Moore, 2008). Behavioral decision researchers delineate the systematic ways in which people psychologically deviate from rational behavior. By revealing common mistakes that can be avoided, researchers can recommend the changes needed to improve society. When psychologists move beyond mere descriptions of behaviors and begin to articulate prescriptions, the power of psychology can be harnessed to improve the public arena.

NOTE

1. There have been some courageous exceptions. For example, in 1997, Lord John Browne, then the CEO of British Petroleum, made clear that he believed climate change existed and was caused by human actions, but this was years after a clear scientific consensus had already emerged on the issue.

REFERENCES

Ackerman, F., & Heinzerling, L. (2004). *Priceless: On knowing the price of everything and the value of nothing*. New York: The New Press.

Aidt, T., Dutta, J., & Loukoianova, E. (2003). *Policy myopia*. Cambridge Working Papers in Economics No. 0344.

Andrade, E., & Ariely, D. (2009). The enduring impact of transient emotions on decision making. *Organizational Behavior and Human Decision Processes, 109*, 1–8.

Antle, R. (1984). Auditor independence. *Journal of Accounting Research, 22*, 1–20.

Baron, J. (1990). Thinking about consequences. *Journal of Moral Education, 19*, 77–87.

Baron, J. (1996). Do no harm. In D. Messick & A. Tenbrunsel (Eds.), *Codes of conduct: Behavioral research into business ethics* (pp. 197–213). New York: Russell Sage.

Bazerman, M. H., Baron, J., & Shonk, K. (2001). *You can't enlarge the pie: Six barriers to effective government*. New York: Basic Books.

Bazerman, M. H., & Hoffman, A. J. (1999). Sources of environmentally destructive behavior: Individual, organizational, and institutional perspectives. In R. I. Sutton & B. M. Staw (Eds.), *Research in organizational behavior* (Vol. 21, pp. 39–79). Greenwich, CT: JAI Press.

Bazerman, M. H., Loewenstein, G., & White, S. B. (1992). Psychological determinants of utility in competitive contexts: The impact of elicitation procedure. *Administrative Science Quarterly, 37*, 220–240.

Bazerman, M. H., & Moore, D. (2008). *Judgment in managerial decision making* (7th ed.). Hoboken, NJ: John Wiley & Sons, Inc.

Bazerman, M. H., Moore, D. A., Tetlock, P. E., & Tanlu, L. (2006). Reports of solving the conflicts of interest in auditing are highly exaggerated. *Academy of Management Review, 31*(1), 1–7.

Bazerman, M. H., & Tenbrunsel, A. E. (2011). *Blind spots: Why we fail to do what's right and what to do about it*. Princeton, NJ: Princeton University Press.

Bazerman, M. H., Tenbrunsel, A. E., & Wade-Benzoni, K. A. (1998). Negotiating with yourself and losing: Understanding and managing competing internal preferences. *Academy of Management Review, 23*(2), 225–241.

Bizman, A., & Hoffman, M. (1993). Expectations, emotions, preferred responses regarding the Arab-Israeli conflict: An attribution analysis. *Journal of Conflict Resolution, 37*(1), 139–159.

Bodenhausen, G. V., Kramer, G. P., & Suesser, K. (1994). Happiness and stereotypic thinking in social judgment. *Journal of Personality and Social Psychology, 66*(4), 621–632.

Bower, G. (1981). Mood and memory. *American Psychologist, 36*(2), 129–148.

Brandt, A. M. (2007). *The cigarette century*. New York: Basic Books.

Chibnall, J. T., & Wiener, R. L. (1988). Disarmament decisions as social dilemmas. *Journal of Applied Social Psychology, 18*(10), 867–879.

Coase, R. (1960). The problem of social cost. *Journal of Law and Economics, 3*(1), 1–44.

Cummings, R. G., Brookshire, D. S., & Schulze, W. D. (1986). *Valuing environmental goods: An assessment of the contingent valuation method*. Lanham, MD: Rowman & Littlefield.

Davies, P. G., Steele, C. M., & Markus, H. R. (2008). A nation challenged: The impact of foreign threat on America's tolerance for diversity. *Journal of Personality and Social Psychology, 95*(2), 308–318.

DeSteno, D., Petty, R., Rucker, D., Wegener, D., & Braverman, J. (2004). Discrete emotions and persuasion: The role of emotion-induced expectancies. *Journal of Personality and Social Psychology, 86*(1), 43–56.

Dovidio, J. F., Esses, V. M., Beach, K. R., & Gaertner, S. L. (2002). The role of affect in determining intergroup behavior: The case of willingness to engage in intergroup contact. In D. M. Mackie & E. R. Smith (Eds.), *From prejudice to intergroup emotions: Differentiated reactions to social groups* (pp. 153–171). Philadelphia: Psychology Press.

Eagly, A. H., Mladinic, A., & Otto, S. (1994). Cognitive and affective bases of attitudes toward social groups and social policies. *Journal of Experimental Social Psychology, 30*(2), 113–137.

Edwards, K., & Smith, E. (1996). A disconfirmation bias in the evaluation of arguments. *Journal of Personality and Social Psychology, 71*, 5–24.

Forgas, J. (1995). Mood and judgment: The affect infusion model (AIM). *Psychological Bulletin, 117*(1), 39–66.

Frederick, S., Loewenstein, G., & O'Donoghue, T. (2002). Time discounting and time preference: A critical review. *Journal of Economic Literature, 40*(2), 351–401.

Gault, B., & Sabini, J. (2000). The roles of empathy, anger, and gender in predicting attitudes toward punitive, reparative, and preventative public policies. *Cognition and Emotion, 14*(4), 495–520.

Geva, N., Mayhar, J., & Skorick, J. M. (2000). The cognitive calculus of foreign policy decision making: An experimental assessment. *Journal of Conflict Resolution, 44*(4), 447–471.

Gordon, C., & Arian, A. (2001). Threat and decision making. *Journal of Conflict Resolution, 45*(2), 196–215.

Gross, K. (2008). Framing persuasive appeals: Episodic and thematic framing, emotional response, and policy opinion. *Political Psychology, 29*(2), 169–192.

Gruenfeld, D. H. (1995). Status, ideology, and integrative complexity on the U.S. Supreme Court: Rethinking the politics of political decision making. *Journal of Personality and Social Psychology, 68*(1), 5–20.

Hsee, C. K., Loewenstein, G., Blount, S., & Bazerman, M. H. (1999). Preference reversals between joint and separate evaluations of options: A review and theoretical analysis. *Psychological Bulletin, 125*(5), 576–590.

Hsee, C. K., & Zhang, J. (2004). Distinction bias: Misprediction and mischoice due to joint evaluation. *Journal of Personality and Social Psychology, 86*(5), 680–695.

Huddy, L., Feldman, S., Taber, C., & Lahev, G. (2005). Threat, anxiety, and support for antiterrorism policies. *American Journal of Political Science, 49*(3), 593–608.

Iyer, A., Schmader, T., & Lickel, B. (2007). Why individuals protest the perceived transgressions of their country: The role of anger, shame, and guilt. *Personality and Social Psychology Bulletin, 33*(4), 572–587.

Johnson, E. J., & Goldstein, D. (2003). Do defaults save lives? *Science, 302*(5649), 1338–1339.

Jost, J. T., & Banaji, M. R. (1994). The role of stereotyping in system-justification and the production of false consciousness. *British Journal of Social Psychology, 33*(1), 1–27.

Kahneman, D., Knetsch, J. L., & Thaler, R. H. (1990). Experimental tests of the endowment effect and the coase theorem. *Journal of Political Economy, 98*(6), 1325–1348.

Kahneman, D., & Ritov, I. (1994). Determinants of stated willingness to pay for public goods: A study in the headline method. *Journal of Risk and Uncertainty, 9*(1), 5–38.

Kahneman, D., & Tversky, A. (1979). Prospect theory: An analysis of decision under risk. *Econometrica, 47*(2), 263–291.

Kanwisher, N. (1989). Cognitive heuristics and American security policy. *Journal of Conflict Resolution, 33*(4), 652–675.

Lerner, J. S., Gonzalez, R. M., Small, D. A., & Fischhoff, B. (2003). Effects of fear and anger on perceived risks of terrorism: A national field experiment. *Psychological Science, 14*(2), 144–150.

Lerner, J. S., & Keltner, D. (2000). Beyond valence: Toward a model of emotion-specific influences on judgment and choice. *Cognition and Emotion, 14*(4), 473–493.

Lerner, J. S., Small, D. A., & Loewenstein, G. (2004). Heart strings and purse strings: Carryover effects of emotions on economic transactions. *Psychological Science, 15*(5), 337–341.

Lerner, J. S., & Tiedens, L. Z. (2006). Portrait of the angry decision maker: How appraisal tendencies shape anger's influence on cognition. *Journal of Behavioral Decision Making, 19*, 115–137.

Loewenstein, G., & Thaler, R. (1989). Intertemporal choice. *Journal of Economic Perspectives, 3*(4), 181–193.

Lord, C., Ross, L., & Lepper, M. (1979). Biased assimilation and attitude polarization: The effects of prior theories on subsequently considered evidence. *Journal of Personality and Social Psychology, 37*(11), 2098–2109.

Malhotra, D., & Bazerman, M. H. (2007). *Negotiation genius*. New York: Bantam Books.

Marcus, G. E., & MacKuen, M. B. (1993). Anxiety, enthusiasm, and the vote: The emotional underpinnings of learning and involvement during presidential campaigns. *The American Political Science Review, 87*(3), 672–685.

Mayer, J., Gaschke, Y., Braverman, D., & Evans, T. (1992). Mood-congruent judgment is a general effect. *Journal of Personality and Social Psychology, 63*(1), 119–132.

Milkman, K. L., Mazza, M. C., Shu, L. L., Tsay, C., & Bazerman, M. H. (June 2009). *Policy bundling to overcome loss aversion: A method for improving legislative outcomes.* Harvard Business School Working Paper, No. 09-147.

Naqvi, N., Shiv, B., & Bechara, A. (2006). The role of emotion in decision making: A cognitive neuroscience perspective. *Current Directions in Psychological Science, 15*(5), 260–264.

Neale, M. A., & Bazerman, M. H. (1991). *Cognition and rationality in negotiation*. New York: The Free Press.

Proctor, R. N. (2001). Tobacco and the global lung cancer epidemic. *Nature Reviews Cancer, 1*(1), 82–86.

Ritov, I., & Baron, J. (1990). Reluctance to vaccinate: Omission bias and ambiguity. *Journal of Behavioral Decision Making, 3*(4), 263–277.

Rogers, T., & Bazerman, M. H. (2008). Future lock-in: Future implementation increases selection of should choices. *Organizational Behavior and Human Decision Processes, 106*(1), 1–20.

Rosati, J. (2000). The power of human cognition in the study of world politics. *International Studies Review, 2*(3), 45–75.

Ross, L., & Stillinger, C. (1991). Barriers to conflict resolution. *Negotiation Journal, 7*(4), 389–404.

Samuelson, W. F., & Zeckhauser, R. (1988). Status quo bias in decision making. *Journal of Risk and Uncertainty, 1*(1), 7–59.

Schelling, T. C. (1984). Self-command in practice, in policy, and in a theory of rational choice. *American Economic Review, 74*(2), 1–11.

Schwarz, N. (2000). Emotion, cognition, and decision making. *Cognition and Emotion, 14*(4), 433–440.

Slovic, P., Finucane, M., Peters, E., & MacGregor, D. G. (2002). The affect heuristic. In T. Gilovich, D. Griffin, & D. Kahneman (Eds.), *Heuristics and biases: The psychology of intuitive judgment* (pp. 397–420). Cambridge, UK: Cambridge University Press.

Sotirovic, M. (2001). Affective and cognitive processes as mediators of media influences on crime-policy preferences. *Mass Communication and Society, 4*(3), 311–329.

Stegemeier, R. (1995). *Straight talk: The future of energy in the global economy.* Los Angeles: Unocal.

Stiglitz, J. (1998). The private uses of public interests: Incentives and institutions. *Journal of Economic Perspectives, 12*(2), 3–22.

Tetlock, P. E., Peterson, R., & Lerner, J. (1996). Revising the value pluralism model: Incorporating social content and context postulates. In C. Seligman, J. Olson, & M. Zanna (Eds.), *Values: Eighth Annual Ontario Symposium on Personality and Social Psychology* (pp. 25–51). Hillsdale, NJ: Erlbaum.

Thaler, R. H., & Sunstein, C. R. (2008). *Nudge: Improving decisions about health, wealth, and happiness.* New Haven, CT: Yale University Press.

Tiedens, L., & Linton, S. (2001). Judgment under emotional certainty and uncertainty: The effects of specific emotions on information processing. *Journal of Personality and Social Psychology, 81*(6), 973–988.

Tversky, A., & Kahneman, D. (1974). Judgments under uncertainty: Heuristics and biases. *Science, 185*(4157), 1124–1131.

Tversky, A., & Kahneman, D. (1981). The framing of decisions and the psychology of choice. *Science, 211*, 453–458.

Tversky, A., & Kahneman, D. (1991). Loss aversion in riskless choice: A reference-dependent model. *Quarterly Journal of Economics, 106*(4), 1039–1061.

Vertzberger, Y. Y. I. (1995). Rethinking and reconceptualizing risk in foreign policy decision-making: A sociocognitive approach. *Political Psychology, 16*(2), 347–380.

Zebel, S., Zimmermann, A., Viki, G. T., & Doosje, B. (2008). Dehumanization and guilt as distinct but related predictors of support for reparation policies. *Political Psychology, 29*(2), 193–219.

15

Where Do Nonutilitarian Moral Rules Come From?

JONATHAN BARON

INTRODUCTION

Heuristics and Biases

The heuristics and biases approach to the study of judgment and decision making originated in the work of Daniel Kahneman and Amos Tversky in several publications in the 1970s and 1980s (for example, Gilovich, Griffin, & Kahneman, 2002; Kahneman, Slovic, & Tversky, 1982; Kahneman & Tversky, 2000). The idea was to compare judgments and decisions in laboratory experiments to normative models and look for systematic departures, which were called biases. Normative models were specifications of the right answer, the standard for evaluation of the responses. Examples of normative models were probability theory, statistics, and expected-utility theory. Many of the biases could be explained in terms of the use of heuristics, that is, rules that are not guaranteed to produce normative responses but were used because they usually approximated such outcomes. Yet sometimes they were quite misleading. An example is judging the probability that an example is a member of a category in terms of the similarity of the example to the category, the representativeness heuristic. This heuristic is often useful but it ignores the size of the category and is thus misleading when possible categories differ in size.

Since about 1990, researchers have applied this approach to moral judgments (for example, Ritov & Baron, 1990; Spranca, Minsk, & Baron, 1991; for some recent examples, see Bartels, Bauman, Skitka, & Medlin, 2009), with varying degrees of commitment to the basic approach. The problem here is that the normative models are controversial. Yet, utilitarianism has often been adopted as a provisional model even by researchers who do not accept it as a moral theory. Utilitarianism holds that the best judgment is the one that is most consistent with producing the best total consequences. It also assumes that when outcomes affect several people we can think of the total consequences as the sum of consequences for individuals. (In this regard, it is a specific form of a more general theory called consequentialism, but something close to the utilitarian form is required for many experiments, which, for example, concern trading some lives for other lives and assume that numbers matter.)

The general finding is that people depart from utilitarian judgments in specific ways. Three that have been studied recently are omission bias, indirectness bias, and contact bias. (Recent literature, such as Cushman, Young, and Hauser, 2006, has sometimes used "action" and "intention" to refer to omission and indirectness, respectively.) Omission bias has been studied in two ways, which we might loosely call judgment and choice. In judgment, subjects are given a scenario in which someone causes harm intentionally, either through action or omission, and the subject is asked which is worse or whether they are both equally immoral. The general finding here is that, depending on the scenario and the subjects, about half of the subjects say that the action is worse and half say they are equally bad. Sometimes a lot more than half and sometimes a lot less. An example is lying versus withholding the truth when you know that the latter will lead to exactly the same false belief as lying.

In choice, the subject compares two options facing a decision maker, one leading to harm through action and the other leading to harm through omission. Usually the harm from omission is greater, so we can think of the action as causing some harm to prevent greater harm. The classic situation is whether to divert a runaway trolley headed for five people to a different track, where it will head for only two people (Foot, 1978). Of interest is the fact that some subjects choose to accept greater harm from omission, that is, not diverting the trolley. The results depend heavily on the details of the situation and the numbers affected.

Indirectness bias has to do with whether a harm is caused directly or indirectly as a side effect (Royzman & Baron, 2002). A clear example in real life is the attitude of Catholic hospitals toward women whose life was threatened by their pregnancy. It was considered immoral to abort the fetus to save the mother but morally acceptable to remove the mother's uterus to save the mother, thus killing the fetus as a side effect (Bennett, 1966). The direct harm to the fetus was the problem. (In both cases, all effects were expected and foreseen, and the harm to the fetus was undesired yet saving the mother was desired, so it is difficult to speak of a difference in intention here.)

The contact effect is that harmful actions are seen as worse if they involve direct contact between the person doing the harm and the person harmed. For example, in the trolley problem, many people accept the option of switching the trolley yet far fewer are willing to push a fat man off a bridge (killing him) in order to stop the trolley and save the lives of five others.

All three of these effects are related, in that they may all be seen as the result of a single principle based on physical causality. In all cases, when the physical relationship between the behavior and its cause is greater or clearer, the morality of causing the harm is worse. Thus we can think of these principles as resulting from a heuristic in which moral judgments are based on direct physical causality, roughly analogous to probability judgments being based on similarity. I shall also speak of a "do no harm" heuristic, where it is understood that *do* means to bring about through physical causation.

I should also note that such moral heuristics are found outside of the moral domain. They may be general heuristics for decision making and for blame, including self-blame, rather than specifically moral ones. Despite this possibility, Sunstein (2005) has called them "moral heuristics."

Moral Heuristics and Public Policy

Moral heuristics are of interest in part because they shed light on public policies that lead to suboptimal outcomes (Baron, 1994; Sunstein, 2005). Consider as an example—in fact the main example discussed in this chapter—the do-no-harm heuristic, which seems to lead us to think of actions that lead to harm as worse than omissions that lead to equal or greater harm (Baron & Ritov, 2004, 2009a; Ritov & Baron, 1990; Spranca et al., 1991). This omission bias leads citizens, legislators, courts, and regulators to support inefficient policies, inefficient because they allow harms to occur that could be prevented by causing lesser harms.

Examples of such policies are the slow approval of beneficial drugs (Baron, Bazerman, & Shonk, 2006), the tendency of government to review proposals for new regulations while ignoring the possibility that regulations are needed that are not being made (Baron, 1999), the lack of concern of research review boards about the lost benefits of the research they prevent (Baron, 2006), low rates of organ donation (Johnson & Goldstein, 2003), epidemics that result from vaccination refusal, rejection of beneficial trade agreements (Baron, Bazerman, & Skonk, 2006), and, more generally, the neglect of the suffering of the distant poor (Singer, 1993; Slovic, 2007).

The claim that moral heuristics affect policies requires an assumption that we might call the "simple effect hypothesis": decisions made by trying to follow principle P usually yield outcomes more consistent with P than are the outcomes of decisions made in other ways. In other words, for most cases, most of the time, at least in matters of public policy, any attempt to follow a principle other than "choose the policy that yields the highest expected utility, all things considered," is likely not to yield the highest expected utility. The simple utilitarian principle is not self-defeating; it is, rather, exactly what we should try to follow if we want the best possible outcomes.[1] This principle may be false, although it is hard to tell from individual cases; most of the apparent counterexamples (such as the use of the atomic bomb against Japan) can be seen as failures to apply the principle correctly.

DEONTOLOGY AND DEVELOPMENT

Omission bias is an example of a class of rules that are also in some cases advocated by philosophers who favor deontology over consequentialism (Greene, 2007). It might be argued that such philosophers are subject to the same psychological biases as are many ordinary people. They use these moral heuristics, such as do no harm, and then they elevate these to principles. Other examples of these rules concern those concerning autonomy and consent, rights, retributive punishment, and fairness.

The question I address here is where these rules come from. If we could answer this question, it might help us to find ways to reduce their deleterious effects on public policy. Some explanations are functionalist, explaining each moral rule in terms of its benefits, compared (usually) to not having any rule. I know of no case in which the utilitarian rule is considered as an alternative. Some of these explanations are based on the idea that we have specific cognitive modules that are the result of evolution, analogous to proposals about linguistic competence (Hauser, 2006; Mikhail, 2009). Of course, utilitarian rules could also be explained in terms of their function, either through biological evolution, learning, cultural evolution, or reflective thought (possibly passed on through culture).

My aim here is to provide an alternative account of the origin of some non-utilitarian moral principles. One reason for seeking an alternative is that these principles appear not to be optimally functional. Moreover, all the principles that I consider are not universally endorsed or followed among people. Many people exhibit essentially no omission bias in questionnaire studies using several hypothetical cases. The variation in other effects is similarly large. If nonutilitarian rules resulted from a hard-wired cognitive module, such as variation, they would be more difficult (although not impossible) to explain. Biases are sometimes called "cognitive illusions," by analogy with optical illusions. But they are quite different in that most optical illusions are universal except for people with identifiable medical conditions, but these cognitive illusions like omission bias are not.

This alternative account does not exclude other accounts, and it may well be that several kinds of mechanisms are at work. In fact, my proposal might be seen as part of a larger proposal containing different accounts. The larger proposal, which I shall not develop here, would suggest that we can divide the development of moral principles into a few rough categories, two of which would be utilitarian and deontological.

Utilitarian rules would arise from perspective taking in the most general sense, including emotions such as sympathy and empathy. As Hare (1963, 1981) has argued, the basis of utilitarian reasoning is the Golden Rule, which asks us to put ourselves in the position of others. Children can learn to put themselves in the position of someone else, and this can serve as the basis for a kind of moral education based on utilitarianism (Baron, 1993, chap. 8); the one additional step required is to apply the Golden Rule to all of those affected, as if you simultaneously took into yourself all of their (conflicting) goals and made them your own. The kind of early training that might be relevant is what many parents do naturally, asking "How would it feel if someone did that to you? " or "Wouldn't it make grandma happy if you …?" Of course, the more advanced stages of such education will involve integrating the positions of all those affected, and ultimately understanding the role of various kinds of disciplinary knowledge (such as economics), but this is not necessary for making judgments of alternative public policies that affect different groups in different ways and certainly not for everyday moral judgments. One implication of the argument I make here, in its most extreme form, is that parents who rely entirely on perspective taking might produce children who grow up to be reasonably sensitive and who are also not particularly tempted to endorse deontological moral rules. These people would show up in studies of moral heuristics as one end of the broad continuum of individual differences.

The deontological type of principle is my main topic here, namely, moral rules such as do no harm that have some basis in consequences (compared to the alternative of no rule at all) but that often lead to systematic suboptimality. Such rules are based on distinctions such as acts versus omissions, direct versus indirect causation (Royzman & Baron, 2002), permissible versus forbidden, obligatory versus optional, and on concepts such as rights and duties. Rules concerning fairness are in this category too (Baron, 2008), in that most of them can be understood as improving consequences relative to some arbitrary distributions. I shall comment on rules of punishment and fairness at the end.

THE FAMILY AND THE STATE

The basis of the idea I propose here is that the family, which constitutes the major moral environment of young children, is analogous to the state. The parents, usually the mother, make laws and regulations in much the way that governments do. As a result, children come to think of moral rules as analogous to laws.[2] Moreover, the nature of these early rules is limited by some of the same economic factors that limit the reach of the law.

Laws Versus Utilitarianism

Consider the first point, the analogy between deontological rules and laws. It is useful to compare utilitarianism with legal principles.

Zero Point   Laws and many deontological rules specify what is forbidden, permitted, and required. The cutoffs between these categories are (theoretically) sharp. It is wrong to go below a cutoff but optional how much to go above it, and there are no degrees of conformity to the rules. Thus, deontological theory has concepts of permission, obligation, duty, and supererogation (going beyond the call of duty). Utilitarianism in its simple form has none of these concepts (although versions of them can be defined). It concerns decisions, and options can be evaluated as better or worse, along a continuum with no natural zero point.

This distinction even carries over into research on moral judgment: Some researchers ask whether a behavior is permissible, whereas other researchers tend to ask which option is better or how would you rate this option on the following scale. Presumably, anyone ought to be able to answer the latter kinds of questions in the sense intended. A serious utilitarian subject might, however, have trouble answering questions about "moral permissibility." Such a subject might reasonably complain, "Are you asking me about the law? If so, I can try to answer your question. But, if you are asking me about morality, I do not know what you mean."

As I shall explain, it would be utterly impractical for the law to rate everyone's choices on a continuous scale, as utilitarianism would do. Thus, even Bentham (the first major utilitarian writer) accepted the general structure of the law as largely limited to specifying what is forbidden and permissible, going on, of course, to analyze the decisions of legislators from a more pure utilitarian perspective.

Acts and Omissions The law distinguishes acts and omissions. Failure to prevent harm to another person, even when the harm is great and prevention has little cost, is very rarely penalized. There are exceptions. In tort law people are routinely held legally responsible for harmful omissions, in particular omissions of due care that lead probabilistically, but not with certainty, to harm. But penalties are levied only after the harm occurs; the negligence itself is not penalized if nothing happens. Moreover, tort law does not penalize the failure to undertake a beneficial activity. Thus, a drug company can be sued for the side effects of a beneficial vaccine but not for deciding not to produce the vaccine at all.

In contract law people are responsible for failure to carry out the terms of a contract. This is of course contingent on making the contract, which is loosely analogous to making a promise (Wilkinson-Ryan & Baron, 2009). And citizens do have certain duties, such as paying taxes and (in some countries) military service. Neglect of these very limited duties is penalized.

By contrast, utilitarianism as a moral system applies to all cases of negligence equally and anything that benefits others, regardless if whether it is defined as a duty or as the result of a contract. When I say "applies," I refer to the fundamental role of evaluating choices. Decisions about punishment (hence also "blame" in some sense) are seen as decisions by the punisher. Thus, it may make utilitarian sense not to punish harmful omissions even if they are, from the perspective of the omitter, far from optimal in their effects.

Trade-Offs Legal prohibitions are usually absolute.[3] In utilitarian analysis, notoriously, any harm can be justified by some greater good. James Bond is a fine utilitarian character, saving the world repeatedly at the expense of harms to others that would ordinarily have him imprisoned.

Parochialism The reach of the law is limited in many ways, one being jurisdiction. We have local laws, state/province laws, national laws, and a few international laws that exist largely because they are affirmed by national laws, but we have no universal laws that apply to all people. Yet, utilitarianism (like many other approaches to normative moral theory) applies to all people and takes the interests of all people into account when they are affected by a choice. This feature of taking all into account is not unique to utilitarianism as an approach to normative ethics, but the point is that it is not typical of the law nor of people's intuitive deontological principles (Baron, in press).

Possible Origins in the Family

Some parents, possibly all, make rules for their children as soon as the child begins to understand them. The following examples of mother–child interaction (from Dunn & Munn, 1985) illustrates the rules that "biscuits don't go on the floor" and "toothbrushes go in the bathroom," and the second example shows that "it's not nice to pull hair."

- First example

[Child (16 months) throws biscuit (cookie) on floor.]
Mother: What's that? Biscuit on the floor? Where biscuits aren't supposed to be, isn't it?

  [Child looks at mother and nods.]

Mother: Yes. Now, what's all this? *[Points to toothbrush and toothpaste on kitchen table.]*

  [Child looks at mother and smiles.]

Mother: Yes, you did. Where does this live?
Child: Bath.

- Second example

Mother: Don't pull my hair! Madam! Don't pull hair. No, it's not nice to pull hair, is it?
Child (18 months): Hair.
Mother: Hair, yes. But you mustn't pull it, must you?
Child: Yes! *[Smiles.]*
Mother: No! No!
Child: No!
Mother: No, it's not kind to pull hair, is it?
Child: Nice!
Mother: No it isn't.
Child: Nice!

Rules like these have essentially all the features of laws. They define what is impermissible. They deal with obligations and duties. Presumably, as stated, these rules are absolute, although of course we know that they can be overridden in emergencies. And of course, they are parochial; they apply only to the household.

They are (mostly) concerned with acts rather than omissions. It is difficult to get data about this, but the following table (from Ross, Filyer, Lollis, Perlman, & Martin, 1994) shows a scoring scheme for classifying disputes involving toddlers. Only the starred items are omissions.

Physical aggression	Children should not physically harm their siblings
Verbal aggression	… not verbally harm their siblings
Nagging	… not annoy their siblings
Lying	… not lie about or lie during interactions with their siblings
Tattling	… not tell their parents about the wrongdoing of their siblings
Disagreeing	… not oppose their siblings' views on matters of fact or opinion

Physical control	... not attempt to control their siblings physically (e.g., hold or manipulate)
Bossing	... not order their siblings to do things
Interfering	... not intrude on their siblings' private activities
Excluding°	... allow their siblings to play with them
Possession	... not take objects currently possessed by their siblings
Ownership	... not use what belongs to their siblings
Sharing°	... let their siblings jointly use the objects they own or are currently using or take turns using objects
Property damage	... not damage anything

It is of interest that many studies of such dialogs involve conflicts with siblings. Parents may find themselves doing a lot more moral instruction and rule making when the toddler has to relate to someone other than the parent.

Another example comes from Gralinski and Kopp (1993), who asked mothers to list the rules they made for their young children. Here is their checklist with examples (p. 576), again with omissions starred.

Child safety	Not touching things that are dangerous.
	Not climbing on furniture.
	Not going into street.
Protection of personal property	Keeping away from prohibited objects.
	Not tearing up books.
	Not getting into prohibited drawers or rooms.
	Not coloring on walls or furniture.
Respect for others	Not taking toys away from other children.
	Not being too rough with other children.
Food and mealtime routines	Not playing with food.
	Not leaving table in the middle of meal.
	Not spilling drinks, juice.
Delay	Waiting when Mom is on the telephone [not interrupting].
	Not interrupting others' conversations.
	Waiting for a meal [not complaining?].
Manners	Saying "please."°
	Saying "thank you."°
Self care	Dressing self.°
	Asking to use the toilet.°
	Washing up when requested.°
	Brushing teeth when requested.°
	Going to bed when requested.°
Family routines	Helping with chores when requested.°
	Putting toys away.°
	Keeping room neat.°

Of interest is the fact that the last three categories, the ones with omissions, were much less commonly used for the youngest children in the study (13 and 18 months), becoming more common at 24 and 30 months. Arguably, omissions become more relevant once the child is old enough to have some responsibilities, but prohibitions of acts are relevant well before that.

ECONOMIC CONSTRAINTS ON LAWS AND HOUSEHOLD RULES

Many properties of household rules can be understood in terms of economic constraints on rule making and rule enforcement. Household rules, like laws, are promulgated by an authority with the power to punish. The threat of punishment, or even reprimand, can be an effective deterrent insofar as the potential offender can learn what behavior will evoke punishment. Thus, rules must be clear, and they are clearest when they make a sharp division. A rule of the sort "if you take too many cookies you will be punished" is not as effective as "if you take more than two ..." This requirement leads to the distinction between what is prohibited and what is permissible, a distinction found in laws and deontological rules but not in utilitarianism.

Duties may well come somewhat after prohibitions. A duty requires the capacity to carry it out. Children are not usually given chores and responsibilities as soon as they can talk. But, once duties are created, the same principle applies as for prohibitions. The authority must make it clear what the duty is in order to use the threat of punishment or disapproval to enforce it efficiently. Duties cannot be as nebulous as the closest utilitarian parallels, such as "Look for what needs to be done and then do it." That is too unclear to serve as a law. It is unenforceable.

More generally, principles that are socially enforced must consider the social costs of enforcement, including the costs of apprehension, judgment, and application of sanctions (Shavell, 2004). The costs of apprehension include, for the state, policing (a major activity of government). The cost of judgment includes the cost of deciding whether a rule has been violated. Clear boundaries—"bright lines"—make this easier.

Clear boundaries also reduce the costs of instruction in the law. Good laws are easy for people to understand, and this is especially true of toddlers. It is possible that very specific rules such as "the toothbrush goes in the bathroom" are easier to learn than general ones such as "things go where they will be used." On the other hand, too many rules can be difficult to keep track of. The state and the family do well to limit legislation to cases that are frequent enough, or potentially harmful enough, for the effort to be worthwhile. This feature of laws and rules helps to create the broad area in which they have nothing to say, the area considered supererogatory.

Another important feature of laws is that they deal with self–other trade-offs. Utilitarianism as a moral theory treats everyone equally. Yet utility theory as a normative model of individual decisions uses only the individual's goals. If these goals are somewhat altruistic, then the goals of others will play a role, but the individual decision maker will usually weigh her own goals more. How do we deal with the conflict between self and all? Utilitarian theory might deal with it by assuming that altruism is an external constraint (Baron & Szymanska, in press). That is, instead of specifying how much altruism each person should have, we assume that self-sacrifice is fixed and then we try to optimize outcomes for others within the constraint. For example, the theory might specify that you should do the most good for others that you can, given your willingness to sacrifice your self-interest.

The law can hardly enjoin people to do this. Rather, it must set reasonable guidelines that, in general, do not demand excessive self-sacrifice except when the sacrifice serves to maintain the power of the state, as in the case of military service or (less so) taxes. The family likewise may demand loyalty to the family, but it does not typically require self-sacrifice to benefit outsiders.

In sum, laws and household rules are limited by economic factors such as being easy to learn, hence clear and not too numerous or detailed, and easy to enforce, hence limited to cases in which infractions are easily detected. Children may come to think of moral principles as having these properties in general.

APPLICATION TO BIASES

The economic principles just sketched can be used to understand the form of many apparently nonutilitarian principles. Some of these principles may be taught to children. Others, though, may gain their support from a general tendency of people to think of moral principles like laws. This tendency arises, I argue, in early childhood, because rules in at least some families are in fact like laws. People then develop a general concept of what laws are like. They may have at least an intuitive understanding of the economic principles just outlined. This is a topic for research: What do people regard as good laws? In particular, do they take relevant costs of learning and enforcement into account?

Omission Bias and Related Principles

Detectability   A major distinction between harmful acts and omissions is that acts are usually more easily detected. This fact would imply that rules against harmful acts would be more efficient than those against harmful omission. Thus, detectability would affect rule creation. People might generalize this principle to their endorsement of moral rules.

Note that this argument about detectability is different from another possible effect of detectability. It is possible that people define the relevant act–omission distinction in terms of detectability. If so, those who display omission bias would tend to regard detectable acts as more wrong than undetectable ones. Spranca et al. (1991) and Baron and Ritov (2009a) found no evidence for such an effect. However, this is not the relevant research question for the general claim here. Rather, it is whether people regard laws against detectable harms as more acceptable than laws against less detectable harms. Detectability can play a role in the development of rules even if it is not part of the rules.

Causality   Although people do not seem to define the act–omission distinction in terms of detectability, many people do seem to define it in terms of direct causality, that is, causality that is accounted for by the application of general principles of causation such as the laws of physics. (But it is beliefs that are relevant, not scientific truth, so direct causation can include such things as praying to God, who then intervenes and answers the prayer.) This type of causality is different from "but-for" causality, which is relevant to much of the law, particularly tort law. But-for causality means that you cause an outcome if it would not have happened but for a choice that you made. The act–omission distinction is irrelevant. But-for causality is, of course, the relevant kind for utilitarianism, which concerns expected outcomes of choices, not any other property of the choices. And utilitarianism is neutral between acts and omissions in evaluating options.

It is possible that the emphasis on direct causality can be understood in terms of economic efficiency. When harm is caused by action, usually no other cause is necessary (in the usual sense of the term *cause*, hence putting aside background conditions that are assumed in any inquiry about the cause of an event). When harm is caused by omission, some other (more direct) cause is necessary. It may be empirically true that the other cause is usually absent. Thus, harms through omission require a special opportunity. If we try to include the opportunity into the rule, we would have many more rules for harmful omissions than for harmful acts. For example, "Do not tell your competitor that he put the wrong address on his mail to his client, thus losing his chance at a promotion ahead of you."

But-for causality may also be harder for young children to learn. The appreciation of it requires evaluation of counterfactuals. Although children as young as five can distinguish cases of causality by omission from noncausality (Schleifer, Shultz, & Lefebvre-Pinard, 1983), the distinction appears to be weak, with only small differences in the tendency to judge causality. The cases were very simple. For example, a store owner did not put salt on the ice in front of his store. In one condition, a customer slipped on the ice and was injured. In the control condition, the customer fell before reaching the ice and was injured. This study (and no study that I have found) has compared causality by omission with causal action in young children's judgments of causality (see also Harris, German, & Mills, 1996, and German, 1999, for other studies of young children's ability to think in terms of counterfactuals).

Direct causality seems also to explain a related bias, the indirectness bias (Royzman & Baron, 2002). Direct harm was judged to be worse than indirect harm, even when both involved actions. For example: A new viral disease is spreading rapidly in a region of Africa. Left alone, it will kill 100,000 people out of 1,000,000 in the region. X, a public health official, has two ways to prevent this. Both will stop the spread of the virus and prevent all these deaths:

A. Give all 1,000,000 a shot that makes them immune to the first disease. The shot will also cause, as a side effect, a second disease that will kill 100 people.
B. Give all 1,000,000 a shot that gives them another disease, which is incompatible with the first disease. The second disease will kill 100 people.

Most subjects thought that option A was better, because the deaths are a side effect rather than part of the mechanism of the main effect.

Protected Values (PVs)   Part of the source of omission bias may come from a tendency to see rules as absolute. Omission bias is greater when *protected values* (PVs) are involved (Baron & Ritov, 2009a; Ritov & Baron, 1999). Protected values are defined as outcomes or features of outcomes that people say they will not trade off. Subjects assent to statements such as, "I would not allow this no matter what the benefit of doing so." Examples include abortion (for those who are against it), reproductive cloning, destruction of original artistic masterpieces, and destruction of animal or plant species. Governments and individuals can honor most PVs if they apply to actions that bring about the outcomes in question. You can refrain from performing or recommending abortions. But it is difficult for PVs to apply to omissions. An omission PV against abortion would require you to take all possible actions to prevent abortions. If you had more than one omission PV like this, you could not begin to behave consistently with them. Thus, stated PVs (those that meet the test of being seen by subjects as absolute values) tend to be limited to actions that bring about the outcomes in question, not omissions (Baron & Ritov, 2009). As a consequence, omission bias is much greater when PVs are involved than when they are not. PVs are thus a source of strong omission bias.

If rules are seen as absolute, then they will be naturally understood as PVs. Children may be especially inclined to see rules this way. Even for adults, PVs tend to be unreflective overgeneralizations (Baron & Leshner, 2000), much like those found in children's early concepts. Adults asked to think of counterexamples will often admit that their rules are not absolute after all. If children see rules as absolute, then they might see them as applying mainly to prohibitions on actions that bring about bad outcomes, rather than as obligations to prevent these outcomes. Children who acquire these sorts of rules might tend to think of moral rules as having the same property. They might think of moral rules like these rules that they first learned. Thus, the tendency to think of rules as absolute, a kind of thinking that may arise from children's tendency to generalize unreflectively (Baron, 1973), would exacerbate omission bias and lead people to think of moral rules as generally absolute.

Retribution Versus Deterrence

Utilitarian accounts of punishment are essentially equivalent to economic accounts; both emphasize deterrence as a major function of punishment. These accounts acknowledge other purposes aside from deterrence, such as incapacitation, rehabilitation, and satisfaction of people's preference for retribution. Yet it is the deterrent function of punishment that is least intuitive. Intuitions often depart from utilitarian theory by following *lex talionis*, or "an eye for an eye." I shall call this "retributive" punishment.

One implication of utilitarianism is that punishment should not occur when deterrence is absent, yet some people ignore this. For example, some people favor tort penalties against vaccines or birth-control products even when the effect of these penalties is to make companies withdraw beneficial products from the market—thus deterring good behavior—rather than making the companies more careful (Baron & Ritov, 1993).[4]

Another implication is that severity of punishment should be higher when the probability of apprehension is lower. Yet many people find this unfair and want the penalty to be fixed (Baron & Ritov, 2009). The result, if this preference is honored, is underdeterrence of offenses that are rarely detected.

Deterrent punishment is also sensitive to intention. Presumably, intentional harm requires greater penalties for deterrence, since the offender presumably benefits from committing the harm (even if the benefit is purely emotional). Children and adults typically do take intention into account, as well as excuses, but the youngest children tend to ignore it (Darley & Shultz, 1990).

Retributive punishment is, however, economically low-cost. We need make no determination of intention, excuses, or probability of apprehension. All we need is evidence of harm. Parents of toddlers may resort to this strategy because of the difficulty of determining the intention of a child who cannot answer detailed questions. Probability of apprehension may remain difficult for parents to estimate, unless the child is honest.

Somewhat analogous to the determination of intention is the determination of negligence in tort law (Shavell, 2004), which can be defined as less than optimal care to avoid harm to others. To determine negligence, courts must have some idea of optimal care, and this can be a costly determination. Thus, one of the arguments for strict liability—holding the injurer liable regardless of the level of care—is reduced cost to the legal system.

In sum, retributive punishment is a natural understanding for young children. They do outgrow this in some ways, particularly with respect to intention. But, in other ways, development is not assured. Of course, as I noted at the outset, all the effects I have described are not universal in adults. Many adult judgments follow utilitarian principles.

Fairness

A number of biases are found in the study of fairness (Baron, 2008). One of particular interest is a preference for ex-ante equality (equality in facing risk, before it is known who will win and who will lose) even when this reduces total utility (by creating losers, whose loss is not compensated by the gains for the winners). For example, many people (again, not all) prefer to give an inexpensive medical test to all patients in a defined group rather than an expensive test to half of the patients picked at random, even though the expensive test could save more lives in total, because it is more than twice as effective (Ubel, Baron, & Asch, 2001; Ubel, DeKay, Baron, & Asch, 1996).

Such a preference for equality, including ex-ante equality (which young children seem to implement by random selection schemes such as rock-paper-scissors [as a reviewer pointed out]), could arise from a simple rule taught to children. Again, the cost of defining and enforcing a rule of equal division is very low, compared to the alternative of looking at expected benefit of unequal division.

CONCLUSION: IMPLICATIONS FOR RESEARCH

The view I have presented has several implications for psychological research.

Concepts of Law and Morality

An important part of the present argument is that people extend their concept of what makes a good law to the question of what makes a good moral principle. In particular, good laws are seen as taking the form of deontological rules. It would be interesting to contrast these sorts of rules with rules that are more consistent with utilitarianism, for example, involving trade-offs and better–worse rather than permitted–forbidden. Do people who use "moral heuristics" also find the form of deontological rules to be better than the form of utilitarian principles?

Positive Duties

Positive duties for children ought to arise later in development than prohibitions. This is consistent with the results of Gralinski and Kopp (1993).

Long-Term Effects of Different Forms of Child Rearing

Parents might differ in their use of rules, as opposed to reliance on emotions like empathy and induction of guilt for harming someone else. Children of rule-using parents might be more accepting of deontological rules when they grow up. Parents that emphasize role taking, putting oneself in the position of others, should produce children who become more willing to accept utilitarianism. Children might move away from these parental influences as they get older. Thus, we might expect family effects to matter more for young children than for older children or adults.

Siblings

Parents might be especially prone to use rules when they need to mediate sibling conflicts. Thus, people who had siblings when they were toddlers might be more accepting of deontological rules when they grow up.

But-For Causality

Children should understand physical causality before but-for causality. This has apparently not been tested directly.

AUTHOR NOTE

The author is supported by a grant from the U.S.–Israel Binational Science Foundation (Ilana Ritov, Co-PI). E-mail: baron@psych.upenn.edu.

NOTES

1. It is also possible that, in following the utilitarian principle, we need to take into account the possibility that our judgment is erroneous. Mill (1859), for example, made this argument for honoring rights even when violating them appears to maximize utility.
2. The argument extends the concept of "simple moral systems" described by Baron (1986).
3. There are some exceptions. You may be allowed to break into someone's house to get warm if you are in serious danger of freezing to death otherwise.
4. These cases were based on real cases in which beneficial products had been driven from the market. But the hypothetical went one step further, specifying that victim compensation could be provided in the absence of tort penalties. Thus, the provision of compensation was also removed as a reason for penalties.

REFERENCES

Baron, J. (1973). Semantic components and conceptual development. *Cognition, 2,* 189–207.

Baron, J. (1986). Trade-offs among reasons for action. *Journal for the Theory of Social Behavior, 16,* 173–195.

Baron, J. (1994). Nonconsequentialist decisions (with commentary and reply). *Behavioral and Brain Sciences, 17,* 1–42.

Baron, J. (1999). Utility maximization as a solution: promise, difficulties, and impediments. *American Behavioral Scientist, 42,* 1301–1321.

Baron, J. (2006). *Against bioethics.* Cambridge, MA: MIT Press.

Baron, J. (2008). *Thinking and deciding* (4th ed.). New York, NY: Cambridge University Press.

Baron, J. (in press). Parochialism as a result of cognitive biases. In A. K. Woods, R. Goodman, & D. Jinks (Eds.), *Understanding social action, promoting human rights.* Oxford, UK: Oxford University Press.

Baron, J., Bazerman, M. H., & Shonk, K. (2006). Enlarging the societal pie through wise legislation: A psychological perspective. *Perspectives on Psychological Science, 1,* 123–132.

Baron, J., & Leshner, S. (2000). How serious are expressions of protected values. *Journal of Experimental Psychology: Applied, 6,* 183–194.

Baron, J., & Ritov, I. (1993). Intuitions about penalties and compensation in the context of tort law. *Journal of Risk and Uncertainty, 7,* 17–33.

Baron, J., & Ritov, I. (2004). Omission bias, individual differences, and normality. *Organizational Behavior and Human Decision Processes, 94,* 74–85.

Baron, J., & Ritov, I. (2009a). Protected values and omission bias as deontological judgments. In D. M. Bartels, C. W. Bauman, L. J. Skitka, D. L. Medin (Eds.), *The psychology of learning and motivation: Vol. 50. Moral judgment and decision making* (pp. 133–167). San Diego: Academic Press.

Baron, J., & Ritov, I. (2009b). The role of probability of detection in judgments of punishment. *Journal of Legal Analysis, 1,* 553–590.

Baron, J., & Szymanska, E. (2010). Heuristics and biases in charity. In D. M. Oppenheimer & C. Y. Olivola (Eds.), *The science of giving: Experimental approaches to the study of charity.* (pp. 215–236). New York: Taylor & Francis.

Bartels, D. M., Bauman, C. W., Skitka, L. J., Medin, D. L. (Eds.). (2009). *The psychology of learning and motivation: Vol. 50. Moral judgment and decision making.* San Diego: Academic Press.

Bennett, J. (1966). Whatever the consequences. *Analysis, 26,* 83–102.

Cushman, F., Young, L., & Hauser, M. (2006). The role of conscious reasoning and intuition in moral judgments: Three principles of harm. *Psychological Science, 17,* 1082–1089.

Darley, J. M., & Shultz, T. R. (1990). Moral rules: Their content and acquisition. *Annual Review of Psychology, 41*, 525–556.

Dunn, J., & Munn, P. (1985). Becoming a family member: Family conflict and the development of social understanding in the second year. *Child Development, 56*, 480–492.

Foot, P. (1978). The problem of abortion and the doctrine of the double effect. In P. Foot, *Virtues and vices and other essays in moral philosophy* (pp. 19–32). Berkeley: University of California Press. (Originally published in *Oxford Review*, no. 5, 1967.)

German, T. P. (1999). Children's causal reasoning: Counterfactual thinking occurs for "negative" outcomes only. *Developmental Science, 2*, 442–447.

Gilovich, T., Griffin, D., & Kahneman, D. (Eds.) (2002). *Heuristics and biases: The psychology of intuitive judgment*. New York: Cambridge University Press.

Gralinski, J. H., & Kopp, C. B. (1993). Everyday rules for behavior: Mothers' requests to young children. *Developmental Psychology, 29*, 583–584.

Greene, J. D. (2007). The secret joke of Kant's soul. In W. Sinnott-Armstrong (Ed.), *Moral psychology: Vol. 3. The neuroscience of morality: Emotion, disease, and development* (pp. 36–79). Cambridge, MA: MIT Press.

Hare, R. M. (1963). *Freedom and reason*. Oxford, UK: Oxford University Press (Clarendon Press).

Hare, R. M. (1981). *Moral thinking: Its levels, method and point*. Oxford, UK: Oxford University Press (Clarendon Press).

Harris, P. L., German, T., & Mills, P. (1996). Children's use of counterfactual thinking in causal reasoning. *Cognition, 61*, 233–269.

Hauser, M. D. (2006). *Moral minds: How nature designed a universal sense of right and wrong*. New York: Harper Collins.

Johnson, E. J., & Goldstein, D. (2003). Do defaults save lives? *Science, 302*, 1338–1339.

Kahneman, D., Slovic, P., & Tversky, A. (Eds.). (1982). *Judgment under uncertainty: Heuristics and biases*. Cambridge, UK: Cambridge University Press.

Kahneman, D., & Tversky, A. (2000). *Choices, values, and frames*. New York: Cambridge University Press and Russell Sage Foundation.

Mikhail, J. (2009). Moral grammar and intuitive jurisprudence: A formal model of unconscious moral and legal knowledge. In D. Medin, L. Skitka, C. W. Bauman, D. Bartels (Eds.), *The psychology of learning and motivation: Vol. 50. Moral cognition and decision making* (pp. 27–100). New York: Academic Press.

Mill, J. S. (1859). *On liberty*. London: J. W. Parker & Son.

Ritov, I., & Baron, J. (1990). Reluctance to vaccinate: omission bias and ambiguity. *Journal of Behavioral Decision Making, 3*, 263–277.

Ritov, I., & Baron, J. (1999). Protected values and omission bias. *Organizational Behavior and Human Decision Processes, 79*, 79–94.

Ross, H. S., Filyer, R. E., Lollis, S. P., Perlman, M., & Martin, J. L. (1994). Administering justice in the family. *Journal of Family Psychology, 8*, 254–273.

Royzman, E. B., & Baron, J. (2002). The preference for indirect harm. *Social Justice Research, 15*, 165–184.

Schleifer, M., Shultz, T. R., & Lefebvre-Pinard, M. (1983). Children's judgements of causality, responsibility and punishment in cases of harm due to omission. *British Journal of Developmental Psychology, 1*, 87–97.

Shavell, S. (2004). *Foundations of economic analysis of law*. Cambridge, MA: Belknap Press of Harvard University Press.

Singer, P. (1993). *Practical ethics* (2nd ed.). Cambridge, UK: Cambridge University Press.

Slovic, P. (2007). "If I look at the mass I will never act": Psychic numbing and genocide. *Judgment and Decision Making, 2*, 79–95.

Spranca, M., Minsk, E., & Baron, J. (1991). Omission and commission in judgment and choice. *Journal of Experimental Social Psychology, 27*, 76–105.

Sunstein, C. R. (2005). Moral heuristics (with commentary). *Behavioral and Brain Sciences, 28*, 531–573.

Ubel, P. A., Baron, J., & Asch, D. A. (2001). Preference for equity as a framing effect. *Medical Decision Making, 21*, 180–189.

Ubel, P. A., DeKay, M. L., Baron, J., & Asch, D. A. (1996). Cost effectiveness analysis in a setting of budget constraints: Is it equitable? *New England Journal of Medicine, 334*, 1174–1177.

Wilkinson-Ryan, T., & Baron, J. (2009). Moral judgment and moral heuristics in breach of contract. *Journal of Empirical Legal Studies, 6*, 405–423.

Author Index

Subject Index